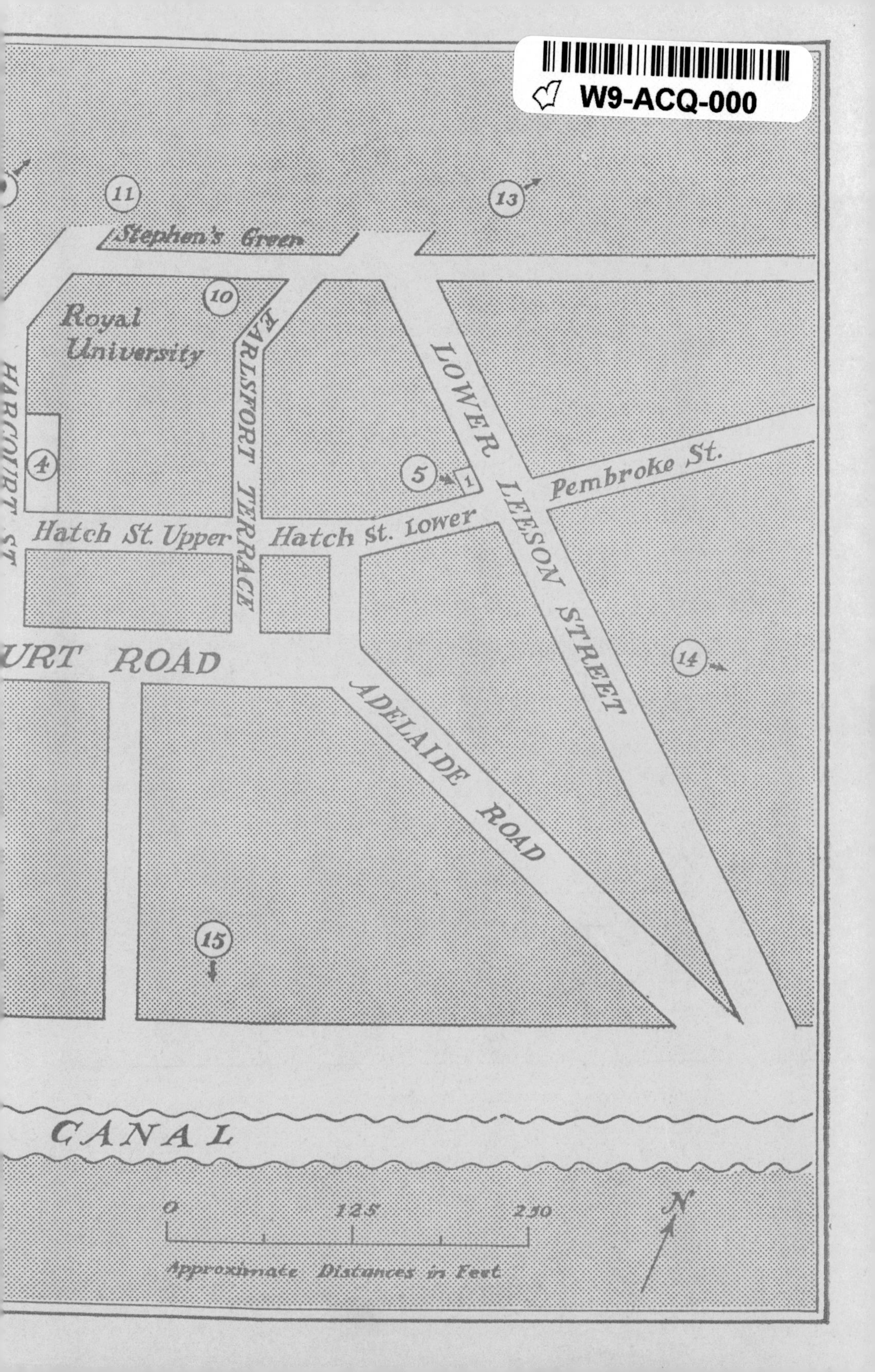

11
13
Stephen's Green
10
Royal University
EARLSFORT TERRACE
HARCOURT ST
4
LOWER LEESON STREET
5
1
Pembroke St.
Hatch St. Upper
Hatch St. Lower
URT ROAD
14
ADELAIDE ROAD
15
CANAL
0
125
250
Approximate Distances in Feet
N

SHAW OF DUBLIN / The Formative Years

SHAW OF DUBLIN

THE FORMATIVE YEARS

B. C. ROSSET

THE PENNSYLVANIA STATE UNIVERSITY PRESS
University Park, Pennsylvania
July *1964*

Library of Congress Catalog Card Number: 63–18892

Printed in the United States of America
Typography and binding design by Marilyn Shobaken

TO IDY

An Angel on Earth

Foreword

THE LATE ARCHIBALD HENDERSON, who between 1904 and 1956 produced three immense authorized biographies of G.B.S., once told me—as he was completing his last book on Shaw—that he had never been to Dublin. The Hendersonian confession suggests one of the reasons why *Shaw of Dublin* is so needed a piece of literary detective work. For the most part, although several have made the pilgrimage—and several others have themselves been Irishmen—when dealing with the Dublin years, Shaw's biographers and critics have accepted the easily accessible documentary evidence, Shaw's own readily offered memories and confessions—and each other's writings. No portrait of Shaw could do without these.

G.B.S.—the persona Shaw created—is very likely the most successfully drawn character in the Shavian portrait gallery. This triumph of self-advertisement forever put into the shadows such earlier (and then still unpublished) self-portraits as Smith, the young newcomer to London, compounded of equal parts of agonizing shyness and intellectual arrogance, who is the hero of Shaw's first major work, the aptly named novel *Immaturity* (1879), written not long after Shaw, aged twenty, arrived in London from Dublin to begin a new life. We remember instead the Shavian partial portraits which seem to contain the essence of the public G.B.S.—John Tanner, *Man and Superman's* author of *The Revolutionist's Handbook;* or Captain

Shotover, the prophetic old navigator of *Heartbreak House;* or Corno di Bassetto, the impudent critic-of-all-trades who brought Shaw to public notice in the music columns of the London *Star* in 1888. When Bassetto moved to *The Saturday Review* and began signing himself *G.B.S.,* the author moved further in spirit from Dublin, for Shaw—as far as he was able to—*became* G.B.S., and the more he trumpeted the imposture the more successful it became.

G.B.S.'s tales of his Dublin years have had the same success. To a large degree it was accomplished through the liberality with which he regaled his readers and biographers with witty memories of persons and places in Ireland. In effect, through his own reminiscences in prefaces and magazine articles (some collected and altered or added to in *Sixteen Self Sketches* when he was past ninety), he wrote his own biography, no more or less accurate than most memoirs. An earlier, unofficial collection of pieces and prefaces went under the misnomer of *Shaw Gives Himself Away*—something G.B.S. seldom really did.

How far Shaw actually has given himself away is a crucial part of both the purpose and the method of Mr. Rosset's study. This close look at Shaw's Dublin years—his parentage, childhood and young manhood—is at the same time an examination of the lacunae and inconsistencies in the versions of Shaw's early life reported by both his major and minor biographer and by the chief research assistant common to all of them, G.B.S. himself. Mr. Rosset's method—perhaps because he is not an academically trained literary scholar—was to be his own research assistant and literally follow the tracks of G.B.S. and his family and friends through Dublin and across the Irish Sea to London.

Mr. Rosset's interest in Shaw began at sea, during his years as a youthful merchant seaman, when he first found *Major Barbara* useful to intellectually enliven dreary intervals in his work as radio operator. Later he settled in New York and turned to teaching and to a busy avocation as Secretary of the Shaw Society of America. But probing into Shaw's beginnings, as a method of better understanding his plays, lured him upon a vacation research trip to Ireland and again altered his life. He decided to stay.

After he settled his affairs in America and returned to Dublin, he sought suitable quarters in the area in which G.B.S. spent his boyhood, and a cooperative Dubliner rented a room to him in an old house at 33 Synge Street. It was the very dwelling in which Shaw was born and lived as a boy; and "Sonny" Shaw's own room, in which Rosset lived for some months, was little changed except for the welcome addition of an electric fire. In the authentic atmosphere of 33 Synge Street—except for an unobtrusive plaster plaque on the front wall, only the TV aerial on the roof reminds one of the 20th century —*Shaw of Dublin* was begun.

Rosset's indefatigable researches included nearly every dusty archive in Dublin and many of its sprawling cemeteries. Family records of Shaw's relatives were opened for his inspection, and even the officials of Shaw's grammar school succumbed to Rosset's persistence. The same pattern of dogged search for facts continued on the Isle of Wight and in London. With the mass of previously published and hitherto unpublished data he has accumulated and organized, and the sometimes controversial inferences he makes from them, a startling reappraisal of Shaw's formative years takes shape, and the familiar cast of characters undergoes a revision of the former starring and supporting roles. On the surface, at least, the setting itself is familiar, as are many of the incidents, for they are the events in and about the household of Shaw's boyhood, with all their tensions and frustrations; and young G.B.S.'s encounters with formal and informal education, as well as with the joys and disenchantments of remunerative employment. For these are the times and the places which shaped Shaw's ironic perspective toward life, and to which his plays—in Rosset's demonstration—appear to be so heavily indebted.

These, to me, are some of the fascinations of this unusual excursion into Shaw's Dublin years, and the early years in London when Shaw had not yet shaken the grip of Dublin. Its findings as well as its controversial hypotheses should provide stimulus for further reappraisals of Shaw's plays, and material for the future definitive biography of G.B.S., which cannot be written until there are more such inquiries into this and other phases of Shaw's many-sided career. His full life spanned ten decades, from a time when Abraham Lincoln was a little-known politician, to the age of atomic bombs and cold war. It is likely to take us at least as long as that long life to take his measure. *Shaw of Dublin* has the virtue of beginning at the beginning.

STANLEY WEINTRAUB

University Park, Pennsylvania
December, 1963

Acknowledgments

I WISH TO THANK the following institutions and persons for their patience and many kindnesses shown to me, often in the face of what may have seemed unpleasant persistency. I can only plead biographer's zeal and, self-delusions excepted, the influence of the Shavian Life Force. It has, for the moment, released me and I hasten to mend my manners.

To the Berg Collection of The New York Public Library, The Boston Public Library, The Library of Congress, The British Museum, The National Library of Ireland and the libraries of Villanova, Harvard, Trinity (Dublin), Yale and Pennsylvania Universities. The Irish-American Historical Association of New York, the Consulate of the Republic of Eire, New York, The Hayden Planetarium and the Society of Authors and the British Trustee of the Shaw Estate.

Also to Rev. Brother W. P. Allen of Dublin, K. Anderson of the North London College, Anonymous of Dublin, the Rev. Burral of Ventnor, I. of W., Niall Boden of Radio Eireann and Kenneth L. Dixon of Phoenix, Arizona. To Henry J. Dubester of Washington, William Evans of Dublin, Dr. Henry George Farmer of Glasgow, Major A. J. W. Fitzmaurice of Carlow and J. J. Fitzpatrick of Dalkey. To Mrs. Lorenza Garreau of Surrey, Grace Goodliffe of Donegal, Mr. and Mrs. Eugene Giblin of 33 Synge Street, Dublin, Dr. John D. Gordan of The Berg Collection, N.Y.P.L., and Mrs. Agnes Hepworth of Ventnor, I. of W. To Edward Keane of Dublin, Francis E. Kettaneh of New York, A. K. of New York, Mrs. Lowry of Dun Laoghaire and Allan M. Laing of Liverpool. To Georgina Meredith of

Dublin, Miss M. E. Macaulay of the Streatham and Clapham High School, London, Frank M. O'Flanagan of Dalkey, Wm. John O'Brien of Dun Laoghaire and Brian Mac Giolla Phadrig of Terenure. To Patrick O'Reilly of Portobello, Gilbert Patterson of Torca Cottage, Dalkey, Barbara Smoker of London, Charles Sawier of Dublin and Miss Mary Shaw, M.B.E. of Churchtown, Dublin. To Dr. P. C. Smyly of Portarlington, Co. Leix, Messrs Townshend of 15 Molesworth Street, Dublin, E. E. Weavers of the London County Council, Anna M. Wallace of Clonmel, Co. Tipperary and C. E. Wade of Ventnor, I. of W.

There are others to whom I owe heavier debts and to these I would like to express the inexpressible. To my mother for her tears. To Lady Geraldine Hanson of Dublin for her generous and gracious co-operation. To the Officers and members of The Shaw Society of America and, in particular, to David Marshall Holtzmann for his consistently warm-hearted support, to Maxwell Steinhardt for his critical examination and wise counselling during the early phases of *Shaw of Dublin* and to Dr. Stanley Weintraub of The Pennsylvania State University and Editor of *The Shaw Review* for his Archer-like encouragement and guidance.

And finally, to Dr. Felix Grendon without whose faith I could never have dared to enter into the staggering task of charting and sounding the endless seas of George Bernard Shaw.

B. C. ROSSET

Introduction

AN INCREASING FAMILIARITY with the works of Bernard Shaw on the part of the earnest biographophile will disclose not only an inordinate preoccupation with and glorification of foundlings, bantlings and so forth but also such parallel themes as the disparagement of fathers, hatred of mothers and a general disapproval of the tables of consanguinity. Shaw deplored the conventional relations of parents and children, brothers and sisters, and urged their total separation as soon as their most basic needs were filled. The cumulative effect of these observations upon me was the conviction that Shaw seriously questioned the role of George Carr Shaw in contributing to his parentage. It is a principal, but not an exclusive, function of this study to examine this aspect of GBS and evaluate its impact upon his works.

Furthermore, although research in Dublin, London and the libraries revealed that literally dozens of persons had written "full-length" biographies—not to mention the scores who made their contributions on a more modest scale—there were persistent and significant gaps and contradictions that seemed, in effect, self-perpetuating.

GBS—alive and dead—has been examined vertically and horizontally, laterally and diagonally, internally and externally, physiologically and psychologically, upside-down, inside-out, cross-sected, dissected and vivisected. Biographers and critics have found him to be a genius and a fraud, a Saint and a Devil, a hero and a coward, a philosopher and a fool, a dramatist and a windbag, a philanderer and a puritan, an everlasting beacon and the briefest of candles. A remarkable man this Shaw, able to stimulate, inflame or unsettle persons of the most diverse convictions and temperaments.

The contradictions of the biographers—authorized and unauthorized—not only in opinions and conclusion but in the facts as well made it desirable that these conflicts be brought together for examination and possible resolution. Despite an extraordinary uniformity of autobiographical comment over sixty-odd years, Shaw was not exempt from inconsistencies which, however, appeared only in certain sensitive areas. These variations may have been intentional, as GBS once declared that no autobiography can be truthful, that it must be, in fact, deliberately untruthful since no one could be "bad" enough to tell the truth about one's family and friends.[1] In another place he confided that some matters were so "personal" that they were difficult enough to talk about let alone write about. He added that there were even more serious objections to revealing them in that they contained experiences for which no expressions could be found.[2] Now these are interesting announcements, since they suggest that the extensive autobiographical stores of GBS contain areas of silence and elements that may be mendacious. Yet apart from a handful of incidents which indicate circumvention rather than falsification, there is, with one possible exception,[3] no evidence of deliberate lying.

However, Shaw as his own biographer was well aware that the withholding of information is not a lie—it is simply less than the whole truth—and he used this device as well as other stratagems whenever he found it expedient. As an example, Shaw at another point in the *Sketches* confessed that for eighty years he had concealed from his wife, biographers and the world a boyhood experience in that as a student he attended the Central Model School in Marlborough Street, Dublin. Now it may be quite true that there was a Marlborough Street episode and it is certainly true that Shaw "confessed" to one. But in calling attention to what GBS would have us believe was a soul-shattering experience affecting his entire life, had he created a diversion to distract attention from more significant matters?

The tactical maneuver of concealing by revealing was superbly employed by GBS. The approach of an inquirer to certain closeted skeletons was the signal for Shaw to fling open the doors to his "public" collection—the hanged rebel, the wife-beater, a bible-reading voyeur, the drunken father, the Rabelaisian uncle and so on. These and other skeletons, vigorously and amusingly shaken by GBS convinced the inquisitive biographer that he had seen the "real" Shaw and, midst much hilarity, he galloped off in other directions. Mencken assumed that everyone was gifted with his own perspicacity. Mr. Shaw, he said, "drags skeletons from their closet and makes them dance obscenely—but everyone, of course, knew they were there all the while." [4] Shaw's tactical effectiveness was inadvertently illustrated by Henderson who had earlier (1904-1910) exhibited a lively curiosity concerning one Dublin amateur conductor of orchestras and operas, but by 1956 Henderson appeared convinced that GBS had nothing up his sleeve.

> A distinctive feature of Shaw's Weltanschauung . . . was his "unnatural" bent for throwing open the doors to the closets where the family skeletons were concealed. Far from feeling the prompting of any instinct for concealment, Shaw found that his comedic sense was vastly stronger than any conventional "duty" of family loyalty dictating concealment of family eccentricity or defect.[5]

Shaw's facility for language, however, remained his chief weapon to halt or deflect the ferreting biographers and his excellence in this respect did not go unappreciated. Archer wrote that GBS "had a wonderful gift of clear exposition," [6] Beatrice Webb marvelled that she had never known anyone to "use his pen in such a workmanlike fashion . . ." [7] Henderson reported that his subject's literary output was the result of arduous labor, "painstaking self-criticism, and fantastically meticulous correction." [8] Even Einstein applauded and compared, relatively speaking, Shaw's prose to Mozart's music, adding that Shaw's every word had meaning "and was exactly in its proper place." [9] Shaw, certainly, was not unaware of his power and declared so publicly on at least two occasions. The reader of his preface to *Back To Methuselah* learned that with the exception of scientific terms the entire vocabulary of the English body of literature from Shakespeare to the then current edition of the *Encyclopaedia Britan-*

nica was so readily available to him that, except on the rarest occasions when he required a third or fourth synonym, he never consulted a thesaurus. The second public utterance was given in a preface expressly written to a subject for which he had the highest regard: language. He declared that his profession was, technically speaking, "that of a master of language."[10] Privately, Shaw was convinced of his supremacy in the forensic as well as the literary world. To Mrs. Pat Campbell he described himself as "a writing and talking machine" which had been operating for almost forty years and had developed its skill until it was almost "devilish"[11] and, in reproaching her for rejecting him at Sandwich, asserted that he was "the greatest living Master of Letters . . ."[12] During the course of this study there will be several examples in which I hope to show how GBS exploited his mastery of language to avoid preciseness in certain areas while yet giving every appearance of answering the question to the entire satisfaction of the inquirer.

The discovery of major discords among the biographers has made an expansion of the original objectives imperative. Where possible, these conflicts have been subjected to analytical attention and, in many instances, their resolution offered. Support or repudiation of one view or another has been sought for in the plays, prefaces, essays, lectures, novels, letters and authenticated conversations of GBS. In the furtherance of these aims, many sources have been drawn upon but, in the main, reliance has been upon the works of Henderson, Ervine, Pearson, Harris and Shaw.

The examination of any person for biographical purposes can and does vary from a fifteen-second reconnaissance as

Solomon Grundy born on Monday
Christened on Tuesday,
Engaged on Wednesday
Married on Thursday,
Took sick on Friday
Died on Saturday,
Buried on Sunday and
That was the end of Solomon Grundy.

to an exhaustive and self-sacrificing effort encompassing a lifetime of exclusive attention to one person by one or more persons. But there are limitations to even the most enthusiastic, meticulous and devoted of biographers. How far can one descend into a human being? How co-operative can that human being be? In the case of Shaw, as in the case of all really great figures, it will be an appalling task and a never-ending labor.

Despite the attention of his many biographers and notwithstanding his extraordinary skill of attracting attention to himself, nothing but the barest outlines are known of Shaw's life up to, roughly, the age of thirty-five. That so little should be known about a man who wrote so much about himself is nothing if not a tribute to his general strategy and skill with language. Purdom believed that Shaw, unlike Granville-Barker, "never tired of writing about his parents, childhood, and youth . . ." [13] while Harris, commissioned to sketch a miniature of GBS, informed his readers that "Shaw has written about his father and mother and about his life in Dublin at such length and with such a wealth of detail that little needs to be added." [14]

Henderson and O'Bolger however, could not be put upon so easily. In his famous (1905) fifty-four-page letter to his authorized biographer, Shaw side-stepped a reasonable request:

> As to my early life, that I also skip; [Shaw avoided questions on his bibliography and on William Morris] and I doubt whether it will be possible to go into it in much detail . . . For the moment I can only tell you hastily . . .[15]

and here GBS offered material largely reprinted later in the preface to *London Music in 1888-1889*. Responding to O'Bolger's request for some early particulars, Shaw expressed surprise that a biographer would be interested in his subject's youth and replied with a touch of asperity:

> But as you want to reconstruct my childhood (God know why!) I must now go back and tell you something about the relations of my mother and father.[16]

and obliged with a duplication of his earlier notes to Henderson with, however, some striking additions. At ninety-two Shaw was still on the alert and, in what he believed would be his last word on the subject, advised the future biographer that all his "goods" were on display and could be found in his books and plays. "What is communicable," wrote Shaw quite truthfully, "has been already communicated . . ." [17] Equally truthful was his observation that all the better autobiographies were confessions and he included in this class the "deep" writers whose works, GBS believed, were in themselves confessional.[18] On that score, George Bernard Shaw wrote deeply indeed.

What has been revealed by Shaw regarding his first three decades is, considering the huge number of words written on it, astonishingly meager. Frequently informed of the date and place of his birth, a few childhood incidents, the schools attended and other scattered tidbits, we know almost nothing of the child, the boy and the young man. What experiences helped to mould the future dramatist and social revolutionary? What did he see and hear in the dingy *salle à manger* of his birthplace in Synge Street and at Torca Cottage that helped make him one of the most remarkable observers and interpreters of human behavior and motives? And what of the effects of the Hatch Street *ménage à trois* upon this artist in embryo? Was Shaw driven by some irresistible and compelling force to reveal his story—to disperse some of that personal history throughout his works? Did he create his hundreds of characters—ventriloquist's children as it were—to do the telling for him? Mrs. Banger, Cashel Byron, Bingley Byron, Leo and Reginald Bridgenorth, the Bishop of Chelsea, Captain Brassbound, Robin Gilbey, Adelaide Gisborne, St. John Hotchkiss, the Inca of Perusalem, Father Keegan, The Man, John Tarleton, Jeff Smilash, Sidney Trefusis and Ann Whitefield—how much of them was Shaw and how much of them members of the family circle? O'Bolger, as other observers, restricted Shaw's dramatic creations to reflections of himself, thus: "He seems incapable at times of presenting any character but his own." [19] Critic Huneker likewise saw Shaws in every direction but, being unacquainted with the *dramatis personae* of Synge Street, saw no others. He asserted that Shaw "instead of closely observing humanity, after the manner of all great dramatists . . . has only closely studied Bernard Shaw"[20] and added (1906) almost prophetically

> He has spoken through so many different masks that the real Shaw is yet to be seen. Perhaps on his deathbed some stray phrase will illuminate with its witty gleam his true soul's nature.[21]

Henderson offered no formal opinions in his major works but in a private letter to Farmer who published it in his book on Lucy Shaw, he gave his private view: "G. B. Shaw" [Henderson wrote] "was incapable both professionally and temperamentally of drawing a true portrait of any member of his family or relative. . . ."[22] Shaw's own view of the matter has been captured by biographer Pearson who, when he suggested that the ninety-year-old Shaw write a play of his own life, reported GBS as smiling when he replied "All my plays are about myself . . . and my friends." [sic][23]

What we do know about the Dublin period of George Bernard Shaw, or rather, what information we have in this area, is not always agreed upon by his biographers. The Henderson chronicles are, without question, the most comprehensive in range and the most detailed in the activities of Shaw Triumphant; an inexhaustible treasury of things Shavian. *George Bernard Shaw: Man of the Century* (1956) written largely after the death of Shaw focuses generally on the period from 1932 to the year of his death in 1950 and contains a somewhat duplicated section on the younger Shaw as it appeared in his first work *George Bernard Shaw: His Life and Works* (1911). Opus number two *Bernard Shaw: Playboy and Prophet* (1932) was mainly concerned with documentation of the political and theatrical history of GBS and did not add anything of particular interest or importance to our knowledge of the Dublin boy. Though there are curious and unaccountable lacunae in all three works, researchers, scholars and lovers of biography in general have every reason to be grateful to Dr. Archibald Henderson.

St. John Ervine's *Bernard Shaw: His Life, Work and Friends* (1956) is a vigorous, interesting, enterprising and well-organized work. It is also imaginative, eager to enter the fray with Shaw's ashes over still controversial political and social issues and, I thought, unduly critical of the dramatist's mother and sister. Alone of all the biographers, Ervine succeeded in prying a brick or two loose from the traditional wall of silence around the Dublin days, but he offered critical judgments which, at times, were strangely at variance with one another. Ervine, who stated that he began his work "long before" Shaw's death, received his subject's approval and blessing on the grounds that he would appreciate the Irish side of Shaw better than any non-Irishman.[24] Shaw was right as usual. Ervine understood and tried to pass that understanding along to his readers. In that respect I hope this study will add to Ervine's efforts.

Hesketh Pearson's *G.B.S. A Full Length Portrait* (1942) and *Postscript* (1950) is included among the major biographies not only because of its many important contributions but because it was completed in Shaw's eighty-fifth year and with his ever-present assistance. Pearson has, in addition, reported events and conversations with an admirable objectivity and unobtrusiveness.

Shaw's own *Sixteen Self Sketches* (1949) was his answer to the repeated requests that he write his own biography. He asserted that as he had never murdered anyone he was, accordingly, unattractive as a subject.[25] Nevertheless, *Sketches* is enormously interesting and enormously important. Containing much new material, it is a frank and revealing *pasticcio* with some interesting revisions of ancient comments. Chiefly remarkable for Chapter Four: *Shame and Wounded Snobbery—A Secret Kept for 80 Years* and the scourging of O'Bolger, the *Sketches* ranged over some of the lesser known and unknown peaks and valleys from an altitude of ninety-two years. One felt that GBS was not as disinterested as he appeared when he casually invited the attention of the psychoanalysts to make the most of it, suggesting that they "may find in such dull stuff clues that have escaped me." [26]

Beside other sources and those referred to above, there remain four works that cannot be overlooked. Each has its particular value or peculiar distinction and must be noted here. The first of these goes under the eye-catching title of *G.B.S.'s Sister and Her Friends: A New Angle on Bernard Shaw* (1959). Brought into existence by Dr.

Henry George Farmer, its appearance made a projected exploration of Lucy Shaw and her relations with mother and brother unnecessary. This is not to say that Farmer's book as such is a serious contribution to the general literature on Shaw—it is not. In his fever to defend Lucy's character and career, the author charged Shaw with the organization and fostering of what he called "that audacious fraud the 'Shaw Story' "; that is (one was eventually able to glean), the promotion of GBS's career at the expense of his sister's reputation.[27] In this adventure Dr. Farmer received support from an unexpected quarter: Dr. Henderson who informed Farmer that Shaw "was jealous of her [Lucy]; and resented even her [minor] successes, and jeered at them." [28] Yet the book is not wholly without merit, for Dr. Farmer has performed an exceedingly valuable service in acquiring and publishing several of the hundred-odd pieces of correspondence from Lucy to her friend Janey Crichton.

Exhibit Two is Stephen Winsten's *Jesting Apostle: The Life of Bernard Shaw* (1956). Winsten, a former neighbor of GBS in the village of Ayot St. Lawrence, is the author of a number of books concerned with Shaw including *G.B.S. 90* (1946), *Days with Bernard Shaw* (1949), *The Quintessence of G.B.S.* (1949) and *Shaw's Corner* (1952). While having their own interest these books are relatively unimportant and are cited now and then. *Jesting Apostle,* on the other hand, acquired value through its author's statement that it was the result of a long series of intimate conversations with GBS. Written in the humanizing manner of the Ludwig biographies, *Jesting Apostle* features quoted conversations among the principals during the infancy of GBS and confidential reports on what the dying Agnes thought of Professor Lee and what Professor Lee thought of young Shaw and so on. Yet Winsten managed to intercept several of Shaw's most significant utterances and will be given appropriate attention.

Third in this group is Frank Harris' *Bernard Shaw* (1931) and subtitled *An Unauthorized Biography Based On First Hand Information.* It contains a profusion of announcements such as a "Dedication" to his ghostwriter; a "Publisher's Note" that the proof sheets "were corrected for the press by Mr. George Bernard Shaw himself . . .";[29] "Credentials" by GBS and a "Postscript by the Subject of this Memoir." [30] The facts behind this literary legerdemain seem to be that a publisher commissioned Harris, reduced in circumstances, to "do" Shaw and assigned Frank Scully to "assist." Shaw, heavily obligated to Harris for giving him work and a free hand on *The Saturday Review,* agreed to cooperate and the way was clear. But Harris took his duties as lightly as he took the publisher's generous advances and left the work to Scully, who later declared, "I wrote it, after ghosting the whole book. . . ." [31] At another point Scully further revealed that he had

> goaded Harris into doing this biog. (Incidentally, I was nursing a two-year-old grudge against Shaw, but that's another story.) I kept writing letters to Shaw for Harris to sign . . . but it was never my intention to pull our punches. Nothing short of a knockout would have satisfied me.[32]

Scully cagily evaded the opportunity to disclose his "grudge" against GBS nor did he explain what he meant by "knockout." Sometime after this dismal affair Shaw, meeting Scully on a train in Europe, is alleged by Scully to have stated that Harris knew practically nothing of his life and Scully even less. However, Shaw went on, the book was factual and accurate and commended it to its readers as "my story." [33] The substance of this was supported by Shaw who, upon re-reviewing the manuscript, wrote that as it contained suppositional matter and serious misstatements he had, consequently, to "rewrite his book myself on matters of fact . . ." before it could be published.[34] With reference to this study, Harris' *Bernard Shaw* will occupy a unique position in respect to certain correspondence from Shaw and in particular to the examination of the influence of his hand in the revision—especially as it touched upon the Dublin scene.

The fourth and final member of this cluster is by far the most provocative—for its effect on Shaw as well as for the correspondence concerning it. Thomas Demetrius O'Bolger, a teacher on the staff of the University of Pennsylvania, developed an interest in Shaw during the first decade of this century and on the basis of that interest submitted in 1913 for his doctoral thesis *The Real Shaw.* Subsequently he wrote another article, *The Social Satires of Bernard Shaw,* neither of which, however, went beyond the confines of the University. It may be seen that by this time O'Bolger was fast in the grip of Shawitis and on the strength of this interest proposed to do a Life. He entered into communication with GBS, with whom he was personally acquainted to "a slight degree," [35] and received a considerable number of letters containing information never before released. In the course of the next six years, O'Bolger wrote in his introduction, he made four complete revisions to meet the objections of Shaw. By 1919 the book seemed to comply with GBS's conditions and it made the rounds of the publishers, one of whom signed O'Bolger to a contract in which he relinquished all of his rights in return for ten per cent of the book's income—providing, of course, it had Shaw's approval. GBS seized on O'Bolger's bad bargain and refused to allow a word of his to be published unless O'Bolger received twenty-five per cent on a sliding scale and retained all the rights appropriated by the publisher. Naturally, the publisher backed down, tore up the contract and, after threatening Shaw, the distracted author wrote revision number five making good his threat by abstracting GBS *in toto.* Offered to another publisher, it again received a warm smile: they would be delighted to issue it—providing, of course, GBS approved of its rather sensational treatment and contributed a "little" preface. Needless to say, Shaw declined the honor, threatened to bring suit against author and publisher if they published it and returned the manuscript accompanied by an abusive excoriation of O'Bolger. To Frank Harris, GBS wrote that in those circumstances he could not consent to its publication; and since Harper's refused to publish it, O'Bolger, assisted by pernicious anemia, died a disappointed biographer—the air surrounding his deathbed ringing with curses for the man who had ruined him.[36] Shaw's fire-breathing opinions of O'Bolger and his "wretched" manuscript, his never-before published comments on the central characters in the Shaw drama and other related matters will be dealt with as they become pertinent to the topic.

Before proceeding to the body of this study, it may be helpful to remind the reader of the members of the Shaw family with whom we will be mainly concerned. George Carr Shaw Esq., gentleman, an unsuccessful merchant in corn and frequently sober. He is the husband of Lucinda Elizabeth, twenty-two at the time of her marriage and sixteen years younger than her husband. Mrs. Shaw is the just Lady made perfect. In addition to possessing a lovely mezzo-soprano voice she has a knowledge of music sufficient to compose ballads and make arrangements for various instruments of amateur orchestras. She is the mother of Lucinda Frances, Elinor Agnes and George Bernard. She is also the pupil and musical aide-de-camp of singing teacher and dynamic conductor George John Lee, perfector of The Method—a system of voice production and preservation. The time: 1850-1896.

B.C.R.

Loch Gowna
November, 1963

Contents

It is certain at least, that he cared little for the relations of kinship. His family do not seem to have loved him, and at times he seems to have been hard toward them. . . . like all men exclusively preoccupied by an idea, he came to think little of the ties of blood. The bond of thought is the only one that natures of this kind recognize.

Ernest Renan
The Life of Jesus

I / George Carr Shaw

I

Of the fourteen children that blessed the union of Bernard Shaw and Frances Carr, George Carr, born on the thirtieth of December 1814 was the eighth child and third son. In 1826 (his fifty-first year) the elder Shaw died—his departure, it was hinted, being hastened by a larcenous business associate who took wing with some £50,000 of Shaw's capital including monies belonging to clients. At forty-three, Mrs. Shaw was left perilously close to destitution with eleven surviving children whose ages at this melancholy period were:

Cecilia	21
Frances	19
Charlotte Jane	17
William Bernard	15
Edward Carr	13
George Carr	12
Robert	10
Henry	7
Emily	5
Walter Stephen	4
Richard Frederick	2

Mrs. Shaw was no stranger to death and, prior to the demise of her husband, had had more than an academic acquaintance with the heavenly summons. In 1813 her second-born, Maria, died in her ninth year, somewhat short of the customary allotment. For Mother, 1818 was a banner year. First-born Sarah Anne joined Maria in her fifteenth year while Richard Osborne died in the year of his birth. For good measure, Robert was born blind. Truly, the cup runneth over.

In view of the difficulties facing the widow Shaw one might surmise that George Carr, twelve years old and in that troublesome time of adolescence, was not overburdened with a mother's corrective influence. Nothing whatever is known of his boyhood or young manhood and so GBS informed O'Bolger.[1] Harris offered nothing positive but offered it in the Harrisian manner—or was it Shaw's busy hand? "Except for playing the role of Prince Consort so that George Bernard Shaw might be legitimately born, George Carr Shaw's life couldn't in any sense be considered important. How he grew up nobody seems to have kept much track of." [2] As to George Carr's education, GBS has referred to it in several places but O'Bolger received what may be described as the "complete" account. His father, responded Shaw, never referred to his education from which GBS deduced that he either had none at all or that it was sketchy and not worth mentioning.[3] All things considered, George Carr's biographical vacuum seems to be justified as he could point only to being a Shaw, a Protestant, a second cousin to a baronet and, as he later refused to engage in retail trade, a gentleman. Unfitted by nature for any detectable purpose, he developed a surreptitious fondness for whiskey and a sense of humor usually described by GBS as anticlimactic in form.

George Carr at forty-six and beyond has been reported on to some extent. Reaching into his earliest years of recall, GBS described his father as a victim of primogeniture. However since his father had died in poverty, it would have made little difference had he been the principal beneficiary. Be that as it may, GBS saw George Carr as being "timid" [4] and having "no inheritance, no profession, no manual skill, no qualification for any sort of any definite social function" but, continued GBS ironically, he had been raised to believe that as a Shaw he had, perforce, inherited the virtue of inborn gentility.[5] Matthew Edward McNulty, boyhood friend of young Shaw and himself a novelist and playwright, is the only other writer known to have personal knowledge of George Carr. In a ten-thousand-word memoir intended for publication, McNulty wrote of him after he had been abandoned by the last of his family to leave him that Mr. Shaw

> had not the mental range of his son, and was not interested in art, literature or science; but he was fairly keen on the current topics of the day. . . . The old man—he seemed old to me then, but was probably not much more than 50. . . . Sometimes we met in the street, and stopped for a handshake and a few words. He always had a smile of greeting. Sometimes, when I passed the Chambers of Commerce in Dame Street, of which he was a member, I saw him seated near a window, reading a financial paper. He always wore his glasses low down on his nose, and used to tilt his head back to get the correct focus.[6]

Since the period of these observations took place after GBS's departure for London, McNulty was mistaken in his estimate of George Carr's age for by 1876 Mr. Shaw was sixty-two.

II

IT IS A FEATURE OF GBS that he exercised a consistent refusal to reveal a three- or even two-dimensional view of George Carr. He never made reference to his height, weight, gait or voice and, apart from a "squint" (polite Irish for crossed-eye), made no mention of any physical characteristics.

McNulty marked the elder Shaw as a "little man" [7] while Ervine, after taking note of McNulty's observation described him as being a "small man." An impression of the relative size of George Carr is afforded in a letter written by him on 4 December 1882 to GBS in London and concerned the gift of a coat from his sister Charlotte (Aunt Cha). Made for her husband, it was found to be a poor fit and when advised by the tailor that an alteration would ruin it, she sent it to her brother. But, wrote Mr. Shaw, it was "too big" for him and he was, therefore, passing it along to son George who had not yet emerged from the early desperate years of the London period.[8] From this, one could draw the conclusion that George Carr's dimensions did not equal the six-feet-one-inch and spare frame of GBS, then in his twenty-sixth year.

O'Bolger, who had somehow managed to charm or annoy GBS into giving him information accorded no other biographer, was particularly honored with an unusual close-up of George Carr. He was, said GBS,

> full of self-reproaches and humiliations when he was not full of secret jokes, and was either biting his moustache and whispering deep-drawn damns or shaking with silent paroxysms of laughter.[9]

This little sketch suggests a George Carr full of whiskey as well as self-reproaches and secret jokes. The alternative conviction being that Mr. Shaw had somehow bridged the gap between puerility and senility with little or no pause at the stations between. Again to O'Bolger, GBS offered another glimpse of the elder Shaw—decent and fatherly, plagued by a memory but not altogether beyond redemption. Mr. Shaw was, wrote GBS, in fact "humane and likeable" and related his confession that in his youth he had let his dog course and kill a stray cat. Still conscience-smitten with this wickedness, Mr. Shaw advised his small son that anyone committing such an act did not merit nor would he ever attain any success or happiness.[10]

III

THE HUMOR OF GEORGE CARR SHAW bears some attention in that it was claimed by some to be the source of GBS's—a claim fostered by the dramatist himself. Writing in the 1921 preface to his first novel,

GBS acknowledged his debt to the elder Shaw in this respect, asserting that "he was in the grip of a humorous sense of anticlimax which I inherited from him and used with much effect when I became a writer of comedy." [11] He added that the elder Shaw's enjoyment of a joke increased if the situation involved matters of convention, thus, by extension, suggesting the evolutionary link to the future iconoclast. To O'Bolger, Shaw disclosed that in addition to composing odd bits of whimsical verse, George Carr made puns, which were then the fashion. In illustration whereof, GBS told O'Bolger that if he were to be introduced to him, Mr. Shaw would, without hesitation, repeat his name backwards as Reglob O'Suirtemed.[12]

The reputation of George Carr Shaw as a humorist rests largely upon the preceding selections and the following anecdotes related by GBS.

EXAMPLE 1. When the firm of Clibborn & Shaw suffered a severe loss due to the bankruptcy of one of its customers, Mr. Shaw "albeit ruined," viewed the disaster in such a hilarious manner that (presumably not to offend his crushed partner) he had to withdraw from their office in haste to a far corner of their granary and there laugh until spent.[13]

EXAMPLE 2. When, during GBS's childhood, the Shaws were visited by a Unitarian named Haughton, the curious Sonny wanted to know what a Unitarian was. Mr. Shaw replied "humorously" that a Unitarian was one who did not believe that Jesus was crucified in that he was observed running down the far side of the Hill of Calvary.[14]

EXAMPLE 3. When, under the influence of his scoffing Uncle Walter and the sceptical Lee, Sonny jeered at the Bible, Mr. Shaw would promptly and in all seriousness admonish the lad, lecturing that it was a mark of an ignorant man to speak thus of a book that was accepted everywhere as a literary and historical work of art. But when he had reached the stage of dramatic solemnity, some inner disturbance would crinkle his eyes and, with a show of impartiality, assure his young listener "that even the worst enemy of religion could say no worse of the Bible than that it was the damnedest parcel of lies ever written . . ." [15]

EXAMPLE 4. The tale of Sonny's first ocean dip in Killiney Bay at the foot of Dalkey mountain. Mr. Shaw concluded a lecture on the necessity of learning how to swim with a personal reminiscence: "When I was a boy of only fourteen," [he told Sonny] "my knowledge of swimming enabled me to save your Uncle Robert's life." [16] Noting the seriousness with which Sonny received this account, Mr. Shaw bent down to have the lad's ear and added "and, to tell you the truth, I never was so sorry for anything in my life afterwards." [17]

Clearly, these accounts do not establish George Carr Shaw as an austere or dour man. Nor do they, on the other hand, portray a particularly gifted humorist. The first sketch conveys a variety of humor suggesting some form of hysteria and would seem to call for a fresh approach to the study of George Carr Shaw. Items two and three are either amusing or sacrilegious as individually determined. Profane or not, they are diverting but I am inclined to believe that Mr. Shaw borrowed his brother-in-law Walter's original material and passed it off as his own to young Sonny. The last tale, apart from its humorous content, may or may not have a particular significance though it suggests that despite Mr. Shaw's amiable disposition (agreed to by all), there were some differences between him and blind brother Robert. Conclusion: if these passages fail to reveal the humorist in George Carr, they do show a man who could appreciate its effects.

GBS's views of Mr. Shaw's drolleries have been absorbed and —more or less faithfully—reflected by the biographers. Hackett reported George Carr's humor to be "acute and mischievous";[18] Ervine had him as a "genial" man whose "sardonic sense of humour and anti-climax [was] a gift which he transmitted to his son . . ." [19] Pearson saw him as one "born with a kind heart" and whose humor —the anticlimactic type—was "so keen that disasters that would have reduced another man to tears reduced him to helpless laughter." [20] Henderson chronicled that the elder Shaw, "an amiable but timid man," had one characteristic which was "reproduced in his son, his antithesis in almost every other respect, [—] a sense of humor, an appreciation of the comic force of anti-climax." [21] While that strange trio of ill-matched voices: Harris, Scully and GBS chorused that

George Carr had "an ungovernable taste for humorous anti-climax which was all he had to bequeath to his son." [22] As none of the writers (excepting GBS, of course) had ever met or seen the senior Shaw, their "humorous" Shaws may be accepted with some reservation and as being variations on the composition by GBS.

Of the same group of biographers only Henderson had met the mother of GBS and, in reporting on that meeting, seemed to have forgotten the source for that one characteristic of George Carr inherited by GBS:

> I remember [wrote Henderson] . . . taking tea with Mrs. Shaw and her son. . . . Her eyes danced with suppressed mirth as she talked, and it is quite easy to see from whom her son derived his sense of humor.[23]

It appears that GBS did not attend Henderson in manuscript for the dramatist held a different opinion of his mother. She, he declared, "had no comedic impulses, and never uttered an epigram in her life: all my comedy is a Shavian inheritance. . . ." [24] Ervine, who had never met Mrs. Shaw, agreed with his subject's opinion of his mother's humorless outlook. He put it that Mrs. Shaw had a "peculiar" brand of humor which might be termed no humor at all, adding elsewhere, in a tone of finality, that "It was from him [George Carr], however, that GBS inherited his wit and sardonic humour: Lucinda Elizabeth had none to leave." [25] There is no evidence whatever to show that Harris had met Mrs. Shaw, but their meeting was not unlikely—at least during the *Saturday Review* days of the eighteen-nineties. He had an opinion of Mrs. Shaw's humor index and expressed it without the direct interference of GBS's revising hand. Ten years before his fall from the throne of literary grace, Harris reported that Mrs. Shaw had "humor, sympathetic humor, extraordinarily developed" [26] but did not offer source to support this assertion. Mrs. Georgina Gillmore Musters, a half-sister to Mrs. Shaw expressed her estimate in a letter to Henderson. Lucinda, wrote Mrs. Musters, "had a great capacity for enjoyment [and] a great sense of fun as well. . . ." [27] William Archer who, as a friend, was possibly Shaw's most affectionate attachment, often visited GBS and his mother in Fitzroy

Square and had ample opportunity to observe. Addressing an audience in New York, he recalled:

> I knew his mother, and a very fine old lady she was, from whom her son undoubtedly inherited, among other things, his sense of humour.[28]

Even GBS was not excepted from joining the dissenters in dissolving a saturnine Mrs. Shaw. To Bland, an early Fabian comrade, he described his mother as a "hearty" and "jolly" [29] person thirty-two years before he characterized her as a dour soul.

As ear- and eyewitnesses, Henderson, Musters and Archer are undoubtedly accurate, suggesting that George Carr Shaw's sense of humor, insofar as GBS discussed it, may have been largely exaggerated and that his mother's sense of humor—ignored as nonexistent—a contributing if not potent factor.

With respect to the doubts raised here as to whom to credit for the humor of GBS, one may well ponder its source, thus leading to the speculation of the acquisition rather than the inheritance of that elusive property. In this consideration, it is suggested that maternal Uncle Walter John seems to have had far more to do with this aspect of GBS than has perhaps hitherto been realized. While formal genealogical accounts give Uncle Walter's year of birth as 1831, school records differ considerably—thus Kilkenny College ("college" being a loose term in Ireland then and now) marked his entrance into that Protestant institution during "1848 aged 10 years, son of W. Gurly, Esq., Stillorgan, Dublin" [30] and, consequently, born in 1838. From Kilkenny, Walter entered Trinity College Dublin and, again from school records, he is reported to have enrolled on 15 October 1852 aged seventeen and therefore born during 1835. There were no details regarding his term in Trinity other than being a paying student, having a Dr. Smith for a tutor and leaving without a degree. He seems to have returned to Trinity (GBS has told that Walter had to resign in order to recover his health after excessive but unidentified debaucheries[31]) to enter the Medical School in 1854. Trinity further stated that in 1863 the degree of M.R.C.S. (Member Royal College Surgeons) was conferred upon him in England and finally, in 1876 he received an "L.M.S.A.A."—a license from Apothecaries Hall and practiced from Grange Park Road, Leyton, Sussex.

To anyone familiar with GBS's treatments of the personality and characteristics of Uncle Walter, it will be apparent how utterly impossible it will be to describe these details adequately in abstract. To those not familiar with Shaw on Uncle Walter, the germane portion of the preface to *Immaturity* and pages 31-33 of the *Sketches* are recommended as superb examples of the character-sketching artistry of Bernard Shaw. Suffice to say that when Uncle Walter was at last released to ply his profession of surgeon, he elected to bestow the blessings of his training upon seamen in the merchant service where he remained for some years. Dr. Gurly, Shaw reported, was observant, intelligent, witty, articulate, artistic, Shakespearean and full of the Bible. He was also blasphemous, obscene, profane, a rake and a scoffer, Falstaffian, Rabelaisian and full of whiskey and he combined all these qualities and conditions without regard to time and place or the complexion of his audience and, whether they were his shipmates or his impressionable nephew, performed before all with an impartial zest. The effect of Dr. Gurly's regime upon the future heresiarch has been given by his most famous patient: GBS.[32] In some serious advice to unheeding biographers, Shaw disposed, I believe, of George Carr as a major influence in the moulding of the man:

> It would be the greatest mistake to conclude that this shocking state of affairs [Uncle Walter's influence] was bad for my soul. In so far as the process of destroying reverence for the inessential trappings of religion was indecent, it was deplorable; and I wish my first steps to grace had been lighted by my uncle's wit and style without his obscenity. My father's comedy was entirely decent. But that the process was necessary to my salvation I have no doubt whatever.[33]

IV

GBS's LOVE OF MUSIC and its influence on him during the early formative years was often summed up by him with a reference to the Shaws as a "musical family" and a suggestion from GBS that his critical faculties with respect to music were a direct Shavian inheritance. In his *George Bernard Shaw: Man of the Century,* Henderson stated categorically that the Shaws were "amazingly musical," each one being able to play "some sort" of an instrument. In his earliest work he was inclined to be more prudent, merely reporting that the principal virtue of the family, apart from their respectability, was their "remarkable aptitude for playing all sorts of wind instruments by ear, even his father playing *Home, Sweet Home* upon the flute," [34] thus restricting the variety of instruments to a particular class. Henderson's use of "remarkable" raises a minor question as to its authorship since it is not likely that young Shaw ever heard members of the Shaw clan individually (except for Uncle William who played in Lee's orchestra) or collectively at any of the musical evenings at Sir Robert's Bushy Park home. Writing in his preface to *Immaturity,* Shaw recalled that he had been to Bushy Park but once and that on the circumstance of Sir Robert's death.[35] He later told his cousin Grace Goodliffe that he got no further than viewing the oak casket in the hall.[36] As Sir Robert died on the nineteenth of February, 1869, young Shaw paid his first and last visit to Bushy Park in his thirteenth year.

In his sixty-fifth year, GBS gave a picture of a musical evening at Bushy Park, suggesting an account from memory. Today's readers, he believed, would be moved to laughter if they were to attend one of Bushy Park's musical evenings for they would see Sir Robert attended by the clan, all of whom were arrayed in a circle around Uncle Barney standing upon an ottoman, solemnly rendering *Annie Laurie* on his ophicleide.[37] But GBS could not have meant his readers to believe he had been an eyewitness to this scene for in the Goodliffe letter he rounded out the cast. His mother, he informed cousin

Grace, once described to him the picture of Uncle Barney perched atop the ottoman and playing, with great feeling, *Annie Laurie.*[38]

The musical aptitudes of the Shaws have been observed and commented upon by the musically-trained Mrs. Lucinda Elizabeth Shaw to her son, the future Corno di Bassetto. Drawing from these early memories, GBS advised his readers that the Shaws were naturally musical. All the ladies, he continued, "could 'pick out tunes' on the piano, and support them with the chords of the tonic, subdominant, dominant, and tonic again. Even a Neapolitan sixth was not beyond them." [39] Now to nonmusical duffers (like myself) this description appears as recondite as Bach in B Minor, but I am assured that it simply means the ladies were equal to providing a left-hand contribution of two or three notes and no more complicated than the rum-tum to *Chopsticks.* Pearson, allowing that the Shaws played every kind of an instrument, believed them to be "illiterate musically" while Ervine saw "nothing remarkable" about their musical tastes or accomplishments. GBS's opinions on the nontechnical level were expressed to Goodliffe and O'Bolger. To cousin Grace he wrote in 1949 that, musically speaking, the Shaws en masse were utterly useless. Symphony, oratorio and opera, he added, had no attractions for them.[40] And to O'Bolger he conceded that they did not know and could not read music.[41]

Contrary to the Shaws, GBS was hopelessly classical in his musical tastes. Surrounded in his childhood and youth, thanks to his mother and her music professor by opera, oratorio and symphony, they were as much a part of his artistic growth as the material necessities were to his physical growth—inconceivably more if one considers the nature of that childhood. His musical education was, like all his education, self-taught. The earliest account of Shaw's musical interest and activity was given to O'Bolger in 1916. Speaking of the period in Dublin when he was left without music as a result of his mother's departure for London, GBS wrote that he had been steeped in music from his childhood "through the ear" and he had once as a small infant "played the *Guards Waltz* with one finger." [42] As no one encouraged the child's musical curiosity—possibly because the piano was considered an instrument exclusively for ladies—he never touched the piano again until his sixteenth year. With Lee and his mother in London, young Shaw found himself music-less but still in possession of the family piano. Upon this unfortunate instrument he made desperate but partially successful attempts to teach himself with the aid of a book containing a diagram of the keyboard. It was this, he admitted later, or musical starvation.[43]

The piano was not the only instrument GBS tried to conquer for he had, at one time, been fascinated by the commanding voice of the cornet. McNulty was familiar with his friend's musical aspirations and noted it in his unpublished memoirs about the end of the century. (Ervine published a briefer account, based upon it.)[44] GBS, McNulty wrote, took instructions from

> Mr. George Connoly, a member of the Theatre Royal orchestra, and to this gentleman's residence in Mount Pleasant Avenue [South Dublin] Shaw used to trudge twice a week, with his cornet wrapped in brown paper under his arm. But this phase lasted only a few months; Shaw explained its collapse by the fact that it was necessary for a cornet player to have his lips of hornlike consistency, and he found that too tedious a process.[45]

Shaw's version? He told O'Bolger that his uncle (probably Walter) presented him with a "very bad" cornet à pistons, and he undertook lessons with an English band musician named Kennedy. When Shaw learned that the instrument would eventually prevent him from singing properly, he gave it to Kennedy.[46] The cornet and sensitive lips of young Shaw were to be recalled a dozen years later, figuring as an amusing detail in "The Serenade" and may be noted in *Short Stories, Scraps and Shavings.*

V

It is a function of this study to trace, if possible, the hereditary and environmental agencies influencing the future dramatist, critic and philosopher. Recall that the musical aptitudes of the Shaws are overshadowed by Henderson's use of 'even' as employed in 'even his father playing *Home, Sweet Home* upon the flute.' This seems to suggest that, according to GBS as quoted by Henderson, George Carr's musical talent was somewhat below the already low Shaw standards. The passage of forty-five years did not confirm this estimate for in *Man of the Century,* GBS is quoted as raising Mr. Shaw to the celestial heights of—but to put it directly, "Mr. Shaw," chronicled Professor Henderson, "could not read music but could play any instrument; and was described by Shaw, by an excessive extension of the word's meaning, as a 'sort of musical genius' (surely 'wizard' would have been a more accurate word)." [47] With the phrase "excessive entension," Henderson pinpointed the blunder and, perhaps out of consideration for his feelings toward GBS, substituted "wizard" which, in its most applicable meaning, is defined as a "clever or skilled person." The quote also contains a declaration that 'Shaw's father . . . could play any instrument,' but neither this nor his musical wizardry is supported anywhere. GBS's own opinions were expressed fairly frequently, but they had an odd sort of consistency. Mr. Shaw, wrote GBS in one of his many variations, "not only played his trombone part, but actually composed it as he went along, being an indifferent reader-at-sight, but an expert at what used to be called 'vamping.' " [48] In another place and at another time, GBS took the elder Shaw down another notch. Gone was the touch of the expert and in its place, a limitation. Mr. Shaw, stated GBS, "played the trombone, and could vamp a bass on it to any tune that did not modulate too distractingly." [49] George Carr's musical level, then, was on a parallel with those of the Chopstick Shaws. Henderson believed that Sonny Shaw cared little for the "infernal cacophony" that Mr. Shaw coaxed from the trombone and reported GBS as observing that his father shattered the peace of his home by intemperate address to the trombone,[50] thus giving, possibly, some reflection of the opinions of Mrs. Shaw. To Jerome Kern's *Nine Questions* GBS, in replying to one of them, gave a miniature but sharp picture of the musicianship of Mr. Shaw who

> *was an amateur of the trombone, and could play "Home, Sweet Home" on the penny whistle or flute in its primitive form.*[51]

—a far cry from a 'sort of musical genius' or 'wizard.'

It was an unknown Irish-American teacher who received the most remarkable report on George Carr's capacity for musical expression. From the University of Pennsylvania to G. Bernard Shaw in London went the thesis of Thomas Demetrius O'Bolger, candidate for the degree of Doctor of Philosophy. Would Mr. Shaw care to comment on *The Influence of Mr. Shaw's Youth On His Views and Personality*? Of course, answered Mr. Shaw and did so in the form of marginal corrections and annotations. In connection with O'Bolger's comments on the musical inclinations of the Shaw clan, GBS noted that Mr. Shaw's instrument was the trombone on which he could produce bass vamps to accommodate the commonplace tunes of the day. Continuing, he recalled that it was considered fashionable to play the wind instrument and the custom for groups of brass-festooned gentlemen to give performances as they wandered up and down the banks of the city's rivers. A member of one of these groups was George Carr Shaw but, GBS had it, Mr. Shaw

> was a fraud, pretending to read the trombone part from notes but really vamping it. . . . It maddened my mother. There was a tune "And *what* a bean and *what* a bean and WHAT a bean your granny was, and *what*" *da capo ad lib* —the ideal Shaw tune. For purposes of domestic bliss my father had better have been born deaf.[52]

It is far more reasonable to seek the seed of GBS's love for music in his mother, her relationship with her singing master George John Lee and the musical environment of the Synge and the Hatch Street homes.

Mr. Shaw's interest in his son's artistic growth was touched upon briefly in the preface to *Immaturity*. His father, said GBS, "encouraged" him to attend the National Gallery, the opera and the theatre "when I could afford it." [53] He once spurred Sonny to read Scott's novels, but there is no evidence that George Carr accompanied young Shaw to any cultural event. It can be reported, however, that this duty was taken up at least once by a thoughtful but unnamed gentleman. "Harris" related that when Shaw was a little boy he was brought to the opera for the first time (by whom he did not say) and described the child's delight when the curtain suddenly rose.[54] In an article written in 1950 and published eight days after his death, Shaw harked back to an incident of his boyhood. The first time he attended the opera, he wrote, he was taken by an "adult" whom he further described as a singing teacher. He remembered the opera to have been *Il Trovatore* and how he expressed his surprise at hearing Manrico render the serenade off stage. Turning to the adult, Sonny asked, "What is that?" Replied the singing teacher-critic, "A pig under a gate." [55]

VI

For one endowed with a surplusage of faults, George Carr Shaw's chief blemish—all biographers acknowledge—was no subject for disagreement. There is no evidence to indicate when or why Mr. Shaw took to drinking, but that he did was a distressing and pervasive fact in the lives of the Shaws of Dublin. Inspection of several bales of Shaw memorabilia at the British Museum produced, as one of the more interesting items, a notebook containing some biographical notes apparently intended for some future effort. Estimated to have been written about 1881, the notebook recorded the twenty-five-year-old Shaw's exercises on his father. The list of beverages consumed by Mr. Shaw were diverse to say the least and included champagne, whiskey, brandy and stout—the last of which he downed in such quantities that it made him ill. While he was never sober, he was never thoroughly helpless and at intervals took the pledge for periods up to sixteen months with, however, the eventual collapse of his good intentions. Once or twice he vanished for several days and on his return his clothing and watch were considerably the worse for the experience. But apart from these excesses, he usually arrived home fuddled with drink, ate his dinner, napped and afterwards made frequent trips to the spirits shop for short ones until bedtime. He never, concluded GBS, did any drinking at home.

But irrespective of George Carr's degree of sobriety or intoxication, he openly exhibited extreme humiliation for his weakness and did not spare himself or his listeners in his self-condemnation. What gave Mr. Shaw's liquorous propensity its peculiar flavor was his sincere conviction that he was a teetotaler—honestly and unalterably opposed to the consumption of alcoholic beverages, thus making, in his eyes, his own addiction all the more reprehensible. Though GBS has described him as a "dipsomaniac," [56] there is no reason to believe him to be an alcoholic in the medical sense since it took a relatively large quantity of whiskey to put him into the category of "disgraceful."

Other particulars of George Carr's changing personality while under Bacchus' influence have been given by GBS. While ordinarily harmless, humane and "the least formidable of men" [57] Mr. Shaw became violent and even dangerous under certain conditions. He seemed to prefer drinking alone but apparently knew when to cry enough. He never reached the condition of senselessness since whiskey did not affect him so and was always able to proceed under his own power. But, added GBS, he was obviously drunk, not in control of himself and moved as if he were walking in his sleep. If scolded at this time he was quite likely to flare up into an unexpected passion, seize anything handy and hurl it to the ground.[58]

George Carr Shaw's teetotalism in theory is hinted at in ACT I of *John Bull's Other Island* wherein the raffish Tim Haffigan avows that while he is a "teetotaler" in principle, he must force himself to accept Broadbent's proffered whiskey and soda because he has bad indigestion and a "wake" heart. *Fanny's First Play* contains a peek at a lightly-disguised George Carr via Robin Gilbey. This occurs in ACT III of *The Play* within the play. As the elder Shaw called young

GBS "Bob" in his early childhood, the use of "Rob" here lends some weight to the assumption that this passage is autobiographical. The reference to Rob and Bob at this time may seem to be stretching the point, but elaboration later may make the assumption more acceptable. In a minor exchange on family skeletons, Gilbey asked the Knoxes whether he had ever told them that his father drank and continued

> My father used to say to me: Rob, he says, dont you ever get a weakness. If you find one getting a hold on you, make a merit of it, he says. Your Uncle Phil doesnt like spirits; and he makes a merit of it, and is chairman of the Blue Ribbon Committee. I do like spirits; and I make a merit of it, and I'm the King Cockatoo of the Convivial Cockatoos. Never put yourself in the wrong, he says. I used to boast about what a good boy Bobby was. Now I swank about what a dog he is . . .

The circumstances of George Carr's transition from teetotaler in principle to teetotaler in fact has been recorded both biographically and dramatically by GBS. Struck down by "a mild fit, which felled him on our doorstep one Sunday afternoon, [it] convinced him that he must stop drinking or perish." [59] The incident being sufficiently impressive to young Shaw to be recalled some thirty years later for use in *The Shewing-up of Blanco Posnet*:

> Blanco
> (to Elder Daniels)
> Dont deceive yourself, Boozy . . . you gave up drink yourself because when you got that fit at Edwardstown the doctor told you youd die the next time; and that frightened you off it.

Now it is not suggested that Tim Haffigan, Robin Gilbey or Boozy Daniels are seriously based on George Carr. These extracts are offered as specimens of actual characteristics and incidents influencing dramatic dialogue and situation. Though GBS denied to O'Bolger that he had ever put Mr. Shaw or anyone resembling him into a play,[60] this study will attempt later to show that in one play at least, George Carr, his wife Lucinda and George John Lee were the principal characters.

VII

THE APPEARANCE OF GEORGE CARR SHAW in the world of commerce has not heretofore been established in point of time and has been said by GBS to have been launched in a clerkship or two, one of them being in an ironworks concern. MacMahon Shaw, who had expressed reservations regarding this prosaic employment for a Shaw, received GBS's annotated assurance that it was true—he had been told so by Mr. Shaw himself.[61] But being a second cousin to the reigning baronet, George Carr was, understandably, unhappy, and prevailed upon one of his numerous brothers or sisters to use their influence in his behalf. Whatever or whoever was responsible, he succeeded in obtaining employment more in harmony with his gentle birth and entered into the Royal Civil Service. Assigned to Dublin's Four Courts (the fountainhead of Irish Justice), Mr. Shaw's title or specific duties have yet to be discovered. At any rate, Mr. Shaw remained with the Four Courts until, according to Pearson, Henderson and Ervine, the year 1850 when the post was abolished as a sinecure. GBS himself was not too certain whether it was the post itself which was abolished [62] or the entire department[63] but in either event, George Carr received a pension claimed to be in the sum of £60 per year as consolation which, Ervine reported, was sold at once for the lump sum of £500. GBS allowed that with his pension "promptly" sold, Mr. Shaw entered into partnership with one George Clibborn and between them purchased an established business in wholesale transactions of corn, flour and cereals.

The notebooks of GBS in the British Museum record that information in these areas was received by GBS from his father on or about 12 August 1872. In 1838 (wrote Shaw), Mr. Shaw entered the employ of "Todhunter's"—quite probably of the ironworks—and stuck it for seven years. From there he went into the Four Courts and "retired" in 1851 on a pension of £44 per annum. GBS further noted that his father subsequently obtained employment with three different concerns all within the space of one year: the "Haughtons," "Wilson" and finally with MacMullen, Shaw & Company, dealers in corn, flour and cereals themselves. The Shaw in this firm, incidentally, being Henry Shaw—an enterprising and sober younger brother of George Carr. Finally, the notebooks recorded that Mr. Shaw sold his annual pension of £44 for £500 to an O'Brien who then sagaciously insured Mr. Shaw's life for £600.[64]

According to GBS's published comments in these matters, there seemed to be some doubt regarding the year in which the partnership between his father and George Clibborn was formed. In his *Sketches,* GBS had it that it was before George Carr's marriage: "On the strength of it [Clibborn & Shaw] my father married in his middle age . . ." [65] Later in the same volume, it appeared to be after the marriage. Speaking of the circumstances that led to Mr. Shaw's proposal of marriage to his mother, GBS reported that Miss Bessie Gurly "caught at the straw. She had heard that he had a pension of £60 a year. . . ." [66] O'Bolger seemed interested in the same question and his curiosity resulted in the following exchange:

> O'Bolger: Was your father in business before he got married?
>
> Shaw: I don't know. It was before my time.[67]

Similarly confusing was Shaw's belief that his father and Clibborn were both novices to the corn trade, but this is not in accordance with the record and will be treated with at an appropriate place in this study.

At thirty-eight, George Carr Shaw, Esq., eager to impart his share to the flourishing Shaw tree and convinced by romantic and other less heavenly considerations that his time had come, proposed marriage to twenty-two-year-old Lucinda Elizabeth Gurly.

II / Lucinda Elizabeth Gurly

I

LUCINDA ELIZABETH—MOTHER-TO-BE of George Bernard Shaw—was born in 1830 to Walter Bagnall and Lucinda Whitcroft Gurly. Her parents' marriage appears to have been something in the nature of a commercial transaction—at least insofar as Walter Bagnall was concerned, for, being in some difficulties, he seems to have chosen his future father-in-law with great care. Ervine believed that Gurly's love for Father Whitcroft's assets was eventually joined by a love for his wife who, the biographer described, was "gentle and pretty, subservient and devoted to her extravagant and chronically impecunious husband. . . ."[1] After ten years of marriage (during which brother Walter followed Lucinda), Mrs. Gurly died in the 14th of January, 1839, at the age of thirty-seven. According to Ervine, her death may have been a severe shock to the irresponsible Walter, for his principal, if not only, merit appeared to be the love he bore his wife, "and he remained a widower for twenty years . . . ,"[2] the inference being that twenty years of widowhood (it was actually thirteen) were twenty years of grieving.

Left in the hands of widower Gurly were their two children, Lucinda (now nine) and Walter either one, four or eight years of age. There is no available information on the history of young Walter, but—up to his entrance into Kilkenny College—it is likely that he remained with his father under whose indifferent eye he grew up into that colorful blackguard so skilfully described by GBS. As to his sister Lucinda, Oughterard, County Galway, was not the place for a young lady without a mother to guide and protect her. It would, of course, be of considerable importance in understanding the relationship between GBS and his mother if something were known about the relations between Lucinda and her mother but, apart from Ervine's views of Mrs. Gurly, there were no intimations from any source. He asserted that Mrs. Gurly's temperament was such that it would have been difficult not to have loved her.[3] One may hope his unrevealed source to be reliable for Lucinda Elizabeth's life after the death of her mother was not one that she would recall with fond nostalgia. To the hump-backed Aunt Ellen went Lucinda—to be brought up in a manner proper to an Irish gentlewoman.

Miss Ellen Whitcroft lived in Dublin's Palmerston Place—which was then and still is a tranquil, working-class street, with a dozen or so identical structures on either side.

Thirty-seven years old at the time she received Lucinda into her iron hand, Aunt Ellen would, as everyone knew, also receive a sizeable sum upon the death of her wealthy father, John Whitcroft. Mr. Whitcroft obligingly departed within four years at the age of seventy-six and is interred with his other daughter, Lucinda's mother, in the Whitechurch Graveyard, Whitechurch, County Dublin. According to GBS, the Whitcroft fortune was founded by the father of John—an unnamed semilegendary figure who had, by the exercise of uncommon enterprise, acquired extensive properties purchased with the profits of a pawnshop he operated *in camera* in the slums of Dublin.[4] In the eyes of his granddaughter, added Shaw, this occupation—disgraceful in itself, was compounded by an even more scandalous matter—a stain on the name of Whitcroft: the family tree could go no further back than the pawnbroker. Ellen, concluded GBS, while pleased with the odor of her own immediate ancestry, wrinkled her nose as she delved into grandfather Whitcroft, the details of whose birth were so vague that there was some question regarding his legitimacy.[5] Ervine reckoned the shadow to be closer to home. He held that the mystery revolved around Ellen's own father who, he added, was reported to be of a "very high-up family" but whose parents had overlooked the customary formalities.[6] *Press Cuttings* may contain a brief reference to Ellen in the character of Mrs. Banger who was described by the author as a forty-year-old, mannish sort of woman having a "powerful" voice and "great physical strength." Mrs. Banger, in an exchange with General Mitchener, flourished her grandmother's pistol and declared somewhat irrelevantly, "Who my grandfather was is a point that has never been quite clearly settled. . . ."

Aunt Ellen, whose natural desires were, perhaps, thwarted by her deformity, was possibly compensated for her loveless existence by the substitution of an inflexible resolve to clear the stain from the Whitcroft crest and to this end viewed the nine-year-old Lucinda Elizabeth as the instrument of that determination. For thirteen impressionable years—1839 to 1852—Aunt Ellen, this "fairylike creature with a will of iron," [7] schooled the child and young woman in the social graces of the times, using methods which did not exclude the employment of "constraints, tyrannies, scoldings, browbeatings and punishments. . . ." [8] To Henderson, GBS described his mother's training as one of extreme severity;[9] to O'Bolger he phrased it as being a period of "ruthless strictness" [10] and in yet another place, he recorded guardedly that his mother had been reared up as carefully as Queen Victoria.[11]

The precise nature of Aunt Ellen's curriculum has, of course, never been revealed; but there is sufficient comment by Shaw to indicate its general form and direction. An early treatment of this subject is contained in the famous fifty-four-page letter to Henderson in 1905 in which he described his mother as having, prior to her marriage, no knowledge of the world nor any idea of the importance of money: GBS charged these deficiencies to her Aunt Ellen's course of study. The most comprehensive account of this period in his mother's life was given to O'Bolger in 1916; but since he did not publish it, Shaw incorporated it into his extremely important autobiographical preface to *London Music in 1888-1889* which he released in 1935. The difference between these two recitals are differences in craftsmanship rather than content and their essences, consequently, will be combined here but documented separately when necessary.

Aunt Ellen's determination to bulwark the social respectability of the Whitcrofts by marrying her niece to nobility is clearly visible in the subjects missing as well as present in the educational regimen of Lucinda Elizabeth. Of hygienics, simple sanitation, knowledge of foods and proper nourishment, of the usages of money, of parenthood or, in fact, of any subject that could be taken care of by any member of any craft, profession or occupation—that is to say, any solicitor, nurse, servant or parent—Lucinda heard no word. True gentility, Ellen could have observed, would be found among those ladies and gentlemen to whom such matters were utterly foreign and, if thought of at all, were left to the creatures born to these tasks. Of the subjects chosen to fill these voids, Lucinda was amply reimbursed with instruction in the pianoforte and in harmony and counterpoint (according to Logier's Thoroughbass System), in French sufficient to deliver the fables of La Fontaine with impeccable pronunciation[12] and how to sit, stand, walk, talk and dress—in short, how a lady ought to behave on any occasion and in any situation according to the then current Irish fashion.[13]

How effective the methods of instruction were, may be gathered from Shaw's wry comment on his mother's fluency in French. Uttered with perfect diction, it was, sadly, limited to "show pieces" and, like her training in the pianoforte, designed to impress mothers of eligible young men with Miss Ellen Whitcroft's cultivated, talented and heavily-dowered young niece. As to her training with the pianoforte and the attendant knowledge of harmony and counterpoint, GBS wrote that his mother fared little better. In what is probably his earliest public reference to her, GBS told his audience of *The World* (14 March 1894) that she had the ill-luck to be taught by that famous teacher Johann Bernhard Logier. From 1839 until he died seven years later, he instructed Miss Gurly in the wrong way to play the piano with such overwhelming success that it became impossible for her to play it with any degree of skill and feeling.[14] He added, with heavy irony, that his mother's failure to rid herself of his "destructive" instruction was a great tribute to Logier as a teacher. We are incidentally informed that on the arrival of her nine-year-old niece in 1839 Aunt Ellen lost no time in launching her program and proceeded to implement her "firm determination to make her a paragon of good breeding, to achieve a distinguished marriage for her, and to leave her all her money as a dowry." [15]

II

LUCINDA'S EDUCATION BEING COMPLETED, Aunt Ellen released her niece into Dublin society which included the usual business of teas, parties and dances. It was possibly at one of these affairs that Lucinda met harmless, unromantic, middle-aged George Carr Shaw. Mr. Shaw was sixteen years senior to Lucinda and probably looked still older despite the preservatory nature of alcohol. The squint or cast to his left eye surely did not increase his appeal and, more significantly—as a peripheral Shaw—he had no money. Appraising the situation, Ervine justly pointed out that Ireland was a land in which the passion of love had been replaced by a passion for money.[16] In an Ireland which had been blessed with more than its share of war, famine and plague, money meant security and, perhaps, a bit of happiness in that unhappy land.

The Shaws of Roundtown and the Gurlys of Stillorgan (then suburbs of Dublin) being members of that ever-decreasing body, the Protestant garrison of Ireland, recognized the existence of each other and, as revealed by later events, seemed aware of the others' sins as well as their virtues. The Gurlys, for example, appeared to be cognizant of George Carr's weakness for whiskey while he in turn was not unaware of the ultimate disposition of Aunt Ellen's fortune, since GBS has described Mr. Shaw as being "emboldened by her expectations" [17] to propose marriage. To Mr. Shaw, the union of Lucinda's youthful beauty and great expectations proved irresistible and, in the course of Lucinda's rounds of the marriage markets, he frequently escorted her. Neither Aunt Ellen nor any of the Gurlys raised audible objections. If Mr. Shaw showed a fatherly interest in Lucinda, Aunt Ellen was pleased. The Shaws were important people—one of them being a baronet—and if Mr. Shaw, the *convenient* Mr. Shaw, would conduct Lucinda now and then to select social functions, why then Lucinda would enlarge her circle of eligibles. Certainly, there could be no harm in that. But while it was obvious to them in its evident logic, they overlooked the fact that Lucinda, who had been brought up as carefully as Queen Victoria, might, in ignorance, be blind to the obvious.

It was about this time that Lucinda's father, widowed now for thirteen years, privately revealed to some members of his family his intentions to remarry. At fifty-two he had discovered the girl of his dreams, one Elizabeth Anne Clarke, the daughter of a crony who was heavily in debt to him—suggesting some sort of *quid pro quo* settlement. To O'Bolger, GBS put it that Grandfather Gurly "perhaps thought it best to cement this financial alliance with a more sentimental one." [18] The necessity for keeping this startling news confidential might be better appreciated if we are reminded that the elder John Whitcroft had been most generous in his subsidies (solemnly acknowledged by I.O.U.s) to his son-in-law. On the death of Whitcroft this policy was continued by his son—though not with the same liberality and, in view of these investments in Gurly, it might seem unreasonable to have expected a brotherly benediction to a profitless marriage.

In his 1916 letter to O'Bolger, Shaw wrote that his mother who thought the proposed marriage highly indelicate (being influenced by Aunt Ellen), "let out" the secret to her Uncle John.[19] In his revisions to that letter as published in the *Sketches,* Shaw made no mention of his mother's complicity, speaking rather of her innocence in the matter.[20] In either case, Uncle John, upon receipt of the unsettling news, flew into a furious rage; had Gurly arrested for debt on the morning of his wedding day and, as Shaw described it, Walter "was torn from his nuptials to a spunging house." [21] It was now Walter Bagnall's turn to be enraged and he charged Lucinda Elizabeth with betrayal in a vain effort to stop the marriage. Lucinda, who was at this time visiting relations in Dublin, heard or possibly felt the shockwaves attending her father's disturbance and was overwhelmed. Faced with the choice of returning to the home of an angry father and an indignant stepmother or retreating to her tyrannous aunt in Palmerston Place, she chose neither—the solution coming from an unexpected quarter. For the climax to this predicament, her son was to write sixty-four years later:

> It was at this moment that some devil, probably commissioned by the Life Force to bring me into the world,

> prompted my father to make a bid for my aunt's property by proposing marriage to her niece. My mother caught at the straw. . . .[22]

Thirty-two years later, this account underwent a major operation: all reference to George Carr's fascination for Aunt Ellen's property had been amputated.[23]

III

IN A DESPERATE PLIGHT, poor Lucinda had snatched at Mr. Shaw's proposal as the best possible answer under the circumstances. It could never occur to her to consider the consequences of an acceptance of such a proposal, largely because her "education" inflexibly rejected contact with the realistic world and its vulgar problems. The biographers as well as the biographee ruled out romance, thus GBS told O'Bolger that there was not the slightest desire on her part to marry him for himself and added that the "tragedy" came from external complications that no one could have prophesied.[24] Henderson reported that Lucinda entered into a hasty marriage when her home was made unbearable by the second marriage of her father.[25] Pearson agreed with Henderson (that the marriage was the answer to her predicament) but prefaced the account with "It is doubtful that she loved him. It is doubtful whether she ever loved anyone." [26] Ervine agreed with both Henderson and Pearson regarding the marriage being a refuge from insufferable domestic circumstances but also asserted that Miss Gurly had no love or affection for her future husband.[27]

It would be an idle exercise to speculate on the manner of the courtship of George Carr and Lucinda Elizabeth. It is highly doubtful that it existed in the usual sense of the word and, as a consequence of this missing element, an impression has been created that Lucinda Elizabeth was incapable of love and scorned its approach. This is a recurring theme throughout the biographies and seems to lose conviction with each repetition. One senses the hand of a gifted dramatist in creating a mother who, for whatever reason the biographers were invited to invent, was destitute of that human desire called, by western nations, love.

Ervine paid the matter close study and, inquiring into the reasons why Miss Gurly would become engaged to an "elderly detrimental" of no qualities, issued his findings. The mother of George Bernard Shaw, he wrote

> did not love easily, if, indeed, she could love at all and it is very certain that she had no feeling for George Carr Shaw that could be called love or even ordinary affection. Ireland was then, and still is, a country in which, outside Ulster, the passion of love is lightly esteemed.[28]

Having raised the central question, i.e., why Miss Gurly became engaged to Mr. Shaw, Ervine proceeded to ignore it, advising the reader that Lucinda Elizabeth was unlikely to love anyone, certainly not George Carr. This deficiency, Ervine intimated, would not have existed had Lucinda been born in any of the Six Counties of Ulster which, by odd coincidence, is the province of St. John Greer Ervine's birth.

Continuing the pursuit for the cause of this hapless engagement, Ervine reversed his technique and offered an answer to a nonexistent question. Speaking of the customary addresses of love notably lacking in this courtship, Ervine had it that Miss Gurly

> could not have been affected by this absence of ardour in Irish wooings, for she was a Protestant gentlewoman, not a Roman Catholic peasant, and her lack of love, therefore, must have been due to some defect inherent in her nature. She was a cold girl, and she became a cold wife and mother.[29]

He saw her, at the time of her marriage to Mr. Shaw, as one

> who had a cold, unloving heart, a ferocious chin . . .

> whose face became less amiable as she grew older . . . a hard and unemotional girl,[30] a cold woman with a deep aversion from all demonstration of affection. . . .[31] She was, in short, devoid of human qualities.[32]

Oddly enough, it was Ervine who struck the first contradictory note in a reference to GBS's sister Lucy who, he declared, while being "Cold and unloving as her mother . . ." nevertheless was the possessor of "a good deal of the charm her mother could display when she felt in the mood . . ." [33] Many people who had a personal knowledge of the mother of Bernard Shaw supported a "warm" theory, but they will be heard from in detail at a more appropriate place.

As to George Carr's role in their dismal romance, he must have had little time or opportunity to play the traditional suitor. There is no information available with respect to the length of the courtship period but under the circumstances it could not have been long enough for the usual premarital adjustments. If, on the occasion of their engagement, Lucinda appeared reserved and unresponsive to Mr. Shaw's timid overtures, George Carr could, in his larger knowledge, well afford to wait patiently for the prize, maintaining, *ad interim,* a dignified, courtly and seemingly sober attentiveness.

IV

LUCINDA ELIZABETH'S ANNOUNCEMENT that she would take Mr. George Carr Shaw for husband shocked the Gurlys into a concert of scolding with Aunt Ellen, no doubt, as conductor. Ervine pictured Miss Whitcroft as "storming" at Lucinda who, nevertheless, remained undaunted in her resolution.[34] GBS originally described this moment to O'Bolger but then adopted it almost word for word in the *Sketches.* His mother, he wrote, placidly endured the entreaties of the Gurlys with total indifference until they, seeing how little effect their words had on Lucinda, approached from a new direction:

> They told her [he] was a hopeless drunkard.[35]

> They told her [he] was a drunkard.[36]

Where commonsense objections to Mr. Shaw on the grounds of his age and general impecuniosity failed to impress, Miss Gurly responded reflexively to her Aunt Ellen's training when Mr. Shaw's refinement was in question. She burst out and denounced it as a fabrication, pointing out that they themselves had spoken highly of him which, of course, they could not deny. However, when they persisted in this charge of drunkenness against her fiancé Miss Gurly, Shaw told O'Bolger, did "the straight thing": she repaired at once to Mr. Shaw's flat at 17 Lennox Street and put the question to him. GBS has noted the answer which, in my opinion, holds the key to the enigma of Mrs. Lucinda Elizabeth Shaw. The answer:

> this monstrous lie[37]

> this whopper[38]

> He swore to her most solemnly that he was a convinced and lifelong teetotaler.[39]

On the twenty-fifth of May 1852 Walter Bagnall Gurly and Elizabeth Anne Clark, being in the sight of God (and, presumably, to the mutual satisfaction of creditor and defaulter) were joined together in Holy Matrimony. Twenty-three days later, on Thursday

> June 17 at St. Peter's Church by the Rev. W. G. Carroll, brother-in-law to the bridegroom, George Carr Shaw, Esq., of Roundtown, to Lucinda Elizabeth, only daughter of Walter B. Gurly, Esq., of Merrion-row, in this city.[40]

The resentful Aunt Ellen, outwitted and outraged, promptly cut her ungrateful niece off without a farthing—not realizing, of course, that one result of the marriage would be to give the world an extraordinary genius.[41]

III / George John Lee

I

LUCINDA ELIZABETH GURLY had probably not yet passed her first birthday when George Lee drew his first breath. Little indeed has been disclosed of this strange figure that limped into the lives of the Shaws to break the heart of one, give joy and happiness to another and, to a third, bequeath the specter of doubt. Guiding Harris' hand, so to speak, GBS admitted that he knew little about Lee's family and background, though he took care not to reveal the "little" he knew.[1] Still curious about him as late as his ninety-first year, Shaw commissioned his "Bibliographer and Remembrancer" Dr. Fritz Erwin Loewenstein to make confidential inquiries from Dublin sources. To Headmaster Brian Mac Giolla Phadrig of the Central Model School (scene of Shaw's *Shame and Wounded Snobbery*) went a request for information on former student George Bernard Shaw and, footnoted Loewenstein,

[16.7.47]

> . . . if you come across a *musician*
> GEORGE JOHN VANDALEUR LEE
> Anything you could *tell me* about him would be of the profoundest interest. . . . Nothing is known about his past, family etc., though he was a conductor of mean merits in Dublin and later in London.[2]

Ervine made some efforts to trace Lee's origins but acknowledged his failure to breach the silence by allowing that "no one now" knew the answers.[3] Farmer took the revolutionary step of visiting the city of Shaw's birth. Though principally occupied with Shaw's sister Lucy, Farmer examined several issues of Dublin's annual directories (apparently beginning with the edition of 1856) and, while observing that they contained nothing of a "George John Vandaleur Lee," noted one G. John Lee in 16 Harrington Street listed as a Professor of Music. The "1873-1874" issue of the directory, he reported, contained a G. V. Lee and mused in a footnote whether the V could possibly be for "Vandaleur." [4] Shaw's published observations on Lee are, considering the mass of general autobiographia, in reasonable ratio. Lumped mainly in the *Sketches* and in the preface to *London Music 1888-1889,* these comments are enlarged by other divulgences widely scattered in Shavian writings. On careful selection and examination of them George John Lee emerges.

II

THE FIRST POSITIVE INFORMATION about George John Lee and his family that adds to the written record, appeared in Thom's *Almanac and Official Directory of Ireland* for the year of 1854. Inquiries at the firm of Alexander Thom & Company, Ltd., Dublin, with respect to the actual periods covered by their Registers were met with the authoritative assertion that the volumes under consideration were actually the reports of the first nine months in the year immediately preceding the year of publication. Thus it may be presumed that the Registers reflect statistics of the previous year and will be so noted.

THOM'S 1854 [1853]

Address	Occupant/s	Notes
3, Synge Street	Shaw, Geo. C.	
11, Harrington Street	Armstrong, John S.	Barrister
	Armstrong, James H.	Solicitor
	Armstrong, George K.	
	Lee, Geo. Jno.	Prof. of Music
16 Harrington Street	Lee, G. Jno.	Prof. of Music
	Lee, H. W. N. Esq.	
	Lee, Mrs.	

These details were exasperatingly vague, but for the first time Lee had been specifically located in the relations of time and place three years before the birth of George Bernard Shaw. Another male member of Lee's family, hitherto referred to by Shaw and his Boswells as a "brother" has been finally supplied with initials—three of them. Most provoking of all, a lady appeared—a Mrs. Lee who, in another Register, was further identified as Mrs. Eliza Lee. No one has mentioned a Mrs. Lee. Was she George John's wife? According to GBS, Lee was a bachelor who lived in Harrington Street with a brother whom he maintained and a servant of all work described by Shaw as a "terrible old woman" [5] named Ellen.[6] Was Mrs. Eliza the wife of H.W.N.? Was she their mother? Or was she the terrible one? Sleater's *Royal National Commercial Directory of Ireland* for 1856 (1855) added to the family with a Mrs. Mary Lee at the Harrington Street address. The inclusion of Lee with the Armstrongs of 11 Harrington Street suggests that Lee used their residence for his professional activities.

There are no changes in the addresses of our principals until 1859 (1858) when Thom's reported the apparent removal of the Lees to Number 48 Harrington Street, but this change proved to be merely a change in numbers. Examination of the dwelling charts in Dublin's Valuation Office showed that the Harrington Street Extension was completed during 1858 and all of the houses on the north side were renumbered—16 becoming 48. In 1861 (1860) Eliza disappeared from the pages of Thom's and, as corroborative evidence later showed, vanished into Dublin's famed Glasnevin Cemetery. Three years later the 1864 (1863) issue of the Register noted, in its negative manner, the passing hence of H.W.N., and one naturally assumed his death to have taken place during 1863. Shaw reported the death of Lee's unnamed brother,[7] but in his several references to this incident successfully avoided relating the death to any particular year while Ervine placed in "about" 1866.[8] A search of the back files of four major newspapers of the times (*Freeman's Journal, Saunders' News-Letter, The Irish Times* and the *Daily Express*) failed to reveal the announcement of H.W.N.'s death. On the assumption (false) that H.W.N., Esq., was an elder son and, consequently, might have had some estate, the Public Records Office, Four Courts, Index to Probate and Administration calendars 1858-1877 were resorted to and on page 460, the following was discovered:

WILL OR INTESTACY
(I)

Lee, Harcourt William Nassau
Registry: Principal—Year: 1867

An imposing name. A Protestant name. Could this be the elusive brother? Cross reference to Administrations 1867 was referred to; page 121 removed all doubts:

> Lee: Harcourt William Nassau
> [260] Effects under £5
> 28 October Letters of Administration of the personal estate of Harcourt William Nassau Lee late of Harrington-street Dublin Gentleman a bachelor deceased who died 7 May 1862 same place were granted at the Principal Registry to Eleanor Leigh of Rathmines County Dublin Spinster for the benefit of George J. Lee the Brother and only next of said deceased.

Thom's street directory for Rathmines County revealed that a Miss Eleanor Leigh resided at 152 Rathmines Road from 1861 through 1866. In 1862 she was joined by a Henry Lee who, in 1864, became Henry Leigh and in 1866 Eleanor had the company of a Mrs. Margaret Leigh. In 1867 Eleanor was dropped from the record and in the following year Henry slipped away, leaving Margaret in Rathmines Road until 1871; here, for the present, we leave the trail. Harcourt may have had some property and the grant was necessary in order to make George John the legal owner. Supporting this suggestion is the evidence that about this time there was in Dublin an army officer, a Lieutenant in Her Majesty's Irish Militia Artillery, named Frederick Ware Corker. A deed in the Registry of Deeds Office (King's Inns, Dublin) dated 1859, Reference: 1859-43-63 recorded that Harcourt made a loan of £220 to this Corker. On the settlement of the estate of Corker's mother subsequent to her death, Harcourt was repaid £150 which he accepted in final settlement. In the same year, Harcourt bought property in the City of Cork from Corker for £350 (Ref: 1859-38-109) and it is possible that George John received some of his income from this source.

It became increasingly evident that the key to George John was, so to speak, within the coffin of his brother Harcourt. Attempts to ascertain the cause of Harcourt's death (Ervine reported him to have been an invalid [9]) were frustrated when officials of Dublin's Custom House advised that compulsory death registrations were only enforced from 1864 onwards and, consequently, Harcourt's age, religion, cause of death and place of burial were as far off as ever. While GBS never referred to Lee's religion—other than to say that music was the only religion he had ever heard Lee profess to—[10] there was nothing to indicate that the Lees were anything but Protestant.

A new avenue of speculation was that, other than George Carr's disgraceful tippling, there may have been an additional cause for Sir Robert Shaw's banishment of the Synge Street Shaws from the Bushy Park conclaves: the presence of Lee in the Shaw household might have been resented on the traditional grounds, that is, of bigotry—*if* Lee had been a Roman Catholic. A fresh sally was initiated into the Registers of Dublin's great Catholic-founded Glasnevin Cemetery and was rewarded by the following entry:

Name	Lee, William
Age	27
Address	48, Harrington Street
Grave No.	FD 103
Location	Glasnevin Garden Plot
Date	10 May 1862

Buried on the third day following his death, William Lee lies in an unmarked grave indistinguishable from any of its jostling neighbors. Four years younger (according to the interment record) than brother George John, William may have borrowed the plumes of Harcourt and Nassau even as George John adopted Vandeleur for the days of his vanity.

Recalling Mrs. Eliza Lee's disappearance from *Thom's Register* in 1861 (1860), we find, on examining the obituary notices in

Freeman's Journal and *Saunders' News-Letter* for 1860, a most important prize in their issues of 7 March:

> March 6, at her residence, 48 Harrington Street, Mrs. Robert Lee, after a protracted illness.

Cross reference to Glasnevin's Grave Registrations revealed that Mrs. Robert Lee was buried as Eliza Lee, aged fifty-five, in Grave No. LE 110 on 7 March 1860. Happily for all concerned, Eliza was not alone in death. Also interred in LE 110: Robert Lee of Caroline Row, buried on 12 January 1843 at the age of forty-one.

Thom's Registers turned up Robert Lee, a Coal Merchant. First detected in 1838 (1837), Coal Merchant Lee was listed in 22, Upper Buckingham Street and, after one or two removals through four years, settled in Number 4, Caroline Row. In 1843 Robert is dropped from the record (having died during the second week in January) and Mrs. Lee is listed in his place. As Mrs. Lee is simultaneously registered among the *Nobility, Gentry, Merchants and Traders,* it may be presumed that she carried on in Robert's coal business. In 1845 Mrs. Lee vacated 4 Caroline Row and for the next seven years may have occupied Shamrock or Shannon Lodge (the names alternate), Booterstown Avenue, in what was then a Dublin suburb. The year 1853 was one of decision. Possibly at the urging of George John who, at twenty-three was eager to embark upon his musical career, Mrs. Lee entered into the last home of her life: 16 Harrington Street—one hundred and twenty-five paces from 3 Synge Street.

It may be accepted with considerable assurance that George John was the Irish son of Irish parents. Ervine, puzzling over Lee's origins, opined that judging from his name and "looks," Lee may have derived from gipsy forbears.[11] However, he may have been influenced by McNulty who had expressed similar views. McNulty, having observed the Professor frequently and at close quarters, recalled that he was "gipsylike" both in appearance and name.[12] Even Shaw was impressed or appeared to be impressed by the "gipsy name" of Lee and so noted it to O'Bolger.[13] Undoubtedly George John was born in Dublin during 1830, and there are sufficient reasons to believe one or both of his parents were Roman Catholic. Although he himself probably rejected the religion of his nonage, he respected it to the extent of burying brother William in Catholic Glasnevin three miles to the north rather than the Protestant Mount Jerome one mile to the south. This is not to say that the Lees' preference for Glasnevin is offered as proof of their Catholicism—it is not. While Glasnevin is in theory and by tradition a Catholic cemetery, it is nonsectarian in intent and offers its comforts to Protestant as well as Catholic souls. Indeed, the number of Protestants reposing in Glasnevin may well equal the number of Catholics who have accepted the reciprocal liberality of Mount Jerome.[14] Proof of the Catholicity of the Lee family has been established beyond a reasonable doubt and will be dealt with presently.

With the exception of one brief but highly significant public record, there were no formal accounts available of the childhood or education of either of the Lee boys. Harris, who had probably never heard of Lee, cannily or uncannily picked up information regarding one or two incidents in the infancy and teen age of George John. He informed his readers that it was then (during the 1830's) the custom for babies to wear particularly large sleeping caps which caught fire now and then. Unfortunately, little George was one of these victims, "and forever after his glossy black hair grew on his forehead like the 'join,' as actors call it, of a wig." [15] At another point, Harris asserted that "Vandaleur" was, like Aunt Ellen and George Carr, afflicted with a physical deficiency which he acquired in his childhood, the result of a fall down a flight of stairs and which, as a consequence, lamed him for life—one leg being "considerably" shorter than its mate.[16] O'Bolger was in receipt of a similar account. "Vandaleur," as GBS consistently misspelled it, received his injury riding down the banister (or something like it), and the mishap left him with one leg "very much" shortened.[17] These recitals are interesting for their uniformity, and they give one the feeling young Lee's lack of proper medical care (his leg was badly dressed) was the cause of his lifelong animosity towards medical science and its practitioners. The reference to George Carr's physical defect is, I take it, to the "squint" in his eye—unless this was Shaw's way of describing the elder Shaw's alcoholism, since it is unlikely, to say the least, that Frank Harris considered addiction to whiskey an affliction.

As to George John's education, Shaw's comments seemed to explain the absence of Lee from the rolls of the likely schools. Again it was the Harris book which first touched upon the subject. One of its three authors declared that as a boy, George John had a tutor whose tenure ended abruptly when, for reasons unstated, he was attacked by his charge brandishing a fishing rod and banished from the Lee household.[18] To O'Bolger, GBS earlier offered substantially the same episode and in addition cleared up some loose ends. Shaw reported that Lee told him that he had never been to school but acknowledged a tutor named Leeson who, upon striking his pupil, was counterattacked with the spike end of a fishing rod. Leeson, added Shaw, angrily ended his tutorial obligations and, presumably, George John thereafter attended to his own educational needs. Here again there is interesting uniformity of accounts, but Shaw's final observation is of far-reaching significance in showing cause and effects. Henceforth, Lee, Shaw wrote, "had nothing good to say of any academic institution." [19]

When Lee told Shaw that he had never been to school, he either lied or phrased it in such a manner as to leave his listener with that impression. He must have had *some* schooling, especially if his parents were Catholic.

Up two streets from No. 4, Caroline Row, there is still a large gray building that melts into the grayness of the area and seems to shrink from sight. One hundred and thirty-odd years have had their effect, but the dedication stone above the main entrance can still be plainly read:

CHRISTIAN SCHOOLS
ERECTED BY THE
CATHOLIC ASSOCIATION OF IRELAND
THE FIRST STONE WAS LAID
BY DANIEL O'CONNELL ESQ. M.P.
ON THE FEAST OF ST. COLUMBA
1828

In the school records of the 1830's appeared the following:

FIRST ADMISSION REGISTER
CHRISTIAN BROTHERS' O'CONNELL SCHOOL
North Richmond Street, Dublin

Number	Name	When accepted	Age	Spelling	Reading	Arithmetic	Residence	Parents' names	Occupation
2671	George Lee	1838	8	6	1	—	Portland Place	Robert & Eliza	Clerk
2672	Wm. Lee	1838	7	6	1	—	Portland Place	Robert & Eliza	Clerk

Here may end the search for the religion into which George John Lee was born. With nonsectarian National Schools and Protestant Schools available, Robert and Eliza preferred to send their sons to the school of the Roman Catholic Christian Brothers where, according to Thom's Registers of the period, the capacity of the O'Connell School was eight hundred boys who were educated gratuitously.

With the discovery of the school records of the Lee brothers, new discrepancies arose with respect to their ages. Harcourt was recorded as being twenty-seven at his death in 1862 thus placing his birth during 1835. The school record however, marked him at seven years during 1838 and therefore, born in 1831. Similarly, George John, declared to be fifty-five at the inquest into his death in 1886 was, accordingly, born in 1831 but as the O'Connell Register declared him to be eight at his entrance in 1838, his birth must have taken place during 1830. Since George and William were undoubtedly enrolled with the Christian Brothers by one or both of their parents, we may take it that Robert and Eliza's answers were the most reliable. With regard to the conflict of Portland Place and Caroline Row, one may assume an unregistered removal between their homes in Upper Buckingham Street and Caroline Row. As to Robert's occupation of "clerk" this may have preceded his advancement to Coal Merchant or, if a fib was involved, it was the little white fib of pretension—a common enough practice anywhere in any period.

III

CONSIDERING THE SCARCITY of information on the appearance, characteristics and personality of George John Lee, his descriptions by undaunted biographers are, if nothing else, splendid gestures of independence. They have declared him to be a genius, an ignoramus, an imposter, possibly a gipsy, a Jew, handsome, unattractive, not wholly unattractive, eccentric, morbid, limited, distinguished, a fraud, a humbug, honest, a charlatan, not particularly scrupulous, a celibate, amoristic, not a man of wide culture, an original, a phenomenon, a man of mesmeric vitality, an innovator, bold, strange, magnetic, very vain, a heretic, a rebel, an iconoclast, and a Svengali.

The enigma of George John is suggested in Ervine's preliminary examination. He held, fairly correctly, that if not for the fact that Lee was mentioned in some of Shaw's prefaces, he would never have been heard of but acknowledged that Lee "played a considerable part" in the early history of GBS. He reported that Lee did not appear in any work of biographical references but believed him to have been an important figure among Dublin musicians, though he discounted his authority elsewhere.[20] Though conspicuously absent from standard works of reference, Lee somehow managed to attract the attention of at least one compiler: a James D. Brown who added nothing to the record and erred in not identifying Lee as Irish.

> LEE (G.). English writer, author of *"The Voice, its Artistic Production, Development and Preservation."* 4to, 1870, 2 editions.[21]

The physical appearance of Lee has been described by several persons not all of whom were qualified for the task. Shaw, of course, was most qualified but also most sparing. Speaking of the pre-London appearance of Lee in *London Music,* GBS described him as having a "clean shaven resolute lip and chin" skirted with black whiskers[22] but to O'Bolger singled out for special attention the "peculiar elegance" of the manner in which Lee limped about without a crutch "carrying it [his lameness] as if it were a quality instead of a defect . . ." [23] Harris' ignorance of Lee proved no bar to the inclusion of a brief sketch. Lee's *upper* lip and chin were clean shaven (wrote the author) and his countenance was "framed with pirate-black whiskers." Further, Lee was always carefully and properly dressed, had physical dexterity and a "personal style." [24]

McNulty was particularly qualified. Novelist and playwright in his own right, GBS's boyhood friend was a skilled observer and, what is even more to the point, on the scene.

> This Lee, [McNulty wrote] who called himself a Professor of Singing, was as gipsylike in appearance as his name: he had dark complexion and eyes, hair luxuriant and jet black in colour, and worn long after the Victorian fashion of poets and artists. He had, in addition, a deformed foot. But his most striking characteristic was a volubility of language which made him easily one of the most tireless (if not tiresome) of conversationalists. Shaw as a boy had a great admiration for Professor Lee, and was impressed by the elderly man's flow of talk.[25]

In a general character sketch of Lee, Ervine added a detail or two which had somehow escaped the notice of McNulty and Shaw. Women, wrote Ervine, (and girls in particular) were not attracted to the Professor because (a) he was crippled; (b) his hair was so arranged that it resembled a wig; (c) he was, in regard to his understanding of life, restricted; (d) he was excessively vain. As to his physical traits Ervine reported that

> His smile was a smirk, a slight disarrangement of the long, hard line of his mouth; his chin was deep and graceless . . . [and] he had alert, bright eyes that glanced about in a quick, enquiring, gipsy fashion . . .[26]

Though one might infer from these particulars that Ervine had had the opportunity of personally examining Lee, such inference could not have been intended, as Lee died in London in 1886 in his fifty-fifth year and in Ervine's third. Ervine's opinions, if not specifically received from GBS, of Lee's tonsorial pattern, world outlook, vanity and physical characteristics come from the same sources available to the reader: the McNulty extract, the several Shavian prefaces and a single photograph.

IV

THE PERSONALITY AND CHARACTERISTICS of George John Lee have been set forth trenchantly by GBS; and although his account lacks breadth, it makes up the deficiency in depth. Lee was a "curious" person, wrote Shaw to O'Bolger, "interesting rather than likeable"—in a class by himself and, added GBS, the only man who reminded him of Lee was the violinist Sarasate.[27] In another place, he described Lee as the "most extreme possible contrast to my father";[28] consequently, he must have been sober, industrious, responsible and efficient. The roster of Lee's idiosyncrasies call to mind Shaw's own eccentricities. GBS's attachment to unusual clothing, his seventy-year-old adherence to vegetarianism and his amusingly derisive and keenly critical treatment of the members of the medical fraternity are strong echoes of Lee's opinionated outlook. The Professor, it is learned, slept with his windows open (in bold defiance of diseases carried by the night air) and urged others to do likewise; refused to eat white bread, insisting on brown (another rash departure); and considered doctors and apothecaries entirely useless, refusing to tolerate them professionally.[29] Elsewhere GBS added to the list of Lee's singularities his scepticism of religion, objections to lawyers and his suspicions of the professions in general. Thus, added Shaw, he (GBS) was reared to regard doctors as pretenders, the clergy as a parcel of pious frauds and barristers as extortionists,[30] recalling Sir Patrick Cullen's observation in *The Doctor's Dilemma* (Act I) to the effect that all professions were conspiracies against the uninformed. According to Winsten, Lee had an especially daring piece of counsel. To the less fortunate, bachelor Lee "was outspoken about sleeping, condemning the double bed and advising married people to sleep in separate beds." [31]

Of particular interest is Shaw's treatment of Lee's lameness as an obstacle to his sexual activity. In writing of this subject to O'Bolger, GBS conducted it with such delicacy that one might pass over it without realizing its full significance. While Lee used no crutch, said Shaw, and limped with a sort of strange grace, "still marriage and gallantry were tacitly ruled out of his possibilities, by himself, I fancy, as much as by other people," [32] adding that when Lee lived with the Shaws he was too busy to concern himself with such matters. Note may be made of Shaw's construction wherein his speculation suggests probability, that is to say, others as well as Lee accepted his lameness *a priori* as a condition precluding "gallantry" and he had, therefore, resigned himself to a life of celibacy. Harris' version of Lee's resignation in the face of his disablement, while not put so fastidiously, was similarly speculative. Lee, wrote the author,

> always walked about with a limp of studied elegance. Possibly this handicapped him completely in the matter of sex: at all events Shaw says that Lee was somehow unthinkable as a married man.[33]

I suggest that Frank Harris would not have agreed that a lame leg would prevent its owner from sexual participation and he might have, perhaps, pointed to Toulouse-Lautrec as an example. I further suggest that in depriving Lee of sexual adventures, Shaw acted in accordance with his total strategy, that is to say, the elimination of sex as an existing possibility in the relations between Lee and his mother. Yet it will be seen that Lee, far from ruling out gallantry, extended his amorous interests to GBS's sister Lucy, twenty-two years his junior.

V

TO SHAW, THE GENIUS OF GEORGE JOHN LEE was not a matter for contention though it was not easy to isolate the exact nature of that genius. In a letter of 14 December 1947 referring to the authorship of *The Voice,* (a Lee-inspired, unfinished manual ghostwritten by twenty-six-year-old Shaw) the ninety-one-year-old added "He was a genius in his way; but not in my way." [34] In 1919 Shaw was of the same opinion. O'Bolger had questioned the genius of Lee and, for his pains, received a Shavian bellow:

> If it does not suit your story to believe that Lee was in his way a genius, better alter your story. I tell you that he was; and I know better than you . . .[35]

Continuing in the same vein, GBS supported his opinions as an expert critic. Having heard all the best conductors and the students of all the best singing teachers he was, therefore, well qualified to recognize musical genius. In response to O'Bolger's claim that there was no evidence of Lee's musical eminence, Shaw countered by asking O'Bolger if he had made any effort to seek that evidence. A German, concluded Shaw in a reference to Teutonic efficiency, could probably (if he wanted to make himself unreadable) stock numerous pages with a catalogue of the concerts and their works presided over by Lee by searching for them in the newspaper files.

Shaw's estimates of Lee's musical prominence, if not his genius, can be confirmed, for his presence and activities are abundantly recorded. Under the general heading of musical societies, Thom's Register for 1856 (1855) contained the earliest evidence of Lee in the public eye.

> AMATEUR MUSICAL SOCIETY
> Antient Concert Rooms
> Gt. Brunswick Street
> Patron: His Exc. Lord Lieutnant—Auditor Chas. Cummins, Esq. Conductor: George J. Lee, Esq.
> Society originated in 1852 for culture of the higher branches of music, independent of professional aid. Music, vocal, and instrumental, selections from Italian and English operas, classical glees, madrigals etc. Society meets every Monday at 8 o'clock. Members admitted by ballot.

Sleater's Directory for the same year was equally aware of Lee and, to his Patron and Auditor, added a President (Rt. Hon. Lord Otho Fitzgerald), a Treasurer (G. F. Codd, Esq.) and a Secretary (William Tracy, Esq.). Of special interest is the year of its organization, thus establishing the existence of the Amateur Musical Society in the year of Lucinda Elizabeth's marriage to George Carr. While the announcements did not state specifically that Lee was a founding member, it would, I think, be quite safe to assume so. Henderson, not one generally given to careless statements, held that Lee established the Amateur Musical Society,[36] this being first revealed by Shaw in his 1905 letter (i.e. that Lee had organized an orchestra and musical society).[37]

The manner and methods of Lee in creating his musical organizations have been dealt with by GBS and offer an interesting sidelight on the Professor as an aggressive as well as an enterprising personality. Speaking before a national conference of the British Music Society 6 May 1920, Shaw coupled this subject to his suggestions for bringing serious music to the people. Individual contributions were quite practical, he stated, and reminisced that he was raised in a city where there were no civic-sponsored or professional musical groups to speak of. Nevertheless his own taste in music was so highly developed before he was ten that it was an ordeal for him to bear with the popular tunes of the day of which the Strauss waltzes were common examples. For this familiarity with the classics, Shaw continued, he was indebted to a man who, like the majority of musicians, was not financially independent and who supported himself playing the piano and by teaching singing. This, however, was not enough for him for if he heard the sound of a musical instrument being played during his walks about Dublin, he would unhesitatingly mount the steps of the building from whence the strains originated, knock on the door and say to the servant: "I want to see the gentleman who is playing the big fiddle [or violin, flute or whatever the instrument was]." When, added Shaw, the frightened wretch appeared, the man would declare, "I am forming an orchestra; you must come and play in it." And, being a forceful character, the man would generally succeed in having his way. In this manner, the man not only put together a small group of musicians but managed, at the same time, to train his singing pupils into a choir. With respect to his orchestra, Shaw reported (driving his point home to his audience) that this conductor did not wait until he had a full complement of musicians but went right ahead and seemed to be quite unconcerned whether the works of Beethoven and Mozart would suffer if the orchestra did not have the required number of kettle drums, flutes, trombones, oboes, trumpets, clarinets, bassoons, horns and a string quartet. This man, Shaw concluded, also taught his mother singing, who, in addition to leading the chorus, sang the major roles, made copies of orchestral parts and, Shaw was sorry to say, made them up from the vocal scores when they could not afford to rent the standard forms.[38]

The depth and breadth of the concerts organized and directed by Lee have been preserved in the excellent newspaper files of Ireland's National Library. Although the advertisements of the Amateur Musical Society did not appear often (an average of three of four per year but increasing after 1868), their scarcity was more than compensated for by their richness of detail. *Saunders' News-Letter* for the week of March 7, 1864, exhibited an announcement bulging with promise.

AMATEUR MUSICAL SOCIETY
Antient Concert Rooms

The Third Grand Concert of the Season will take place on FRIDAY EVENING, the 1st April next.

Henry Parkinson, Hon. Sec.

N.B.—Performing Members are requested to be punctual in their attendance at the Rehearsal on This (Saturday) Evening, the 12th March, at Half-past Seven o'Clock, when the first issue of Tickets to Members will take place.

SHAKSPEARE.

COMMEMORATION OF THE TERCENTENARY. The Committee of the AMATEUR MUSICAL SOCIETY have made arrangements to give a Musical and Literary Entertainment to the Public, at the ANTIENT CONCERT ROOMS, on the Evening of SATURDAY, the 23d of April next, the 300th Anniversary of Shakspeare's Birth, on which occasion the Programme will comprise a Recitation by Mr. Bell of Elrington's much-admired Ode to Shakspeare, illustrated by a choice Selection (both Vocal and Instrumental), from the Music of "Macbeth," "The Tempest," "Midsummer's Night Dream," and other compositions in connection with the writings of Shakspeare. The proceeds of the entertainment will be given to the Governors of the City of Dublin Hospital, for the purpose of founding a bed or beds for the exclusive use of poor Actors and Musicians. Tickets to be had on and after Monday, the 14th Inst., at the Messrs. Pigott's Musical Warehouse, 112 Grafton-street.

Reserved Seats, 4s. Unreserved, 2s. 6d. each.

HENRY PARKINSON, Hon. Sec.

N.B.—Ladies and Gentlemen wishing to assist in the Chorus will please forward their Name and Address to the Conductor, Mr. Lee, 48 Harrington-street.

In *Saunders' News-Letter* for the following week, the Society released their program for celebrating the three-hundredth anniversary of Shakespeare's birth, thus revealing some of the scope and intensity of Lee's musical interests. Note correction of *"Midsummer's Night Dream"* of previous announcement and the respelling of Shakspeare:

Celebration of the
TERCENTENARY OF SHAKESPEARE
by the
AMATEUR MUSICAL SOCIETY
(Conductor—Mr. Lee)
On Saturday, 23d April, 1864
The Programme will include—
Mendelssohn's Wedding March. Midsummer Night's Dream
MUSIC FROM "THE TEMPEST"—PURCELL.
Introduction—Orchestra.
Air—Come unto these yellow sands.
Chorus—Hark! the Watch Dog's Bark.
Air—Full Fathom Five Thy Father Lies.

Chorus—Sea Nymphs Hourly Ring His Knell
Chorus—The Cloud-cap'd Towers.
MUSIC FROM MACBETH
Introductions, Solos, Choruses, &c.
ODE TO SHAKESPEARE
By S.N.Elrington, Esq.

To be recited by Professor Bell, who has kindly consented to render his valuable assistance on this occasion. By the kind permission of Colonel Best, the Band of the 86th Regiment will perform

Selections .... Othello
(Under the direction of Mr. Savage).
The Programme will also include the following—
MISCELLANEOUS SELECTIONS

Duet—I Know a Bank .... Home
Trio—It Was a Friar of Orders Grey Callcott.
Song—Bid Me Discourse .... Bishop
Quartette—Under the Greenwood Tree
Duet—Tell Me Where is Fancy Bred. Sir J. Stevenson
Song—Hark! Hark! the Lark at Heaven's
Gate Sings .... Schubert
Duet—As it Fell Upon a Day .... Bishop
Song—Blow, Blow, Thou Winter Wind. Sir J. Stevenson
Trio—O Happy Hours .... Shield

&c., &c., &c.
A PROLOGUE
(Written specially for the occasion
by William Scribble, Esq.)
Will be delivered by the Author
Tickets to be had, and places secured, at
Messrs Pigott's Music Warehouse, 112 Grafton-street
Reserved Seats, 4s.; Unreserved, 2s. 6d.
H. PARKINSON, Hon. Sec.

Nor were Lee's activities confined to the paid advertisements. Not a few of his concerts were reported in the regular news columns of those journals observing the musical scene in Dublin. As *The Irish Times* of Saturday 6 May 1865 reported, Professor Lee was one of the sparkling diamonds in Dublin's cultural crown.

> AMATEUR MUSICAL SOCIETY
>
> The above society gave a concert last evening at the Antient Concert Rooms, in aid of the funds of the Whitworth Hospital, Drumcondra. There was a numerous and fashionable attendance, owing, no doubt, to the fact of the concert being for a charitable purpose, and more particularly to the expectation of a rich musical treat, as might be anticipated from a glance at the programme, and the prestige enjoyed by the society as a musical institution in the city. Mr. Lee conducted with characteristic accuracy and efficiency. The concert opened with Mendelssohn's Wedding March, then came in succession, selections from other composers, including Gounod, Sir John Stevenson, and a few compositions by Mr. G. J. Lee, which were listened to with marked pleasure, which the audience indicated at intervals by applause. The second part of the concert was more varied still, commencing with the "Village Choristers," arranged by Mr. G. J. Lee, and embracing many agreeable items. The vocalism throughout was of a high order, and the society have in fact much reason to congratulate themselves on the success of last evening's concert.

O'Bolger's skepticism concerning Lee's talents is contrary to the record and nullified by an expert but perhaps partial witness: George Bernard Shaw.

In 1905 Henderson was advised by Shaw that his mother became associated with "an energetic genius." [39] Eleven years later GBS wrote O'Bolger that Lee was a "conductor of genius" [40] and thus identified at least one of Lee's talents. Afterwards Shaw had an assortment of variations. Dynamic, efficient, a man of energy, spirit and mesmeric vitality—an artist of exceptional temperament endowed with mesmeric energy were some of the expressions used by GBS to support his claim of Lee's genius. According to Shaw, Lee's genius extended to the critical appraisal and emendation of at least one Master. Writing in his preface to *London Music* in 1935, GBS recalled that during his own musical development as a critic, he had examined an old vocal score of *Don Giovanni* belonging to Lee and had been "shocked" to discover that Lee had removed all the repetitive phrasing Mozart incorporated as part of the conventional sonata structure. With the passing years, Shaw's "pedantic" view changed and, he concluded, "I now see that Lee was a century before his time in this reform . . ."[41] As to whether Lee himself played any instrument Shaw appeared reluctant to say, but he reported in one instance that his sister Lucy had "quarrelled" with Lee when he attempted to give her piano lessons.[42] Fortunately, Lee as a musical executant has been commented upon by at least one source. *Freeman's Journal* for 27 May 1873 reviewed a "Grand Charity Concert" given for the Meath (Dublin) and City of Dublin Hospitals conducted by G. Vandeleur Lee. Observed the reviewer: "Mr. G.V.Lee conducted and presided at the pianoforte with much skill and taste."

The question of Lee's genius, at this distance, is not a subject to be entered into lightly—at least not for the record—and it is with a certain sense of relief that one passes to the examination of Lee's musicianship in general.

VI

As a conductor, Lee must have been blessed with an extraordinary talent since from the academic point of view he was completely disqualified for that function. Shaw tells us that as far as he knew a full score never passed before Lee's eyes and that he conducted from either the first violin or a vocal score. Further, GBS believed that Lee had no training (in the modern sense), nor had he a firm concept of orchestration as an integral part of a composition; but he had that quality so essential to a conductor (and here Shaw quoted Wagner): the ability to give the right time to those under his direction. More than this, when the orchestra (all amateurs like himself) stumbled into difficulties, Lee was able to shepherd them into safety through "sheer mesmerism." [43] While the newspapers reported him to have composed and arranged some music, I suggest that Mr. Lee had relatively little part in this, probably leaving such matters to "his right hand"—a lady versed in these intricacies and to whom appropriate attention will presently be accorded. Still, Lee's musical competence cannot be judged entirely by his use of mesmerism as a substitute for correction and example, since his chief strength seemed to rest in his reputation as a teacher of singing and it was here that Lee may have earned the laurels of genius. Shaw himself recognized the limitations of Lee's effectiveness in music and, in noting his narrow cultural interests (he "never" read anything but a treatise on sound and recognized no art but music), reported that Lee's musical compass was "limited" to its vocal branches.[44]

So little is known of Lee's childhood and youth that any effort to account for his talent in and preoccupation with music and the voice would be highly presumptuous, but it may be noted for the record that Thom's Registers list one Signor de la Vega, a Professor of Music in Number 13 Caroline Row during the period of the Lees' occupancy of Number 4 Caroline Row. Lee himself, it appears, did not sing; Shaw reported that while Lee never sang a note within his hearing, his artistic judgment of singing was, nevertheless, "classically perfect." [45] He added that Lee, in his quest for the secrets of the singing voice, not only queried all the teachers within his reach but also extended his search into actual dissection of human as well as animals' throats.[46] By 1859 the twenty-eight-year-old Lee seemed to have exhausted Dublin's stock of vocal knowledge (all conflicting, of course) and journeyed to Italy where he contracted malaria as well as culture in the furtherance of his musical education. On his return to Dublin by way of London, Lee attended the opera and heard Italian baritone Cesare Badiali from whom, it appears, Lee received the secrets of his singing. Badiali, or Badeali as GBS (and Harris) spelled the name, was the possessor, according to Grove's *Dictionary of Music and Musicians,* of a remarkable voice of great beauty (which he retained for some years after his retirement) and an excellent "method." Writing in *The World* for 23 July 1890, Shaw had something to say of Methods and his "late friend" Professor Lee. As he reproduced it in *Music In London,* GBS recalled a conversation in London wherein he asked Lee how he had come by his method. The reply was that he had developed it as the result of his study of "the physiology of the vocal organs." When Shaw openly scoffed and pointed out that Huxley and Foster had done no less and did not, on that account, pretend to a knowledge of singing, Lee retreated. He then told Shaw that when he discovered that the singing teachers (to whom he wished to serve his apprenticeship) knew as little of the subject as himself, he struck out on his own. One of the three or four only known direct quotes of Lee:

> "I pottered over anatomy, and experimented on myself and my pupils until I could tell by watching a singer exactly how he was doing it. Then I watched all the opera-singers, and found that those whose voices wore badly sang differently from those whose voices wore well. I heard old Badeali, when he was nearly eighty, sing with the freshness of a young man. Accordingly I taught my pupils to produce their voices as Badeali did, and to avoid doing what the others did. The plan answered perfectly . . ." [47]

Returning to his reader, GBS would not vouch for the truthfulness of the second account, since Lee had, said Shaw, "the artistic temperament." [48] According to MacMillan's *Encyclopedia of Music and Musicians,* Badiali was born in Imola about 1810 and made his debut on the operatic stage of Trieste at the remarkably early age of seventeen. Grove's work did not mention the year of his birth, but noted that he visited London during 1859 and died in the city of his birth on 17 November 1865. Thus, if the sources are accurate, Lee may have exaggerated the singer's age possibly to impress prospective students with the system used by Badiali and called by Lee, The Method.

The application of Badiali's system by the enterprising and energetic Lee did not endear him to his professional rivals. Henderson asserted that they regarded him "with the greatest contempt, even hatred . . ." [49] Henderson's source declared that every teacher of singing in Dublin held Lee to be his enemy and he retaliated ardently.[50] But this was an atmosphere in which Lee thrived and, whether his unpopularity was due to his Catholic aura or his fervid denunciations of his rivals as voice-wreckers,[51] the Professor and his Method proved a successful combination; for, in addition to carrying the major expenses of a large town house in Hatch Street, he was simultaneously able to afford Torca Cottage in Dalkey.

The effect of Lee and his method upon the Shaws has not remained unobserved by the major biographers. "Harris" noted that Lee had developed a system of singing "known in the Shaw household as The Method." [52] Pearson reported that the Professor had "discovered" a method of teaching singing which became his religion and to which Mrs. Shaw "soon" became converted.[53] Henderson stated that Mrs. Shaw, her daughter Lucy, Lee's pupils and Shaw himself all put their trust in "The Method." [54] Ervine almost succeeded in capturing the substance as well as the spirit of the method as it affected the Shaw family:

> The Method—the term always used by his followers in referring to this system—was mentioned in [Mrs. Shaw's] house in hushed tones that could not have been more reverential if they had been applied to the holy and undivided Trinity.[55]

Playwright Shaw, chuckling to himself perhaps, may have reincarnated Lee as the Royal Musician to Cleopatra in ACT IV of *Caesar and Cleopatra* completed twelve years after the death of the Professor. The master of the harps is summoned by the Queen of Queens:

> CLEOPATRA
>
> I want to learn to play the harp with my own hands, Caesar loves music. Can you teach me?
>
> MUSICIAN
>
> Assuredly I and no one else can teach the queen. Have I not discovered the lost method of the ancient Egyptians, who could make a pyramid tremble by touching a bass

> string? All the other teachers are quacks. I have exposed them repeatedly.
>
> CLEOPATRA
>
> Good: you shall teach me. How long will it take?
>
> MUSICIAN
>
> Not very long: only four years. Your Majesty must first become proficient in the philosophy of Pythagoras.

Some forty-five years before this caricature was drawn, George John Lee became the friend of the Shaw family, and Henderson was the first to be informed. His mother, wrote GBS, was disappointed with marriage. She sought and found salvation in music and "She became the right hand of an energetic genius . . . by name George John Vandaleur Lee . . ."[56] Henderson has thrice given the occasion his thoughtful attention:

> Not long after her marriage to Mr. Shaw, she became the right hand of an energetic genius . . . George John Vandaleur Lee.[57]

> It was not long after her marriage that Mrs. Shaw became the right hand of the energetic genius George John Vandaleur Lee.[58]

> It was not long after her marriage that Mrs. Shaw became the right hand of that energetic genius, George John Vandaleur Lee.[59]

With three opportunities over a span of fifty-one years, Henderson offered no opinions on the length of time between Mrs. Shaw's marriage and her meeting with Professor Lee.

IV / Dublin I

I

No. 239	Names	Age	Condition	Address	Father's Occupation
1852	George Carr Shaw	Both of	Bachelor	17 Lennox St.	Solicitor
June 17th	Lucinda Elizabeth Gurly	full age	Spinster	Stillorgan	Gentleman

Witnesses: W. B. Gurly
Geo. H. MacMullen

Clergyman: W. G. Carroll[1]

WITH THE BENEDICTIONS of the Reverend William George Carroll still reverberating within the walls of the church, Mr. and Mrs. George Carr Shaw emerged from fashionable St. Peter's on Aungier Street and stepped into a carriage which awaited the newlyweds. The bride was given away by her father, who seems to have forgiven her for her part in his arrest on his own wedding day.

Inside the carriage, the hitherto patient Mr. Shaw, observing that the prize was at last within his grasp, approached flying the usual signals but reckoned without his bride's breeding. Requested by O'Bolger to comment on his doctoral thesis, GBS gladly obliged with an additional detail to halt O'Bolger's speculations. When, wrote GBS, Mr. Shaw "offered" to fondle his bride, Mrs. Shaw was "disgusted or indignant." Going further, GBS marvelled that after thirty or forty years, his mother could still allude to this incident with an unmitigated umbrage and concluded, somewhat anticlimactically, that

Mr. Shaw's eyes must have opened wide at her lack of "mately" affection.[2]

There is no evidence to show that Mr. and Mrs. Shaw spent any part of their honeymoon in Dublin. They seem to have driven at once to the North Wall of the Liffey where they embarked for Liverpool. How or why this city was chosen was a source of bewilderment to GBS and understandably so. Whatever Liverpool is today, Liverpool in the 1850's—bursting with potteries and mills, bustling with vans and ships—was hardly the romantic spot in which to store a bride's mind with memories to be cherished. Ervine reported the Shaws to have taken accommodations at one of the city's hotels[3] while Winsten fastened them upon distant relations—whose relations in particular he did not say.[4] In either case, the bridegroom, eager to share in the traditions of the Shaws, performed his first and, not inconceivably, perhaps his last husbandly obligation by contributing his services in the principal function of marriage.

Gratified by the knowledge that he had not failed in his duty, or perhaps in the optimistic contemplation of his future, George Carr celebrated the event by the resumption of his bibacious pursuits. Though he made some childish effort to conceal his drinking Lucinda soon discovered the signs and her son, some years later, received her confidences. Writing in his *Sketches,* GBS said his mother once told him that during the honeymoon she found Mr. Shaw's wardrobe to be "full" of empty bottles.[5] Pearson held it to be a "number" of empties cached in a cupboard.[6] Ervine, agreeing with the cupboard, restored the number to full.[7] Winsten was not to be outdone. He asserted that after a few days of honeymooning Mr. Shaw had forgotten he had a wife and returned home one night in so advanced a stage of intoxication that he had to be undressed and put to bed by his wife who, when putting his clothes away in the wardrobe, found it then to be filled with empty bottles.[8] GBS's account of the wardrobe being full of empty bottles is unquestionably an accurate quote of his mother's natural exaggeration of several bottles. In any case, one is led to believe that either the honeymoon was considerably extended or that George Carr's capacity for alcohol has yet to be realized. It may be additionally deduced that Mr. Shaw, described by GBS as a lonely drinker at the public house, supplemented that practice by extending it to his own lodgings and, by further extension, to his future home in Synge Street. One cannot account for his clumsy efforts to conceal the empty bottles without concluding that, as a gay dog, George Carr was more dull than sly.

As the full meaning of the wardrobe's shocking contents struck home, Lucinda's first reaction may have been an ungovernable submission to a wave of shame. Her second was a desperate and hysterical act. GBS related that his mother ran from the house to the dock area with the apparent intention of shipping as a stewardess on one of the vessels. This, to me, suggests two things: first, that the hotel (or distant relative's home) was near the waterfront; and second, that the notion of leaving her husband may have occurred to her before the wardrobe incident. Howsoever that may be, Lucinda did not have her chance to actually inquire into employment opportunities since some burly 'longshoremen frightened her away with some personally tendered compliments.[9]

Forced to return to the scene of her honeymoon, Lucinda may have reviewed her predicament. Her family and friends were right—they had warned her that Mr. Shaw was a drunkard. He had rejected their accusations with genuine horror[10] and had sworn that he was a life-long abstainer. And now she was face to face with the truth, trapped into a dreadful marriage by the monstrous lies of a gross, foul-smelling and disgusting drunkard. Were there other such disappointments in store for her in the tomorrows to come? Thirteen years with Aunt Ellen had not prepared her for this—the Brilliant Future envisaged for Lucinda had contained no hint of a world of lies and ugliness, at least not for an Irish Protestant young lady of gentle birth. There were to be only charming ladies and gentlemen, cultured and refined with soft hands, sweet breath and musical voices. How had she stumbled into this hell? How was she to get back to the world planned for her? Pearson suggested that Lucinda had had enough of the world as it was and would content herself within the confines of her own imagination—a condition "which was incomparably better than the world of reality that had treated her so harshly." [11] One might be tempted to accept this popular, convenient and modern

(1942) view, but Lucinda's solution was not the classic withdrawal of the schizophrenic. Pearson's further observations did not support his opinions. He also noted that Mrs. Shaw possessed qualities which could not be reconciled with his withdrawal theory; namely, her "mental independence, imaginative self-sufficiency and ability." [12]

Other biographers and on-the-scene observers had similar views. Thus McCabe described her as being "capable, self-reliant and audacious," [13] Hamon saw her as an "intelligent, energetic and persevering woman" [14] and Hackett gave her a "strong personality and a decisive character." [15] There were few direct observers and fewer still who were moved to record their impressions. Henderson noted her independence and self-reliance,[16] McNulty used "masterful" to describe his friend's mother[17] and daughter Lucy viewed her as "shrewd and fearless." [18] Some of the comments indeed, pictured Lucinda as a sort of Vivie of *Mrs. Warren's Profession* or, for that matter, any of the numerous "Shaw women" created by GBS and dismissed by the critics as impossible females. Henderson glowed as he rose to the subject. Mrs. Shaw was independent in the "extreme," vigorous, resolute, aloof, able and had an "unquestionable power of leadership," [19] and at another time announced her as being, in many ways, the precursor of the " 'new woman' of our own day." [20] Rattray typed her as emancipated and added that she was not "of the marrying sort." [21] Hackett analyzed her as being "made of sterner stuff." [22] Ervine added a new note to an old theme: "The cold, hard young heart [he wrote] became colder and harder, and she announced herself an atheist." [23] As to GBS himself, the terms he used to describe his mother hinted at a woman who had pride as well as strength and were phrased in a style that has been made familiar by the biographers. Mrs. Shaw (he said) was neither "weak or submissive," [24] possessed large reserves of an inner force which encouraged the growth of her "self-sufficiency and power of solitude." GBS surmised that these characteristics could be attributed to her deprivation of love and affection during the early motherless years and to the many disappointments she suffered.[25]

Mrs. Shaw now confronted the problems before her with the rudiments of many, if not all, of these qualities, and they did not fail her. Divorce was out of the question and, apart from a direct appeal to one of the houses of Parliament, there was no existing machinery in mid-nineteenth century for dealing with twentieth-century dilemmas.[26] Her method and manner of resolving her situation has been dealt with by the second-best authority: first in a letter to O'Bolger and later, with slight changes, in the *Sketches*. Shaw responded with perceptible annoyance to the American professor's persistent inquiries regarding the Lee-Shaw household. Replying that although he had mislaid O'Bolger's letter, he could guess the nature of the question and proceeded to give the best sketch of Lucinda Elizabeth Shaw extant. Everyone, wrote Shaw, had either deceived her, disillusioned her or oppressed her, yet she had not been embittered by these experiences. No matter what the provocation—whether hurt through malice or the victim of someone's anger or "passions" (Shaw substituted "tempers" in the *Sketches*)—her equanimity in and superiority to the circumstances were never affected. Being by nature "long-suffering," she never made "scenes" and never revealed her complaints. She would not bicker or scold and, if wounded, refused to exact reprisal. She never sought revenge, Shaw continued, nor did she ever forgive. Further, if one misbehaved, one was catalogued among those persons who behaved so and was treated as such. Finally,

> if at last you drove her beyond even her patience to the point of forcing her to break with you, the breach was permanent; you did not get back again.[27]

I suggest that when GBS typed these lines to O'Bolger and later publicly released them in the *Sketches,* he had his mother's relationship to her husband particularly in mind. I believe that when George Carr stood exposed as a drunkard and a liar, Lucinda Elizabeth had been driven beyond the breaking point, and the little that held them together was permanently breached. I finally suggest that Mrs. Shaw detached herself from her husband, rejecting him in every sense including, possibly, the sexual sense.

II

THE SHAWS RETURNED TO DUBLIN to settle down and endure each other for the next twenty years. Mr. Shaw had taken a house in Synge Street about two miles south of the River Liffey in a quarter known as Portobello—a district more rural than urban at the time. Although both Thom's and the *Post Office Dublin Directory* for 1853 (1852) list one Thomas Moyers as the occupant of Number 3 and do not register George Carr until the following year, it can be assumed that the newlyweds moved into it during the latter part of 1852 or early in 1853. There is some possibility that the house was not available to them and they may have stayed for a short time in Mr. Shaw's bachelor quarters at 17 Lennox Street (officially described as "tenements") and just around the corner from Synge Street. A few yards up Lennox was brother Henry Shaw in Number 31 where, during 1850, George Carr lived for some time.

While Synge Street of today is a tidy and respectable three-block-long thoroughfare of many homes and an impressive-looking Roman Catholic Christian Brothers school, it was not so in the 1850's, being then only one block in length and consisting of eleven residences and the works and timber yard of their builder, William Moyers. By 1864 expanding Dublin, after centering its attention on the more fashionable streets, reached into its lanes and byways and Synge Street was extended from Lennox across Harrington, Grantham and Pleasants Streets where it ended abruptly. Renamed in characteristic Dublin style Upper, Middle and Lower, the streets were also rezoned and Number 3 was rechristened the number it bears today —33.

The class nature of the Synge Street neighborhood has come under the scrutiny of Henderson. He reported it to be inhabited by civil servants, merchants, moderately successful professionals and city clerks, all respectable enough but smacking of shabby gentility.[28] MacManus had a similar description and included the city clerks to whom GBS took exception.[29] Synge Street, wrote Shaw, was beyond the means of city clerks, being for the most part populated by merchants of modest prosperity though with pretensions of social superiority to retail tradesman.[30] Of the eleven householders listed by Thom's for 1852 only three are identified by their occupations (a barrister, a carpenter and a dressmaker); consequently, we do not get a clear picture of Synge Street's social face.

Built in the 1840's Number 33, like its sisters, has stood the years well. Quietly acknowledging the earlier Georgian influence in the modest scroll-like carvings to either side of the door, it is sturdily constructed with the saffron-hued bricks and stepped chimneys that link it to the early nineteenth century. The interior of 33 has been accurately described by its most distinguished former inhabitant. Writing to Harris on 20 June 1930, GBS set forth its main features. Beginning with the basement which contained the kitchen, pantry and the servant's bedroom, Shaw ascended to the street floor and pointed out the parlor, nursery and the "return room." [31] In the upper story were the drawing room and the master bedroom "and that was all." [32] From the front of the house the windows of the drawing room and the single one of the parlor stare impassively into Synge Street whilst the kitchen window, as if an apology for its effrontery, sinks below the street level. In the rear and from the vantage point of the "garden" (about ten by ten feet), one may still see, on the right, the outdoor W.C. now happily superseded by the conversion of the pantry. To the left of the garden door is the servant's room, above which is the nursery window. To the right of the nursery and directly above the converted pantry is the "return room" which Mr. Shaw used as a dressing room and which was also used by Sonny Shaw as his bedroom when his advancing years separated him from his sisters in the nursery.[33] Surveying all of this from the uppermost floor was the window of the master bedroom from where the first sounds uttered by George Bernard Shaw issued forth.

III

THERE IS SOME POSSIBILITY THAT GBS might have been mistaken regarding certain circumstances of George Carr's entrance into business as a corn factor (commission agent). According to the account in his preface to *Immaturity,* GBS asserted that Clibborn and his partner Shaw were both new to the business in that Mr. Shaw knew nothing about corn and Clibborn (who had been pressed into the cloth trade) knew even less if possible. He added that the business (an office and warehouse in Jervis Street and a mill in Dolphin's Barn) was acquired as a going concern and despite the fumblings of the new proprietors, continued to function "automatically." [34] Ervine agreed, terming the partnership "a joint incompetence." [35] Yet, examination of the directories of the period seems to disclose some discrepancies, at least with regard to Clibborn. They show that a George Clibborn was a partner in the firm of Clibborn & Moncrief (variously spelled with one or two f's), Corn Factors of 67-68 Jervis Street from 1850 until 1853 when Moncrief's name was replaced by Shaw. Cross reference to Thom's listings of Nobility, Gentry, Merchants and Traders for the same years show that Clibborn, George, Esq., Corn Merchant lived at 10 Upper Leeson Street. The possibility exists, of course, that the Clibborn of Clibborn & Shaw could have been a son and heir of the Clibborn of Clibborn & Moncrief but then, this lessens the likelihood of his being an apprentice to cloth or that he knew even less about corn factoring than did Mr. Shaw. As to Moncrief (identified in Thom's as Alexander Rutherford Moncrief Merchant, office 67 Jervis Street), it is reasonable to assume that it was his share in the business that Mr. Shaw bought with the proceeds of the sale of his pension. That GBS was no stranger to the name of Moncrief is revealed through his practice of selecting names for his works contemporaneous with his Dublin memories, and a Moncrief appears as the name of the headmaster of the school attended by Cashel Byron.[36] It seems that George Carr did indeed enter into the corn and flour trade immediately after his marriage, but Thom's somehow neglected to note and record the change.

IV

If Mr. Shaw were not engaged in the corn trade at the time of his marriage, his income then may have been his pension of £44 per year. Undoubtedly advised and influenced by his enterprising brother Henry,[37] George Carr sold his pension for a cash settlement and invested the proceeds as previously described. The income from Mr. Shaw's investments of his money and talents cannot be precisely determined. Hamon saw Mr. Shaw as a "poor" man and did not believe that he earned more than two or three hundred pounds a year,[38] and GBS recalled that the "impecunious" corn merchant never paid his bills on time—a characteristic not necessarily a sign of impecuniosity.[39] Elsewhere, GBS's opinion of George Carr's economic situation was given a subjective flavor. Writing in his preface to *London Music,* he avowed that Mr. Shaw's income was insufficient and accordingly "humiliating" [40] but in another place explained by, despite a reasonably comfortable income, it was nevertheless embarrassingly inadequate. Suggesting that his father did not know how much money he earned, GBS admitted his own knowledge to be even more uncertain but allowed that the corn merchant's income ran into "at least" three figures—"four, if you count in dollars. . . ." Concluding, GBS added that what really impoverished him was the delusion of the social grandeur synonymous with being a Shaw and (it followed) his extravagances in living up to that concept on only one-half or one-third of the income required.[41] Elsewhere he put a ceiling on Mr. Shaw's income by expressing a doubt that he ever earned more than three or four hundred a year[42] and to MacMahon Shaw he wryly noted that the Shavian affectations for aristocracy ("colossal") were not always equal to their incomes.[43] GBS did not illustrate the manner in which Mr. Shaw supported his social pretensions, but conceivably it may have taken the form of ill-afforded carriages, elaborate parties and fashionable clothing.

The fixing of Mr. Shaw's income would not establish the economic picture or living level of the family, for there is no way of setting their cost of living. Attempts to determine the exact rental of

3 Synge Street failed when the present land agents[44] advised that after the closest examination, they were unable to supply the facts. They cited the Moyers family as being in full control of the neighborhood from 1842 until 1900 when they disposed of the houses leaving no records of tenants and rents. According to *Griffith's Valuation* for 1853, 3 Synge Street (occupier George Shaw, Lessor William Moyers) had a rateable annual valuation of £18 which, in the judgment of an official of Dublin's Valuation Office, indicated that an annual rental of twice that figure would not be too far off an estimate.

In his 1919 blast at O'Bolger for suggesting, among other things, that George Carr, faced with the infidelities of his wife, turned to whiskey for solace, GBS inquired of that "buffleheaded idiot" whether it was necessary to tell him the story over again—and did so, thereby adding some new facts in the retelling. Mr. Shaw, wrote GBS, rented the Synge Street house at about £30 a year.[45] By the crude and speculative rule of thumb that rent absorbs one quarter of one's income, Mr. Shaw's annual earnings came to £120—a reasonably comfortable sum for the period. Admittedly this method of estimating George Carr's income may contain fallacies, still it might be agreed that his original capital of £60 a year had indeed been shrewdly invested to obtain an income of "at least three figures."[46]

The use of servants in the Shaw household cannot (as held by some commentators) be construed to mean their employment was a contradiction of a "poor" Shaw. Full-time servants were then available, GBS tells us, at £8 a year or at about seventy-five cents weekly; yet, while scandalously low, this outlay must still be considered as one of the "necessary" unnecessary expenses in supporting the Shaw pretensions. Moreover, such servants (as bad as they were) were indispensable to the household, since Mrs. Shaw, having been brought up as an Irish carriage lady, could under no circumstances stoop to the duties reserved for the serving classes.

Except on special occasions, it was unlikely that the Shaws employed more than one servant at a time, but as the turnover may have been high, the impression could have been received of a larger staff. Over and above such domestics, a nurse or a governess would be engaged whose duties would include those of a tutorial nature and who would be paid by the hour. Taking all into consideration, George Carr Shaw may have had a difficult moment or two in keeping the wolf at a respectable distance.

V

IT IS MOST UNLIKELY that Mrs. Lucinda Elizabeth Shaw used any part of her inheritance to help her husband in either their home or business—even had she had the desire and presuming she had an inheritance. George Carr's premarital optimism regarding his betrothed's marriage settlements collapsed in an early postmarital period of sober reality when Aunt Ellen's much promised dowry was angrily withdrawn. In its stead, Aunt Ellen handed over to her niece a wedding gift in the shape of a large packet of I.O.U.'s signed by the sporting Walter Bagnall who, in a heaven-sent opportunity afforded by Lucinda, seized and thrust them into the fireplace. The precise size of Aunt Ellen's fortune has been variously estimated but only Ervine took the trouble to find the facts and he reported it to be about £4000. While the will of Aunt Ellen was proved on the 24th of June 1862 in a sum of under £2000, it was re-sworn six days later as being under £4000.[47] Evidence regarding its final disposition could not be uncovered.

With respect to Lucinda's inheritance from grandfather John Whitcroft, there seems to be some discord as to its size, control and division. According to Henderson, "not a penny" of it belonged to Mrs. Shaw, but during the grim days in London she was forced to draw upon "assets totalling £4000"—indeed, obliged to do so under the terms of the will—to spend it in the interest and welfare of her children and for her own maintenance.[48] Harris reported that Whitcroft settled an unspecified sum on his grandchildren and that Lucinda's father—who had the power of appointment—schemed to divert it into his own pocket. The author further reported that Walter Bagnall's solicitor, out of pure solicitorial perversity, refused to permit his client to do his worst and "fixed" it so that Lucinda's children, if any, would receive $25000 (£5000) as they reached their majorities while, at the same time, depriving Lucinda of any use of it for herself.[49] Ervine believed the Whitcroft bequest to be £5000 but held that this had been reduced to £4000 by the rapacious Walter Bagnall who, waxed Ervine, "should have been imprisoned for his crime." It was Lucinda's solicitor, he reported, not her father's, who rescued the £4000, and in further contradiction to the Harris version, Ervine asserted that it was Lucinda who had the power of appointment and that the will contained clauses empowering her to spend not only the interest on the principal but the principal itself as each child came to his or her majority and with his or her consent. Nor were these Ervine's only dissents. He additionally stated that the children "were of considerable financial benefit to her" in that Mrs. Shaw was able to "make use" of each child's share as they came of age. He supported this implication by asserting that the share of Mrs. Shaw's second daughter "may be said to have been pure profit to her mother, for Agnes died within a week or two of her twenty-first birthday." [50] Shaw's own explanations account for some of the confusion. In 1921 he stated, in connection with the difficult early London years, that his mother was forced from time to time to draw on a "maternal" inheritance of £4000 over which she had the power of appointment.[51] In 1949 he changed his mind and gave the power of appointment to Walter Bagnall who attempted to deprive his daughter of the entire bequest (no sum was mentioned) but was thwarted by the Gurly "family" solicitor who, Shaw wrote, managed to salvage about £40 a year for her.[52] O'Bolger received the earliest and, consequently, the most accurate account. Her father, Shaw wrote, had the power of appointment which he used in an attempt to defraud his daughter of her entire portion, but the Gurlys' solicitor thwarted this attempt and managed to save "a couple of thousands pounds." Mrs. Shaw, added GBS, regarded her father as selfish, uninterested in her welfare and, within the confines of his social level, a blackguard of the lowest order.[53]

As for the £40 per annum story, it may be discounted as an error, since GBS wrote it when he was in his nineties and may have confused the Whitcroft bequest with certain properties in Carlow which brought his mother about £40 annually.

The record of the Whitcroft bequest exists in the form of a "Memorial," that is to say, a subsequent and supplementary document, wherein those concerned seek legal implementation of an original agreement of "indented deed." This Memorial states that the Marriage Settlement of John Whitcroft upon his daughter Lucinda Whitcroft and her husband Walter Bagnall Gurly was vested in and undertaken by his son John Hamilton and one Joseph Fishbourne (an official of the Gt. Southern & Western RR). Fishbourne may be related to Robert Moore Fishbourne, a fellow employee of GBS in the land agency of Townshend & Company and who posed with his friend just before his departure for London in 1876. The following is an extract from the Memorial stripped of some of its legal terminology:

Book 1869 37 35

> A MEMORIAL OF AN INDENTED DEED OF APPOINTMENT . . . 30 October 1869 between Walter Bagnall Gurly of Clareville . . . of the first part Walter John Gurly of Liverpool, England, Medical Doctor son of said Walter Bagnall Gurly of the second part George Shaw of Hatch Street Dublin and Lucinda Elizabeth Shaw otherwise Gurly his wife of the third part Reciting a certain Indenture of Marriage Settlement dated 26 December 1829 made upon the marriage of Walter Bagnall Gurly with Lucinda Whitcroft his late wife and Reciting a trust . . . vested in John Hamilton Whitcroft and Joseph Fishbourne Trustees . . . that if there should be more than one child issue of said intended marriage that they should levy and raise a sum of four thousand pounds for the portion or portions of such children to be paid to them at such age or respective ages and in such shares and proportions as the said Walter Bagnall Gurly should . . . direct and appoint and Reciting that said marriage took effect and there was issue thereof the said Walter John Gurly . . . and Lucinda Elizabeth

> Gurly now the wife of George Shaw Esquire and one other child who died an infant . . . said Walter Bagnall Gurly was desirous to exercise the power of appointment given to him . . . [and] in consideration of the love and affection which he hath for his said children . . . hath given granted conveyed . . . the said sum of four thousand pounds in manner following that is to say to his son Walter John Gurly his executors administrators and assigns a sum of two thousand five hundred pounds and to his said daughter Lucinda Elizabeth Gurly otherwise Shaw a sum of one thousand five hundred pounds the remaining part of said sum for her own sole and separate use and free from the debts control or engagements of her husband Signed and Sealed Walter Bagnall Gurly in presence of Michael Driscoll Solicitor . . . [who] saith that he is a subscribing witness to the Deed of which the foregoing is a Memorial . . . [Done] Friday 3rd day December 1869 at the hour of twenty minutes to two o'clock . . . [and] sworn before me this third day of December 1869 at the Registry of Deeds Office.[54]
>
> T. M. Ray, A. R.

The biographers, it can be seen, have erred in the size of the bequest to Lucinda Elizabeth. Contrary to Henderson and Ervine's four thousand, Harris' five thousand and Shaw's annual forty pounds, the record shows the sum to be no more or no less than fifteen hundred pounds. Both Henderson and Ervine reported Whitcroft's great-grandchildren (GBS and his sisters) to be the beneficiaries but the Memorial supports Harris and Shaw in that the trust speaks specifically of the grandchildren; to wit: Walter John and Lucinda Elizabeth.

One can only speculate on the reasons why Father Gurly waited until his daughter's thirty-ninth year and the seventeenth year of her marriage to call upon the trustees. Was it because he felt his time was running short (he was then sixty-nine) and that the fortune he perhaps felt rightly belonged to him was slipping through his fingers? Or did he withhold it as an expression of his disapproval of George Carr, his estimable son-in-law? Shaw's assertion that Walter Bagnall tried to swindle his daughter of her inheritance seems to be refuted in the Memorial which, verbally at least, demonstrates that Father Gurly, far from trying to cheat her, actually protected her by specifically denying its use to her husband—an unheard of breach of Victorian privilege. However, these records may not reveal the whole truth and I am strongly disposed to accept Shaw's report that Gurly schemed with the solicitor to relieve his daughter of most if not all of the £1500. There is no evidence as to Gurly's designs, if any, on his son's portion.

Apart from the operations of Clibborn & Shaw there does not seem to have been any other source of income during the first ten years of their marriage, though it is possible that Lucinda's brother Walter may have contributed during his stays with them in Synge Street between voyages.

VI

WHATEVER GEORGE CARR'S innermost thoughts and reactions were to his marriage—particularly during its earliest years—GBS offered no opinions. As to Mrs. Shaw's state of mind, her son proved less reticent. In a review of the "tragedy" of that marriage to the disbelieving O'Bolger, GBS invited him to conceive of his mother's arrival in shabby-genteel Synge Street with a drunken husband as a descent into hell.[55] Imagine—for that is all we can do—the hell for both Lucinda and George Carr: Lucinda's frigid silences, her thoughts as she daily grew larger with the child of a liar and drunkard, George Carr's redoubled guzzling in some pathetic effort to insulate himself against his wife's forbidding aspect.

The biographers were relieved of the need for excursions into their imaginations as Shaw's brief but coruscating references set the motif. Thus Henderson recorded that Shaw's mother harbored a "bitter disappointment" towards her husband who, he added, was a "confirmed alcoholic."[56] Hackett echoed his subject closely. Mrs. Shaw was "disappointed with her husband's feebleness" and disgusted with his "morose conviviality."[57] Ervine, noting Lucinda's "disdain" for her husband and her disgust in realizing that she had conceived his children,[58] sounded a pious note as he took up the defense of Mr. Shaw. As Ervine put it, "With a more congenial mate, one who was less intent on herself, kindlier and more tolerant of a man's little habit of taking a drop too much now and then, his life might have been very agreeable . . ."[59]

However, Ervine's inference that the unhappiness of the marriage was due to Lucinda's unfriendly, unkindly and intolerant attitude towards George Carr is admissable only if she entered into that marriage with a full awareness of George Carr's weaknesses.

VII

IF, AS SHAW AMUSINGLY SUGGESTED, George Carr was prodded into proposing marriage by some imp of hell driven by the Life Force to bring GBS into the world, then that imp was also scheduled to influence Lucinda Elizabeth. Her son had it that the change in his mother's fortunes occurred at least five years after her marriage and coincided with the appearance of George John Lee. The time of this appearance in the affairs of the Synge Street Shaws has not received appropriate attention and in general has either been entirely ignored or phrased in what might be described as literary mumbling. Henderson, as Shaw's official biographer and as a competent and conscientious writer, could not avoid the subject altogether. He reported that "not long after" Mrs. Shaw's marriage she became an indispensable adjunct to Lee. In the fifty-five years covering the period of his three major works on Shaw, Henderson's treatment of this event remained unchanged. Since Mr. and Mrs. Shaw separated after twenty years, the phrase "not long after" the marriage assumes a coy unwillingness to stand and be measured. Ordinary usage of the phrase would imply the meeting time to be anywhere between a few months to two or three years—perhaps four.

Ervine offered a freshly-worded opinion on the meeting of Mrs. Shaw and the Professor. He believed that they met during "the first years of her marriage." [60] Two paragraphs later Ervine was more certain, venturing that her immersion into Lee's world of music "did not come immediately after [her] marriage": she had first to bring her three babies into the world, thus placing her meeting with Lee some time after 1856.[61] O'Bolger was also convinced that Lee came on the scene some time after July 26, 1856. While he had frankly charged Mrs. Shaw with having an adulterous relation with Lee[62] he dismissed the notion that the alleged relation could have existed prior to his subject's birthdate and gave his reasoning:

> . . . I entertain no whiff of a doubt that he is the reputable son of George Carr Shaw—if for no other reason than that I believe he arrived before Lee.[63]

It is in Shaw's own comments that one finds reason to sympathize with the biographers in their struggle to produce substance out of shadow. Shaw set the pace in his 1905 letter to Henderson. Here for the first time he described some of the circumstances leading up to and away from his mother's wedding day. Disappointed in marriage (wrote GBS), Mrs. Shaw sought and found escape in music and "She became the right hand of an energetic genius . . . by name George John Vandaleur Lee." [64] Shaw's next reference was ten years later and given in response to one of two questions put to him by O'Bolger. "When," inquired the doctoral candidate in his first question, "was the *ménage à trois* that included G. J. Vandaleur Lee set up at your father's house in Dublin?" Denying (quite accurately) that the *ménage à trois* had been established in Synge Street, GBS added that "When I first became conscious of him, he lived in the next street to us . . ." [65] and recalled that when Lee's brother died, Lee attempted suicide (on or after 7 May during the year of 1862). He further advised O'Bolger that "By that time [1862] my mother had become indispensable to Lee's public musical activities." [66] Shaw's earliest memory of Lee seems to be linked to his sixth year while Mrs. Shaw's first meeting with Lee could have taken place at any time between June 1852 and May of 1862. To O'Bolger's second question, "How did your mother come to know Lee?", Shaw replied that he did not know but presumed the meeting took place when she went to him for instruction in singing.[67]

In his 1919 letter to O'Bolger, GBS lashed out at him for his "defamatory" treatment of the Shaw family and conferred his "hearty curse" on him for extorting still another letter. Bidding him to leave Lee out of the picture for the moment GBS reported, not without justifiable sarcasm, that Lee had not yet turned up when George Carr was still the bachelor and reviewed the situation up to and into the marriage. Financial difficulties, social excommunication, three children, a drunkard of a husband with no prospects and a house leased at about £30 a year—all these, wrote Shaw, were his mother's liabilities "when Lee, roaming in search [for musical talent] discovered her voice and trained it." [68] In this arrangement, Shaw pointed out that Lee only appeared some time after her children were born and seemed to suggest that George John was a sort of itinerant impresario of no fixed abode who had wandered into Synge Street more or less haphazardly.

Sixteen years were to pass before Shaw once again turned his attention to this topic. In what is a substantially repetitive comment, Shaw asserted that when his mother realized what it meant to live on insufficient funds with three children, she was "disillusioned" and, as singing lessons in Dublin were "cheap," she then went to Lee to be taught how to sing correctly.[69]

Shaw's final observations on this subject were published in his ninety-third year as he reviewed the history of the Shaws for the last time. Here his remarks tended to nullify the impression of a gipsy music-man wandering about for talent and reported that when his mother went to Lee for singing lessons, the Professor was "already well established in Dublin as an orchestral conductor . . ." [70] Therefore Lee's "roaming" may be accepted in the figurative sense and as being conducted in and from his home in Harrington Street. But despite these minor discords, Shaw's major theme remained dominant and unmistakeable: his mother and George John Lee did not meet until her three children were born. There is no evidence to the contrary; however, their meeting *could* have taken place during the last three months of 1853 or any one of the years that followed. Review of the record will show that both the Shaws and the Lees occupied their respective houses in Synge and Harrington Streets during the same year (1853) and, as may be observed in the Street Plan, they were within two hundred and fifty feet or about one hundred and twenty-five paces of each other for the next thirteen years, until they joined cooperatively in Hatch Street. Further examination of the Street Plan illustrates the sparsely-settled nature of the neighborhood: sixteen houses on both sides of block-long Harrington Street and eleven houses on both sides of block-long Synge Street. Under such conditions all members of this little community were, at the least, aware of each other. It would have been highly improbable for Mrs. Shaw to have been unconscious of the musical activities of Mr. Lee in the three years prior to 1856 or to have failed to notice the Professor as he walked the streets with that "peculiar elegance" which characterized his movements.

I suggest that Mrs. Shaw yearned for release from her husband and from the squalor of her home and resolved to resume her music studies at the first opportunity. That opportunity, I believe, came within eighteen months of her marriage.

VIII

Tuesday March 29, 1853

On the 26th inst., at No. 3 Synge-street, the wife of George C. Shaw Esq., of a daughter.[71]

PROBABLY NAMED AFTER HER MATERNAL GRANDMOTHER, Lucinda Frances arrived into the world precisely 281 days after the marriage of her parents—a normal carriage—thus establishing conception during an early moment of the honeymoon. With the postnatal period behind her (her second baby was some twenty-one months off), I think Mrs. Shaw felt that the opportunity to rise out of the hell in Synge Street had come and, in my opinion, applied at this time to Professor Lee for lessons in singing. Winsten was the only biographer to comment on Mrs. Shaw's application to the Professor. While placing the occasion well into the 1860's, he told his readers that upon hearing tales of his "miracles" with persons of no talent, "Mrs. Carr Shaw" went to Lee in the hope that he could help her salvage something of her life.

> She asked his advice and for the first time told of her desperate plight and opened her heart to a stranger. This man not only understood but offered to teach her if she gave in return occasional help as he had a bad housekeeper who repulsed many pupils.[72]

Mrs. Shaw, implied Winsten, had no talent or believed she had no talent and sought Lee's advice in this connection. His reply, presumably, was so encouraging or so sympathetically given that Mrs. Shaw went into deeper confidences with the stranger whose compassion then moved him to the extent of waiving his usual fees for lessons—but on the condition that Mrs. Shaw assume the duties of his housekeeper now and then. Winsten did not report the response of Irish carriage-lady Lucinda Elizabeth, daughter of Walter Bagnall Gurly, Gentleman.

The birthdate of Mrs. Shaw's second daughter could not be ascertained. Ervine reported it to be unknown, and all concerned support this in the negative sense by shedding no light on the question. Examination of her death registration and headstone at the cemetery of St. Catherine's Church, Ventnor in the Isle of Wight, proved fruitless in this respect. Yet perhaps some idea of the date can be coaxed out of the available information. In an inquiry into the uses and divisions of the Whitcroft bequest, Ervine asserted that she died within one or two weeks of her twenty-first birthday.[73] Henderson put her death in her twentieth year;[74] earliest biographer (1907) Holbrook Jackson reckoned her passing "just as she came of age,"[75] which may be taken to mean twenty-one or just short of it. GBS himself was not at all certain. In 1916 he informed O'Bolger that his younger sister died at twenty "or thereabouts" [76] but, when publishing portions of that letter thirty-three years later, dropped "or thereabouts," fixing her age at the time of her death at twenty,[77] thus leaving us no better informed as far as the month was concerned. But assuming that Jackson and Ervine received their information *viva voce,* it can be seen that if Mrs. Shaw's youngest daughter died (27 March 1876) within a week or two of her twenty-first birthday, she could have been born between the 26th of March and the 8th of April, 1855.

Though brunette-haired [78] Lucinda Frances may have been named after her grandmother, there seem to have been no Gurlys who lent their names to red-haired Elinor Agnes (known within the family as "Yuppy," "Yup" or "Aggie"). Examination of the Gurly genealogy[79] produced five Elizabeths, two Annes, two Lucindas, one Constance, one Georgina, one Florence but neither Elinor nor Agnes. As to the other side of the family, several days spent in the warrens of Burke's and Henderson's genealogies and other sources found the records swarming with Marys, Rebeccas, Janes—and one Ellinor born about 1770 to an obscure off-shoot of the Shaws. Noted elsewhere was Eleanor Leigh who, at the death of Harcourt William Nassau, was named administrator of his estate for the benefit of George John Lee.

IX

Monday July 28, 1856

> On the 26th inst., at 3 Synge-street, the wife of George C. Shaw, Esq., of a son.[80]

SATURDAY'S CHILD, AUBURN-HAIRED GEORGE BERNARD, was probably conceived during the month of October 1855, perhaps seven months after the birth of Yuppy. According to the Harris biography, GBS was "named George after his father" and Bernard after Uncle William

Bernard (Barney) the ophicleidist. Henderson reported that in his childhood GBS was called "Sonny"—never Georgie or Barney but added that his sisters often ragged him by chanting the traditional teaser of "Georgie Porgie." He offered the opinion that Lucy and Yuppy baited their brother in this wise not on account of the jingle's sentiments but possibly because they knew he "hated" his Christian name.[81] Ervine wrote that the young Shaw answered to the name of Sonny but when an infant was called "Bob" by Mr. Shaw. Bob, asserted Winsten, was the name preferred by Mr. Carr Shaw[82] but when the lad developed to some degree of individualism he insisted on Sonny and strongly objected not only to Bob but to "Copperhead," "Ginger" and "Bullocksoup" as well.[83] MacMahon Shaw's *Bernard's Brethren,* published seventeen years before Winsten's *Jesting Apostle,* reported that Shaw's boyhood companions dubbed him Copperhead and Ginger both of which, however, were denied by GBS.[84] Acknowledged historian of Dalkey Frank M. O'Flanagan obtained a refreshing interview for Radio Eireann with one Billy Meegan in the year of Shaw's death. In his nineties, Meegan described himself as a boyhood playmate of GBS and recalled, among other things, that when he knew him on Torca Hill in the years between 1866 and 1874 "the Vegetarian of the future was nicknamed 'Bullock's Blood' because he was always boasting of the *meat soup* he got in Torca Cottage!" [85]

Writing in his *Sketches,* Shaw acknowledged that he was called Sonny but could not remember being called Bob.[86] Sonny seems to have been the family's favorite name for the lad: Mr. Shaw may have been the only one to call him "Bob." In focussing on the question of this independent use of "Bob" by the elder Shaw, I am suggesting that Mr. and Mrs. Shaw did not see eye-to-eye in the selection of a name for their infant son and I offer the following reconstruction to account for this alleged disagreement.

According to a major premise of this study, Mrs. Lucinda Elizabeth Shaw had been culturally associated with Professor George John Lee for two to three years before the birth of her son. I think it reasonable to assume that during this period, the master-pupil relationship had altered to the extent of becoming less formal and had moved towards the freemasonry of professional people. More particularly, Professor Lee was delighted with Lucinda's beautiful voice, her enthusiasm and her competency in assisting with the various technicalities attendant upon the preparation of concerts. Not without some pride, GBS wrote that his mother "soon" became indispensable to the Professor. She was not only his prima donna and choirmistress but auxiliary-in-chief as well, writing the band arrangements, improvising missing instrument parts and, in general, compensating for Lee's technical deficiencies.[87] In short, Lee would not be Lee without Mrs. Shaw.

For her part Lucinda admired, respected—respected? say rather, revered this genius, her High Priest of the Vocal Arts. Winsten had it that the Professor called her "Bessie" [88] and that Mrs. Shaw reciprocated by calling him "Lee" and openly worshipping him.[89] Henderson believed that in her reaction to "domestic disappointment," Mrs. Shaw sought and found a haven in music.[90] Archer, who had often visited mother and son in Fitzroy Square during the early London years, told a New York audience that Mrs. Shaw, having a very good voice which had been trained by a genius, became a leading figure in a circle which gave performances of opera.[91] GBS has himself recognized his mother's debt to her teacher. He reported that Lee believed in his Method as others believed in the Bible, that is, as holy and as a religion which, Shaw observed incidentally, was the only religion Lee ever "professed." Mrs. Shaw, GBS continued, studied and espoused this religion, repudiating all other beliefs as dreary and false doctrines.[92] Elsewhere he declared that music was her "salvation" in that Lee who had cultivated her voice with his Method had thus given her "a Cause and a Creed to live for." [93] Clearly, Professor Lee had made it possible for Lucinda to find a release from her wretched home and husband and to enter into a new and sparkling world of music and beauty, of cultured and dedicated people—in short, Lee had given her freedom, happiness and purpose.

Examination of Henderson's massive genealogical chart of 1911 (prepared by GBS) reveals no precedent for a Shaw to name his first son after himself.

Did George Carr depart from the traditional Shaw refusal to pass on their Christian names to their first sons? I do not believe he did so willingly. I suggest that George Carr wished to name the infant Robert after his distinguished second cousin Sir Robert Shaw, Bart., perhaps in an effort to curry favor in the hope of profiting by this form of flattery. I think he viewed his wife's insistence on naming her son George with objections and suspicions. Far from being a gesture (as Lucinda may have declared) of wifely love and affection for him, he may have replied that it was, in fact, a sign of—he hesitated—a sign of her indebtedness to that Lee fellow.

Henderson's recognition of the young Shaw's dislike of his Christian name raised a sensitive and significant question. It was true—from Sonny to Sage, GBS hated the name George. Though his name has been variously affixed to his works as George Bernard Shaw, Bernard Shaw, G. B. Shaw and G. Bernard Shaw, only the last had his approval and was the only one used for formal and legal purposes. Thus there was a clause in Shaw's printed publishing agreements which stated that his name as author was to appear in his works as "Bernard Shaw" and he specifically forbade "George Bernard Shaw." "Bernard Shaw," the agreement stipulated, must be used on all title pages, advertisements and other publicity matter released or controlled by the Licensee.[94]

Shaw's objection to George down the years was consistent and undeniable. Earliest complaint was to Ellen Terry in 1896 when he coyly protested to her request that he cease calling her Ellen and to use instead Nell or Nellen. Was it essential that he must henceforth eschew Ellen? Out of the question. Ellen Terry, he said, was the loveliest name in the world—it was like a bell, chiming through the final quarter of the nineteenth century. It had, he continued, a wonderful rhythm—"Not like 'Jorj,' which is so horribly ugly and difficult that all attempts to call me by it are foredoomed to failure." [95] To Ellen, Shaw's objection to the name of George was found in his disapproval of ugliness and cacophony in general.

The submission of Henderson's ms. of *George Bernard Shaw, Playboy and Prophet* to GBS for his approval brought a surprise to the biographer. Shaw, he said, had written across the proof sheet of one of the illustrations "Why all these Georges? I loathe being Georged. Please immortalize me as Bernard Shaw, or even G.B.S. but NOT as Jorge Bernard Shaw, a detestable phrase. It doesn't sing." [96] Final title: *Bernard Shaw, Playboy and Prophet.* To "ugly" and "difficult," GBS added "detestable" and unmusical, implying that the remainder of the name sang. Pearson allowed that Shaw had a personal objection to his first name and, after quoting the Terry extract above, reported him to have stated that he was never more exasperated than when he was Georged in type. Winsten recorded GBS as saying, "George has a bad sound" and that he didn't like it and had long ago tried to eliminate it—even going to the extent of putting a bracketed George in *Who's Who?* [97] Patch informed her readers that everyone, including Charlotte, called him "G.B.S." and everyone, that is, but his own family who persisted with "George," were requested to refer to him as Bernard Shaw. In her opinion this objection was aesthetically understandable and she added that his signature to formal documents and checks was "G. Bernard Shaw." [98]

GBS's disapproval of George as a name may not have been based upon its alleged stridence—his dislike of the name may have had its origins in his earliest memories of the Synge Street, Hatch Street and Torca Cottage households. Possibly Shaw's objections to the name arose out of the coincidence of two Georges—George Carr and George John both living under the same roof with his mother. Constantly aware of the two Georges, Sonny could not fail to be impressed by the contrast between them. On the one hand there was George Carr—indolent, lethargic, repellent, drunk and a liar. On the other hand there was George John—resplendent, energetic, brilliant, fascinating and sober. And while George John occupied the center of the stage deep in intimate conference with Mrs. Shaw on a forthcoming concert, George Carr might glower at them from the furthest corner, muttering to himself with many movements of his head in punctuation of heaven knows what imaginary thrusts and parries. Ignored by his wife, shunned by his children, in disgrace with the Shaws, reduced to nullity at home, his position and authority arrogated by a Roman Catholic who was on uncommonly good terms with his wife, frustrated by his own guilt, George Carr must have indeed thought himself an unhappy man. And perhaps there were times when Sonny might have seen his father reach for his penny flute and, with simple irony, convey his feelings to his little world:

Observing the cordiality and friendliness of his mother with George John, Sonny could not help being struck by the contrast of his mother's indifference towards her husband. It may have been under such circumstances that his attention, oscillating from one George to another, was drawn to the question, "Which George am I named for?" Sickened by its inherent implication, he lashed out in a reasonable rejection of both Georges, thereafter so hating that part of his name that he tried repeatedly to strike it out and refused to respond to its employment.

Baptized in Jesus' name George Bernard, GBS may have been named after the merchant or the musician, but in either case, I believe that George Carr continued stubbornly to call the child Bob up to the threshold of GBS's recorded memories.

X

MRS. LUCINDA ELIZABETH SHAW continued her visits to 16/48 Harrington Street in pursuit of her musical advancement until, at some unspecified time, Lee either insinuated himself, or was invited, into the home of his star pupil.[99] Previous to this event, Thom's for 1854 (1853) registered the Professor at two different addresses. He was located with his family at 16 Harrington Street and, in addition, appears to have had a studio at 11 Harrington just around the corner from Synge Street and occupied by a family of Armstrongs. The record for 1855 (1854) disclosed that Lee had cleared out of the Armstrong home—possibly at their urgent invitation, since the utility of Lee's rent may have been outweighed by the caterwaulings of exercises in The Method. Thereafter, however, Lee is listed annually to 1864 (1863) as plying his profession from his home.

Winsten's version of the meeting between Bob and the Professor indicated an exclusive source of information—the alternative conclusion being that Winsten possessed an ability to transfer himself at will to selected periods of the nineteenth century. He reported that Bob, during a raid on someone's apple orchard, noticed his mother "talking excitedly" with a lame and beardless man who shortly afterwards came to the Shaw home.[100] Shaw's report is recorded in his preface to *London Music*. He wrote that "soon" after his mother went to Lee for singing lessons, the Professor made his way into their home first by giving her lessons there and then by making use of the drawing room for band and opera rehearsals. GBS seemed to be puzzled as to the reason for the transfer of these activities from Harrington Street to Synge Street but offered a "guess" that the cramped quarters of his home were preferable to the "inadequacies" of Lee's housekeeper Old Ellen and, possibly, the "incompatibilities" of Lee's brother.[101] Since the Harrington Street house was, for the Professor's purposes, far superior to 3 Synge Street, Shaw's puzzlement is understandable and the moment bears a share of attention. The reason for the shift of Mrs. Shaw's singing lessons and the band rehearsals to Synge Street can never, of course, be known with any degree of finality, but a study of the circumstances can yield several hypotheses. None of them can be considered seriously, however, unless one admits a relationship between Mrs. Shaw and the Professor that could be construed as socially censurable. Since Lee continued to instruct other pupils in Harrington Street, I suggest that either or both Old Ellen and Harcourt raised objections to the presence of Mrs. Shaw, thus forcing her to continue her lessons in her own home. As to the rehearsals being held in Synge Street, I hold that Mrs. Shaw, as its arranger and copier of parts, was essential to the effectiveness of the band and, consequently, if Mrs. Shaw couldn't come to the rehearsals in Harrington Street, the rehearsals would have to come to her.

With respect to Old Ellen, it may be pointed out that she was probably one of those family retainers who sometimes dominate the roost and that Shaw's recollection of her as a "terrible old woman" may have been based on actual experience. For example he told O'Bolger that Lee lived with "a terrible old housekeeper named Ellen (at least she terrified me)." [102] This strongly suggests that Sonny visited Lee's house (possibly on an errand for his mother) and that Old Ellen expressed, in one way or another, her disapproval of the son of that woman. His sensitivity on the subject of Old Ellen is interestingly illustrated in his later accounts. In 1935, he reported her simply and directly as "a terrible old woman who was his servant of all work." [103] But Shaw gave no hint as to how or why she was terrible. In 1949, he avoided any responsibility for that characterization and described her merely as an old housekeeper "reputedly a terror." [104]

In consideration of the heavy traffic through the front doors of 16/48 Harrington Street and the continual comings and goings of singers and musicians, one could hardly expect a naturally sour temperament to sweeten in such service. Old Ellen may have been perpetually (or so it seemed to her) on the go attending the arrivals and departures, cleaning up after visitors with bohemian habits, to say nothing of her regular duties. To perform such services for the Protestant Mrs. Shaw may have been the last straw and down may have come the Catholic foot.

The time of Lee's entry into the Shaw household for the first time may be fixed by estimating the age of young Shaw in GBS's own narration of the meeting. He recalled that when his mother first introduced the Professor to him, the occasion turned into a state of combat between the two. It seems that Lee's concept of a happy child was one whose face was embellished with moustaches and beards and he proceeded at once to put his theory into practice with a piece of burnt cork. To say that Sonny objected to these attentions would not be putting the case fairly. GBS had it that "in spite of the most furious resistance I could put up, our encounter was not a success . . ." [105] and implied that thereafter he gave Lee a wide berth until the passage of the years placed them on a more equal footing.

A child who was helpless enough to be held captive and subjected to such indignities probably could not have been more than six—particularly this lad who was undoubtedly tall for his age. I think it would have been difficult, indeed dangerous, for Lee to have pressed these attentions on a squirming, kicking, howling boy. GBS has more or less pinpointed the year himself. Writing in *The World* under the dateline of 1 June 1892, he remembered that "it is now thirty years since I first met a singing-master . . ." [106]

XI

THE EARLIEST ACCOUNT OF GBS in his infancy has been given by George Carr in a series of fourteen letters to his wife and revealed for the first time in the *Sketches.* Although the letters seem to have been considerably abbreviated, my examination of the originals in the British Museum indicated that GBS's editing in no wise concealed or affected the apparent intentions of George Carr. Containing a few affectionate expressions ("Thusella, honey"), they were, in the main, without salutations and signed simply: GCS. Such excisions as were made by GBS dealt with matters of little or no interest to the present work and he released those parts that concerned the infant Shaw.

Mrs. Shaw, leaving the two youngest children in her husband's care, had departed for the west of Ireland in the summer of 1857 on a month's visit to her father then in Kinlough, County Leitrim. While Shaw gave no reason for the visit of his mother,[107] it was quite possibly in response to Walter Bagnall's invitation to come and spend a holiday with him. Winsten had an explanation which again suggested a confidential source. He reported that Mrs. Carr Shaw, in her desire to escape from Synge Street, seized upon the complaint of four-year-old Lucy that her clothing was poorer than her neighbors and carried her off to her father "hoping to persuade him to take the children, for she would gladly have handed over all three to anyone willing to adopt them." [108]

Arriving in Kinlough, Lucinda was in receipt of almost daily letters from her husband which she kept until her death and which eventually passed into GBS's hands through Lucy's death. Referred to as "Their correspondence," all fourteen exhibited are actually from George Carr to his wife, and we may take it that GBS either could not or would not bring his mother's replies to light. Introducing the correspondence, Shaw fastidiously declined to certify to its truthfulness, since he did not have the slightest recollection of being dubbed "Bob" or learning to walk. Among the fourteen chosen by Shaw, the following are selected for attention here.

[I]

22.7. [Wednesday][109]

Nurse is in great blood about having the young chap able to walk when you come back, besides I am sure she thinks it will be a great relief to herself. He made a famous attempt this morning. They were all to have gone up to your Aunt's to-day. [Aunt Ellen Whitcroft].[110]

[II]

24.7. [Friday]

. . . Nurse says that Bob walked in great style for your Aunt.

[III]

27.7. [Monday]

Nurse got a new hat for Bob and nothing short of a Tuscan would do her so I had to hand over 10/-. However it was his birthday and so I will say nothing. . . . Yup and Bob both fell out of bed yesterday morning on the tops of their heads; neither appear to have been hurt, but they might have been.

[IV]

28.7. [Tuesday]

Bobza honors me with his company and we have walking

matches together. His exploits in that way have not yet extended beyond a couple of yards which he performs in a plunge from Nurse to me and back again to Nurse or Caroline Brabazon [G.B.S.'s godmother]. His hat is very grand but I think Nurse will be walking into you for feathers for it when you come home.

[V]

30.7. [Thursday]

I brought the two youngsters out yesterday morning and gave them a drive in the perambulator which they, indeed I too, enjoyed greatly. Bob is growing very unruly. The *threshing season* is approaching and he had better look out or I'll flail him.

[VI]

3.8. [Monday]

I will feel disappointed every morning that Bob does not stagger into me with a letter from you—and desperate fighting there is to get it from him. The young ruffian tore the newspaper this morning. . . .

[VII]

6.8. [Thursday]

I was home in the middle of the day and had a good ½ hour's fun with Yup and Bob. . . . Cecilia [his sister, G.B.S.'s Aunt Ciss] has called to see the children.

[VIII]

8.8. [Saturday]

I delivered your kisses to Yup and Bob but contrary to your instructions I fobbed a few for myself—you know how sweet a stolen kiss is!

[IX]

11.8. [Tuesday]

Poor Bob had a narrow escape on Tuesday morning. He was sitting on the kitchen table in charge of Nurse, who merely, she says, stooped to pick up something off the floor, when he suddenly fell back and his head went slap through a pane of glass and against the iron bar outside; miraculous to say he was not even scratched; had he fallen with his face against the glass he would have been ruined. I was in my dressing room at the time, and when I heard the crash I ran down and found Nurse so paralysed with terror that she could hardly lift the poor fellow up. I do not know how the poor fellow escaped; but it does not appear to have given him even a *pane* in his head.

[X]

15.8 [Saturday]

Poor Bob is annoyed with his teeth, and is consequently very uneasy both day and night.

Considering the impression created and given by GBS and by McNulty concerning Mr. Shaw's limited literary interests and general impotence, the letters are surprisingly well written and if they had not been actually examined, it would be difficult to believe that they had not been retouched. Containing touches of light humor and a flair for dramatic narration—even a certain elegance—the letters are free from the expected husband-wife commonplaces and, except for their artless simplicity, certainly cannot be admitted as having no seed for some hospitable soil.

As pointed out earlier, GBS referred to the packet as "Their correspondence" but exhibited no letters from his mother to Mr. Shaw. That there were such letters may be noted in Letter VI wherein George Carr expressed his vexation at not receiving word from his wife every day; and in Letter VIII he acknowledged, in effect, receipt of a letter by replying that he carried out its instructions. Further examination of the correspondence suggests in Letters I and II an Aunt Ellen considerably mellowed from her earlier characterizations by GBS while number III is the sequel to Bob "flittering" his hat to pieces. Letter IV is delightful and charmingly written but is included here (with VIII) chiefly to show the presence of members of the

Shaw clan in Synge Street. Mr. Shaw's punning humor is illustrated in V in which he felt it necessary to give notice to Mrs. Shaw that there was a joke in "threshing" by underlining it but overlooked treating "flail" in the same manner. Letters IX and X are reproduced for their glimpses into the infancy of GBS and as further examples of Mr. Shaw's epistolary expressions which may reflect some part of his personality. Letter VIII is provocative in the extreme because of its possible implications. Here, Mr. Shaw must have been requested to tell the children their mother sent them kisses but was apparently directed not to kiss them himself, perhaps because Lucinda did not want the children to be sensible of his whiskey-laden breath. Nevertheless, he cannot refrain from helping himself to a few kisses, nor can he resist reminding his wife how sweet a stolen kiss can be. Whether this last was a reference to some premarital or postmarital gallantry is, however, a question that can be left to the school of dramatized biography.

Winsten believed that with the arrival of Letter IX, Mrs. Shaw abandoned her efforts to persuade her father to take the children and, after taking little Lucy into her confidence, decided to return to Dublin. Fortunately for posterity, someone was within earshot:

> After reading her husband's letter to Lucy, she said: "Bob has had a tumble. I expect your father wants us to return." There was nothing for her but to go back to the home where she felt so alien.[111]

XII

ADDA SHAW TYRRELL was the daughter of Professor George Ferdinand Shaw, LL.D., a Fellow of Trinity who, with his family, lived at Number 11 Harrington Street. While the Harrington Street Shaws were not particularly friendly with the Synge Street Shaws, Adda and Lucy Shaw became the closest friends, and when Lucy died in 1921,

Adda and GBS "adopted" one another. Born two years before GBS, Adda outlived him by five and was the recipient of many a card and letter from the famous dramatist. Some estimate of how far their threads ran back may be sensed in a letter from a ninety-four-year-old Shaw to a ninety-six-year-old Adda. Mrs. Tyrrell, being resident in Devon, had expressed her desire to see GBS. Impossible, replied GBS—both of them would soon be the oldest human beings on the planet—and even if he could go further than his garden gate, it would be just as well they did not meet since he'd prefer to be remembered by her as "Sonny" instead of that "ghastly old skeleton of a celebrity I now am." [112]

Queried by Adda in his seventy-second year concerning a certain Dublin family, GBS confirmed their existence but, caught up in a wave of memories, bitterly recalled that "Except in my secret self I was not happy in Dublin; and when ghosts arise up from that period I want to lay them again with the poker." [113] He added, in his soft Irish way, that Adda was not one of those unwelcome memories. What the nature or the identities of those ghosts were can only be surmised for GBS has never revealed them nor did Adda Shaw Tyrrell —if she shared that knowledge. In his eighty-sixth year Shaw had an additional comment on the period, but this time it concerned his sisters as well as himself. In a miniature review (it was confined to one postcard) of Lucy's relations with Adda's children, he released one of the reasons for his unhappiness with an emphasis unknown in the canon of Shavian prose: "And the way we were brought up, or rather not brought up!!! It doesnt bear thinking of." [114]

Patrick O'Reilly, famed as Shaw's "Cultured Dustman of Dublin," conducted a one-man campaign to honor a prophet in his own country. He proposed exhumation of Troubetzkoy's delicate standing figure from the catacombs of the National Gallery for mounting in Stephen's Green. Unthinkable, declared the Gallery's director—the man is still alive! Appealed to, Shaw agreed with the Gallery—the Troubetzkoy must wait until he was dead. Nothing dismayed, O'Reilly sailed in on another tack: a plaque to commemorate the birthplace of a great Irishman. Unwilling or unable to give an outright no, GBS yielded; but with a condition: the plaque must not go beyond the barest statement of fact, to wit: that Shaw was born in the house.[115] Upshot was an awkward compromise. Executed by C. G. Sawier and subscribed to by Shavians in Ireland, Great Britain and the United States, the plaque was mounted and elicited the following comment from the ninety-three-year-old GBS to his second cousin Grace Goodliffe:

> The house where I spent my not at all happy childhood has just been decorated with a tablet commemorating my birth there. I would see it blown to smithereens without the faintest regret, in fact, with exultation . . .[116]

The childhood of George Bernard Shaw has been summed up in a letter to Ellen Terry who, as a sort of Oedipean goddess to GBS, received many of the dramatist's confidences. Often quoted but little understood, Shaw's cry gushed forth as from some inner hell. "Oh," he wrote, "a devil of a childhood, Ellen, rich only in dreams, frightful and loveless in realities." [117] Written in his forty-first year, the passing years would not and did not lessen the pain of that memory. If, as Einstein put it, every word of Shaw's had meaning and was exactly in its right place then what meanings are we to gather from "frightful" and "loveless"? That the childhood of GBS was loveless in the modern sense, has been plainly evident to the readers of Shavian autobiography and will be analytically dealt with presently—the frightfulness, *passim*.

Although Shaw's references, in many minor asides, to his unhappy childhood have gone unnoticed, even his serious and more revealing utterances on the subject have been neglected or ignored, chiefly because of his skill in verbal obfuscation. In 1935, fifteen years after the death of sister Lucy, he published the preface to *London Music* and included the best account of his childhood we have. Here he remembered the period prior to Lee's arrival in Synge Street as an era when Mr. Shaw ruled in undisputed authority as "sole chief" of the house, even leading the family in prayer. After a few ironies at the expense of *The Book Of Common Prayer* and its catechistic discords in the Shaw household, GBS recalled that he and his two sisters were handed over to the servants and "abandoned entirely" to their care. Barring Nurse Williams of his infancy whom he remembered to be a decent and conscientious woman, the servants were totally unsuited to be in charge of three cats, much less three children. His food was eaten in the kitchen and consisted largely of beef stews (which he abhorred), improperly cooked potatoes of questionable quality and huge quantities of oversteeped tea which he may have sweetened with stolen sugar. He was never hungry, he said, because Mr. Shaw, who was frequently underfed in his youth, had such a dread of children going hungry that he always maintained an instantly-available supply of bread and butter for their use. GBS further declared that he hated the servants but

> liked my mother because, on the one or two rare occasions when she buttered my bread for me, she buttered it thickly instead of merely wiping a knife on it.[118]

One may only guess at the depths of cynical bitterness with which GBS wrote of his mother's maternal attachment to him.

Continuing in the *London Music* account of his childhood, Shaw added that his mother's

> almost complete neglect of me had the advantage that I could idolize her to the utmost pitch of my imagination and had no sordid or disillusioning contacts with her.[119]

This may be one of the best examples of Shaw's use of language to conceal. Unwilling to tell all the truth and unable to fill in with a falsehood, the subject matter is formed so that the reader receives and retains an impression that Mrs. Shaw was an object of worship to Sonny. Second glance at this quotation shows that GBS considered his mother's neglect as an advantage in that he could then adore her —in his imagination—thus revealing (to me, at any rate) its inner truth, to wit: that she was not an object of idolization in reality. Finally, Mrs. Shaw's son did not explain how any contact with his mother could be sordid or disillusioning—that explanation was sealed in the memory of Sonny—". . . rich only in dreams, frightful and loveless in reality."

XIII

INCOMPARABLE MASTER of precise and meaningful language when he chose, GBS did not select the word "abandoned" without cause. It was true—the children were deliberately abandoned by their mother. But before one is carried away by a picture of the Shaw babies lying forlorn and neglected in their cribs, it would perhaps be well to establish, if possible, the time, the nature and the reasons for that abandonment.

While the biographers showed various degrees of interest in the reasons for Mrs. Shaw's rejection of her maternal responsibilities, not one seemed to trouble himself with the question of when this rejection took place. Possibly it was because they assumed the abandonment began with umbilical severance or, what is more likely, the absence of inspiration due to the scarcity of Shavian comment. There are several vague observations by Shaw touching upon the time of abandonment in a general way such as, for example, Captain Shotover's assertion that the human animal's affection for its offspring ended in its sixth year.[120] Yet GBS was specific on one occasion. According to the Harris book Shaw was reported as fixing the time during a recital of the middle years in Synge Street. GBS, wrote the author, said that Mrs. Shaw put up with the children, with her husband, with his drinking, with the poverty and with everything else

> ". . . leaving them to the servants (and, my God! what servants!—except old Nurse Williams), and to Providence, and taking no interest in them after, say, six years old." [121]

From this it would be reasonable to gather that Mrs. Shaw gave some degree of motherly attention to her children during their first six years after which she lost "interest." Consequently, the period of abandonment can be said to have begun, for Sonny, in 1862.

The nature of the abandonment is not as easily ascertained. Writing in the *Sketches,* GBS recorded that his mother did not trouble herself "much" about the children, since she had never been "taught" the science of motherhood, and he seemed to discount or ignore her possession of the mother instinct. He added that it was of little or no importance to her what the children ate or drank and she left the decision up to illiterate servants[122] who, as GBS has already pointed out, were unfit to care for and feed an equivalent number of cats. In the preface of *London Music,* Shaw described his mother as being, in the practical sense, "the worst mother conceivable" in that she had no concept whatever of even the most basic principles of raising children. Equally unimportant to Mrs. Shaw, according to her son, were the less material needs of her children—thus to be taken by her for a visit or even a walk was considered a rare favor.[123] As to Mrs. Shaw's influence in the ethical sphere, GBS reported in an article written for the press entitled *How to Become a Model Parent,* that he could not recall "having ever heard a single sentence uttered by my mother in the nature of moral or religious instruction." [124] From these limited accounts we may, fairly, assume that the nature of the abandonment consisted of a voluntary withdrawal by Mrs. Shaw from the day-to-day performance of her maternal duties: Mrs. Shaw, shortly after GBS's sixth birthday, no longer concerned herself with her children's food, hygiene, education, entertainment or, presumably, any other duty normally rendered in the ordinary course of rearing children.

The reasons for the "abandonment" have attracted the attention of several of the biographers but not all of their views merit serious attention. In 1932 Henderson offered the opinion that Shaw's mother was not the domestic type and that the Teutonic concept of children, churches and kitchens was abhorrent to her.[125] In his last biography, the Professor jettisoned his *Kinder, Kirche und Küche* theory and observed that Mrs. Shaw, in reacting against her Aunt Ellen's military-puritan regime, "allowed her own children every opportunity to develop naturally and freely." [126] Ervine proposed an entirely different theory and suggested that Lucinda abandoned her children in some sort of reprisal. Reporting that there seemed to be little doubt that the children were deprived of the love that was their right, he declared the explanation was simple: Mrs. Shaw was "cold." Further, she had an extreme repugnance for sentimental demonstrations, which repugnance was aggravated by her contempt for her husband and by disgust at the thought that George Carr was the father of her children. He concluded that these were the considerations which "turned her away from her son and daughters as surely as it turned her away from her husband." [127] Additionally, Ervine believed that although Mrs. Shaw severed the ties to all the children, she had a particular disaffection for her son and in an ill-considered moment placed a "fact" on record: "The fact that her son physically resembled his father seemed to make her more antipathetic to him than she was to his sisters." [128]

With the exception of Henderson, the biographers in general have reconstructed the mother from the blueprints of a badly-understood or ignored GBS. Hamon, McCabe and Pearson saw nothing amiss while Ervine explained Lucinda's withdrawal to be the result of her natural coldness made colder by George Carr's inadequacies and, he alleged, the resemblance of Sonny to her husband. Whatever the validity of the various biographers' opinions, it can not be held that they were uninformed, for GBS has given the subject a fair amount of his attention. The earliest discoverable public comment by Shaw appeared in a contribution to Frank Harris' second series of biographical sketches of contemporary figures in 1919. Although he did not mention Aunt Ellen by name, it is clear that he had her in mind when he reported that his mother, reared in an atmosphere of the harshest discipline, "had such a horror of her own training that she left her children without training at all." [129] The next references were buried in the preface (1921) to *Immaturity*. The first was given a rather oblique and ironic phrasing. He had been badly trained (he wrote) because his mother had been so well trained, and he linked this cause and effect to her rigid and unloved childhood.[130] The second reference was direct and to the point. His mother's humorless clergymen left her with such a remorseless loathing for religion that she was "resolved that it should not do the same to them." [131] A resolution that does not illustrate an indifferent mother.

The third expression was contained in the *London Music* preface and here GBS seemed to approve of his mother's revolt against her Aunt Ellen's Spartan regime. He put it that in her "righteous reaction" to her Aunt's rigid disciplines, she drove the pendulum in the opposite direction so energetically (knowing no other alternative) that she produced what her son termed "domestic anarchy." [132] Another Shavian comment was that his mother "detested" her Aunt Ellen and was convinced that everything taught her in the name of religion and discipline was despotic and enslaving. Being by nature most humane, (she could not bear cruelty to children, flowers, or, for that matter, anything or anybody) ". . . she abandoned her own children to the most complete anarchy." [133]

While Shaw made much of his mother's abandonment of the children, his unpublished views gave support to the hint of approval in the "righteous reaction" extract. For example he told O'Bolger that his mother's adoption of a hands-off policy as the substitute for Aunt Ellen's methods was, in general, "better" (he preferred "easier" in the revised version for the *Sketches*) and was intended to be kinder. "Indeed," he added, "it *was* very much kinder, but not so much as my mother thought." [134] With respect to the final effects of his mother's abandonment upon the children, Shaw declared that Lucy was the one who really suffered from it, since she was not exempt, as he and his mother were, from the conventional yearning and need for correct social behavior. Concluding, Shaw admitted that his mother's "process" which proved disastrous for Lucy's ambitions was "in fact the process that was the making of me . . ." [135] but this admission did not appear in the revised version of the *Sketches*. A further acknowledgment of indebtedness to his mother's abandonment was given publicly in his advice to parents. Avowing that his own parents assumed no moral obligations for him, he went on to say that neither did they fret and fume "uselessly" over the sort of person he would grow into; and, consequently, he did not suffer from the unbearable officiousness of "conscientious" parents. Concluding, Sonny—now well advanced as octogenarian Bernard Shaw—had a word of wisdom to the parents in his audience.

> Be advised by me: do as my parents did: live your lives frankly in the face of your children according to your own real natures and give your sons a fair chance of becoming Bernard Shaws.[136]

In summarizing, I would suggest that Shaw's use of "abandoned" to describe his mother's withdrawal from her maternal duties, while technically acceptable, was not the most accurate description available. Quite the contrary. Mrs. Shaw, in reaction to her own childhood training and experiences, completely and utterly rejected the lessons of Aunt Ellen and with the arrival of her own children, resolved that they would be spared a repetition of her history. Knowing nothing of mothering as a science or, for that matter, mothering of any sort, Mrs. Shaw could see only one alternative to the Ellen method of tyranny and slavery: total freedom; in short, anarchy. I am convinced that Mrs. Shaw, far from abandoning her children, acted in their best interests, according to her lights. Her launching and prosecution of her intentions cannot be construed as abandonment but must be regarded as a well-meaning, if injudicious, program of a mother who carried out her responsibilities as she saw them. Shaw's use of "abandonment," while neither wholly accurate nor inaccurate, seems carefully chosen to divert attention from the principal reason for his hostility towards his mother: her association with Roman Catholic George John Lee, the constructions that could be placed on that association and the deductions that might be drawn from it.

XIV

MR. SHAW'S RELATIONS WITH THE CHILDREN have not received the attention accorded to Mrs. Shaw though there is little evidence that he performed the conventional parental duties any more than did his wife. Yet he must have been an affectionate parent as may be detected in his letters to Mrs. Shaw on her visit to her father during 1857. He loved to play with the children, but when they had grown to that age when they could distinguish between his sober and drunken moods, they gave him less and less satisfaction.[137] Winsten offered a direct quote in which he reported GBS as comparing Mr. Shaw and Professor Lee insofar as their interest in Sonny was concerned. While describing Lee as the more vigorous of the two, GBS is quoted as saying he was better understood by the titular head of the house, adding, incidentally, that he was not demonstrative.[138] Elsewhere GBS described his mother as singularly free of moral and religious advice but allowed that George Carr "made an effort or two" and proceeded to illustrate his advice to parents. When Mr. Shaw (who smoked a pipe) observed little Sonny puffing upon a toy pipe in imitation, he advised the boy, in his most serious manner, never to use him as an example in anything, thus, by his sincerity, so impressing his young listener that to the end of his days, George Bernard Shaw neither smoked, nor used intoxicants. Nor were these the only subjects Mr. Shaw discoursed upon for the benefit of the attentive Sonny; he also instructed the child in other less commendable matters (to be dealt with shortly) and looked upon himself as a failure and a victim of a large number of unbecoming practices. He held himself up not as a good example but as an object lesson of what one ought not to be. As a matter of fact, concluded GBS, in his ardor to prevent Sonny from adopting his habits Mr. Shaw blackened his own character far in excess of its actual shade

> and I now [1946-90] perceive that this anxiety on his part was altogether admirable and lovable, and that he was really just what he so carefully strove not to be: that is, a model father.[139]

GBS's contention that Mr. Shaw was a figure to be modeled upon cannot be taken seriously, and I believe that his late recognition of George Carr's fatherly qualities was penitent in essence and due to his eventual realization that Mr. Shaw's role in the tragedy of Synge Street was that of a pawn.

George Carr Shaw's concern for the welfare of Sonny did not end with his exhortations on the evils of smoking and other Shavian frailties. From his earliest years Sonny was the target of the elder Shaw's lectures on the Shaw clan, its divinely appointed Protestant supremacy and its consequent exalted social position. Sensitive to the subject himself, O'Bolger early recognized the signs of indoctrination.

He thought the boy might have grown up to be arrogantly proud—well, if not actually so, he must have been confused with the "constant home admonishments to think of himself always as a Shaw and a Protestant . . ."[140] Henderson seemed to avoid certain aspects of the subject. He noted only one of Mr. Shaw's pretensions and that one in the most general way, i.e., that as a merchant engaged in *whole-sale* trade, George Carr Shaw considered himself in a class apart from and above those in the *retail* trades. Nor did Henderson relate this as an influence upon GBS. That he was aware of this acutely significant and absorbing topic is clearly shown in the seriousness with which he viewed the Central Model School incident.[141]

Ervine has been the only writer who seems to have realized the importance and effects of the religious and economic dissensions upon the health of Ireland. He accurately pointed out that for all practical purposes, Ireland was divided into two solid antagonistic groupings whose relations were further complicated by supplementary social, political and economic divisions. These two groups, he advised, consisted of Protestants and "Roman" Catholics—the latter designation, presumably, being used to distinguish them from their brethren of the Eastern Church. He identified the Shaws as being of the Ascendancy and, consequently, Protestants. In commenting on the inner feelings of young Shaw when he found the Central Model School to be swarming with Catholics, Ervine seemed unwilling to discuss the question and referred the reader to Shaw's "reference" to it in the *Sketches.* Himself a product and example of Ireland's social and religious conflicts, Ervine concluded that there was little likelihood of non-Irish or nonresidents realizing the nature of Sonny's deep-rooted torments when he learned of the religious composition of the Central Model School. Ervine tried to drive his point home with an excellent but unfortunately futile illustration. "Tell a high-caste Indian," wrote Ervine, "that it is absurd to throw away his food because it has been contaminated by the shadow of an Untouchable," and you will receive for your pains a glance of contemptuous disdain that Sonny would have given, had you chided him for his own haughty presumptuousness.[142] Ervine's tacit admission that he was unequal to the task of explaining these forces to a non-Irish world would not have been necessary, had he read and studied his subject's own views on the topic. O'Bolger's treatment, as given in his 1919 untitled life of Shaw, differed from Ervine's in that the latter reported factional Ireland from the Ulster Protestant view while O'Bolger dealt with it from the position of a Southern Catholic. He held that George Carr was one of a large clan who talked much of the Shaws and, though they had never been to England, "they were, nevertheless, in their own estimation, the immeasurable superiors of all merely Catholic Irish." [143]

The earliest reference by GBS to this facet of the influences in his childhood appeared in T. P. O'Connor's *Mainly About People* for 1898. Mr. Shaw, wrote GBS, had nothing whatsoever to recommend him for membership in any useful society—except that he had been imbued with the conviction that all the Shaws (as champions of William the Conqueror) were royally, if not divinely, endowed with the virtue of gentility.[144] In his 1905 letter to Henderson, GBS described his family as Protestant with George Carr's position among them ("a very damnable one") as that of an impoverished member of that particular section of the *haute bourgeoisie* which made vigorous efforts to scale the ladder of social success. His family—who were many and fruitful—were likened unto planets orbiting about and basking in the solar prominences of Sir Robert Shaw, Bart., and who always referred to themselves as "the Shaws" with an air of inborn superiority.[145] In 1921 GBS offered an extra fillip to the importance with which the Shaws considered themselves and were considered. While proclaiming his "enormous contempt" for their assumptions, he reported that the Shaws' estimates of themselves were accepted by those about them in Ireland who regarded the name of Shaw with as much deference as others in different spheres regarded the awesome names of Valois, Hapsburg, Bourbon, Hohenzollern and Romanoff.[146]

Australian cousin Charles MacMahon Shaw was the recipient of some extended remarks on the matter. MacMahon, who had decried his cousin's characterization of the Shaws as snobs, was gently corrected by the chief figure in his *Bernard's Brethren.* Like all Protestants, said GBS, the Shaws had to be snobs and declared the snob lines were sharply defined:

> No Shaw could form a social acquaintance with a shopkeeper nor with a Roman Catholic; and naturally the Shaw parents impressed that fact on their children and thereby made arrant snobs of them.[147]

According to this, both George Carr and Lucinda Elizabeth could have seen eye-to-eye in the matter of protecting the children from social and religious contamination. I cannot believe GBS intended to mean that his mother was responsible with Mr. Shaw for the children's (and his own) arrant snobbery and I suggest his expression must be attributed to the caprice of age (83). Twenty years earlier, in response to direct questioning by O'Bolger, GBS unequivocally rejected the notion that his mother was in sympathy with the Shaw pretensions:

> O'Bolger: Did your mother share the Shaws' satisfaction with themselves?—the Hohenzollern—Romanoff conceit?
>
> Shaw: Not in the least—had the greatest contempt for it.[148]

As to Mrs. Shaw's attitude towards and relations with Catholics, the abundance of reports and reminiscences of her son clearly and unquestionably establish her freedom from bigotry—or, at least, from bigotry with respect to Catholicism and Catholics. As this particular topic will be dealt with at length elsewhere in this study, the evidence of Mrs. Shaw's associations with those untouchables of Irish-Protestant society of mid-nineteenth century will be limited at the moment to one example, one dramatically revealing a profoundly disturbed GBS.

Despite Shaw's persistent corrections to O'Bolger, the Kilkenny-born professor seemed determined to press certain allegations in regard to the Lee-Shaw household—one of the lesser of these allegations being that Mrs. Shaw's attitude towards Catholics was one of "obdurate prejudice and superciliousness." [149] Of course GBS blasted away at O'Bolger for what he called his "insane" treatment of the *ménage à trois* and charged that it contained "monstrous falsification" and "outrageous calumnies" against almost everyone involved.[150] Naturally, GBS was forced to block publication and in their ensuing quarrel treated the distraught O'Bolger to a transatlantic amateur psychiatric examination. Psychoanalysts, wrote GBS, would declare the professor's precarious mental state as being due to a "Resentment Complex"—a condition, he asserted, quite common in Ireland. Thomas Demetrius had, Shaw continued, the poor man's resentment of the rich man, the Catholic's resentment of the Protestant, the schoolmaster's resentment of the critics of schools and the Lord knew how many secret resentments of

> which you have made me and my father the whipping boys and my mother the whipping girl . . . you hate my mother, the gentlest of women, the friend of priests and the singer in their churches, and imagine her a bigoted snob.[151]

Concluding, Shaw advised O'Bolger to seek a psychoanalyst (providing he could discover one who was not a quack) to track his complex down to its beginnings, charm it out of existence and, finally, to complete the cure by writing his autobiography. If he did not do these things, he would (GBS assured him) most certainly become as mad as a hatter. Elsewhere, GBS in his nineties recalled that his own bigotry towards Catholics vanished as a result of his mother's musical activities.[152] Mrs. Lucinda Elizabeth, who was friendly to priests, participated in their musical masses and stood as a model of tolerance for her observant son, could not and did not encourage her son to despise any social class or religious order. These latter obligations, I suggest, were undertaken exclusively by George Carr Shaw.

While it is not unlikely that Sonny received admonitions from other members of the Shaw clan,[153] there can be little doubt that George Carr was instructor-in-chief by virtue of proximity and opportunity, if not by authority. Yet the record, though not altogether bare of such evidence, is singularly free from a precise identification of Sonny's moral counsellor. Cousin MacMahon was told that when the elder Shaw discovered the boy playing with a schoolfellow whose father kept an ironmonger's shop, he informed Sonny that such associations must cease.[154] In other places, Sonny's adviser was not so specifically identified, particularly where his advice dealt with the relations of a Protestant Shaw to Catholics. Thus, for instance, in the same letter to MacMahon, GBS reported that he (Sonny) was convinced that Catholics were some sort of subhuman creatures predestined for Hell and with whom no Protestant Shaw could associate. This, said GBS, was "told" to him—by whom he did not say; but since this account followed on the heels of the incident in which the ironmonger's boy was involved, it is almost certain that George Carr was the lecturer. In his preface to *On The Rocks,* GBS came closest to naming his moral patron. He recalled that he,

> being the son of an Irish Protestant gentleman, found myself, at the dawn of my infant conscience, absolutely convinced that all Roman Catholics go to Hell when they die . . .[155]

In the *Simpleton* preface he recalled that by the time he left the child's world of hob-goblins and banshees, he was already convinced that all his Catholic fellow children would sizzle eternally in blazing brimstone.[156]

On the seventy-fourth birthday of GBS, one Edward Monks, aged eighty, wrote from Dublin and offered congratulations. Did Mr. Shaw remember him? And did he recall an occasion in Synge Street when Shaw—then six years old—playing with a group of children became enraged at a little girl who insisted on joining in their play? Sonny, exasperated, turned on her, threatening dire consequences if she persisted. Off ran the terrified child to return with noble knight Edward who reminded Shaw that he was twice his age so he'd better mind his manners! Did Mr. Shaw remember? Yes, Mr. Shaw remembered:

> 30/7/30
>
> It is a long time ago; but I still remember the names of

> Crofton (the madman next door), Savage (the other next door), Magrone, whose infant I told that she would go to hell for being a Catholic, and Monks.
>
> And *you* are Monks, no longer more than twice my age. Well, well!
>
> G. Bernard Shaw

Yes, Mr. Shaw remembered. Nor did he forget the lessons taught him by the man whom he regarded, as Henderson put it, with "unbounded admiration amounting to reverence." [157] Stocked with the seeds of clan conceit and religious intolerance, Sonny's infant soul would, on some not too-distant day, be shattered with the humiliation of the Shaws of Dublin.

XV

SONNY'S "REVERENCE" FOR MR. SHAW was not merely biographers' fustian—it was quite true. Although McNulty reported that from an early age his friend "hated and despised his weak and inefficient father," [158] it is certain that he referred to Shaw's teen years since the two lads did not meet until 1869. Speaking for himself, GBS acknowledged in his *Sketches* his childhood belief in the perfection and omniscience of Mr. Shaw[159] and in another place told his readers that the elder man was (to him) infinitely wise and incapable of error.[160] The worship by the child, however, could not have extended over too long a period and seemed to have vanished entirely with the discovery that George Carr, despite his own impressive sermons on the evils of drink, was himself a member of the tribe he had been denouncing. Ervine expressed surprise at Sonny's obtuseness in not recognizing this sad fact earlier than he did. He held that the boy appeared to be "well past the age at which [Mr. Shaw's drinking] would certainly have been observed by a less remarkable child.[161] There was nothing in GBS's own comments, to suggest such a deficiency. According to the account given to Ellen Terry, Sonny could not have been more than five and was probably closer to four. Writing to Ellen in his forty-first year, GBS confided to her that "as a tiny child," the first moral sermon he could remember was delivered to him by Mr. Shaw and dealt with the horrors of drink. In that connection, he recalled that he, being then "about as tall as his boots," was taken out for an evening stroll during which a shocking and unbelievable suspicion gradually dawned upon him. When he arrived home, he ran to his mother and, in a frightened manner, whispered

> "Mamma, I think Papa's drunk." She turned away with impatient disgust and said "When is he ever anything else?" [162]

Elsewhere, GBS filled in the picture, adding a detail withheld from Miss Terry—that when Mr. Shaw took him for a walk, he picked up Sonny and with make-believe movements threatened to throw him into the canal. When they came home, Sonny observed to his mother that he thought Papa was drunk. "When is he anything else?" she retorted.[163]

Winsten offered some fresh particulars unaccountably overlooked by GBS. He reported that when Mrs. Shaw visited her father with Lucy in 1857, she left Yuppy and Bob behind to be cared for by Mr. Shaw. Unlike his wife, Mr. Shaw so loved his children, Winsten continued, that he refused to attend to his corn business, preferring instead to take the children for extended walks beside "evil-smelling riverside streets." He must have had an especially tender regard for Yuppy since to amuse her he would make a grand show of tossing Sonny into the river. Indeed, Winsten concluded, on one occasion Mr. Shaw actually fell in taking Sonny with him to the accompaniment of a shrieking Yuppy.[164]

When disillusionment came, GBS wrote, the scoffer was born and he never again believed in "anything." [165] In a comment to O'Bolger GBS illustrated his earlier childlike faith in and unqualified acceptance of Mr. Shaw. When he was a small child, he noted, he was "persuaded" that Mr. Shaw was a teetotaler and was now convinced that even had he had his pipe actually in his mouth, Mr. Shaw could have induced him to believe that he never smoked.[166] In the *Sketches,* GBS granted that to say that he never again believed anybody or anything was, rhetorically speaking, exaggerated, but that when his faith in George Carr's perfection and infinite wisdom was destroyed and he realized that his father "was a hypocrite and a dipsomaniac [the discovery] was so sudden and violent that it must have left its mark on me." [167] If it were not altogether true that Bernard Shaw never again believed anything or anybody, then it may be fairly said that the mark left on him by disillusionment helped prepare him for the task of seeing the world without its illusions.

XVI

THIRTY-THREE SYNGE STREET was a busy place with Professor George John Lee's continued visits there in the furtherance of Mrs. Shaw's musical development and the activities of the Amateur Musical Society. Colbourne saw the period as one almost continuously occupied with musical matters. Lee, he wrote, swept Mrs. Shaw off her feet with his music and between them they seemed to turn the Shaw home into a rehearsal hall whose walls oscillated in resonance with the voice exercises, music scales, operatic scores and musical soirees so much so that the neighbors complained of the "din." [168] MacManus held similar views, enlarged to include Lee's band as well, thus providing GBS with some material for his *Biographers' Blunders Corrected.* Here GBS advised MacManus directly and Colbourne incidentally, that the supposition of orchestral rehearsals in the little Synge Street house was ridiculous. These rehearsals, he said, were held in the Banner Room of the Ancient Concert Rooms, and when rehearsals were held in Synge Street, the piano was used. Moreover, added Shaw, there were no complaints from the neighbors since the music was more than satisfactory and "there was no 'din.' " [169] In his unpublished memoirs, McNulty reported that young Shaw was steeped in music from his childhood, since his mother, being Dublin's leading amateur singer, had made their home a "popular resort for musicians." [170] In an article accepted for publication McNulty reinforced this report and described Mrs. Shaw as "the foremost amateur singer in Dublin and her house the centre round which musical Dublin revolved." [171]

What George Carr Shaw thought of all this is, or perhaps was, a fascinating mystery. According to GBS's account in the preface to *London Music*, the invasion of the Shaw household by Lee posed no particular problems, in fact one somehow received the impression that the relations between Mr. Shaw and the Professor were little short of cordial. Here he admitted that in addition to annexing "all" of his mother's interests and activities, Lee "supplanted" Mr. Shaw as the authoritative element in their home. Nevertheless, he added, the Professor was so preoccupied with his professional duties "that there was no friction and hardly any intimate personal contact between the two men: certainly no unpleasantness." [172] It would be difficult not to assume from even a careful reading of this that Mr. Shaw had no objections to the presence of Lee in his home, despite Mrs. Shaw's complete absorption in the Professor's musical affairs and despite Mr. Shaw's reduction to an insignificant figure.

Elsewhere GBS held that Mr. Shaw's "position" in his own home, insofar as the relation with the children were concerned, "was just what he was capable of taking: he was Papa in the fullest sense always; and the dynamic Lee got none of the affection Papa inspired." [173] Shaw, in this instance, using his language facility to create the appearance of a George Carr capable of asserting his authority as Papa, an authority which, as will be shown, was as close to zero as it is possible to approach without actually attaining it. To MacMahon Shaw, GBS reported that George Carr was reduced to "nullity" through Lee's hypnotic vigor and initiative but placed this eclipse as coincident with the establishment of the *ménage à trois* in Hatch Street.[174] Harris was in receipt of similar information. Speaking of Lee and his influence upon the Shaws, GBS wrote with deceptive casualness that "With my mother he of course, completely sidetracked my father . . ." [175] and denied, incidentally, that she substituted one for the other.

But it was in an earlier letter that Shaw revealed the attitude of the corn merchant towards the Professor. O'Bolger had inquired of GBS the nature of their relations and put it in the form of a direct question. Replied Shaw:

> You ask whether my father liked Lee. He certainly did not, and would not have tolerated the arrangement if he could have afforded a decent house without it, or if he could have asserted himself against my mother . . .[176]

O'Bolger's treatment of Shaw's reply served to express his interpretation. He had George Carr "this drunken man, hating the Lee arrangement intensely . . ." [177] which, it seems to me, was rather melodramatically rendered and not, I think, wholly justifiable. GBS explained that Mr. Shaw was, in the first place, opposed to it; but as he was unhappy with his shabby Synge Street home, he was willing to tolerate the Professor in return for improved or more fashionable living accommodations. In any case, his objections would have been in vain, since he had to defer to Mrs. Shaw's wishes.

It would not be seemly to advance to the next link in the affairs of the Shaws without paying respects to the views of Ervine. Again the only biographer to give some heed to Lee's relations with the Shaw family, Ervine raised the possibility that Lucinda's interest in Lee was not confined entirely to The Method. He offered that "Lee's advent to the Shaw household was less pleasant to the Shaw children than it was to their parents, and especially to their mother, who liked his money and his music." [178] If, by his phraseology, Ervine meant that the children were displeased, then it must be granted that this opinion is supported by sufficient evidence, for Shaw himself has asserted the children had no affection for the Professor,[179] with his sister Lucy having an especially intense aversion.[180] Ervine's second opinion, if interpreted in harmony with his first, conveys the assurance that Mr. Shaw was pleased with Lee's presence but not quite so pleased as his wife. In view of Shaw's published discords on the subject, it seems reasonable to gather that George Carr could have been pleased with Lee's company, but Ervine's concurring conclusion is not strengthened by his comments at large. Speaking of the

Shaw-Lee household, Ervine advised his readers that George Carr's suggestions, when given, were of no use and ignored,[181] that he was eclipsed by the dominating and acquisitive Lee[182] and tolerated in his own home solely because his ejection was not worth the trouble.[183]

The union of Lee's energy and ambition with Mrs. Shaw's love for and technical knowledge of music heralded a period of cultural activities that flourished increasingly until the collapse of the Hatch Street household in 1873. O'Bolger was of the opinion that Lucinda not only devoted herself to Lee but exploited her family as well [184] and that the success of their combination was due in considerable degree to Lucinda's "essential energy." [185] Whatever the ratio of their particular contributions, the effectiveness of their partnership must have been gratifying to Lee, and it was especially so to Lucinda. If Lee was in his Dublin glory, Lucinda was in the happiest years of her life. Childbearing and rearing (such as she was capable of) were behind her, and she threw herself completely and joyfully into the world of music created by Lee. Their musical assemblages were, in addition to being artistically impressive, sometimes social events of some magnitude. GBS remembered that as a boy he attended one of their concerts in the Antient Concert Rooms at 42½ Gt. Brunswick Street. Everyone, he said, was in evening dress and he recalled the presence of the Lord-Lieutenant attended by his courtiers in blue facings.[186] Winsten seemed to be in possession of further details and proceeded to enliven the solemnity of Shaw's account with a touch or two of human interest. He reported that Mrs. Carr Shaw, after singing several solos, was thanked personally by the Lord-Lieutenant and in full view of a large and ecstatic audience. Mrs. Shaw, Winsten continued, was so gratified by all this that her pleasure "overflowed even to the point of showing affection to her three children. Bob shrank from her touch because he suspected that she was intoxicated." [187] Judging by Lee's own comment on this occasion (as recorded by Winsten), it was not outside the realm of possibility that he too had sampled the festive drop. Equally gratified, he predicted that Mrs. Shaw would one day sing before the Queen herself and he so assured the children.

Some conception of the scope and nature of Lee's early musical undertaking may be recalled by reviewing the Dublin press. *The Irish Times,* for example, of Tuesday 30 May 1865, reported in its general news columns the activities of Lee's organization in a manner that surely reflected the respect and esteem with which it was held:

> THE AMATEUR MUSICAL SOCIETY
>
> This favourite Society has just brought its season to a close with a fifth grand concert, if possible, more successful than any of those which preceded it. The Society includes many of the most distinguished amateur vocalists in the city, and the concert of last evening, which embraced a carefully and pleasingly selected programme, afforded not only a good opportunity for the display of their vocal powers, but also a fair test of the merits of the orchestral accompaniment . . . On few previous occasions has the Antient Concert's Music Hall contained a larger and more fashionable attendance. The programme included some of the choicest music from Donizetti, Meyerbeer, Beethoven, and others of the most eminent composers, the concert was conducted by Mr. Lee . . . The principal instrumental parts were the overtures to "Marianiello" and "Figaro" which were admirably executed . . . The cavatina "Robert Toi que J'Aime" from Meyerbeer, with a harp obbligato by Mr. Fitzgerald, was an excellent piece of vocal execution. Balfe's "Lo, The Early Morning," and Mozart's "To Rome's Immortal Leader" were no less admirably realised, and the concert was in every respect most judiciously carried out.

The importance of Mrs. Shaw to Lee as his musical adjutant has already been dealt with. Her participation in his musical adventures has also attracted the attention of the press. Both *The Irish Times* and *Freeman's Journal* reported at length on a gala affair in one of Dublin's fashionable suburbs which, it appears, was conceived by the

Very Reverend Walter Lee, Canon, P.P., and possibly related to the Professor. *The Irish Times* for Wednesday 17 January 1866:

> AMATEUR CONCERT, BRAY
>
> A short time ago some of the principal residents at Bray formed the intention of giving entertainments in the shape of a concert and amateur theatre whose proceeds were to be [donated?] to the relief of the poor of all [denominations?] throughout the extensive district of which Bray is the centre . . . The use of the largest room in the International Hotel was obtained and it has been appropriately fitted up for the occasion. . . . The concert took place last night and as regards the nature of the entertainment presented, the manner in which the programme was carried out, and the number of the audience, must be described as a remarkable success. The room was crowded to the doors, and the applause was frequent, cordial and well deserved. Amongst the principal vocalists were . . . Mrs. Shaw. . . . Mr. Lee, known to be a conductor of considerable ability, held the baton. . . . The famous quartette from Rigoletto was assigned to Mrs. Cliffe, Mrs. Shaw, Mr. Comyns and Mr. Martelli, and very neatly rendered. In a new song entitled "The Parting Hour" by a lady who composes under the 'nom de plume' of Hilda, and who is favourably known as a vocalist to Dublin concert goers . . . Mrs. Shaw and Miss Doyle happily interpreted Rossini's famous duet "Quis est Homo?" . . . In the delightful air from "Les Huguenots," "Nobil Donna," Mrs. Shaw sang with artistic grace and expression. . . .

The *Freeman's Journal*'s account of the Bray concert was substantially the same as that of *The Times* but written more in recognition of individual rather than collective performances. Particularly impressed by Mrs. Shaw, the *Journal*'s reporter ventured a guess at the identity of Hilda:

> Mrs. Shaw, so well known in musical circles as a gifted

> vocalist, sang the "Nobil Donna" from The Huguenots delightfully, and kept the ears of all present attentively listening, and at the termination of the piece the applause was loud and general as the performance of the gifted deserved. She is, we believe, the authoress of a charming little song, brim full of merit—"The Parting Hour," published as the production of Hilda. It was done every justice by Mr. Cummins, to whom it is dedicated, and we think that the fair composer was right in making the godfather of her song a person who could "stand" to it.[188]

If the newspapers were reluctant or coyly unwilling to give Mrs. Shaw full credit for music by Hilda, Mrs. Shaw's son saw no reason to conceal that fact thirty-one years after her death. Adda Tyrrell had inquired of GBS whether he possessed any of his mother's songs. No, he did not and explained that there may have been a few copies in sister Lucy's home, Champion Cottage, but it had been bombed during the war, and the contents had been stored with Judy Musters in Surrey (a daughter of his mother's half-sister). Concluding, he reminisced that "In the old days in Synge Street my mother had two songs published as by 'Hilda.' One of them began 'The Night is Closing Round, Mother.' "[189]

XVII

THE MUSICAL SPHERE of the Professor and Mrs. Shaw's activities was not always confined to the general public and social affairs. The pious-minded citizens of Dublin also put in their bid for the talents of at least one member of the Amateur Musical Society: Mrs. George Carr Shaw. While there are no indications of her participation in the services of any of Dublin's Protestant churches (of which there were no fewer than thirty-five), there is considerable evidence of her presence and activity within the chapels and churches of the Catholic faith (of which there were then no more than eleven). Ervine reported, without giving any ratio, that Protestants and "Papists" fraternized in a friendly fashion at the meetings of Lee's society. Harris was supposed to have written that when Lee made the Shaws' home a focal point for his musical interests, the patrons were "largely" Catholic.[190] To O'Bolger, Sonny's home was "all day long" the resort of the children of Belial, that is, hell-bound Catholics.[191]

Shaw's own statements were, with one exception, uniformly consistent. Writing *In the Days of My Youth,* GBS admitted that his earliest misgivings regarding God as The First Protestant Gentleman were set in motion by his observation that, insofar as they combined with his mother's voice, the Catholics had been granted the best voices. Not only was the Divine Protestantism brought under review by the future critic but His Gentility as well, since it was evident to Sonny that several of the Society's best singers were undeniably engaged in the abhorred retail trades.[192] To O'Bolger, Shaw wrote that the members of Lee's organization were his own pupils who were "almost all" Catholics.[193] Cousin MacMahon Shaw was in receipt of the news that Mrs. Shaw was not interested in consorting with her husband's relations, since she was occupied exclusively with those who had musical interests in common with her own and who were "mostly Catholics." [194] The last public attention GBS paid to this topic was in his corrections to MacManus who was advised that "nearly all" of the Professor's best vocalists were Catholics.[195]

It was to another cousin that GBS made the exception. To Mrs. Grace Goodliffe he reviewed the relations between the Synge Street Shaws and the Bushy Park Shaws and adjusted the ratio of Protestants to Catholics by eliminating the former entirely. He wrote that Lee's concerts were rehearsed in the Shaws' home and added that "the tenors, baritones, basses and sopranos, as it happened, were all Catholics. Shaws [Protestants] were of no use . . ." [196] Whatever the ratio of Protestants to Catholics, it may be seen that it was preponderantly in favor of Catholics, and I suggest that this fact had much to do with the banishment of the Synge Street Shaws from all intercourse with the Bushy Park gentry.

The nature of Mrs. George Carr Shaw's occupation with the

Catholic churches of Dublin has been clearly set out by her son and was confined to participating in the musical portions of their services. The full significance of this occupation by a member of the Protestant Ascendancy cannot be appreciated by weighing it in the balances of twentieth-century liberalism. It must be appraised from *within* the brass-bound class distinctions of the nineteenth century—and an Irish century at that. His mother, wrote GBS in 1898, had no alternative: if she wished to work with music seriously she had, perforce, to join with those who had similarly serious desires, irrespective of their social or religious complexions. Further

> She must actually permit herself to be approached by Roman Catholic priests, and at their invitations to enter that house of Belial, the Roman Catholic chapel, and sing the Masses of Mozart there.[197]

The effect of what could be termed (from the Bushy Park point of view) a Papist invasion of the home of one of their number has not been fully dealt with by Bernard Shaw. In discussing the excommunication of the Synge Street Shaws from the councils of Bushy Park, GBS exhibited an almost undetectable evasiveness by shifting its major cause from Lee and his Catholic brood of singers and musicians to George Carr's desperate overindulgence. In 1921 Shaw gave something of the history of the relations between his family and that social luminary Sir Robert Shaw. Writing in his preface to *Immaturity,* GBS chronicles that in the "early days" (evidently 1852-1860) Sir Robert, being unmarried, made himself and his home readily available to the clan—even unto his second cousins. Mrs. Shaw, socially very acceptable, was according to GBS, "made welcome in all directions" and received the special regard of Sir Robert himself. Describing a typical evening at the gathering of the clan, GBS went on to say that the time eventually came when Sir Robert's door was closed to George Carr and, therefore, to his wife who, he explained, could not very well be invited without her husband. The cause for Sir Robert's exclusion order, GBS implied, was George Carr's behavior when under the influence of alcohol and which he described in some detail. Sir Robert's disapproval of George Carr appeared to spread to the rest of the Shaws, for GBS reported that, beyond his early childhood, he could not recall an instance of visiting the home of a relative. So limited was the family's social life that GBS declared that if the house caught on fire, the children would be less astonished than if their parents were to dine out or to go to a party.[198]

In general, the biographers have accepted and echoed their subject's explanation. Ervine had it that George Carr's "chronic intoxication" converted Dublin into a social desert for his family.[199] Pearson believed that it was the "habits" of Mr. Shaw that made his numerous relatives cut him and his family socially.[200] Henderson, it seemed, overlooked or refused to accept Shaw's instructions and suggested another and quite reasonable explanation for the severance of relations. He saw Mrs. Shaw as a victim of persecution and held that her "ill-treatment and ostracism by some of the closer Shaw relatives [was] because of her musical 'infatuation' for Lee . . ." [201] but unfortunately, Professor Henderson did not offer any examples to support his persecution theory nor did he explain why he chose "infatuation" in place of "association."

Shaw remembered having been at Bushy Park on only one occasion and that one to attend a funeral. "Their drinking father," wrote Harris, "got them all dropped socially until Lee made the house a center of musical society. And that, being largely Roman Catholic, was not tolerated by the snobbish Shaws." [202]

I suggest that when GBS prepared the Harris book for publication, he intentionally inserted the note on Lee and his Catholic associates as being a contributory, if not a major, reason for Sir Robert's decision to ban his Synge Street cousin from the baronial precincts. Since GBS knew how difficult—even impossible—it would be for future researchers to distinguish Harris from Shaw, he must have felt quite secure in this and other inclusions. Moreover, if it was the hand of Harris that put it in, the hand of Shaw did not exercise its privilege of excision but passed it through in proof.[203]

O'Bolger, while not granting the presence of Catholics in Synge Street as the *causa causans* for Sir Robert's interdict, believed them to be a supplementary offense to Protestant nostrils. His interpretation, though honestly enough stated, did not, I think, accurately reflect the contents of the original source material. In response to his question regarding the *ménage à trois* and the relations between George Carr and Lee, GBS replied with a thirty-page letter packed with what he later described as "unique literary matter inaccessible elsewhere." [204] One part of this matter unavailable anywhere else was imbedded in some of his recollections of the early days in Synge Street. He recalled a newspaper whose black-bordered columns told the story of Prince Albert's death (thus, he said, fixing the year as 1861 and his age as five). It was during this period that George Carr read the family prayers and Sonny, indistinguishable conventionally from other little boys, was sent regularly to church and Sunday school. He was on visiting terms with all his uncles, aunts and cousins, but he thought that by this time his mother had already been excluded from the Bushy Park family dinners and musicales because of Mr. Shaw's tipsy arrivals at these functions. Then, continued GBS, came Lee and the shattering impact of his influence—the gift of Torca Cottage, the fine house in Hatch Street, his musical society with its

> continual rehearsing of music by a set of acquaintances who were Lee's pupils and who were almost all Catholics (and therefore from the point of view of the Shaw family unfit for human intercourse) with the incidental result of a complete dropping and estrangement of cousinly relations which must have been rather hard on my father, who had no part in the musical proceedings, though he had been an amateur trombone player.[205]

Closer attention to Shaw's recital seems to show that Sir Robert's expulsion order was put into effect in two stages: partial and total. Shaw thought that in or around 1860, that is to say prior to the arrival of Catholics en masse in Synge Street, Mr. and Mrs. Shaw had already been dropped from the Bushy Park parties, but when their home became a nest of Catholics, it resulted in "a *complete* dropping and estrangement." This conveys the impression that Sir Robert—not one to be deluded by George Carr's claim to teetotalism—may have suggested to his weak-willed cousin that if he was prepared to arrive in a respectable condition and leave equally respectable he would be welcome at Bushy Park but until then it would perhaps be better if he absented himself. I believe that although Sir Robert held the gate open for a sober cousin, he clanged it shut when George Carr permitted his home to be invaded by Catholics to the everlasting disgrace of the Shaw clan.

Bernard Shaw's publicly-pressed claim that the Synge Street Shaws were socially disowned by their aristocratic relations because of the elder Shaw's drunken misbehavior was the truth but not, in my opinion, the whole truth. I suggest that the presence of Lee and his Catholic associates in Synge Street were at least equally responsible and that GBS's attempts to suppress or evade this circumstance was due to his desire to conceal the Catholicity of Lee and formed part of Shaw's total strategy.

XVIII

PROFESSOR GEORGE JOHN LEE was invited into the home of the Shaws. Was George Carr the responsible agent? On the basis of the logic of the situation alone, he must be ruled out. Lecturer-in-chief to Sonny on the natural and divinely-granted supremacies of the Shaws, George Carr could never descend to exchange even the normal decencies with God's despised, much less invite them into his home. Invite into his home this Lee, this musician, this teetotaler, this Catholic Lee? Make his home a den of damned Papists? Disgrace himself before Sonny and be rejected by his own people? Impossible. GBS noted the blamelessness of George Carr. He reported that there was never any quarrelling between Mr. and Mrs. Shaw (over household policy, I presume), since

> my mother went her own way, which happened to be the musical way of Lee, just as Lee went his: and my father could only look on helplessly, just like Mr. Jellyby in Bleak House. He cannot have liked it; but he could do nothing to alter it.[206]

On the basis of the logic of the situation—and the evidence—Mrs. Shaw must be acknowledged as totally and solely accountable. She had nothing but scorn for her husband's aristocratic pretensions and grand airs. While the immediate reason for this attitude might be ascribed to an extension of her opinion of her husband, the underlying cause was obvious: Aunt Ellen. Thirteen years in the hands of that iron maiden had not inured Lucinda to the iniquitous instructions that went into the making of an Irish Protestant lady. Her son reported she abominated her aunt and considered the religious and social matters taught to her as both oppressive and repressive.[207] In reaction to her aunt's detested regimen Lucinda, in a pattern reminiscent of her "abandonment" of her children, again drove the pendulum far and forcibly in the opposing direction. If she had been taught that tradesmen and Catholics were beyond the pale, then, if it suited her purpose, down would come that pale. Her criterion would not be their religion or their occupation but their ability to sing or play an instrument or their love and appreciation of music. And if the best voices and musical talents were somehow allotted to Catholics, so much the worse for the Protestant gentry.

Henderson's opinion that Lucinda Elizabeth was a target of the Shaws' opprobrium was, if he had no supporting evidence, an excellent shot in the dark. Testifying to Henderson's accuracy was Shaw himself. Writing in the preface to Winsten's *Salt and His Circle,* Shaw recalled that George Carr's relatives, though engaged in quarrelsome combat among themselves, "combined against my mother" [208] but went into no details as to the reason for their coalition or why it was directed particularly against his mother. In illustration whereof, GBS described a visit by his mother to one of his aunts whose cordial welcome must have come as something of a shock to a young lady as carefully brought up as Queen Victoria. Announced by his aunt's servant, Mrs. Shaw could not help overhearing her sister-in-law respond, "Oh, that bitch!" This, said Shaw, ended all relations between the Synge Street and the Bushy Park Shaws, and thereafter he himself came to regard all of the elder Shaw's relations as odious. In his *Sketches,* GBS identified the gracious hostess as his Aunt Emily, sister to George Carr.

By his uselessness, by his burden of guilt with regard to his lies and drunkenness, by his inability to capture her interest or to do anything to invite the respect of his wife and by suffering the presence of Professor Lee, George Carr Shaw forfeited his share in the leadership of the family. With the assumption of full powers, Lucinda Elizabeth brushed aside her husband's feeble protests, ignored the scandalized Shaws and, in general, disregarded the conventions by her open association with bachelor Lee and his band of social outcasts.

XIX

THE DEATH OF PROFESSOR LEE'S BROTHER HARCOURT seemed to have been the signal for the establishment of the Shaw-Lee household in Hatch Street. Although it has not been possible to ascertain the cause of Harcourt's death, his youth at the time of this dolorous event suggested that he had fallen a victim to one of Ireland's ancient enemies: tuberculosis. The reaction of George John to his brother's passing bears some attention, since perhaps it reveals something of his character. Neither Henderson nor Pearson saw anything worthy of comment, but Ervine found that when his brother died, it was "much to Lee's distress" [209] and Harris put it that Lee went almost "insane with grief." [210] In his own comments, GBS went further than either Ervine or Harris. In the preface to *London Music* he reported that Harcourt's death brought George John "to the verge of suicide." Nineteen years earlier he confided to O'Bolger that if it had not been for the intervention of a Reverend Ben White, Lee would have succeeded in taking his own life, adding that the good Reverend's wife (thus identifying him as no son of the one true faith) was his first experience of an American lady and a southern one at that.[211] Since Sonny had not yet reached his sixth birthday at the time, it may be taken that details of this episode reached him indirectly although it appears that he had been introduced to the Reverend's wife. In attempting to account for the presence of the Whites in Lee's Harrington Street home, I suggest that with the death of Mrs. Eliza Lee two years earlier, her sons let one or more of their six rooms to lodgers of whom the Reverend and Mrs. White were their guests at the moment. As regards George John's suicidal urge, it might be explained as an incidental product of self-pity at being alone in the world—a condition from which he soon recovered. Harcourt's interment amongst strangers in one of Glasnevin's least expensive graves without a headstone in a monument-conscious community does not support the image of a genuinely bereaved brother.

The launching of the *ménage à trois* in Hatch Street which, Shaw informed his readers, took place after Harcourt's death, has been dealt with in a manner that made it difficult to extract the essential facts. He wrote that "after the death of Lee's brother . . . we left our respective houses and went to live in the same house, number one Hatch Street . . . We also shared a cottage in Dalkey . . ."[212] Thus we are left with three or four questions that dangle provocatively. Elusive was the year of Harcourt's death, the year of the household amalgamation, whether their removals to Hatch Street were simultaneous (as almost implicitly stated), and lastly whether Dublin or Dalkey was the scene of the first *ménage à trois*. As the year of Harcourt's death has since been found to be 1862, an inquiry to establish the year in which the Shaw family joined with Professor Lee under the same roof may begin at that date.

Writing in his *Sketches,* GBS discussed the question of whether or not he was "educated"—meaning whether he had received a full and formal academic education. No, he declared (in effect), he had not and attributed his intellectual eminence to famous paintings, great books and majestic music. He would have been even more ignorant than he was, he continued, but for his "removal at the age of ten from the street in which I was born . . ." to the commanding heights of Dalkey Hill. Here, from Torca Cottage, he could see with his own eyes what Shakespeare meant when he sang of that "majestical roof fretted with golden fire" and could not believe that Shakespeare might have written this without having been to Dalkey Hill himself.[213] Sonny's "removal" from Synge Street to Torca Cottage in 1866, while not necessarily carrying with it the implication that the Shaw family left their Synge Street home for another, does suggest at least that a removal of some sort had been made to Dalkey. Henderson, Harris and Pearson did not fix the removal from Synge Street in any specific year, but Ervine and Rattray offered their views. Ervine appeared to be uncertain—he asserted that the Shaws moved to Hatch Street "about the year 1866, when GBS was ten." [214] Rattray confidently held that the Shaw family "removed to 1 Hatch Street, in 1867, when Shaw was 11" [215] but prefixed this earlier with the news that Torca Cottage "which Lee had bought in 1866, when Shaw was 10, [was] for Mrs. Shaw for the summer." [216] According to Shaw's published account as given in *London Music,* it might seem that all those concerned repaired to Hatch Street and, more or less concurrently, shared Torca Cottage. For O'Bolger, Shaw arranged the events in a sequence without, however, reference to any time. Here GBS said that Lee had left Harrington Street and moved into Hatch Street, but that when the Shaws left Synge Street, they went directly to Torca Cottage and "spent a whole year there, winter and all; and then we went to Hatch Street and used the cottage only in summer." [217]

Examination of the domicile records (Dublin Post Office Directories and Registers, Alex Thom, Printer & Publisher, Dublin) confirms the movements in and out of Torca Cottage, Hatch Street, Harrington Street and Synge Street. It should be recalled that the information listed for a particular year was gathered in the first nine months of the year preceding the year of publication. Thus the actual years are enclosed in brackets below. Furthermore, it should be noted that Synge Street houses were renumbered in 1864 after an extension had been completed.

Year	Address	Occupant	Notes
1864 [1863]	3 Synge Street	Shaw, Geo. C. Esq.	
	48 Harrington Street	Lee, G. Jno.	Prof. of Music
	1 Hatch Street		Vacant
	[Torca Cottage]		[Not listed]
1865 [1864]	33 Synge Street	Shaw, George C. Esq.	
	48 Harrington Street	Tomlinson, Mrs.	
	1, Hatch Street		Vacant
	Torca Cottage	Byrne, Mrs.	

Year	Address	Occupant	Notes
1866 [1865]	33, Synge Street	Shaw, George C. Esq.	
	48, Harrington Street	Tomlinson, Mrs.	
	1, Hatch Street	Dunne, Mr. William	
	Torca Cottage	Byrne, Mrs.	
1867 [1866]	33, Synge Street	Shore, Mrs.	
	48, Harrington Street	Tomlinson, Mrs.	
	1, Hatch Street	Dunne, Mrs. William	
	Torca Cottage	Shaw, George C. Esq.	Merchant
1868 [1867]	1, Hatch Street	Lee, G. J.	Prof. of Music
	Torca Cottage	Shaw, George Esq.	

While the directories had frequent and discouraging omissions and conflicts, some measure of their accuracy with respect to the above may be gathered by earlier references to them in this study. One example is the Amateur Musical Society's announcement in *Saunders' News-Letter* for the week of 7 March 1864, in which a footnote appeared inviting those having choral aspirations to apply to Mr. Lee at 48, Harrington Street, thus pegging the Professor in place and time. The week of 3 December 1864, it happened, contained another announcement of the Society in *Saunders' News-Letter* which, apart from an additional view of the Professor's prominence in Dublin's musical affairs, revealed him at a new address:

> AMATEUR MUSICAL SOCIETY
> Antient Concert Rooms
>
> Patron—His Excellency the Lord-Lieutnant The First grand CONCERT for the season will take place on FRIDAY EVENING, the 16th inst. Tickets will be issued This Evening at the above Rooms, from eight to Ten o'clock, to Members having paid their Subscriptions. Candidates for admission as Performing Members are subject to the opinion of Mr. Lee, No. 1 Hatch-street, and Non-Performing Candidates should communicate with the Hon. Sec., HENRY PARKINSON, 112 Grafton-street. Performing Members are requested to attend the Rehearsal at Eight o'clock sharp this Evening.

Therefore, sometime between the seventh of March and the third of December, 1864, and two years after the death of Harcourt, Lee left

Harrington Street for his last home in Dublin—1 Hatch Street. The official domicile record also shows Lee to have vacated Harrington Street during 1864, relinquishing it to a Mrs. Tomlinson, but it did not relocate him in Hatch Street, as one might have expected. Reference to the records of the Valuation Office in Dublin established final confirmation. Here Number 1 Hatch Street was described as a multiple dwelling and was owned by a Mrs. Anna F. Fraser who rented part of the premises to one George Lee otherwise unidentified and, probably, fellow-lodger to William Dunne.

The time of Lee's acquisition of Torca Cottage and, consequently, its occupation by the Shaws, is not so easily or accurately ascertained. In fact the time can be estimated only by putting the cart before the horse, that is, by knowing when the Shaws entered it. A study of the documents concerning the rates record of Torca Cottage did not establish a connection to Lee until his actual purchase of it in 1872, hence it may be presumed that he rented the cottage on a monthly, semiannual or annual basis. Turning towards the domicile records for evidence of Torca Cottage's tenancy and the Shaws' movements we find, in 1865, a Mrs. Byrne in command at the Cottage and Mr. Shaw, if not in command, at least present in Synge Street. By 1866, however, both Mrs. Byrne and Mr. Shaw have disappeared from their accustomed hearths. Where Mrs. Byrne went is neither interesting nor relevant but Torca Cottage is now under what appears to be the tenancy or possession of George C. Shaw Esq.

There seems to be little doubt that the Shaw-Lee *ménage à trois* was first constituted in 1866 and, contrary to the biographers' unanimous statements, existed for one year in Torca Cottage prior to its more permanent establishment in Hatch Street. Located in the Commons of Dalkey, but high up on Torca Hill, the Cottage was (and is) about nine miles from Dublin and could be reached in those days by the Dublin & Kingstown Railway or by pony and trap or carriage. Consisting of four reasonably sized rooms, a "return room" (for Sonny), a kitchen and a pantry into which they jammed the servant's bed, Torca Cottage snugly accommodated Mr. Shaw, Mrs. Shaw, Lucy, Yuppy, Sonny, Professor Lee and a servant. All things considered, life may have had its difficult moments as the Professor and the corn merchant left the Cottage for their respective employments in the city: George Carr to his Jervis Street office and George John to his Hatch Street studio.

In the light of Lee's prior presence by three years, the question of whether he and the Shaws moved into Hatch Street simultaneously dissolves into insignificancy.

XX

IF THE ESTABLISHMENT of the Protestant Shaw-Catholic Lee household in Torca Cottage shocked the Shaw clan, the transfer of that scandalous liaison to Dublin proper must have shaken the Bushy Park stronghold to its very foundations and calls for some attention insofar as determining its prime mover. The biographers viewed this bone with various degrees of contention—Pearson being the only writer to take a neutral or perhaps, detached view. He reported it straight: when Lee's brother died, "he shared a house with the Shaws . . ." [218] Harris was almost as noncommittal, but his construction went just a bit further. After his brother died "Lee lived with the Shaws . . ." [219] thus implying that Mr. and Mrs. Shaw may have been the principals in Hatch Street. Rattray had no doubts as to the initiator. He reported that it was Lee who first broached the subject and that the Shaws agreed to live with him.[220] Lady Hanson may have given a radio audience a different impression. She reported in a broadcast over Radio Eireann on the centenary of Shaw's birth that when the Shaws left Synge Street to take up their new home in Hatch Street, Lee was part of the household and "a large room was allotted to him in which he gave instruction to his numerous pupils" [221] thus placing the control with the Shaws. Ervine was convinced that Lee controlled the Hatch Street house—that the Professor "proposed" to Mr. and Mrs. Shaw that they should all take a larger house in a more fashionable neighborhood to which proposal the Shaws agreed and, Ervine added, "they thereupon removed to No. 1 Hatch Street . . ." [222] Winsten was equally convinced: it was Mrs. Shaw who opened the negotiations. On the death of his brother, wrote Winsten, Lee wished to move to a larger house but was deterred by the problem of what to do with Old Ellen his housekeeper—the terrible Old Ellen; then "Mrs. Carr Shaw came forward with the brilliant suggestion that they should set up house together and that the housekeeper could go to her Great Aunt Emily [sic], the tyrant of her childhood and thus tyrant would be matched with tyrant. The plan succeeded . . ." [223] As Aunt Ellen had been dead for five years one dare not speculate on the means George John and Lucinda employed to dispatch Old Ellen to Aunt Ellen. Colbourne named Lee as the agent. The energetic conductor wasted no time—he removed the entire family "promptly" to Hatch Street which he shared with them without, however, the slightest scent of scandal.[224]

Whatever Henderson's private views, his earliest public ones were patterned on his subject's guiding lines as laid down in 1905. Speaking of his mother's indispensability to Lee and their extensive musical activities, GBS made no mention of Lee's brother but explained that in order "to facilitate all this, [she] kept house for him by setting up a joint household . . ." [225] which could be construed to mean that his mother was the activating force. Henderson's 1911 treatment was well disciplined. The musical association between Lee and Mrs. Shaw, he echoed, was not as effective as it could be under improved circumstances therefore "in order to facilitate matters, Mrs. Shaw kept house for Lee by setting up a joint household." [226] In his final work, Henderson loosened the restraining shackles (GBS being dead) and reported that when Lee's brother died, the Professor "found himself with a house much too large and expensive for his purposes, and arranged to live with the Shaws. The new house they decided to share, No. 1 in handsome Hatch Street . . ." [227] This version returned the active role to Lee and played down Lucinda's desire to facilitate their musical labors. The decision to combine was probably reached when several rooms in Hatch Street became vacant and the logic of uniting became evident to both.

The union of Lee and the Shaws at Hatch Street invites further attention for its motivating forces. Henderson put the move to Lee's need for economizing, that the size and overhead of the Harrington Street house forced the Professor to seek less commodious and consequently less expensive lodgings. If this were true, Lee failed to achieve his ends, for No. 1 Hatch Street had, in addition to the basement, two rooms more than the Harrington Street house and had, into the bargain, an annual tax rating of £35 as compared to Harrington Street's £32. Henderson's change of opinion from his original one in 1911 may be traced to one of two sources. The first one came from Shaw who, in 1935, offered justification for the Lee-Shaw alliance by pointing out the practical considerations. He declared "The arrangement was economical: for we could not afford to live in a fashionable house, and Lee could not afford to give lessons in an unfashionable one . . ." [228] For speciosity of exposition, this specimen is rare indeed in the works of Shaw. While we receive an impression that the move was an economic necessity, it is on examination, nothing of the sort. If we are to take its real sense seriously, we must believe that the Shaws' move to Hatch Street was provoked solely by a dissatisfaction with the unfashionableness of their home in Synge Street. Moreover, we are almost invited to sympathize with Lee who it seems would suffer professionally were he to continue his activities under circumstances less grand than those in Hatch Street. This explanation, however, loses all force when one recalls that the Professor has been settled in Hatch Street at least two years before the amalgamation. Furthermore, the record has shown that the Shaws had vacated Synge Street one year before their move to Hatch Street, having already spent that year (1866) with Lee in Torca Cottage. The decision to return to Dublin (leaving Torca Cottage occupied only during the summers) was undoubtedly made partly because of the rigorous nature of Torca Cottage's isolation but principally on account of the difficulty of Mrs. Shaw's commutation to Dublin in connection with her musical ambitions there. If one looks for the central core of truth which is in the heart of every Shavian sentence, one is drawn to the conclusion that there were three possibilities open to Mrs. Shaw and Professor Lee towards the end of their year in Dalkey. First, they could go to separate homes as heretofore with its attendant disadvantages, that is to say, Mrs. Shaw's return to unfashionable quarters and inconvenient communications between conductor and adjutant. Second, Lee could share unfashionable quarters with the Shaws, thus maintaining perfect communications but risking the loss of his pupils. Finally, the Shaws could join Lee in Hatch Street and enjoy the happy combination of perfect communication and a fashionable address.

The second source for Henderson's change of opinion might have come from the Harris book, which reported that Lee,

> needing a good address, had a house too big for him and too dear for the Shaws. So they combined forces and set up a joint household. In handsome Hatch Street this strange triangle based, as Shaw says, not on Adultery but The Method, had its heyday.[229]

If the hand responsible for this "Harris" statement was Shaw's, the house must have been the Hatch Street one, since GBS knew, of course, that Lee was no longer in Harrington. In my judgment, this extract bears the unmistakeable marks of Shaw's attention and has the desperate evasiveness of a man struggling between an unwillingness to speak frankly and an equal unwillingness to commit actual falsehood to paper even when that falsehood might never be traced.

GBS's reference to the economic motive in the move to Hatch Street raises some question regarding the sharing of the costs as well as the comforts. Henderson saw Lee as generous. He believed that Lee contributed more than was necessary but offered no supporting comments.[230] Ervine ventured no opinion on the size of Lee's contribution but pointed out that with the Professor's departure for London the Shaws could not afford to remain in Hatch Street nor could they continue to use Torca Cottage rent-free.[231] Writing to Harris, Shaw brought out the superiority of Hatch to Synge and allowed that "the rent, of course, was much higher. Without Lee's contribution it was beyond my father's dwindling means."[232] This could be construed as suggesting that Lee's share of the responsibility was a minor one. But to O'Bolger's harassing tactics, GBS stumbled into an unguarded admission. When Lee's brother died and Old Ellen had been disposed of ("I don't know how"), it became plain that the logical and economical thing to do was to join under one roof and, added Shaw snappishly,

> By this means *we* obtained a decent house, and *he* got it kept for him & occupied. I don't know what the pecuniary arrangement was; but Lee paid the rent.[233]

I do not draw the inference that this necessarily establishes Lee as solely and totally responsible for the maintenance of Hatch Street. I believe that George Carr contributed at first a sum equal to the cost of the maintenance of 33 Synge Street—a sum, however, which diminished in proportion to his dwindling means.

XXI

IT WOULD SEEM THE PROFESSOR stood to lose nothing by this arrangement. His day-to-day services and needs, hitherto handled more or less irritably by Old Ellen (who could now be eliminated), would be supervised more or less haphazardly by Mrs. Shaw assisted by one or two servants. Further, Mr. Shaw would contribute towards the rent, thus dispensing with the need for lodgers. Best of all, Lee would be able to further his professional and amateur activities with the constant, sympathetic and competent assistance of Lucinda. Quite possibly, the Professor may have believed he had the best of the bargain. O'Bolger thought otherwise. Recalling GBS's disparaging view of his mother as a housekeeper, he held that "Unless the good man had very modest tastes he must often have thought that he had the poorer end of the bargain." [234]

What of Mrs. Shaw's outlook and attitude towards sharing a house with two men? The prospect of leaving Synge Street for a spacious and more presentable house in a fashionable quarter would have her enthusiastic approval. Further, as her alliance with Lee became closer her musical interests would expand and her ambitions would be closer to realization. Together, she and Lee would fill the city with music and song and the period would one day be hailed by all as a glorious page in Fair Dublin's cultural history, and Lucinda Elizabeth Shaw would be the Queen Cockatoo of the Cultural Cockatoos. As to the proprieties (coming down to earth), the approval or disapproval of base-minded persons would mean less than nothing to her. Indeed, in her reaction to the tyrannies of her cruelly-repressed youth she might have independently chosen for her own proud pennant the defiant words of Lord George Keith, Earl Marischal of Scotland—the words that adorned her son's fireplace at 10 Adelphi Terrace years later: THAY SAY. QUHAT SAY THAY? LAT THAME SAY!

Lucinda's disregard of public opinion is a characteristic mirrored by several of the biographers. As Henderson was the only biographer known to have met Shaw's mother, their opinions must have been formed in personal interview, correspondence or by their interpretation of Shaw's own published comments.

Shaw's own views of his mother's nonconformist behavior were expressed with the elusiveness one now expects when the subject dealt with members of the family circle or with the Dublin days. Writing to Henderson in 1905, GBS revealed for the first time the existence of the joint household which, he took pains to point out, was

> a sort of blameless *ménage à trois;* for she was the sort of woman who never troubled herself about gossip, and consequently might have had a dozen men in her house without more scandal than any hotel keeper would have raised.[235]

Study of this treatment of his mother's role as the woman in a house with two men will show it to be a carefully-constructed non sequitur. Henderson was informed that the family in which his subject was brought up differed from the standard household of husband and wife in that this household consisted of a *ménage à trois*—a circumstance guaranteed to produce fresh interest in any flagging biographer. But, added Shaw, there was no need for this fresh burst of attention; the biographer could safely return to his original state, since the conditions of this *ménage à trois* were without blame, thus suggesting that the Hatch Street household of three was entirely free of any violation of the conventional proprieties. This was followed by what seemed, at first glance, an explanation of why the arrangement was blameless, but second glance did not confirm its promise. It was blameless not because of Shaw's denial of any breach in marital fidelities (a simple and effective method) but because his mother was a woman who neither indulged in nor took any notice of "gossip." This was succeeded by an additional conclusion as misleading as the previous one. Since his mother was unaffected by gossip it followed (as a matter of course) that there would be no gossip in her community whether she harbored one or a dozen men in her home.

Shaw's second affirmation of the virtuous nature of the Lee-Shaw household was delivered eleven years later to O'Bolger and while similar in substance to his earlier treatment, incorporated a firmer note. In this account he substituted the atmosphere of a military installation for that of the hotel. His mother, wrote GBS in response to O'Bolger's nagging insistence for more light on the *ménage à trois,* "was one of those women who could act as a matron of a cavalry barracks from eighteen to forty and emerge without a stain on her character." [236] He added that there was nothing particularly strange regarding the Lee-Shaw living arrangement and not any more scandalous than Coleridge among the Gillmans or Spencer with the Potters. Inquiries into the affairs of Coleridge and Spencer being quite beyond the scope of this study, I must confine myself to Lee among the Shaws. But apart from the unShavian naivete that any female of any species could be safe from the attentions of cavalrymen, the general impression one receives is the inner agitation of GBS.

The third example of son on mother is contained in the 1935 preface to *London Music,* wherein Shaw touched twice on the theme of her impeccable behavior in Hatch Street. At one point, he explained that it would be necessary to stress the part played by The Method because without this clue his mother's relationship with Lee and the subsequent *ménage à trois* would be "unpleasantly misunderstood." [237] Thus, like "Harris" quoting his friend, GBS rejected carnality for melody as the cornerstone of the Hatch Street establishment. At another place Shaw, apropos of nothing in particular, plunged into the subject and discussed it in a manner that served as a pattern for several impressionable biographers. Mrs. Shaw, he said, "went her own way with so complete a disregard for and even unconsciousness of convention and scandal and prejudice that it was impossible to doubt her good faith and innocence." [238] Shaw had put it to the reader, as from one gentleman to another, with supreme illogic. Premise: Mrs. Shaw either deliberately ignored or was blithely unaware of peoples' wagging tongues and censorious airs. Conclusion: Mrs. Shaw had good faith and was innocent.

Suspicious of Shaw's reasoning, Alick West, a good man fallen among Leninists, argued that in addition to George Carr's alcoholism there was another reason for scandal. Mrs. Shaw, he wrote, having a remarkably pure soprano voice and wishing to cultivate it, went to the highly-regarded Professor Lee. To further effect their growing association, Lee came to live with them in the same house and, continued West, though her son said his mother was never the sort of woman who concerned herself with gossip "some gossip there must have been, and the conduct of the wife would not have inclined Dublin society of the 1860's to close its eyes to the failing of the husband." [239] West's suspicions were the only ones to reach the printed page.

The biographies unanimously ignore or deny any infraction of sexual propriety within the Hatch Street home. Rattray was thoroughly convinced—either by his studies or by GBS. The *ménage à trois,* he wrote, "was entirely free of sex." [240] Pearson had nothing to contribute while Henderson, except for one curiously-worded paragraph, similarly avoided the subject in all three of his major works. Ervine dealt with the matter frontally and forthrightly—any allegation of sexual infidelity by Mrs. Shaw with the Professor was a "myth" but, with biographer's responsibility, reported that both Harris and Henderson entertained lively misgivings concerning the conjugal sanctity of the Shaw household. Ervine may have his lead from GBS himself. Speaking of the occasion of Lee's flight to London in search of success, Ervine allowed that when Mrs. Shaw followed him there, "some" persons were convinced that Lee was her lover but that when GBS heard of this theory, he "scoffed it into disrepute." Ervine added that Shaw experienced difficulty in ridding Harris' mind of his conviction that Mrs. Shaw was Lee's mistress and concluded that "even Dr. Archibald Henderson was deeply suspicious." [241]

That Henderson was indeed suspicious of the relations of Mrs. Shaw and Lee cannot be denied, despite the conspicuous absence of suspicions from his works. Responding to O'Bolger's relentless inquiries into the Hatch Street household, GBS submitted a labyrinthine line of reasoning to disprove any allegation of intimacy between his mother and Lee. He himself, he told O'Bolger, bore a strong resemblance to his father:

> Sir Horace Plunkett has often reminded me of my father; and the other day I saw myself for the first time on a cinematograph film and was struck by my resemblance in certain ways to Sir Horace. You may therefore abandon all Hendersonian speculation as to whether Lee did not play Wagner in a Tristan & Isolde romance like the one in Zurich.[242]

GBS's shifts in his efforts to halt or turn aside O'Bolger's inquiries are evidenced in the almost hysterical abandonment of his customary perspicuity. His assertion that his own resemblance to Plunkett who seemed to have some resemblance to George Carr constituted additional proof of a consanguineous link to his father is, in my judgment, a non sequitur and is symptomatic of his inner distress.

At another point in Shaw's thirty-page letter to O'Bolger, he returned to the subject of Henderson's suspicions in a summing up of the life and death of George John Lee and his relations to the Shaw family. The story of Lee he said, could now (1916) be freely revealed as his mother was dead (d. 1913). For her sake, he continued, he had to be more reserved with Henderson who, consequently, "wrote nonsense about 'the man Lee' which I fortunately stopped in time) and imagined that he was a serpent in our domestic ashes." [243] With the exception already noted, Henderson's suspicions did not reach print, even when the death of Shaw removed all earthly objections—an omission due, perhaps, to a fear of some posthumous Shavian thunderbolt.

Whatever O'Bolger's opinions were in his Shaw-damned fourth version of the Life, his fifth and final revise made handsome amends. Stung by Shaw's threat to bring suit against all concerned if use were made of any of his letters or biographical material, O'Bolger hurled a counterthreat. He would blast Shaw's reputation by abstracting in its entirety revision number five and thus revenge himself for Shaw's destruction of his hopes with Harper's and for his refusal to write a "little" preface for Liveright. Battle won (no reputable publisher would dare to challenge the law-wise GBS), Shaw breathed easier: "Blast away, my dear Demetrius . . ." [244] and thus was born, or rather stillborn, a Life of George Bernard Shaw.

As it exists today, O'Bolger's final work shows the scars and grafts of its many surgeries. Trenchant, shrewd, sensitive yet petulant, bitter and even savage at times, O'Bolger's Life deserves to join the assemblage of major biographies. Shaw's social, educational, political, cultural, artistic, economic and dramatic views all came under his close, but not always objective or even competent, examination. As to his treatment of the Hatch Street *ménage à trois,* O'Bolger had come a long way from his earlier belief that a state of adultery existed between Mrs. Shaw and the Professor—so far had he come that not even GBS would find fault. Mrs. Shaw, O'Bolger now wrote, was not the sort of woman who would appeal to the sexual appetite of men or, for that matter, not the sort to invite it for itself. Lee, he thought, was not cut from the same cloth, but of Mrs. Shaw he had no doubts—no doubts whatever: "I have no disposition on earth to see in her relations to Lee any infraction of sexual propriety . . ." [245] It seems unlikely that GBS was familiar with the contents of Number Five for he continued to rake O'Bolger from stem to stern for some time after it was completed. For example, in 1922 and one year before O'Bolger's death, Shaw warned him (in a manner somehow faintly reminiscent of Sonny's prediction to the Magrone child) that if he persisted in his vain pursuit of sin in Hatch Street he would surely end up in an uncomfortably warm climate:

> When you begin rooting about in those circumstances for sexual scandal, you produce a quite frightful effect on me.

> You will certainly go to hell when you die. Anyhow, you won't go where my mother is.[246]

It would, I think, be a mistake to dismiss these expressions as mere effusion, for I believe they illustrate the profoundest disturbance of the composer. It is difficult to accept the sixty-six-year-old Shaw as being genuinely concerned with his mother's reputation unless it somehow affected him, and I suggest that he was not so much interested in the defense of the innocence of his mother as he was in staving off the specter of personal contamination. His reference to a hellish reward may have been chosen for its deterrent effect on Catholic Demetrius.

Ervine's specific rejection of the suspicions of Harris, Henderson and "some" people received further support of a more positive nature as he applied himself to the job of exploding the "myth" of adultery in Hatch Street. He held that none of these persons observed the elementary "fact" that Mrs. Shaw—despite having brought three children into the world—

> was not only a cold-blooded woman who was describable in the words of the Thirty-nine Articles, as having neither body, parts nor passions, but also the wife of a man for whom she now felt nothing but contempt. The whole business of sex had become repellent to her. . . . [furthermore] Lee took little interest in sexual relations. The larynx was his love.[247]

Ervine's friendship with Charlotte Shaw, his many opportunities for personal conversations with GBS and his own considerable talents combined to afford him a position unique among Shaw's many biographers. Consequently, his views should, in general, be taken with a seriousness proportional to these qualifications. In the present matter, however, Ervine called on his readers to discard critical objectivity and to accept seriously a trio of opinions represented as facts. In an incredible comparison of Lucinda with the sixteenth-century Anglican concept of God, Ervine reiterated his conviction of her natural frigidity. Mrs. Shaw he declared, was sexually deficient—that is to say, that while presumably fitted with the customary kind and number of feminine particulars, said particulars did not serve the functions for which they were evolved. In short, Mrs. Shaw was unwomanly if not unhuman. But, continued Ervine, this unhappy condition was not always so, since sexual activities *"had become"* objectionable to her, thus implying, perhaps inadvertently, that they may have been attractive at another time. Finally, Ervine added, Lee's libido was almost as extinct as Mrs. Shaw's—such interests being almost if not entirely sublimated to his interest in music. His conclusion: Sexual intimacy in Hatch Street? Preposterous, even impossible. There was nothing between the asexual Lucinda and the undersexed Lee.

The happy fortuity of biographer Ervine's friendship with the Shaws was aptly illustrated by his receipt of Shavian views not recorded in print. He quoted Shaw directly as "informing" Harris that Henderson could not rid himself of the notion that George John Lee was a blackguard who had debauched his mother. Shaw's own remarks regarding the character of a person capable of such an act were interestingly phrased. Any man, he is reported to have said, who was capable of violating his mother would not be above seducing the wooden Virgin at Nuremburg and repeated the now familiar homily that his mother was the sort of woman who (had she operated a lodginghouse) could have fed and quartered D'Artagnan and his three musketeers for twenty years without ever realizing they were not of her own sex.

In preparation for his portrait of Shaw, Harris wrote for information regarding the joint household in Hatch Street. Judging by the contents of Shaw's reply, Frank must have put it bluntly indeed to produce the following response which, on its surface, appeared to be a blanket denial of sexual misconduct. Wrote Shaw:

> There was no sex in the atmosphere; it was never discussed or even thought about as far as I could see; you had only to hear my mother sing Mendelsshon's "Hear My Prayer," or even listen to one note of her voice to understand that she might have been the center of a ménage à mille et trois without an atom of scandal sticking to her no matter how hard it was thrown.[248]

Eager and able to speak out fearlessly, brilliantly and, to his opponents' discomfort, Shaw seemed to lose these qualities here.

Although Shaw's denial of sexual impropriety in Hatch Street could have been presented in a more positive manner, it was nevertheless (and because of his obsessive refusal to lie) as truthful an account as could be made under the circumstances, since it was based on the observations of Sonny between ten and sixteen years of age as recalled by him in his sixty-third year. Further, there was every possibility that Shaw's oddly-phrased denial was, in fact, totally truthful, for if an intimate relation existed between Lucinda and George John, it probably developed during 1855 or before. Consequently, when the Hatch Street household was established in 1866 that relation could have been in force for eleven or more years. I suggest, rather, that if there had ever been any signs or sounds of sex in the atmosphere, they had long since dissolved in their day-to-day activities.

The suggestion that Hatch Street was "sexless" derives from another passage in the Harris book, a passage that seems to be indebted to Shaw. Speaking of Lee in Chapter Five: "The Innocent Triangle," the author described in some detail how the Professor came to develop his system of voice production. By dissecting throats (presumably human) he became thoroughly familiar with the physiology of the larynx. Then by observing the baritone Badiali he evolved the system of singing referred to as The Method which, the author continued,

> came very shortly to be Mrs. Shaw's religion. It would be easy to hint that she swallowed The Method to get at Lee. But the fact is, she was through with men as men. The bond between Lee and her was The Method. Any sex tie would not have lasted a year, Shaw says. The Method was eternal.[249]

Unless Frank Harris, at some time during his last remaining days on earth, put the Devil behind him and thereafter trod the paths of righteousness, it is highly improbable that his was the hand that formed this passage. Boudoir-fancier, buttock-pincher, early and vigorous advocate of pornography for art's sake, author of a shockingly-candid autobiography, Sybarite Frank Harris would not have been so easily convinced that any woman—short of an octogenarian prioress—would be through with men as men. Nor would he present as a "fact" that the association between Lucinda and Lee was exclusively a musical one. Rather, he would have gleefully seized on those circumstances and thoroughly enjoyed a flight into some prurient Paradise.

But Harris, Shaw declared in the postscript of his friend's book, was almost totally ignorant of the facts in his life, did not have the application necessary for research, nor did he even trouble himself to glance into the "monumental" work of Henderson and, consequently, "put in a good deal of guesswork. His guesses were not always successful: some of them were miles off the mark." [250]

It was *Shaw,* "Harris" reported, who said it was The Method and only The Method which kept them together—that a sex bond would not have lasted a year. Whether this was or was not the work of Harris seems immaterial. Clearly, if it was not Shaw's work, it nevertheless received his imprimatur, for he did not choose to exercise modification or excision and passed it through in proof.

If Shaw had wished to deny a sex link between his mother and Lee, he could have done so in a manner which could not lead to confusion or lend itself to other interpretations. For example, if he had wanted to dispose of this irksome question once and for all, he could have done it by stating flatly through Harris,

> The bond between Lee and her was The Method. No sex tie existed, nor could it have existed, Shaw says. The Method was everything, eternal.

I suggest that a sexual relationship did exist between Lucinda Elizabeth Shaw and George John Lee for a time during the first four years of the Shaws' marriage and that GBS either knew of this or suspected its possibility. I further suggest that, in his attempts to conceal this, he developed and pursued strategy and tactics based on the sound doctrine that the defense of his mother's virtue was the first line of defense.

GBS at 31.

A.

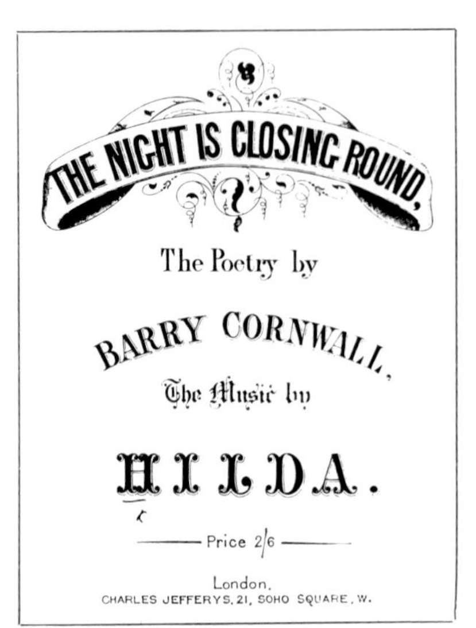

B.

C.

D.

A. Lucinda Gurly and George Carr Shaw at the time of their marriage.

B. Title page of music composed by Lucinda Elizabeth Shaw, 1865.

C. Facsimile of Lee's signature on a memorial assigning Torca Cottage to Julian Marshall, 1874.

D. G. J. V. Lee (seated, center) with Lucinda Shaw (far left) and George Carr Shaw (far right), 1865.

A.

B.

C.

D.

E.

A. Number 33 Synge St.

B. Detail showing plaque at 33 Synge St.

C. Interior view of lower floor showing return room door at end of passage.

D. Servant's bedroom showing door to garden and pantry window.

E. Exterior view showing return room extension (right), master bedroom window (top), and nursery window (bottom).

A.

B.

C.

D.

E.

A. Original doorway of 48 Harrington St.

B. Doorway at 1 Hatch St.

C. Original building of Clibborn & Shaw at 67–68 Jervis St.

D. Office of Townshend & Co. showing the original cashier's desk and stool at which Shaw worked.

E. Christian Brothers' O'Connell School.

A.

B.

C.

D.

A. Original building of the Wesleyan Connexional School: "My Curse on it."

B. Original buildings and children's playground of the Central Model School.

C. Gate of the Central Model School: "All hope abandon, ye who enter here."

D. Building and site of the former Dublin English, Scientific and Commercial School at 55 Aungier St.

E. Carmelite Church, Whitefriars and Aungier St.: "A terrific crash of glass."

E.

A.

B.

C.

D.

A. McNulty and Shaw in 1874.

B. Elinor Agnes at 19 (probably taken at Ventnor).

C. Lucy and GBS (Isle of Wight, 1876).

D. Elinor Agnes' headstone at St. Catherine's in Ventnor.

A.

B.

A. George Carr Shaw in his last years.
B. A late photograph of Lucinda Elizabeth Shaw.
C. Lucy Shaw at about 20, Dublin.
D. Family headstone, Mt. Jerome Cemetery, Dublin.
E. Charlotte Payne Townshend one year before her marriage to GBS.

C.

D.

E.

A.

Mr. G. B. Shaw

The Edison Telephone Company of London, Limited,

Mansion House Chambers
11 Queen Victoria Street, E.C.

From 14th November 1879
To 5th July 1880

B.

No.

The Edison Telephone Company of London, Limited

WAY-LEAVE.

17th February 1880

TO THE MANAGER

With reference to your Memorandum No. 29

I beg to inform you that for Wire No. 29

From

To

the following Consents have been obtained

G. B. Shaw

C.

A. Mrs. Patrick Campbell.

B. Shaw's telephone company employee identification card (front and back).

C. A report of telephone company representative G. B. Shaw.

XXII

THE LIFE-LONG ANTIPATHY OF GBS towards his mother was not, in my opinion, based primarily on his uncared for and unloved childhood, though he made considerable efforts to so impress his audience. In the main his biographers echoed and re-echoed Shaw's intentions and thus contributed to the long list of self-perpetuating half-truths encircling GBS. Ervine's treatment was fairly representative. He asserted that Sonny was "starved" for love—a starvation which left its mark "dark and deep" on the boy's mind and ventured that it was not surprising to find mothers treated so caustically in his plays. Ervine added that while Shaw had a "curious and dispassionate admiration" for his mother, he always remembered his miserable childhood and her part in it. Henderson was not altogether in agreement with his colleagues and seemed unwilling to accept Shaw's estimate of his childhood. He reported to his readers that Shaw's relatives (the Bushy Park ones, I suppose) were outraged by their famous kinsman's published announcements that his was a deplorable childhood made so by the "inhuman neglect" of both his parents but explained that Shaw's descriptions were in the nature of natural by-products of his subject's dramatic talents.[251]

I do not believe that Shaw's animosity towards his mother developed into its final form until his early years in London convinced him that something—which he was to identify later as the Life Force—had singled him out for an extraordinary commission: to save the English drama fallen from its seventeenth-century high estate. I do believe that the origin of Shaw's attitude towards his mother was his belief that a sexual intimacy between her and Lee did exist or could have existed, and that he knew or suspected himself to be the product.

Up to the end of his school days, young Shaw's dissatisfaction with his circumstances was translated into the usual adolescent transgressions, that is to say, poor or indifferent progress at school, rebellious behavior towards his schoolmasters, questionable companions and delinquent conduct in general. George Carr's drinking sprees and his consequent inability to retain the respect and affection of his children and Lucinda Elizabeth's planned withdrawal and her occupation with musical affairs forced the children to seek substitutes for their fatherless and motherless world. I do not know whether Lucy and Yuppy succeeded in finding compensatory satisfaction, but some record of Sonny's search for love and romance has been preserved. Earliest hints of the secret life of Sonny Shaw were given in articles appearing in *The Candid Friend* during May of 1901 and were, in part, reproduced in the *Sketches.* Already famous as a playwright specializing in social and religious heresies, Shaw defended his asceticism as the better way of life. Cigars, champagne, fashionable clothing? He could well afford them all but dismissed them as Bond Street extravagances and in no way to be compared with the luxuries of his imagination. Before he was ten, wrote GBS, he had completely exhausted his store of romantic reveries, and the novelists of the day were then writing the tales he had told to himself (and sometimes to an audience) before the emergence of his second set of teeth. "Some day," he added, "I will try to found a genuine psychology of fiction by writing down the history of my imagined life: duels, battles, love affairs with queens and all." [252] He compared his imaginary adventures to the voluptuous excesses of Sardanapalus, ancient King of Nineveh and Assyria, and admitted that there would be some difficulty involved in publishing these histories since the greater part of his adventures were "too crudely erotic" to be exhibited by an author of refinement.

Henderson was the next to receive the confidences of Sonny Shaw. To him GBS described himself as a "cowardly little brat" thumped by his nurse for pinching sugar. But at night there came a wonderful change; the realities of the unhappy day slipped away and the cowardly brat was transformed into a triumphant hero, an Admirable Crichton and a great lover, and he likened himself unto Alnaschar the dreamer.[253] Other biographers were attracted to Sonny's *fantasie nocturne:* for example, McCabe and Pearson. McCabe, in 1914, responded with a relatively conservative air. He saw Sonny as escaping into the world of his imagination and, in his wanderings around the "dreary Dublin suburb," engaging in tremendous battles and glorious adventures in which the love of queens were the prizes. The usually cautious Pearson succumbed to the possibilities, adding a few extra flourishes and sounding the note sinister. The child Shaw, he wrote in 1942,

> began to create a world of his own which was full of fantastic and burlesque happenings. He was the hero of every incident, fighting duels, conducting battles against kings and conquering them, making love to their queens and winning them. He was all powerful and always victorious, supreme in war, irresistible in love. There were no relations, no friends in his dreams; he stood alone, a foundling, a superman.[254]

Sonny's imaginary exploits first appeared in the Harris book (published eleven years before the Pearson biography) and were dealt with in dramatic—not to say sensational—manner. Here one of the authors touched upon the lad's early cultural influences and recited information of such a restricted and exclusive nature as to suggest it was directly inserted by GBS. Sonny's analytical faculties, wrote the author, developed simultaneously with his pubescence, and his interests turned towards science and physics. He read Tyndall on Helmholtz's experiments with light, heat and sound, and studied the squabbles between science and religion as published in the *Westminster Review* and in John William Draper's work on the collision between Darwinism and Fundamentalism. But before all this, added the shadowy author, the child Sonny had, through the liveliness of his imagination, been immersed in a world of fantasy far removed from the world of reality. In this fictive fairyland, continued the writer, Sonny

> was as free from the need of money as Amadis de Gaul. He was eminent, fearless, powerful, victorious, a great fighter, a great lover, and everything else that, as a matter of cold fact, he was not. It was a secret life: its avowal would have made him ridiculous. It had one oddity. The fictitious Shaw was not a man of family. He had no relatives. He was

> not only a bastard, like Dunois or Falconbridge, who at least knew who their parents were: he was also a foundling.[255]

Nor was this the only reference to Sonny's rejection of his parents. Elsewhere in the Harris book the subject again reared its head. Speaking of the romance of GBS and Charlotte Payne-Townshend, its author gave details which Harris could not have known nor would have known during the lifetime of Charlotte. Shaw, said Shaw or Harris, would spend his disengaged evenings with Charlotte at her apartments in Adelphi Terrace, and, "as the Terry correspondence shows," she assisted him as his voluntary secretary. Plainly, continued the author, if it could not be said they were engaged, they were certainly the next thing to it. However, implied the writer, there were snags on the road to matrimony; Shaw, to say the least, was not the marrying sort, and the readers were reminded that "in that imaginary life of his, he was never a husband and a father, never even a son or a brother. He was a foundling . . ." [256] Here the writer recalled another gentleman who was not of the marrying sort either and wondered aloud whether Shaw had not patterned himself unconsciously (in this respect) on George John Lee.

Now quite apart from the Rabelaisian gusto with which Harris would have handled the theme of playwright and secretary in the secretary's flat, these passages once again raise the question of Shaw's responsibility for their existence, and once again I suggest that it matters very little whether the hand that formed those words belonged to Harris or Shaw. Considering the care with which GBS prepared his own manuscripts and examined those of his biographers, it does not seem reasonable that these paragraphs would have escaped his notice—assuming, of course, that he himself did not write them in the character of Frank Harris—an exercise in which Shaw had had some publicly acknowledged experience.[257] Further, the probability (if not actual certainty) that Shaw himself was the agent is suggested by the anachronistic reference to the Terry-Shaw correspondence. Since Harris died on the 26th of August, 1931, and the Terry book was not published until September of that year, he could not have been (without additional Shavian collaboration) privy to its contents—that knowledge belonged exclusively to GBS and his publisher.

The author of the "Harris" extract added to Sonny's dreamland rejection of friends, relatives and parents the additional and more specific categories of husband, father and brother and again called attention to young Shaw in the shadow of bastardy. Of even more interest was the line implying that while Dunois and Falconbridge, were both of illegitimate issue, both, at any rate, knew that identity of their parents. But Sonny, he concluded, was deprived of even this knowledge.

The references to Sonny's dream life in which he constantly plays the role of bastard and foundling were apparently passed and approved—if not written—by Shaw, and they reveal his profoundest torment: that is, his uncertainty regarding which of two men was his father, an uncertainty that haunted George Bernard Shaw to the last day of his ninety-four years.

XXIII

THE DREAMWORLD DRAMAS of Sonny's lonely but splendid bastardy did not end with his entrance into adolescence or, for that matter, with his arrival into manhood, for the hero-foundlings of his childhood kept pace with his advance into his literary career. Shaw's deepest inner disturbance becomes evident in his fictive and dramatic treatment of children and fathers. The children, by and large, when not actively disliking their fathers, either question their own legitimacy, suspect themselves to be the children of men other than their putative fathers or are completely in the dark concerning any father. Shaw's observations on fathers and fatherhood are similarly striking, taking as they do various forms of disparagement and denial and destruction of fathers in and out of lawful marriage.

The earliest Shavian view of fathers was given in *Immaturity* written by a twenty-three-year-old Shaw. Subdued and deceptively insignificant, the subject was raised in connection with the death of Harriet Russell's father. Robert Smith, eighteen, slender, yellow-haired and gray-eyed, is engaged as a clerk in a capacity similar to that of Shaw's occupation with the land agency of Townshend & Company, Dublin. He despises his employment, is dissatisfied with the smallness of his emolument but will not descend to the vulgarity of retail trade where he could earn considerably more. Rejecting Byron for Shelley, Robert attempts to embrace vegetarianism and makes plans to found a new religion based in a Spartan dedication to Truth. By nature Robert is curious and observant. He possesses a colorless baritone, is proud of his cynical views, cannot abide the sound of an Irish brogue, avows he is an Englishman and is as imaginatively romantic as Sonny ever was. For example, having spent an evening in the Alhambra Theatre, Robert has been temporarily smitten by the sundry attractions of the dancing star. Oh! mused Robert—if only he could pick pockets he would steal her purse, restore it and thereafter receive the reward of her everlasting gratitude. Or perhaps an opportunity might arise to rescue her from peril by somehow snatching her out of a wildly-careening brougham whose horses had gone out of control. Or the Alhambra might be fired—he could then carry her through the flames to safety. Shipwreck! Together they would face the danger! Other disasters ran through his ingenious mind and in each he was the hero. But eventually the dancer faded and, being enamored of Harriet (they were both lodgers in the same rooming house) Robert sought to probe their landlady, Mrs. Froster. Miss Russell, Robert forced the question, was then greatly upset by her father's death? Mr. Smith would not think so if he knew her, replied Mrs. Froster, adding that while Miss Russell always spoke coolly of her father as if he were alive, her feelings could be compared to those of a stone. Nevertheless Mrs. Froster absolved her of implied callousness by pointing out that it was quite excusable since her heart had never been touched.[258]

In *Cashel Byron's Profession* (1882), GBS approached the subject directly, and the auburn-haired, blue-eyed Cashel's uneasiness regarding his origins was laid open. Cashel, a student in Dr. Moncrief's select school for the sons of gentlemen, has not measured up to that institution's standards in academic proficiency, nor has he adjusted to communal discipline. The master summoned Cashel's actress-mother for a consultation and, after giving her a rather dismal view of the son's general indolence, tactfully implied that he held little hope for the young man's future and suggested that perhaps the parents were better qualified to chose a profession for him, adding

> ". . . I am, of course, ignorant whether his relatives possess influence likely to be of use to him . . ."
>
> "I am the only relative he ever had, poor fellow," said [Mrs. Byron], with a pensive smile. Then, seeing an expression of astonishment on the doctor's face, she added quickly, "They are all dead." [259]

Considering the manner of Mrs. Byron's response, it is not to be wondered at the manifestation of surprise appearing on Dr. Moncrief's face. It could likewise have appeared on the faces of Shaw's readers. Mrs. Byron might normally have said "I am the only relative he *has,* poor fellow, [etc]." Attention to Shaw's phrasing will show that Mrs. Byron is actually saying that her son never had any relatives (other than herself) and amending it a moment later to say that the relatives he never had were dead. That this construction was accidental or attributable to literary awkwardness is, in my opinion, unlikely. I believe Shaw struck precisely the note he desired in an artful suggestion of an unknown father.

Cashel—dissatisfied with life in school, escapes from Moncrief House, adventures to Australia and, after a few years, returns to England a well-trained and formidable professional boxer. In the course of events he plunges into love with the intellectual, wealthy and aristocratic Lydia Carew who returns the affection, though in a somewhat more rational manner. Discovering Cashel's socially impossible occupation, Lydia decides against the alliance and forbids him her home. Cashel, however, is not so easily discouraged and forces an entrance, despite the valiant objections of that admirable butler, Bashville. Face to face with Lydia, Cashel launches into a remarkable defense of his profession (in effect a moving diatribe against vivisectors and social parasites) and winds up with a five-page brief on his personal history. He was, related Cashel, the "most unfortunate devil of a boy that ever walked" but gave no details of his misfortunes. He confessed that he was afraid of his mother who, he said, was a first-rate professional actress and intimated that he feared her because she was most particular about his appearance and behavior and because she never permitted him to go to the theatre. Although it is difficult to see cause for fear in this reasoning, a genuine basis for fear nonetheless existed, for his mother's personality was, to say the least, rather unstable. She seemed, for example, to regard her maternal duties as satisfactorily performed if she started breakfast by bashing him to the far side of the room and ended the meal with divers promises and endearments. Cashel recalled a particular instance. Referring to his socially ineligible background for marriage to her, he frankly declared ". . . I know nothing about my people or hers; for she boxed my ears one day for asking who my father was, and I took good care not to ask her again. . . ." [260] I cannot say whether this fictive episode had any basis in fact, nor do I even suggest it, since Mrs. Shaw has been described by her son as being unable to maltreat any child, flower or animal or, for that matter, any living thing.[261] I do, however, suggest that Shaw's introduction of the topic was sympathetic and symptomatic of his own feelings when he tortured little Cashel with a shadowy father.

As the novel draws to a close, Cashel and his mother meet after being separated for seven years. Unknown to them, this meeting had been arranged by Lydia who, after observing the amenities, vanishes discreetly, leaving mother and son alone. Up to the scene that follows, Mrs. Byron has demonstrated her professional talents by exhibiting various emotions to suit and has, for the moment, settled on a pose exuding sympathy. At first discomfited by the presence of his mother, Cashel turns abruptly to the matter uppermost in his mind and announces his wish to marry Lydia.

> "*You* marry Miss Carew!" Mrs Byron's tenderness had vanished; and her tone was shrewd and contemptuous. "Do you know, you silly boy, that—"

"I know all about it," said Cashel determinedly: "what she is; and what I am; and the rest of it. . . ." [262]

Cashel's interruption is neatly timed and Mrs. Byron does not pick up the thread of objection—thus we never discover what she and her son knew. Yet Cashel is not to be deterred and vows nothing shall stand in his way. Overwhelmed by his forcefulness Mrs. Byron, after sitting in silence for some time, tries a reversal of attitude. On second thought she could see no reason why he should not marry Lydia—after all, it would be a very good match for him. Quite so, agreed Cashel, but allowed that it would be a very bad one for her.

"Really I do not see that, Cashel. When your uncle dies, I suppose you will succeed to the Dorsetshire property."

"I the heir to a property! Are you in earnest?"

"Of course, Old Bingley Byron, disagreeable as he is, cannot live forever."

"Who the dickens is Bingley Byron; and what has he to do with me?"

"Your uncle, of course. Really, Cashel, you ought to think about these things. Did it never occur to you that you must have relatives, like other people?"

"You never told me anything about them. Well, I *am* blowed! But—but—I mean—Supposing he *is* my uncle, am I his lawful heir?"

"Yes. Walford Byron, the only brother besides your father, died years ago, whilst you were at Moncrief's; and he had no sons. Bingley is a bachelor."

"But," said Cashel cautiously, "wont there be some bother about my—at least—"

"My dearest child, what are you thinking or talking about? Nothing can be clearer than your title."

"Well," said Cashel blushing, "a lot of people used to make out that you werent married at all."

"What!" exclaimed Mrs Byron indignantly. "Oh, they *dare* not say so! Impossible. Why did you not tell me at once?"

"I didnt think about it," said Cashel, hastily excusing himself. "I was too young to care. It doesnt matter now. My father is dead, isnt he?"

"He died when you were a baby. You have often made me angry with you, poor little innocent, by reminding me of him. Do not talk of him to me."

"Not if you dont wish. Just one thing though, mamma. Was he a gentleman?"

"Of course. What a question!" [263]

The sudden materialization of the brothers Bingley and Walford only twenty-odd pages before the book ends underlines the clumsiness of the contrivance and suggests that this was, in the creator's judgment, the best of a number of unsatisfactory terminations. Other examples of patchwork may be noted in the unexpected appearance of the live uncle, contrary to Mrs. Byron's assertion that all of Cashel's relatives were dead, and in the reactions of mother and son. Mrs. Byron is made to express surprise at Cashel's ignorance of his uncle, surprise at his ignorance of his family, surprise that there is any question of Cashel's right to the family fortune and surprise that her marital status has been under suspicion by many persons. Finally, recognizing the inherent hazards in continuing the discussion of a nameless and faceless father, novelist Shaw dismisses him through the device of a mutual agreement between mother and son never to mention him again. Further examination of the exchange between Mrs. Byron and Cashel discloses conclusively that he not merely suspected but was certain that his birth was irregular, a certainty reinforced by the recollection of a pair of boxed ears. As to Cashel's responses to his mother's unexpected disclosures, he expressed astonishment that he was an heir and, surprise upon surprise, learned that he not only had a real and proper father but also rich and eminent families on both sides. According to Mrs. Byron, Cashel was "perfectly well connected" through her, implying titled nobility, while on the Byrons' side of the family, though descending from one of England's oldest families, there were only commoners.[264] Thus assured, Cashel was able to certify to Lydia that his blood had none of the common red. ". . . My birth," said Cashel, "is all right; I'm heir to a county family that came over with the Conqueror; and I shall have a decent income. . . ." Byronian legitimacy and gentility firmly established, the noble Cashel marries Princess Lydia, and all is serene in the dreamworld of Sonny Shaw.

Nineteen years after the completion of the novel, the dramatization of *Cashel Byron's Profession* offered GBS a new opportunity to deal with the mysterious father of Byron. In rewriting it for the stage, Shaw, in order to protect his copyright, rendered it into Elizabethan verse because (he said) it was so ridiculously simple ("hence, by the way, Shakespear's copious output") that he was able to do in one week what would have taken him a month in prose.[265] In this version, Cashel has broken a promise to Lydia never to fight again and has participated in an illegal prizefight with one William Paradise. Surprised by the police, Cashel has taken refuge in the home of Lydia, much against her will. Enter Cashel's mother (under the stage name of Adelaide Gisborne), a Policeman and two culprits under arrest—Paradise and Cashel's trainer Mellish. Adelaide, sensing the drama of the moment, glides into the role of anxious mother and, in a voice that can be heard by Cashel, declaims that Heaven had blessed her with an only son whose adoration for her was equalled by her devotion to him—

POLICEMAN

Hark! did you hear an oath from yonder room?

Piqued, Adelaide reproaches the Policeman for his interruption and admonishes him to respect a mother's shattered heart. Ten years, she continued, ten years of tears to which her aging face could testify she had spent and called upon one and all to bring her son back to her that she might take him home. Applauded by all, Adelaide graciously acknowledges their appreciation with thanks as Cashel emerges from hiding eager to surrender to the Law. Lydia's offer to go his bail is declined:

CASHEL

Never, I do embrace my doom with joy . . .

and avows that he preferred prison to being with his mother and concluded with an impassioned plea for a hemisphere delivered of his mother.

ADELAIDE

Ungentlemanly!

CASHEL

I am no gentleman. I am a criminal,
Redhanded, baseborn—

ADELAIDE

Baseborn! Who dares say it?
Thou art the son and heir of Bingley Bumpkin
FitzAlgernon de Courcy Cashel Byron,
Sieur of Park Lane and Overlord of Dorset . . .

and went on to relate how her husband dispatched himself upon discovering that more than three months of heavenly bliss with her was beyond the capacity of his earth-bound soul.[266] Fog-shrouded in the novel, Cashel's father receives new dimensions in the play but certain confusions are thereby revealed. For example, Byron senior is never mentioned by name in the novel—the reader merely being told that he had two brothers: Bingley and Walford. In the transition from novel to play, Walford, being dead, may reasonably be omitted without disturbing the play's main structure, but Bingley disappears as Adelaide's brother-in-law and reappears as her husband.

The problem of explaining the absence of the elder Byron faced GBS for the second time. Re-examination of the novel will show that Byron "died" while Cashel was still an infant, but in the play he is reported as having committed suicide at least six months before his son was born. Adelaide's account of her late husband brings up yet another point. Reeking of Park Lane wealth and respectability, Seigneur Byron is likewise Squire of a Dorsetshire estate and one may assume that upon his death all his wealth and property would have passed into the hands of his wife but this, evidently, did not take place, since the Widow Byron entered a profession not quite approved by Victorian society. However, I see no particular significance to these minor discrepancies other than attributing them to oversights of GBS caused by the pressure of transforming the novel into a play within one week.

But by far the most interesting feature of *The Admirable Bashville,* insofar as the purposes of this study is concerned, is Adelaide's response (and lack of response) to her son's public confessions. Rejecting his mother's offer of comfort in favor of a guaranteed motherless jail, he justified his "ungentlemanly" behavior by denying his gentility. Note may be made of Adelaide's apathy:

CASHEL

> I am no gentleman. [Silence] I am a criminal, [Silence] Redhanded, [Silence] baseborn—

Adelaide seems to have no interest in the deficiences of her son. Cashel not a gentleman? Not honest and law-abiding? Apprehended *in flagrante delicto?* Well, what could one expect? But when Bernard Shaw sounds Pavlov's Bell, Adelaide springs into animated protest, offers a timely explanation and thus Cashel, cleared of the stain of an ignoble birth, is elevated to grace.

Of incidental yet significant interest was Shaw's endowment of Father Byron with a multiplicity of names thus attesting to the blueness of the Byron blood. But here the author had his little joke with the insertion of FitzAlgernon. Shaw's recurring use of names prefixed by "Fitz" indicates, in my opinion, his familiarity with its ancient usage. As defined in respectable sources—

> Fitz– a word in use from the 12th century in names of English families (esp. of French origin), meaning *son;* . . . used esp. for illegitimate sons of kings and princes of the blood . . .

Fitz appears frequently enough in the fictive and dramatic works of GBS to attract attention and in addition to FitzAlgernon, we find: Fitztollemache, Fitzambey, Fitzfassenden, Fitzjones, Fitzgerald, Fitznightingale, Fitzthunder (coined by the anagrammed Redbarn Wash for a member of the rival Socialist League) and, of course, Fitzgeorge.[267]

Hero Sidney Trefusis of *An Unsocial Socialist* (1883) waggishly lies about the circumstances of his birth, telling a curious curate he has no idea who his parents were. As a matter of record, according to the novel, Sidney is the son of Jesse Trefusis, M.P., a millionaire with a palace at Kensington and a mother who came from a "county family"—one of the "oldest families" in England.[268] Sidney has inherited a good deal of his father's money, a good deal of early Shavian culture and is the possessor of a class-conscious soul. He is, consequently, dedicated to the elimination of the class of which he is a member. Overcome by the same force to which John Tanner (Ann Whitefield; *Man and Superman.* Act IV.) succumbed, Sidney abandons his bride of six weeks in revolt against the stifling restrictions of marriage insofar as it interfered with his occupation as a socialist propagandist. Adopting the name of Jefferson Smilash, he flees to some rustic region where he occupies a battered and ramshackle Swiss cottage. From this base he offers his services as painter, decorator, glazier, plumber, gardener, piano tuner, waiter and in "general domestic engineering"—in none of which could he have truthfully claimed any experience. To support these pretensions, Sidney dresses as a common working man and sports a *reddish-brown* beard of one week's growth. In order to complete his disguise, he suppresses his educated accent and adopts a sort of hybrid speech from the English and American peasantries. He seems to enjoy spouting this barbarous jargon. At the moment, a sudden summer shower has forced two curates and a number of young ladies from a near-by college to take refuge in his cottage. Subjected to Smilash's leg-pulling garrulity, Curate Fairholme attempts to impose his station upon the coarse fellow and haughtily inquires of him from whence he came. Brixtonbury, replied Jeff, almost pulling his forelock,

> "Brixtonbury! Wheres that?"
>
> "Well, sir, I dont rightly know. If a gentleman like you, knowing jography and such, cant tell, how can I?"
>
> "You ought to know where you were born, man. Havent you got common sense?"
>
> "Where could such a one as me get common sense, sir? Besides, I was only a foundling. Mebbe I warnt born at all." [269]

With many a more plausible answer at the tip of his facile pen, GBS preferred his hero to don the mantle of illegitimacy.

The Miraculous Revenge (1885) concerns, in part, an unwashed, disreputable, boozing and—even worse—atheistic blackguard known as Brimstone Billy, so named, no doubt, in certain knowledge of his ultimate destination. Described as having no family, GBS added that his real name was (appropriately) Wolfe Tone Fitzgerald and that his "antecedents did not transpire." [270]

The Adventures of the Black Girl in Her Search for God (1933) is not free from the Shavian opinion of fathers. Meeting the Conjuror at a well, the Black Girl admires his skill in causing the drinking cup to appear and disappear. Believing him to be a great magician, she tells him of her search for God and inquires as to God's whereabouts and is told He is within her. Fairly reasonable, thought the Black Girl, but *what* is He, she persisted. Our Father, replied the Conjuror. Puckering up her face in disappointment, the Black Girl ponders a moment and asks captiously, why not Our Mother? It was now the Conjuror's turn to pucker, and he expressed his belief that mothers expected their children to place them above God and went on to explain that if he had listened to his mother he would have become a rich man instead of the pariah and itinerant he was, but he would not have discovered God. The Black Girl however, did not appear to be listening for she kept to her theme on fathers. Her father, she said, beat her as a child until she grew strong enough to beat him instead and declared ". . . I have always refused to say 'Our father which art in heaven.' I always say 'Our grandfather.' I will not have a God who is my father." [271] Jesus, thinly disguised here as the Conjuror, also exhorted his listeners to call no man father unless it was his Father who was in heaven (Matt. 23:9). Shaw went further. Having rejected parents in the dream world of his childhood, he continued to reject them in the drama world of his maturity—excluding even the concept of God the Father.

Among the plays of GBS, *Mrs Warren's Profession* (1894) presents the earliest evidence of what I consider to be his preoccupation with the subject of illegitimacy. Kitty Warren is the child of an unknown father, and she has one sister and two half-sisters. Her mother, Kitty said, ". . . called herself a widow. . . . I suppose our father was a well-fed man: mother pretended he was a gentleman; but I dont know." [272] Born and reared in the slums of London, Kitty deliberately chose the profits of prostitution to the poverty of respectability. Highly successful as an organizer and manager of many thriving establishments throughout Europe, Madam Warren has, at the same time, managed to have her daughter Vivie raised to young womanhood in complete ignorance of her occupation. But Vivie has discovered the nature of her mother's employment and in a scene exploding with emotion, probes into her private life. Was she actually her mother? Mrs. Warren is shattered. She swears it is so and, on her knees, begs Vivie to believe her. But Vivie is relentless, the playwright's knife cuts deeper:

VIVIE

Who was my father?

MRS WARREN

You dont know what youre asking. I cant tell you.

As the play comes to a close, Vivie, still in ignorance of who her father is, severs ties to her mother and to her young man Frank Gardner (revealed as the son of one of her mother's lovers) and moves bravely into a world in which there "is no beauty and no romance," since now anyone might be her own half-brother.

Bluntschli, professional soldier-hero of *Arms and the Man* (1894) seems to have little love for his father. After receiving a telegram from home that his father is dead, he appears more concerned with his inheritance than with his bereavement, moving the saucy Louka to observe that Bluntschli has no feelings and not a syllable of sorrow for his poor father.[273]

You Never Can Tell (1896) contains those two irrepressible imps, Dolly and Philip Clandon who, for their eighteen years, have been kept in darkness concerning their father. Dolly, being in need of dental attention, is escorted by Philip to Dr. Valentine—a young dentist now facing his first patient. Extraction completed, the twins, in a whirlwind of entreaties, cajoleries and commands, invite the doctor to their hotel (they are on a visit to Devon from Madeira) for lunch. Dazed by the rapidity of events, he manages a protest: it is socially impossible to lunch with total strangers. Philip is quick to fill in the vacuum with formal introductions. Struck by their family name,

Valentine inquires whether they were the children of Densmore Clandon of Newbury Hall:

DOLLY

[vacantly]

No.

PHILIP

Well, come, Dolly: how do you know youre not?

DOLLY

[cheered]

Oh, I forgot. Of course. Perhaps I am.

VALENTINE

Dont you know?

PHILIP

Not in the least.

DOLLY

It's a wise child—[274]

This seems to put an entirely different light on the propriety of dining with the twins and their mother, and Valentine is convinced that neither of them is aware of the seriousness with which English society views certain breaches of seaside punctilio. Warming to his subject, Valentine proceeds to lecture the Madeirans. One may bicycle in knickerbockers and the rector's wife may wear health boots and urge dress reform, but there was one condition that must be observed: when at the seashore, one must have a father "alive or dead." The twins' private reaction to this disquieting news is given shortly after. Left alone for a moment, Philip approached the operating chair and bestowed a kick on it "as if it were Valentine," and Dolly ill-humoredly complained that it was all just too horrid—all the English were interested in was whether one had a father. Philip was in entire agreement:

I wont stand it either. Mamma must tell us who he was.

DOLLY

Or who he is. He may be alive.

PHILIP

I hope not. No man alive shall father me.

Philip's unwillingness to be "fathered" is not, I suggest, merely in the nature of an orotund dramatic phrase but the conscious rejection by GBS of any father.

Shaw's play on an episode in the American war for independence has, as an unimportant member of its cast, Essie, a girl of sixteen or thereabouts. Her part, while fitted expertly into *The Devil's Disciple* (1897) seems to have been inserted without regard to necessity. The natural daughter of Peter Dudgeon who has just died, Essie is in the hapless position of being left on the hands of his sister-in-law—that paragon of virtue, Mrs. Annie Dudgeon. Given the opportunity to call attention to Essie's birth, Mrs. Dudgeon makes the most of it. She reminds the child that her history is not fit for her own ears and sends her off to bed with the stern admonition not to forget to say her prayers. To her second son Christy (who, not being too bright, knows nothing of Essie's origins) Mrs. Dudgeon explains testily that when Peter died, the girl would have gone to her bed as though nothing out of the ordinary had occurred. Christy is puzzled. He allows that she couldn't be expected to have the same feelings as if she were one of the family, could she?

MRS DUDGEON

> What are you talking about, child? isnt she his daughter—the punishment of his wickedness and shame? [Christy is incredulous] Why else should she be here? D'ye think Ive not had enough trouble and care put upon me bringing up my own girls, let alone you and your good-for-nothing brother, without having your uncle's bastards—

CHRISTY

> Sh! She may hear you.[275]

Captain Brassbound (*Captain Brassbound's Conversion*—1899) is a hero of the type that could have been plucked whole out of Sonny's dreams. Captain of the schooner *Thanksgiving,* he was better known as the infamous Black Paquito, so christened, according to that cockney cutthroat "Brandyfaced Jack" Drinkwater, at the knee av his blessed mawther, bless 'is little awt! Smuggler—possibly a slaver and pirate—Brassbound has dark eyes and is olive-complexioned, both characteristics, it was suggested, inherited from a Brazilian mother. Apparently fathered by Miles Hallam, an English planter, the Captain hated the name and forbade Lady Cicely to address him so. Told by her that he bore strong resemblances to the Hallam family and to Sir Howard Hallam in particular, Brassbound flew into a passion. If he believed that, he said, he would slash his veins to drain them of his black blood, adding,

> I have no relations. I had a mother: that was all.[276]

With the exception of one play (*The Fascinating Foundling*), it will be seen that when the subject of illegitimacy arose, it had little if any bearing on the plays' major or minor themes. Smoothly incorporated into the story structures, the topic was dealt with in a manner that attracted no undue attention. A typical but particularly significant example was *Major Barbara* (1905). An amusing sidelight in connection with this drama was told by GBS's good friend Gilbert Murray, the famous Greek scholar. Writing in *The New Statesman and Nation* on "The Early G.B.S.," Professor Murray recalled that Shaw turned up at Oxford once to inquire whether he was a foundling. "No!" cried Murray. Well, then, did he mind his saying that he was a foundling? "Not in the least," he replied and received the explanation that Shaw had just finished a new play, *Murray's Mother in Law* (Lady Carlisle), which was to be retitled *Major Barbara.* Might he read it to the Murray family to see if there were any objections to it? and added facetiously, "I don't mind about *you.*" [277]

Central character in *Major Barbara* by virtue of his devastating logic, shocking iconoclasms, awesome personality and his occupation (dealer in Death and Destruction), is Andrew Undershaft who dominates its stage, whether or not he is actually on it; and, as one may expect, he is a foundling. His wife, Lady Britomart (they have been separated for many years), knows the facts and has told them to their son Stephen. The Undershafts, she said, were founded around the beginning of the seventeenth century, during the reign of James I, when an armorer in the parish of St. Andrew Undershaft adopted a foundling who eventually succeeded to the business. Undershaft the

First was so grateful or otherwise obligated that he adopted another foundling to succeed him, thus establishing the tradition. Here Stephen interrupted to inquire whether the Undershafts ever married and if there were any legitimate sons to which his mother replied that they did marry, but they always left the cannon foundry to some adopted foundling.[278] The current master of the Undershaft enterprises made no effort to conceal his humble history—rather he flaunted it aggressively. He was proud of his lack of education, proud of the good blood that "probably" ran through his veins and proud of his nameless birth. Being the seventh foundling in direct succession, he selected for his personal motto: UNASHAMED, which, I think, GBS chose as applying as much to Undershaft's bastardy as to his pride in the profession of wholesale slaughter. In adopting the artifice of illegitimate birth as a condition for eligibility to the control of the Undershaft munitions empire, I suggest that Shaw, with equal facility, could have chosen albinos, vegetarians, dolichocephalics, brachycephalics or even pacifists. By choosing illegitimacy as a prerequisite, GBS sustained the leitmotiv which pervaded his life and works.

Of the more than fifty plays written by Shaw, *Getting Married* (1908) was, in my opinion, his chief vehicle for transferring something of the fascinating drama of the Shaws of Dublin to the stage. Because of its special interest, it will be examined more fully in its own section. While avoiding the subject of Mr. and Mrs. Reginald Bridgenorth's children (none are mentioned), *Getting Married* has its shadowy as well as its brightly-lit moments. Cecil Sykes, one of the play's lesser lights, is a young gentleman about to be married to Edith Bridgenorth. But before this happy event can take place, there ensue two hours of delightful and edifying discussion on Victorian marriage, morals and associated topics. One of these deals with the marriage contract: both Edith and Cecil refuse to go through the ceremony unless each receives contractual assurances against certain contingencies. Cecil insists on a clause indemnifying him against libel suits incurred by Edith in the course of her vigorous participation in the labor movement. And Edith is equally adamant. She will not take a step towards the altar unless the terms of marriage include provisions for divorce if Cecil should become a murderer, a thief, a forger or an atheist. This leads into arguments for and against marriage.

General Bridgenorth, aghast at this turn in the discussion (which to his mind implies some form of treason) appeals to his brother the Bishop of Chelsea to exert his office and call a halt to it. The Bishop, however, confesses that he too has had his doubts about the wisdom of English marriage law and soberly observes that unless the law be adapted to human needs it will never reach its intended divine station. The Bishop's wife is not, however, impressed by her husband's exalted position. With a touch of impatience she instructs him to be sensible—after all, people must marry and (with GBS at her ear) asked him what he would have said had the parents of Cecil not been married?

THE BISHOP

They were not, my dear.

Hotchkiss	Hallo!
Reginald	What d'ye mean?
The General	Eh?
Leo [Mrs. Reginald]	Not married!
Mrs. Bridgenorth	What!

Cecil's response is quite natural. He rises in amazement, demands of the Bishop what on earth he meant and denies that his parents are unmarried. Hotchkiss is quick to remind Cecil that his memory is perhaps faulty in this respect, but Cecil staggers on. Never, he continues, has he asked his mother to produce her marriage certificate—what son ever did? To stem Cecil's mounting hysteria the Bishop offers him some words of comfort or, at least seems to: there is no real cause for alarm and explains that the Sykes', not being members of the Anglican Church, have taken part in a ceremony of marriage which does not have the Holy Sacrament of the true faith and, consequently, are unmarried. Fortunately for the plot of this little episode, Cecil was converted to the true faith in his second year at Oxford and is, therefore, further soothed by the Bishop who then asks him whether, as an Anglican, he considers his parents married?

CECIL

Great Heavens, no! a thousand times no. I never thought of that. I'm a child of sin. [he collapses into chair] [279]

Laboriously contrived, Shaw's signature is apparent despite the levity in Cecil Sykes's illegitimacy.

Shaw's little comedy on England's suffragist movement *Press Cuttings* (1909) has, among its jocundities, Mrs. Banger's doubts concerning the identity of her grandfather, but in a one-act playlet written during the same year, Shaw carried his obsession with children of nobody boldly into the title. *The Fascinating Foundling* is principally concerned with Horace Brabazon, a handsome young man, and Anastasia Vulliamy, a beautiful young woman—unknown to each other and both foundlings. While there are mysterious references to the circumstances of Horace's beginnings, Anastasia's history is clearer. Found on a doorstep (could happen to anyone, you know), Anastasia snobbishly resents the slur that it was the doorstep of a common workhouse: it had been one of the most fashionable houses in Park Lane, thank you. Brought together by dramatist Shaw, Horace and Anastasia meet in the office of the Lord Chancellor who is charged by law with the welfare of orphans of the realm. In this mad and charming scene Horace and Anastasia become romantically interested and examine each other as matrimonial prospects. Anastasia admits she has no money but offers instead evidence of membership in an exclusive aristocracy; her illegitimacy:

BRABAZON
[excited and hopeful]

A foundling?

ANASTASIA

I havnt a relation in the world.

BRABAZON

Mine! mine!! MINE!!! [280]

Presumably, there was an end to foundlings insofar as the Brabazon-Vulliamy union was concerned.

Misalliance (1910), "A debate in one sitting," harbors references to parents and families as bitter as can be found anywhere and may possibly account for some of the biographers' comments on this score. Pearson, for example, reported that Shaw questioned the wisdom of filiation and seemed to recommend that children should not know who their parents were. His suggested method for achieving this end, Pearson continued, was to bring large numbers of healthy men and women together in (I presume) one huge but darkened boudoir. Duties performed, the participants would proceed in their separate ways.[281] Henderson held that GBS was brought to this view through Shelley who, he said, believed that there was a hostility between child and parent which was neither abnormal nor wicked but perfectly natural.[282] Drama critic Huneker discerned this element in Shaw early and, in keeping with his profession, put it dramatically as well as critically. Like some all-powerful deity, he wrote, Shaw set out to destroy the family, thundering

> I will teach children to renounce the love of their parents; parents to despise their offspring; husbands to hate their wives; wives to loathe their husbands; and brothers and sisters will raise warring hands after my words have entered their souls.[283]

Yet it must be reported that Shaw denied that he wished to destroy the family. Duffin also noted this Shavian propensity and was selected as one of the blundering biographers to be corrected. He had no desire to dissolve the family, replied Shaw in rejecting Duffin's verdict, the community of a father, mother and their children, though narrow and unfriendly in itself, "is the natural social unit." [284]

The number and complexity of themes in *Misalliance* (exceeded only in *Heartbreak House*) make it almost impossible to follow the biographical rabbit through the warrens of this work. Hypatia Tarleton, a "properly" brought-up young lady, is in revolt against her environment and its restrictions. Her opinions of home, family, parents and duty take form in an immoderate outburst somewhat out of proportion to its causes. Bored, listless and useless, Hypatia wishes to be released from her duties of attending to the wants of her mother and father and thus escape the inevitable fate of dried-up spinsterhood. To a friend of the family Hypatia pours out her resentment. No one, she says, could realize the dreadful waste of youth on the selfishness of the old—it is worse than ordinary wickedness—

> Oh! home! home! parents! family! duty! how I loathe them! How I'd like to see them all blown to bits!

Father John Tarleton is not too far behind his daughter in these opinions. For example, he does not believe there can be a close and useful relation between parents and children because of a moral barrier to uninhibited exchange. He declares that there is a ten-mile-long-wall ten-feet thick between them preventing such a desirable but impossible condition and concludes that before a thousand years have passed, social changes will occur, and children will grow into maturity without ever knowing who their parents are. At another point, Tarleton delivers himself even more forcefully. After a desperate quarrel with Hypatia, who has ceased to recognize his authority, Tarleton confesses his defeat and rages

> Parents and children! No man should know his own child. No child should know its own father. Let the family be rooted out of civilization! Let the human race be brought up in institutions!

Nor was *Misalliance* limited to expressions of bitterness towards the family unit. The appearance of new members of the cast (in this play of many plots) and new situations brought new opportunities to raise old subjects. Hypatia and Joseph Percival (the boy with three fathers) occupy the stage for a few minutes of Shavian fun. Hypatia wishes to be wicked. Joseph wishes to remain proper. Hypatia advances to the attack. Joey retreats and runs off stage with Hypatia in hot pursuit. Hidden spectator to all this is a revolver-brandishing stranger who has been hiding in a recently-uncrated portable Turkish bath. Though obviously bent on mischief, the prowler may be supposed to be at least a primly conventional one, since during the aforesaid proceedings he can be seen by the audience in the act of peering at the two and showing signs of moral disapproval. However that may be, the intruder's purpose in coming thus armed is soon revealed. Tarleton enters and, having been forced to exercise himself unnaturally on the trapeze, is exhausted. He mops his brow and leans against the Turkish bath—his nose only inches away from the prowler's and in a moment their eyes meet. Tarleton shrinks at the sight, cries aloud that his brain has cracked under the strain but recovers quickly as the man, pistol in hand, springs into full view warning Tarleton that if he utters another sound it will be his last. In complete command of himself, Tarleton cooly inquires who the devil he might be and what, pray, was he doing in his new Turkish bath?

THE MAN
[with tragic intensity]
I am the son of Lucinda Titmus.

As disclosed by later events, Tarleton pretended to be unimpressed by this announcement and adopted an attitude of humoring a lunatic. To come to the point, the would-be assassin charges Tarleton with seducing and abandoning his mother to her "shame." Tarleton suggests that he sounds as if he had been saturated with melodramatic literature and confesses that in his own youth he was similarly partial to stimulating fiction and remarks how odd it is that both of them should enjoy such tastes. Could he explain this extraordinary coincidence?

THE MAN
No. What are you driving at?
TARLETON
Well, do you know who your father was?
THE MAN
I see what you mean now. You dare set up to be my father! Thank heaven Ive not a drop of your vile blood in my veins.[285]

The biographical link of *Misalliance* with members of the Shaw family seems to me to be, from Shaw's point of view, plainly—even dangerously evident. Tarleton's opinions on the raising of children are not unlike those of Mrs. Shaw's; they both permitted their children to grow up without parental supervision or interference. Joseph Percival, the boy with three fathers, has his origins in Sonny Shaw. To Frank Harris, GBS acknowledged that he would never have thought of the idea had not he himself had three fathers, i.e., his "official" father, Professor Lee and Uncle Walter.[286] But perhaps the most striking resemblance is between Shaw and The Man who, when not stalking the man who disgraced his mother, is employed as a cashier in a position similar to the one occupied by young Shaw with land agents Townshend & Company in Dublin. Like Shaw, The Man hated his work, hated his imprisonment in an office counting other people's money and, like Shaw, was never out a farthing in his accounts. Finally, Shaw's most daring step was in directly identifying The Man's mother's Christian name with that of his own mother.

Written in connection with a movement to found a National Theatre, Shaw's play about Shakespeare and Queen Elizabeth, *The Dark Lady of the Sonnets* (1910), manages to include dialogue reflecting on the birth of the bard himself. Keeping a tryst with his Dark Lady at the Palace, Shakespeare mistakes a cloaked lady who has been walking in her sleep (and quoting mangled Macbeth from that as yet unborn masterpiece) for his Mary. Soon awakened, the cloaked lady unwittingly charms Shakespeare (that snapper-up of unconsidered trifles) by the music in her speech, moving the poet, despite her admonitions, to make love to her. This is the moment the Dark Lady chooses to arrive and, taking in the situation with her first glance, flies at both with upraised fists. The cloaked lady receives her left and Shakespeare is sent sprawling to earth with her right, both to the musical accompaniment of Elizabethan malediction: *he* is a "false lying hound" and *she* a "filthy trull." Fuming with rage, the cloaked lady throws aside her cloak revealing herself as the Queen and pronounces the assault as high treason punishable by decapitation. While Shakespeare is concerned only with the unspeakable outrage to Shakespeare, the Dark Lady is terrified, falls on her knees and implores Shakespeare to save her.

QUEEN ELIZABETH

> Save you! A likely savior, on my royal word! I had thought this fellow at least an esquire; for I had hoped that even the vilest of my ladies would not have dishonored my Court by wantoning with a baseborn servant.

SHAKESPEAR

> Baseborn! I, a Shakespear of Stratford! I, whose mother was an Arden! baseborn! You forget yourself, madam.

Battle lines drawn, the Queen and Shakespeare proceed to hurl charges, countercharges, invective and threats at one another. The dramatist refuses to temper his tongue and will not, he vows, humor any sovereign who dares to impugn the honor of his family. Continuing with the defense of the Shakespeares' good name, one may note some semblance between John Shakespeare and George Carr Shaw. William admits that his father was a bankrupt but implies it was due to his inborn gentility that forbade him from entering trade. True it is that he never paid his debts but no one could say that he refused to own them and it could be sworn that he had given his creditors bills which, unfortunately for him, proved his downfall when pressed to the wall. But the Queen has little interest in the past misfortunes of Shakespeare senior; she is more concerned with the imminent misfortunes of Shakespeare junior and vows that the son of John will be taught his place by the daughter of Henry VIII. Heretofore on the defensive in his denial of the Queen's allegations regarding his station in life, Shakespeare shifts to the offensive. He admonishes her not to mention that glutton in the same breath with solid citizen John Shakespeare of Stratford, for he married but once whilst that rake of a Tudor entered marriage six times—indeed a daughter should blush at the utterance of his name.

ELIZABETH

Insolent dog—

SHAKESPEAR

[cutting her short]

How know you that King Harry was indeed your father?

ELIZABETH

Zounds! Now by—[she stops to grind her teeth with rage].

SHAKESPEAR

Learn to know yourself better, madam. I am an honest gentleman of unquestioned parentage, and have already sent in my demand for the coat-of-arms that is lawfully mine. Can you say as much for yourself? [287]

I suggest that Shaw's inclusion of the question was deliberate, if not compulsive, rather than topical.

Fanny's First Play (1911), authored by Xxxxxxx Xxxx (signed thus to confuse critics who reflexively attacked any new play by

Shaw), does not overlook the opportunity to question parentage. Juggins, footman to the Gilbeys, gives notice, explaining to his employer that his brother who had recently suffered a death in the family was now lonely and wished his company. Gilbey grumbles at the news and offers increased emoluments which Juggins must decline as, he explains further, his brother has objections to his employment as a servant. Gilbey sarcastically suggests that perhaps his brother is a duke. Sad to relate, Juggins replies, he *is* a duke and in response to the ringing of the doorbell, excuses himself. He ushers in the Knoxes and after providing seats for the newcomers, withdraws to give them the opportunity of receiving the unsettling news. Serving tea, Juggins is the object of covert inspection and on returning to the kitchen for the tea cakes, Knox inquires *sotto voce* whether it was proper for Juggins to serve them, adding suspiciously that, after all, anyone might be a son of a duke—was he legitimate? As Juggins returns with the cakes, Gilbey whispers to Knox:

> You ask him.
>
> KNOX
>
> [to Juggins]
>
> Just a word with you, my man. Was your mother married to your father?
>
> JUGGINS
>
> I believe so, sir. I cant say from personal knowledge. It was before my time.[288]

It is further ascertained that Juggins' mother was actually a duchess; any remaining doubts regarding his birth are put to rest.

Mutilated, musicalized and muted, *Pygmalion* (1913) stars that unbathed hoyden Eliza Doolittle whose ignorance of elementary social behavior was equalled by her ignorance of her parents. One may recall that memorable scene in Covent Garden under the portico of St. Paul's Church, when with Liza at his elbow, Higgins boasts to Pickering that in three months (later extended to six) he could change that bedraggled baggage into a duchess.[289] This seed does not fall on barren ground for Liza appeared at Professor Higgins' laboratory the following day, eager for metamorphosis. Higgins is delighted to have his boast taken up but housekeeper Mrs. Pearce expresses both moral and practical objections. She cannot permit this wickedness and orders Liza to go home to her parents. Aint got no parents, replied Liza, she that put her out to work was her sixth stepmother but she was a good girl she was. As the play progresses, Higgins is visited by garbage collector Alfred Doolittle, one of nature's sociologists, who lives with his "missus." When asked by Higgins the purpose of his visit, Doolittle adopts a theatrically menacing attitude and declares that he wants his daughter, see? Later Doolittle again calls attention to the claim that Liza is his daughter by insisting on his rights as her father, that is to say, a five-pound note would allay his uneasiness as to whether his daughter was in proper hands. Up to the present, Liza has had a mother (surely), six stepmothers and a father—ostensibly Mr. Doolittle. At play's end, Doolittle's own transmogrification has taken place. No longer a carefree collector of garbage or a loyal member of the undeserving poor, his reputation as an authority on the social castes has been appreciated by a rich American cheese magnate to the value of £3000 annually for a series of lectures on Moral Reform. But his troubles do not end there. With the turn in his fortunes his "missus" turns respectable and she now insists on marriage. Agitated beyond all measure, he asks Pickering to see him through the ordeal.

PICKERING

But youve been through it before, man. You were married to Eliza's mother.

DOOLITTLE

Who told you that, Colonel?

Pickering admits he just "naturally" assumed it but Doolittle argues that while such as assumption would be quite natural for those in the middle classes it would not be true for his class—the class of the undeserving poor. Returning to the central question he concludes

> But dont say nothing to Eliza. She dont know: I always had a delicacy about telling her.

While strongly implying that Alfred *is* Eliza's father, it unquestionably establishes Eliza as being born out of wedlock.

The collapse of the Eastern front in the war to end wars was followed by two noteworthy events in rapid succession: the Russian revolution and a topically titled play by George Bernard Shaw, *Annajanska, The Bolshevik Empress* (1917).[290] Annajanska—the Grand Duchess Annajanska—most beloved of all the Little Father's children had joined the Bolshevists and was now Comrade Annajanska. Former Imperial General Strammfest, dragooned by the Revolutionary Council to lead them, is secretly loyal to the deposed "Panjandrum." He lives only (he declares privately) to destroy the revolution, restore the Imperial family to their throne and hang his own solicitor—the man who appointed him as Commander-in-Chief of the Bolshevik forces. Annajanska, in her efforts to join up with the main revolutionary forces, has disguised herself as an officer of the Imperial Guard and thus expedites her capture and delivery to the General. Horrified that Her Imperial Highness has gone over to the enemy, scandalized by her cries of "Long live the Revolution," provoked by her waving of a red handkerchief and her seditious utterances in general, Strammfest's anger gets the best of him:

> "You always had low tastes. You are no true daughter of the Panjandrums: you are a changeling, thrust into the Panjandrina's bed by some profligate nurse. . . ." [291]

For all its breath-taking range, *Back To Methuselah* (1920) confines itself to its author's intention: a testamentary drama promulgating his belief that there could be a tomorrow better than today if only mankind were willing to stretch its will as the progenitor of Lamarck's giraffe stretched its neck. One of the improvements in store for tomorrow seemed to be in answer to an earlier plea by John Tarleton who called for the destruction of the family and the dissolution of the ties between father and child. In Part III—*The Thing Happens,* the far-sighted Chief Secretary Confucius explains to the short-sighted Accountant General Barnabas how disastrous some of the consequences would be if there were a general increase in the span of life from threescore and ten to three hundred years . . .

> ". . . terrible things. The family will dissolve: parents and children will be no longer the old and the young: brothers

> and sisters will meet as strangers after a hundred years separation: the ties of blood will lose their innocence."

In the fourth book of Shaw's "metabiological pentateuch" the disaster has taken place. The scene is placed in Galway during the thirty-first century A.D.—Ireland being Shaw's tongue-in-cheek selection as the world's most advanced country. Central figure of the moment is The Elderly Gentleman, a traveller from Britain who has been driven to the point of suicide through his futile efforts to explain his own nineteenth-century outlook. Saved from self-destruction by his ninety-four-year-old male nurse who has been assigned the task of keeping him out of mischief, Elderly Gentleman declares he shall go mad trying to reply to their "childish" questions and suggests they may as well call him "Daddy" and get it over with. The nurse responds with surprise that he did not know the old man's name was Daddy. Elderly Gentleman retorts that is *not* his name; he is Joseph Popham Bolge Bluebin Barlow, O.M., but this array fails to impress the guard who replies that he prefers to call him Daddy.

> THE ELDERLY GENTLEMAN
>
> People will think I am your father.
>
> THE MAN
>
> Sh-sh! People here never allude to such relationships. It is not quite delicate, is it? What does it matter whether you are my father or not? [292]

The fatherless society suggested here in which, as a matter of good taste, fathers were neither referred to nor mentioned, received further support in Part V: *As Far As Thought Can Reach.* Here parthenogenesis is at last established and babies are produced oviparously.

Made to order for Shaw's interest in illegitimacy were France's Charles VII and Jean Dunois, bastard son of Louis, Duc d'Orleans. In these instances, Shaw made theatrical capital over the doubts surrounding the birth of Charles as well as the undenied illegitimacy of Dunois. *Saint Joan* (1923) opens with Gentleman-at-Arms Poulengey arguing with Captain de Baudricourt. He believes that Joan should be given a chance to show what she can do against the English—after all, he pointed out, they occupy half the country as well as Paris itself. As to the Dauphin, he was holed up somewhere like a rat, except that, unlike a rat, he refused to fight. And no wonder, Poulengey continued, he might not even be a real Dauphin for his own mother denied his right to the throne, and who else would know better? Just think of it, he concluded, the Queen declaring her own son illegitimate! At his court in Touraine, the Dauphin (really Charles VII but as yet uncrowned) is not treated with the deference due to him as a royal personage. He grumbles that they deal with him as they please because he is not a fighter and because he owes them money but, let them remember, through his veins ran the blood royal.

THE ARCHBISHOP

> Even that has been questioned, your Highness. One hardly recognizes in you the grandson of Charles the Wise.[293]

Receiving news from Captain de Baudricourt that a Saint is coming to raise the siege at Orleans, drive out the English and crown him King in the Cathedral at Rheims, the Dauphin exults that as holy as he is, the Saint is coming to see himself and not the Archbishop—*she* knows the blood royal. So certain is the Dauphin that the Maid will recognize him that he arranges for a public demonstration of her infallibility: he will change places with one of the court and the Maid will choose. On her arrival Joan sifts the crowd of courtiers and pounces unerringly on the Dauphin who then declares triumphantly

> You see, all of you: she knew the blood royal. Who dare say now that I am not my father's son. . . . [?]

Prominently featured in the play is French General Jean Dunois who is described in the stage directions as being well built, having a broad brow and a pointed chin which gave his face a triangular effect. His natural expression is one of friendliness, but one also gains the impression (writes the author) that this is also a capable man who, if he ever had them, has long ago shed all false illusions and affectations and, consequently, has little patience with the ignominy attached to his illegitimacy. When Joan, seeking him out at the battlefront on the River Loire, inquires directly whether he is the Bastard of Orleans, Dunois replies "cooly and sternly" by directing her attention to the bend sinister on his war shield. Additional touches to the sketch of Dunois are given through Bluebeard who, when discussing the military situation, paints him in a manner somehow reminiscent of the heroes in Sonny's dreamworld. Commanding the troops, said Bluebeard, was Jack Dunois

> "the brave Dunois, the handsome Dunois, the wonderful invincible Dunois, the darling of the all the ladies, the beautiful bastard."

Pamphilius, secretary to King Magnus of *The Apple Cart* (1929), does not believe that one can ask one's father anything about himself, while Boanerges knows neither father nor mother. Paying his respects to Magnus on the occasion of his appointment to the Cabinet, Republican Boanerges confers with the King in the matter of ruling the country. The King, he declares, must withdraw from active participation in government affairs and content himself with being a rubber stamp monarch. Magnus, who has apparently been up against republicans before this, easily leads Boanerges about by the nose through his intellectual superiority and by his skillful use of flattery at a level tailored to his latest minister. He congratulates Boanerges on his rise from political obscurity to King's minister and contrasts this extraordinary achievement with his own accidental accession to the throne which could not have been his, if he had had to depend upon his own merits. On the other hand

> If I had been born as you were in the—in the—
>
> BOANERGES
>
> In the gutter. Out with it. Picked up by a policeman at the foot of Captain Coram's statue. Adopted by the policeman's grandmother, bless her! [294]

Too True To Be Good (1931) delights in a secretly-ordained clergyman turned burglar whose father is an atheist. Answering to the name of Popsy, he and his companion in crime (a lady called Sweetie) have planned to rob The Patient (victim of a doting mother) of her necklace but instead, they invite her to steal it herself (which they will sell) and for a fifty per cent commission they will help her to sunshine, freedom and LIFE. The Patient, secretly delighted, is outraged. Fifty per cent! Why, it's out-and-out robbery. But believing herself to be dreaming, agrees—reasoning that if she awakens she will never escape from her family and social position and adding parenthetically that it was all very well for Popsy and Sweetie since they were not ladies and gentlemen. The burglar is quick to point out that on this score she could rest easy. His own rank, he asserted, was even higher than hers, for her people made their money in trade whilst his were either landowners or in the administration of Crown Colonies. As for Sweetie, she might have been born to the purple

> but for the unfortunate fact that her parents, though united in the sight of heaven, were not legally married.[295]

In his seventy-eighth year, Shaw again dispensed with parents by again producing a child who owed nothing to anyone, but this time conception and gestation took place within a test tube instead of the confining walls of an eggshell. *The Simpleton of the Unexpected Isles* (1934) has its stage blessed by the presence of another clergyman who goes by the distracting name of Phosphor Hammingtap. So baptized, he mourns, because he was not a "natural" baby but a nitrogen baby and explained that his "father" was a famous biological chemist, thus giving the reader (or playviewer) to understand that he was manufactured in the laboratory.[296] Further to Hypatia and John Tarleton's impassioned prayers for the extirpation of families, GBS obliged with a dramatization of Judgment Day. An Angel has trumpeted the Call from Heaven and, armed with a flaming sword, dispenses fiery justice to the useless, the selfish and the mischievous, with England being among the first victims. Pra receives the reports by telephone and repeats them to her audience. Disappearance and panic are the keynotes. The Stock Exchange is closed—all but two members have vanished. The House of Commons is bloody with corpses, only fourteen members being saved, none of Cabinet rank. The House of Lords is more fortunate—fifty remain whose one virtue in common is the fact that not one of them has ever attended his own offices. Mayfair is a Sahara and six hotels are guestless.

Westminster Abbey is jammed, but the congregation evaporates with such speed that the dean is left sermonizing the choir. Sir Ruthless Bonehead, professor of Mechanistic Biology, announces that he will lecture on the current epidemic of disappearances. He disappears himself before he can utter the first syllable. The medical fraternity as a class vaporize without a single exception whilst the bar and clergy are, for the most part, unaccountably exempted. And, of course

> Happy husbands and fathers disappear from the family dinner with the soup.[297]

The garden had been weeded.

As many another Shakespeare addict, Shaw thought the fifth act of *Cymbeline* not as convincing as it could be and, at someone's suggestion, supplied a new ending in his *Cymbeline Refinished* (1937). A comparison of these two endings shows certain differences that contribute to the significance of these studies. Briefly, according to Shakespeare's account of the kidnapping of King Cymbeline's two infant children, Belarius confessed to Cymbeline twenty years later that it was he who stole them, but though he had brought up the children as his own, he would sacrifice his love for their sake and return them to their rightful father. Cymbeline accepted the explanation, was reunited with his sons Guiderius and Arviragus and granted Belarius full pardon for his splendid heroism in recent battle. Throughout these confessions, pardons and general exchanges, neither Guiderius nor Arviragus had expressed his gratification or disappointment with the proceedings, and it may be reasonably assumed they accepted this change in their destiny with fortitude if not with happiness. The Shavian treatment of reunited father and sons is, in the light of this section, no surprise; and if Guiderius and Arviragus were somewhat reserved in the Shakespearean account the Shavian version compensated with measure to spare. Belarius has urged Guiderius and Arviragus to offer their love and loyalty to Cymbeline:

GUIDERIUS

We three are fullgrown men
    and perfect strangers.
Can I change fathers as I'd change my shirt?

CYMBELINE

Unnatural whelp! What doth thy brother say?

ARVIRAGUS

I, royal, sir? Well, we have
reached an age
When fathers' helps are felt as hindrances.
I am tired of being preached at.[298]

Nettled, Cymbeline inquires of Belarius whether this insolence can be traced to his tutelage, but before Belarius can reply, Guiderius interjects that they have been taught to speak the truth. For his part, Belarius avows that he is at a loss to explain their unseemly behavior but philosophizes that neither Cymbeline nor himself can know what is in the minds of children and accepts the blame for their disrespectful address. Guiderius, however, will not have it. He would place the blame where it belongs—with God and adds, in a denial of sire,

I am of no man's making. I am I:
Take me or leave me.

Iachimo is so impressed by these sentiments that he counsels Lucius to note Guiderius well for, mark you, he has just heard the future king of England. This does not escape Guiderius who retorts that the prospect of being England's monarch has no charm for him, recalling that when he lived in a cave he dreamt of a palace filled with seers renowned for their wisdom, soldiers famous for their might, all living the lives of holy saints and all, if he were their prince, under his command. But, he continued, since then he has been awakened. To be a real prince one must be an oafish lout, a Cloten (an ass who "cannot take two from twenty, for his heart, and leave eighteen"), be tormented by the babbling of a retinue of sycophants, be forced to revere and adore gods trumped up by the priests, be compelled to marry a woman not of his own choosing and be ordered at every turn by ancient dodderers who cry "Don't!" or, even worse, "Do!"

Oh no, sir: give me back the dear old cave
And my unflattering four footed friends.
I abdicate, and pass the throne to [Arviragus].

ARVIRAGUS

Do you, by heavens? Thank you for nothing,
Brother.

I cannot affirm that Shaw's refinishing of *Cymbeline* was a more satisfactory conclusion or that the revolt of Guiderius and Arviragus was an essential part of that reconstruction. But it can, I believe, be said that Shaw's manner of treatment was predictable, that is, that sons would be either foundlings or reject their fathers.

The dramatic procession of evidence illustrating Shaw's preoccupation with illegitimacy cannot be really completed without a glance at two items that are, properly speaking, outside the domain of his strictly creative efforts. In the preface to *Misalliance* subtitled *Parents and Children* (1910), Shaw went into the subject of the family and its internal relationships at great length, from which the following is the briefest of abstracts and in itself restricted to one of many facets. He asserted that until the family unit as it is presently known disappears, no one will "dare" to analyze the difference between parental affection and ordinary human fellow-feeling. He believed that when that parental affection continued into a period unnecessary to the child's well-being, the child might become "morbid" and might be permanently injured if parents persisted in this direction. The proper course, he continued, was for the children and their parents to break off these relations when they are no longer needed. In support of this proposal he offered the observation that one is not surprised to learn

> that some people hold that blood relationship should be kept a secret from the persons related, and that the happiest condition in this respect is that of the foundling who, if he ever meets his parents or brothers or sisters, passes them by without knowing them.[299]

While avoiding personal involvement with the conviction of "some people," I suggest that GBS held this view himself, a position that followed logically from his own uncertainties.

The second example outside the canon is manifested by Shaw's sensitivity to a charge made in *My Dear Wells, A Manual for the Haters of England*. Its author, Henry Arthur Jones, formerly one of GBS's closest friends, severed his relations with Wells, Shaw and others as a result of the impact of World War I upon Socialists and writers. He was bitter to the point of hysteria in his denunciation of all those who were critical of England's war policies, paying particular attention to the seditious GBS. Unable to understand the universalist outlook of Shaw and unable to treat him critically, Jones tried to account for his "eccentricities" by the use of poetic metaphor. Shaw, he said, was

> a freakish homunculus germinated outside lawful procreation. For no issue are you of human parentage. The hag Sedition was your mother, and Perversity begot you; Mischief was your midwife, Misrule your nurse, and Unreason brought you up to her feet—no other ancestry and rearing had you.[300]

Shaw was aware of Jones's intent to impugn his intellectual legitimacy; but his reaction suggested that he was disproportionately disturbed—possibly because he believed that Jones's outburst could be construed as reflecting on his physical legitimacy. Writing in *The* [London] *Sunday Chronicle* for 20 November 1921, GBS "reviewed" the book by knocking out Jones with a dazzling display of literary haymakers—one of which, however, missed its target and headed straight for the chin of G. Bernard Shaw. Calling his article *The Invective of Henry Arthur Jones,* GBS battered Jones from corner to corner without (to carry the metaphor further) affecting his own respiratory rate. He was a patient man, said Shaw, and timid by nature—but this time old friend Jones had gone a bit too far. He had produced a book of fulminations in which he (Shaw) and Wells were the principal victims. Such vilification, GBS continued, had not been seen in English literature since Milton and Salmasius exchanged views on republicanism and monarchy. After systematically demolishing Jones's "political" criticisms, Shaw turned to the book's more vituperative aspects. Wells, reported Shaw fairly, was described as "a mischievous and brainless ignoramus." As for his opinion of Shaw,

GBS accurately quoted Jones's characterization of himself as "a freakish homunculus germinated outside lawful procreation" but neglected to supply the context which nullified its otherwise plain meaning that GBS was a human oddity conceived and born outside the institution of marriage. Focussing upon these seven words Shaw advanced aggressively. By the way, he casually noted, Jones's statement regarding his birth had already influenced several persons to conclude that either (a) Jones was hopelessly insane or (b) Shaw's mother was, *sui generis,* of the mothers of Falconbridge and Dunois. In contradiction thereof, Shaw offered that his family could trace their lineage to Shaigh, Macduff's third son of whom Shakespeare sang, was "from his mother's womb untimely ripped." He ventured that it must have been some remembrance of this genealogical gem that inspired Jones to so shameful a defamation adding

> I protest I am the unquestioned lawful heir of my mother's property and my father's debts; and if Jones will come to tea (or any other meal) with me, not only will he be cordially welcomed, but he can inspect the family photographs, which will convince him that, extraordinary as I am, I am none the less unmistakeably the son of my reputed father.

Expressing his belief that Jones's publishers would never have dared to gamble on such a "roaring libel" without Jones's express assurance that they could count on his friendship with GBS, Shaw concluded that he was, of course, quite right—there would be no action.[301]

Jones would have had little difficulty in expressing himself precisely had he wished to question the circumstances of Shaw's earthly conception and birth, but that this was not his intention can be seen specifically in the second sentence: "For no issue are you of human parentage." Nevertheless, it deeply affected Shaw, whose normally razor-sharp wit must have been, I suggest, badly blunted with fright. His claim of descent from Shaigh,[302] while unsmilingly couched, could not have been issued seriously and may have been a ruse to disarm through humor. Further, the consternation wrought within the breast of GBS by Jones's unfortunate metaphor was dramatically illustrated in his publicly-tendered invitation to Jones to come and inspect evidence which would prove "unmistakeably" that GBS was the son of his father. The evidence: a comparison of the living features of bearded George Bernard Shaw to the photographs of the long-deceased (1885) and bearded George Carr Shaw. Nothing could be more reasonable—for what son or daughter could hope to produce better proofs?

When the specter of irregularity with regard to his birth appeared (whether real or fancied), Bernard Shaw automatically rose to do battle. Further, his consistent absorption with illegitimacy and associated matters in twenty-five novels, stories, plays and articles over a period of fifty-eight years, in my judgment, constitutes presumptive evidence that Bernard Shaw harbored grave misgivings regarding the circumstances of his own conception.

V / Dublin II

I

THE EARLIEST EVIDENCE of Shaw's preschool education can be traced to his mother and strikes a pleasant note amid the perpetual janglings of her alleged coldness and unmotherliness. He reported in the *Sketches* that she taught him a half-dozen nursery rhymes[1] and in a half-forgotten nook of dusty recollections confirmed the picture of a patient mother urging her son to read. Writing in *T. P.'s Weekly,* Thomas Power ("Tay Pay") O'Connor's publication, for December 19, 1902, GBS obliged that journal with an account of the encouragement his mother gave him to struggle through the preliminary portions of *Robinson Crusoe* until he landed on the desert isle, after which he experienced no further difficulties.[2] Quoting Shaw, Henderson recited even a possibly earlier lesson that Sonny received. When he was four years of age, GBS told him, he was taught that all matter could be classified into one of four "elements," i.e., fire, air, earth and water, but who taught Sonny these Empedocletian concepts was not revealed.[3]

Expanding on the subject of the literary diet of his childhood, GBS further informed the readers of *T.P.'s Weekly* that he could not remember what his first book was any more than he could remember his first meal, nor could he remember a time when he did not (and could not) read anything that came his way. He remembered that the two literary sensations of the day were *The Pilgrim's Progress* (which he read with great interest at the age of five)[4] and *The*

Arabian Nights. He added that these selections proved that as an infant he was as good a critic as he was now (at forty-six), but that he could not then offer such artful support for his opinions. Continuing, he wrote that he seemed to have come into the world having a familiarity with *The Ancient Mariner, John Gilpin* and, for some reason unknown to him, Baron Trenck and his escapes from prison. He also developed an appetite for Shakespeare from the little scraps printed under Selous' illustrations, but for children's books he had no use—from the "accursed" *Swiss Family Robinson* onwards. These, he said, he always despised and loathed for their hypocrisy, sickly immorality, dishonesty and their damned dullness, concluding that his moral sense, like his literary sense, was a healthy one.[5] Before his sixth birthday, he had read all the fairy tales he could lay hands on[6] and Charles Lever's *A Day's Ride* and had picked up a knowledge of the multiplication and pence tables; he had learned (through the Reverend William George Carroll, his maternal uncle)[7] Latin declensions and conjugations before he was ten; and by the time he was thirteen years of age, he had gone through Dickens' works. If GBS did not remember the first book he read, he did remember the first one he owned: the Bible, a gift with which he became quite familiar and which, as a boy, he read from cover to cover, simply because he wished to do what no other boy had done.[8] An example of Shavian precocity was illustrated in his account of a rainy day on the quays of Dublin's River Liffey. He, being then small enough to be carried in his father's arms, "electrified" the crowd sharing the shelter from the rain by reading aloud all the bills.[9] The ubiquitous Winsten, apparently one of those electrified, reported the occasion, adding a festive note not recalled by Shaw. Mr. Carr Shaw, wrote Winsten, "beamed with pleasure and celebrated the achievement by sharing his drink with the little fellow." [10]

Shaw's oft-repeated assertions that he did not remember a time when he could not read bears a moment in passing. Typical specimen was his comment in the preface to *Misalliance* wherein he stated that he had no recollection of receiving instructions in reading and writing and, consequently, presumed that he had come into the world with both these faculties ready for employment.[11] At the age of ninety he suddenly realized that this belief of many years was "nonsense" and gave credit where due: Miss Caroline Hill. But before this he had, in a touching sketch, described how Miss Hill performed some of her duties and ended on a theme boldly trumpeted throughout his life. Miss Hill, Shaw wrote, attempted to instill into Sonny and his two sisters a love for poetry by declaiming before them "Stop; for thy tread is on an empire's dust," but, alas, the poor lady only succeeded in awakening in them a sense of mockery. When they were saucy, Miss Hill would "punish" them with little strokes of her fingers the gentleness of which, Shaw said, could not have disturbed a fly. On occasion, however, she would convince Sonny that he had been naughty and he, therefore, would be obliged to feel disgraced and weep. It was Miss Hill, he wrote, who taught him the basic arithmetical functions of addition, subtraction and multiplication but somehow failed to impart the intelligence in division, because she never explained what "into" meant as used in "four into eight," "three into nine" and so forth. This deficiency, reported GBS, was repaired in his first day at school and he thereafter declared "solemnly" that this was the only knowledge he ever received in school.[12] At the age of seventy-seven Shaw remembered Miss Hill by placing her poetic declamation into the Second Conversation of *Village Wooing* but it was not until his ninetieth year that he came to realize how much Miss Hill had taught him and (she being long deceased) he became a contributor to the Governess's Benevolent Institution.[13] In his ninety-first year he admitted at last that it was she who also taught him his alphabet.[14]

II

SOMETIME BEFORE SONNY'S NINTH BIRTHDAY—that is to say, while the Shaws were still in Synge Street, the decision was made to enroll him in some section of Dublin's chaotic school system. In the main, the primary schools were (and are) sectioned into three general groupings and consisted of Christian Brothers Schools (secular educational arms of the Roman Catholic Church), National Schools (open to all classes and denominations) and a sprinkling of schools sponsored by various Protestant institutions catering to children of the elite. As his family was of the Protestant Ascendancy, Sonny's enrollment in either the Christian Brothers Schools or the National Schools was, of course, unthinkable, and it thus came to pass that the Wesleyan Connexional School must be debited for instilling in young Shaw his hatred of schools. According to Harris, this school was chosen by George Carr because it was one of the "genteel" Protestant schools.[15] If so (and it was undoubtedly so), then its gentility was not in the slightest danger of being eclipsed by its pedagogical pretensions.

Founded in the 1840's, Wesleyan was then located at 79 St. Stephen's Green, just less than a mile from Synge Street, and had provision for "boarders" and "day-boys" each group calling the other "skinnies." The year of Sonny's entry into his first school has not found the biographers in agreement with the record. Pearson reported it to be at the age of ten or in 1866;[16] Ervine had it in 1867.[17] Henderson was more specific, quoting from, presumably, official sources. He reported that, according to the roll book at Wesleyan, Shaw was entered for the first time on April 13, 1867[18] which, it happens, was a Saturday. Examination of the roll books of Wesleyan (since absorbed by Wesley College) disclosed the following:

Name	Quarter Ending	Tuition	Books & Stationery	Elocution	Total
Shaw, G. B.	31 July 1865	2 Gns	3/6	2/6	2 gns 6/
Shaw, G. B.	31 Oct 1867	2 Gns	3/6	2/6	2 gns 6/
Shaw, G. B.	30 Apr 1868	2 Gns	3/6	2/6	2 gns 6/
Shaw, G. B.	31 July 1868	2 Gns	3/6	2/6	2 gns 6/
Shaw, G. B.	31 Oct 1868	2 Gns	3/6	2/6	2 gns 6/

According to these records,[19] it will be seen that young Shaw entered school for the first time on or about 1 May 1865 and was, therefore, aged nine. He seems to have lasted for but three months, not returning until two years had passed. Reenrolled on or about 1 August 1867, he again left at the end of the quarter to come back three months later on about the first of February, but this time he completed nine months in unbroken succession before shaking the dust of Wesleyan from his boots. No facts were available to account for these entrances and exits, but perhaps they expressed his unhappiness with the curriculum and activities of the school.

The scholastic record of day-boy Shaw at Wesleyan was not available as such and existed only in the meager recollections of one of the school officials and in the richly-charged memory of GBS. To Henderson came a letter in 1909 from Principal Crawford of Wesley College who wrote that according to predecessor Dr. Crook, Shaw seemed to be continuously at or near the bottom of his class, except for one surprising burst of scholarship that distinguished his otherwise undistinguished sojourn. Commenting on this, Shaw confided to Henderson that it was only because of his familiarity with the Bible that he was enabled to do exceptionally well in an examination on Scriptural knowledge.[20] The Reverend Gerald G. Myles, Principal, also contributed some information, though on examination it proved to be more in the nature of opinion than fact and may have been influenced by Shaw's gruff and contemptuous dismissal of Wesley College as an institution dedicated to "learning and decency." Myles, in response to a fellow divine's request for information, offered:

> . . . the school records are of the scantiest nature, and Shaw was regarded as such a disreputable character by my respectable predecessors that nobody thought fit to enquire into his school career. . . . The staple academic diet in those days was Latin, to which was added as side-dishes, English, Arithmetic and Scriptures. . . . as to the books studied there is no record . . .
>
> Rev. Gerald G. Myles, M.A.
> Principal Wesley College

As Myles's predecessors had long disappeared before his succession to the principalship, leaving records of the "scantiest nature," it could have been difficult, conceivably, for the Reverend to document his source for the behavior and character of the young Bernard Shaw.

Shaw's own memories of his days in Wesleyan were touched

upon at odd moments but were always expressed in a manner in which ambiguity played no part. In his last prose work of major importance, GBS discoursed on education in general and at length reached the particular. Here he admitted—well, perhaps bragged—that he was not quite the model student. He was, he wrote, "a shamelessly unscrupulous liar" when it came to finding excuses for undone lessons and exercises, giving as his real reasons his occupation with reading readable books and otherwise absorbing culture.[21] Such laudable interests were not, however, Sonny's only activities. Elsewhere, he disclosed that he formed friendships with members of gangs that made mischief for mischief's sake. They were, he concluded, engaged in a grand conspiracy directed against schoolmasters as well as policemen.[22] He reported, in a more direct attack, that the school's curriculum was created and operated in the belief that a knowledge of Latin was the sum and substance of all wisdom. Moreover, the Wesleyan method of teaching Latin was at once both ineffective and "barbarous" in that the boys were required to learn the declensions and conjugations by drill, and failure to do so meant a caning or staying on after classes. Like Shakespeare and Dickens, he concluded, he left school with little Latin and less Greek.[23]

After the passage of years had brought fame to G. Bernard Shaw, Wesleyan, in March of 1901, paid homage to him as one of its distinguished sons. Replying to the honor by telegram, he assured a Reverend E. G. Seale that he was quite right in claiming him as a distinguished former pupil, adding that he was distinguished all right—distinguished as the idlest boy in Wesleyan, as any of his fellow students, if they were still alive, could testify. He would never, he said, never forget the Wesleyan Connexional for laying the basis of his firm belief in the need of a drastic revision of teaching methods and with that he wished to be remembered to all his fellow victims—both old masters and old boys. Not so friendly was his response on 16 May 1945 to the Reverend J. Lynham Cairns who, on the centenary celebrations of Wesley, wrote to Shaw asking him to say something pleasant about his alma mater, coolly requesting that he also "send a few thousand pounds sterling for the advancement of learning and decency in [Wesley's] second century." From Ayot St. Lawrence came a bolt in the form of a postcard. Would Mr. Shaw say something complimentary about the school in which he spent some of his happy childhood? There was nothing, barked Shaw, absolutely nothing, to be said in favor of the Wesleyan Connexional. Jammed with boarders, it was an ordinary dwelling house having a large schoolroom in the rear with a long areaway doing duty as a play yard. Sanitation? Primitive. Teaching paraphernalia? None. Lectures? None. Explanations? None. Teaching? Consisted of asking questions (largely concerning Latin vocabulary) and caning for incorrect answers. Classes? Overcrowded with barely enough time for one question per student per lesson—in short

> Everything that a school ought not to be; nothing that it ought. My curse on it. Forget it.
>
> G. Bernard Shaw

III

SONNY'S FIFTEEN MONTHS AT WESLEYAN were educationally more retrogressive than progressive. The Shaws—now living in Hatch Street in three-part harmony—somehow learned or suspected that Sonny was deriving no benefits, for his uncle and first Latin tutor, the Reverend William George Carroll was called in for consultation. In this connection, there seems to be some doubt as to the person showing the most interest in the case of Sonny and his schooling. GBS has himself recorded that Lee, despite his preoccupation with musical affairs, found time to "think" that something should be done. The Harris book expressed it similarly. Lee, someone wrote, now and then "protested that nothing was coming of the schooling" but, being too busy with his teaching, concerts and operas, did not "interfere seriously." [24] Winsten offered a different view. He held that the Reverend Uncle was invited by Mr. Carr Shaw to step in at this time to prepare Bob for Trinity College and for his eventual admission into the

Church. Carroll, wrote Winsten, "was only too happy to do this, for in his heart he wanted to counteract the influence of Vandeleur Lee, whom he called 'The Jew.' "[25] Uncle William George examined Sonny and found that not only had he learnt nothing but that he had forgotten the Latin he had taught him.[26] If the Reverend suggested corrective measures along with his report on Sonny, they are unknown. At any rate, Sonny left or was withdrawn from Wesleyan and, for some period between 1 November 1868 and 31 January 1869, attended a private school in Glasthule,[27] a small community near Dalkey where the family probably spent that summer and fall in Torca Cottage.

With the return of the Shaws to Hatch Street, the question of Sonny's education must have been raised again, and this time it appears that Professor Lee played an important if not the leading role. Henderson's treatment of this event suggested that he either did not know the identity of Sonny's benefactor or that he was bound not to divulge his name. He reported that "a friend of the family," knowing that Sonny was not doing well in school and acquiring knowledge in matters not normally within the compass of the Wesleyan syllabus, consulted an acquaintance who taught drawing in the Central Model Boys School—a unit of the National Schools of Ireland. Whatever Henderson's reason for avoiding Lee's name in this connection, it could not have achieved its purpose, since Lee had already been named as the friend some eight years earlier by Shaw himself. What marked Henderson's omission as noteworthy was that, according to his footnote, the information came straight from the book and page in which the name of the friend was given as "George John Vandaleur Lee."[28] Not sharing Henderson's delicacy, Ervine flatly declared that responsibility for Sonny's "incarceration" in the Central Model must be laid at Lee's door.[29] Winsten likewise asserted that it was Lee who paved the way into what he called the "Catholic School," incidentally noting that Sonny had to bring tuition fees to the sum of five shillings at regular but undefined periods.[30]

Shaw's own account served as the model for all. Lee, he said, while deeply involved with his musical interests, believed that something should be done about Sonny's school problem. It was clear,

GBS continued, that his attendance in Wesleyan was teaching him nothing, except what he should not have been taught. It was at this moment that Lee struck up an acquaintance with a Mr. Peach, a drawing master on the staff of the Central Model Boys School in Marlborough Street. Mr. Peach, it seems, had impressed Lee with the professional level and integrity of Central Model as compared to the more genteel schools which, Mr. Peach claimed, were worthless. Central Model, Shaw went on informatively, was "undenominational and classless in theory but in fact Roman Catholic" whose pupils, when their parents could afford it, brought five shillings at regular but undefined periods for their tuition and, when their parents couldn't afford it, received a caning in lieu thereof.[31] Apart from the reference to the "Catholic" nature of Central Model, the foregoing is chiefly remarkable for the solicitude of Lee for Sonny's welfare in contrast to the apparent lack of interest on the part of Mr. and Mrs. Shaw.

IV

BERNARD SHAW MARKED HIS ENTRANCE into the Central Model Boys School as one of the most extraordinary events in his life. The gravity with which GBS regarded—or would have the world regard—this catastrophe to a Shaw is evident in the electrifying heading to Chapter Four of *Sixteen Self Sketches*:

SHAME AND WOUNDED SNOBBERY
A Secret Kept For 80 Years

Head thrown back, eyebrows bristling, GBS advanced to the podium and, with just the right touch of his soft voice, laid bare his haunting secret:

> I now confess to an episode in my boyhood formerly so repugnant to me that for 80 years I never mentioned it to any mortal creature, not even to my wife.[32]

He gave a review of his education, an account of his induction into the Central Model and an exposition of the social, moral, economic and religious aspects of caste systems in general. Was this the confession? It must be—there are no other possibilities:

> So I was sent to Marlborough Street, and at once lost caste outside it and became a boy with whom no Protestant young gentleman would speak or play.[33]

Twenty-eight words in length, this sentence distills the thirty-five-hundred-word Chapter Four into what GBS offered as his "confession." It states that he attended a certain school and for eighty years thereafter believed that he would be disgraced, should it be discovered that he had gone there, before he was prepared to release the information himself. His presence in a school or, for that matter, in any sort of body of which the social composition was not exclusively genteel and Protestant was unthinkable for him or any other Shaw, and GBS has expressed this fact with trenchancy. Recording his first impressions of Central Model, he declared that, from the Shaw point of view, it was "inconceivable" that he—the son of an Irish Protestant gentleman and merchant—would in any way mingle with the Catholic sons of lower middle class Catholic tradesmen and shopkeepers.[34]

Ervine accepted Shaw's confession without reserve. He explained that the Central Model, though "nominally non-sectarian, was, in fact, Roman Catholic, since the majority of its pupils belonged to that denomination." [35] This condition, Ervine asserted, was sufficient reason for Sonny's humiliation but offered little hope for those who had never lived in Ireland to understand its full significance. "Horror" was Winsten's key word. Sonny was "horrified" when he discovered that most of his schoolmates were sons of tradesmen and petty shopkeepers and, as recorded earlier, designated the Central Model as a "Catholic" school.[36] Henderson gave considerable and respectful attention to Shaw's confession but, with admirable independence of mind, would not accept it within the confines of Shaw's explanation. He held that Shaw's suppression of the Central Model incident from his wife, his biographer and from the world constituted a "pretty problem" for the psychiatrist, since the humiliation went "far deeper," and he asserted that Shaw harbored a complex in which he supposed the disclosure of this incident would reduce his aristocratic wife's respect for him. By 1949, Henderson argued, there was no further reason for Shaw's silence, as Charlotte had died six years earlier, and, consequently, his objections to the release of his shameful secret were no longer valid. Henderson additionally implied that Shaw, knowing quite well that he would eventually become the object of a "floodlight of research," realized it would be pointless to withhold the secret further, since it was bound to be discovered.[37]

Henderson brought out an excellent point, but I suggest that Shaw's fear of offending his wife's sense of class was only a part of a greater fear: that independent and unrestrained research might lead to frightful consequences. Finally, Henderson's belief that Shaw released the Marlborough story, *because* it would ultimately be discovered is unconvincing for two reasons: (a) it would have been extremely unlikely that Shaw's presence in Central Model would have been uncovered and (b) even had it been uncovered, the "floodlight of research" would reveal nothing but the simple fact that Shaw attended a school which was *not* a Roman Catholic school and *was* what the record and the registrations declared it to have been: "undenominational and classless."

Several visits to the Central Model were necessary before the dusty archives yielded, and it might have been impossible to open them but for the sympathetic and energetic offices of retired headmaster Brian Mac Giolla Phadraig to whom I am deeply indebted. From the roll book in which Sonny's name is entered, the following bloc of enrollees was selected as being a group typical of the whole and is reproduced here exactly (less individual identities) as written nearly a hundred years ago.

[Monday,] 1 February 1869

Reg. Nr.	Name	Age	Religion	Address	Father's Occupation	Blank
4688			E.C.		Carpenter	
4689			E.C.		Civil Engineer	
4690	Geo. Shaw	12½	E.C.	1, Hatch St.	Corn Merchant	Left 11 Sept '69 No reason given
4691			E.C.		Hotel porter	

[Monday,] 1 February 1869 (continued)

Reg. Nr.	Name	Age	Religion	Address	Father's Occupation	Blank
4692			E.C.		Farmer	
4693			R.C.		Shopkeeper	
4694			E.C.		Carpenter	
4695			R.C.		Butcher	
4696			R.C.		Solicitor	
4697			R.C.		Clerk	
4698			E.C.		Sgt. Royal B'racks	
4699			R.C.		Bricklayer	
4700			O.D.		Gaol Warder	
4701			E.C.		Hatter	

With regard to the religion and occupation of the lads' fathers, this page is representative of the whole. In this particular bloc there were eight members of the Established Church, five of Roman Catholic persuasion and one whose "O.D." suggested him to be a member of "Other Denomination," but, as someone with a saving Irish wit remarked, perhaps it stood for "Orthodox Dissenter." In any case, if anyone had cause for resentment, no one could have been more justified than the son of the gaol warder. With respect to its commercial complexion, the group had a heavy list to the less genteel occupations, but proper assessment of this aspect could not be realized without equivalent examination of fathers' occupations in Shaw's two other schools and these were not available.

In pursuit of Shaw's purpose in alleging a traumatic disturbance apprehensively secreted for eighty years, I suggest that, though Sonny was genuinely dismayed in finding himself in an institution with social untouchables, he adapted himself to his environment and accepted at least some of its conditions. His recorded impressions of the Central Model tell us something of his feelings. It was, he wrote, a huge place faced with high unclimbable iron gates and picketings which, so far as he was concerned, might well have been surmounted by the Dantean caveat "All hope abandon, ye who enter here." For him to pass through these iron gates and actually mix with its "hosts" of Catholic children was, from the viewpoint of the Shaws, unimaginable.[38] Nonagenarian Shaw told his confessors that even before his admission to Central Model, Sonny had already been impressed with the paradox of The Merchant and The Tailor. Speaking of his wretchedness in finding himself inside the hated gates, he acknowledged that he was already in rebellion against the snobberies of the Shaws and acutely aware that his father's tailor was able to afford a cottage in Dalkey, a "yacht" in Dalkey Bay, dress and equip his sons far better than Mr. Shaw and, more, send them to costly schools and colleges. To class the tailor as the social inferior of his unprosperous father who never paid his bills on time was as ridiculous to him at twelve and a half years of age as it was now in his nineties.[39] As to his religious prejudices, Shaw appended to the account that he, at this time, was not in the least the arrogant Protestant—in fact he was proud of being the Boy Atheist who had already ceased "irrational" praying. Further, he gave credit to his mother and her musical circle for sweeping his mind clear of his bigotry towards Roman Catholics as well as his instilled belief that when they died they were dispatched forthwith to hell.[40] Further evidence of Sonny's rejection of unreasoning bias against his fellow Catholics was given to Cousin Goodliffe. In his ninety-third year Shaw recalled proudly that his mother was a well-known amateur singer who discovered that Providence had given musical talent to Catholics as well as to other religious factions. Her participation (as a singer) in Catholic church services, in the concerts of the Amateur Musical Society and their rehearsals which were held in his home all had salubrious effects on the preteen-age Shaw and he frankly acknowledged the effect:

> In this way I learnt early that the Catholic bourgeoisie, instead of being, as I had been taught, an inferior class on its way to hell, was in fact more cultivated and much kinder and better mannered than the Protestant.[41]

Snubbed by his friends, young Shaw was perhaps compensated by the consciousness of his own developing superiority. In a comparison of Sonny at Central Model with Sonny at Wesleyan, GBS wrote that the two were altogether different persons. At Wesleyan, he never had the slightest inclination to learn his lessons or to tell the truth to that universal enemy and hangman—the schoolmaster, whereas at the Central Model the evolutionary development which he had described in *Man and Superman* as the "birth of moral passion" had begun to flower within him and he declared it was here that his scruples began.[42] Behind him forever was the "gangster" and "shameless liar" phase, and within the forbidding gates of Central Model he learnt his lessons (and disagreed with Irish history as written by English historians), made friends with the teachers and, during playtime refused to play, spending this period pacing back and forth with the teachers in their private compound.[43]

Apparently satisfied with the content of Chapter Four, GBS skillfully capped his confession and simultaneously lectured the psychoanalyst fraternity. For eighty years, he said, he had been unable to mention the Central Model affair to anyone, but now that he had broken the habit of shameful silence, he was "cured." Not a shadow of his early shame remained, for it had survived not as a complex but as a habit dismissed with no trouble whatsoever. This, he concluded, was an example of the defects as well as the effectiveness of psychotherapy, since instilled habits are curable while hereditary complexes are not.

Summarizing this examination of "Shame and Wounded Snobbery," I submit that Shaw's Marlborough Street confession was the playwright's device to forestall posthumous inquiries into the subject of his origins. What he said, however, is not, in any real sense, a confession at all. Sinned against rather than sinning, Sonny's experience may have given him some severe moments when his young Protestant friends rejected him, but their attitude, far from inducing a trauma, accelerated his adjustment to and recognition of the realities and absurdities of the world—an enormously important contribution to the growth of George Bernard Shaw. I do not think that his entrance into Central Model was so dreadful a shock as he would have us believe, for he had had considerable preparation for it in his victorious battle with the Shaw snobberies. Sonny's rejection of both social and religious distinctions—strengthened to a considerable degree before his enrollment in Central Model—at least cushioned if it did not cancel the shock engendered. I suggest that, in support of his life-long struggle to halt or deflect the analyst, the biographer or the merely inquisitive, Shaw, with a calculated strategy, confessed to a childhood event truthful enough in itself but extravagantly out of proportion to its significance. In offering an opinion to account for the confession of Marlborough Street, I am sensible of the danger of bending every word and every experience in favor of one's hypothesis, nevertheless I also suggest that there lodged within Shaw a very real psychic disturbance connected with his belief or suspicion that he was the son of his mother's musical colleague George John Lee. In confessing what he would have his audience believe to be his life's "abhorred secret," GBS hoped to block future inquiries into his Dublin days. Darkest confession trumpeted to the world, would it not now be clear to all that further probings could only be fruitless?

V

THE ATTITUDE AND CONDUCT of George Carr Shaw with respect to Sonny's entrance into an institution not up to the Shaw standards of gentility bears upon the education of George Bernard Shaw. If George Carr made any effort to prevent the boy's enrollment into the Central Model, the record does not show the manner of his opposition, but he was opposed to it. Henderson was the only biographer to comment on Mr. Shaw's temper and he drew a cooperative father: meek, mild and sanguine. He, wrote Henderson, knew the nature of the Central Model and was "concerned" by it but hoped that its academic reputation would more than compensate for the loss of caste.[44] Speaking of his own unwillingness to return to the Central Model, GBS reported that he bore his unhappy lot from February until September of 1869 when, for the first time, he set his foot down and regardless of all arguments and persuasions brought to bear, refused to return to that school. His father, he added, who was "as much ashamed of it as I was, and much less resolute, let me have my way . . ." GBS puts a veiled suggestion into this passage that he and his father had some disagreement on the question of his continuing in the Central Model or withdrawing from it. Judging George Carr from GBS's portrait of him, we would expect him to be opposed to his son's remaining in that school, and I believe Shaw used hazy phrasing in an effort to conceal, without actual falsification, the roles of his mother and Lee at this time. It is much more likely that the disagreement was between George Carr and Sonny on the one side and Lucinda and Lee on the other.

There are no official reports available on the progress or conduct of young Shaw in the Central Model, although the roll book included a note that on his admission he was graded into the third form and moved into the fourth three months later, a movement that does not suggest a laggard, uninterested or unteachable boy. None of the major biographers was able to throw light on Sonny's educational development in this school—and Winsten abhorred that vacuum. Being Shaw's neighbor in Ayot St. Lawrence, Stephen Winsten had (his readers were told) many conversations with GBS, and he drew upon them to enrich his *Jesting Apostle.* He stated that the drawing master, Mr. Peach, reported to his friend Professor Lee that "George Bernard Carr Shaw," despite all inducements to learn, showed no disposition whatever for any subject. Lee, continued Winsten, entreated Mr. Peach not to give up so easily and persevere in his encouragement to the boy, since "they" were at a loss as to what to do with him. Peach agreed and broadened Sonny's horizon by trips to the Dublin Art Gallery where he familiarized his pupil with the works of the old masters, discussed famous men and took him along on his painting journeys. Sonny's response to all this, added Winsten, was to be critical of his teachers. Peach went still further and, to satisfy friend Lee, invited young Shaw to join him in the teachers' private walk during playtime. This, Winsten concluded, merely increased Sonny's "conceit," thus convincing Peach that the boy was an unteachable snob, and he passed this opinion on to Lee.[45]

Ervine noted Sonny's unhappiness in the Central Model. He commented that it was the only school of which there was no mention in Shaw's autobiographical notes other than *Sixteen Self Sketches* and observed that GBS did not appear to have developed any friendships there or even have any memory of anyone associated with that place.

He illustrated Sonny's discomfiture in the Model school by pointing out, rather sympathetically, that an Etonian did not feel the social gap between himself and a Borstal Boy as "a boy of G.B.S.'s class and creed felt at being a pupil in the Central Model School, mixing on terms of equality with Micks!" [46]

Ervine's opinion that Shaw did not appear to have remembered anyone connected with the Central Model was accurate enough insofar as the available information allowed. But besides remembering drawing master Peach, GBS also recalled three other members of the Model school staff. Loewenstein, Shaw's High Commissioner of bibliography and memorabilia in general,[47] helped prepare the groundwork for *Shame and Wounded Snobbery* by entering into "Strictly Confidential" correspondence with Mac Giolla Phadraig, then headmaster in Marlborough Street. Writing (I suppose) from his private address in London, Dr. Loewenstein posed an undated (but received in Dublin 30 June 1947) and innocent query. Was the school the same one that existed during the eighteen-sixties? If so, were the records of students and teachers still available? Having received an affirmative reply, Loewenstein sent letter number two (written 7 July 1947 and on GBS's Ayot Saint Lawrence stationery) which prefaced that the matter was most delicate and could under no circumstances be released before Mr. Shaw published it himself toward the end of 1948. The headmaster was next informed that Mr. Shaw was a former pupil. Mr. Shaw said the name of his headmaster was Joist and that two of his teachers were named Bell and Ryan. Could the headmaster oblige by confirming these names, establish the dates of Mr. Shaw's admission and discharge, his class, subjects taken, his scholarship and his home address at this time? The last letter in the group bearing on this subject gratefully acknowledged receipt of the headmaster's reply and noted that both he and Mr. Shaw read it with great interest and were looking forward to receiving further information. Loewenstein expressed astonishment that the headmaster was not surprised at finding GBS on the school's roll, since he was raised as a Protestant but complimented him on his "perspicacity" in guessing one Geo. Shaw, Hatch St., to be GBS. Evidently disappointed at not receiving answers to some of his questions, Loewenstein commiserated in a letter of 16 July 1947 with Mac Giolla Phadraig on the destruction of records during the firing of the Four Courts and admitted being frustrated elsewhere; he could obtain no information regarding George Carr's civil service career, nor was he able to get confimation of Shaw's birth and baptism, since all these records went up in the smoke of the Easter Rebellion.

As Ervine further observed, Sonny formed no friendships at the Model which GBS saw fit to mention in his autobiographical notes. His reaction towards his classmates was probably in the nature of a complete withdrawal from all unnecessary contact with the children of Belial. As his arrogant and haughty manner isolated him from the usual pursuits of high-spirited schoolboys he, consequently, no longer found it expedient or amusing to continue his opposition to the schoolmasters. Cut by his former friends, Sonny's channelized energies raised him to eminence within the classroom and here the first signs of the dissenter appeared. In a reminiscence of multiple significance, GBS recalled that when there were readings in history he noticed that Ireland was treated with disdain while England was described in the loftiest terms, and when his turn came to read he would always substitute one for the other. The other lads would wonder what the teacher would do to him, but, added Shaw, the teacher would merely smile and say nothing. Sonny, GBS concluded, "was, in fact, a young Fenian in [his] political sympathies, such as they were." [48] Shaw's comment, apart from being an early example of his intellectual valor, again showed the influence of Lee. Writing in the Harris book, one of the ghostly hands recorded that "Shaw admits" Lee's influence made a radical change in the Shaw household. If GBS slept with his windows wide open it was because Lee advocated the fresh night air. If Shaw did not regard the medical profession with respect, it was because Lee expelled the apothecary and his purgatives when GBS was an overdosed youngster and because Lee restored his mother's health through "mesmeric induction of his own vitality." Finally, if GBS was an Irish nationalist "it was because Lee's family had sheltered Fenians 'on the run.' " [49] Though no evidence whatever was uncovered in the search for the Lees to connect them actively with Ireland's struggle for freedom, there were some indications of Professor Lee's personal views in this area, particularly as they were affected by the strangling of Irish culture by her many invaders. Writing in his treatise on singing, Lee boldly, yet with delicacy of expression, identified himself as a true son of Erin. The genius of Ireland, he wrote,

> has always been for music, poetry, and the arts generally; our pastime was ever that military glory which is inspired by these; our ambition the attainment of that high state of mental culture—that refinement of intellectuality—which is consistent alone with national freedom and independence; and had we been till now an unfettered people, there is no knowing to what extent our fine natural propensities might have led us in the direction of art. We can now only speculate as to what could have been, by what has been done in poetry and music, despite the centuries of oppression which we have suffered.[50]

Assuredly, considering the times, these were seditious sentiments.

On 11 September 1869 the thirteen-year-old Sonny left the Central Model School for what he chose to call his last school prison.

VI

TOTALLY PROFITLESS WERE THE VISITS to the Church of Ireland Representative Body in Stephen's Green; no records of the Dublin English Scientific and Commercial Day School were preserved. Inspection of Shaw's comments did not sustain the promise in this school's impressive title. Situated on the corner of Aungier and Whitefriars Streets, it was about a half-mile from Number 1 Hatch Street and only a few doors from St. Peter's, scene of George Carr and Lucinda Elizabeth's blissful union. This school, said Shaw, was as thoroughly Protestant and genteel as Wesleyan but, unlike that institution, made no pretensions to being a steppingstone to the university;

frankly, it trained her pupils for business and, equally as frankly, barred Latin and Greek from its courses.[51] Perhaps it was for this reason that Henderson thought there were grounds for suspecting that Mr. and Mrs. Shaw intended Sonny to embark on a business career.[52] At any rate, in addition to excluding the classics, Dublin Commercial [53] seemed to have excluded other subjects as well, since Shaw reported that though he elected drawing at a cost of four shillings per quarter extra, the drawing master gave no drawing lessons or even troubled himself to keep order. Bible classes, continued Shaw, were conducted once a week during which the class played pranks on the clergyman and no one showed the slightest interest in religion. In the mathematics class (possibly the only class in which something was taught), a few of the older and more advanced pupils occupied a corner of the room as a group and taught themselves, for no one made any pretense of teaching them. The headmaster remained in his office and, except for exercising his time-hallowed duty to cane, had no contact with his charges. As to the method of teaching, GBS brusquely dismissed it with the assertion that it was no different from the Wesleyan system.[54]

Ervine's account was far more detailed than those of his colleagues; but while introducing some refreshing material gathered together by Edward McNulty, a boyhood chum of Shaw, Ervine treated the section on Dublin Commercial in a manner that made it difficult to determine where McNulty's reminiscences left off and his own contributions began. The school chum had prepared a manuscript of Sonny's association with this school, a version of which was published in *The Candid Friend* of 6 July 1901.[55] The original manuscript from which this article was drawn, Ervine said, was in the possession of a collector of Shaviana who also owned a GBS-annotated copy of *The Candid Friend* version and, presumably, both were examined by Ervine. There were many faults in McNulty's article due to his bad or failing memory, Ervine noted, but allowed that GBS's memory was similarly faulty and that it would be difficult for one to decide which was the more accurate account. This school, Ervine wrote, was a large building, formerly Lord Aungier's town house. It had large rooms, broad staircases, ceilings whose artistically ornamented stucco designs were executed by Italian artisans and, in the best Georgian manner, mantelpieces of oak. The Dublin English Scientific and Commercial Day School, he added, had a proficient staff supervised by headmaster James de Glanville of Trinity College where he had been a mathematics scholar. One of his staff members was a junior master—a David Anderson (whose name may have been used by Shaw for the clergyman in *The Devil's Disciple*). Sonny, continued Ervine, received more from this school than from any other institution. In fact, he concluded, Sonny was no longer to be found at the bottom of the class as was the case at Wesleyan, and it was here that the boy shot to the top or, at worst, into second place.[56]

Bernard Shaw at thirteen was an object of absorbing interest to classmate Matthew Edward McNulty. In his later years an author and playwright, McNulty prepared an untitled and unpublished memoir dealing with his impressions and recollections of young Shaw and his family in Dublin. Fortunately, a copy of this memoir has been preserved by one of his descendants (and I gratefully acknowledge indebtedness to this person who wished to remain anonymous). Examination of both this memoir and the *Candid Friend* article confirm and conflict with Shaw's autobiographical notes.

McNulty recalled the day on which Sonny Shaw came to Dublin Commercial which, he wrote, was in Aungier Street and on the opposite corner to a large and beautiful Catholic church. The school, which has long ceased to exist, enjoyed a social standing similar to the Wesleyan and was housed in a large building once Lord Aungier's town residence. It was fitted with broad staircases, stately rooms, oaken mantelpieces in the finest Georgian style and richly-ornamented ceilings with central stucco garnishments designed by Italian artists. Headmaster of this establishment was a noted mathematical scholar of T.C.D.: James de Glanville; second master was a Mr. Thacker and a David Anderson was junior master. In addition there was a Herr Cramer, Instructor in German; a drawing master named Murray and an unnamed gymnastic instructor.

On the day Shaw arrived, McNulty, being previously warned by classmate Frank Dunne that a boy was coming who would "knock the stuffing" out of him, looked around during play time but saw no sign of any new boy. Returning to class after playhour, Dunne

> nudged me and nodded darkly towards the open doorway through which some laggards were arriving.
>
> "There's Shaw," he whispered.
>
> I then saw for the first time he whom I took to be the late Wesley[an][57] heavyweight champion, talking to three other fellows.
>
> "That's Shaw?" I repeated in astonishment.
>
> Instead of the burly, beetle-browed ruffian I had expected I saw a tallish, slender youngster, with straw-coloured hair, light greyish-blue eyes, a skin like that of a baby and lips like those of a beautiful girl.[58]

Shaw was assigned the seat directly in front of McNulty who, after gazing at his head for some time, initiated aggressive overtures. According to the *Candid Friend* article, McNulty first attempted to kick Shaw's ankles but failing this, pulled his hair. The original manuscript made no mention of kicking but detailed the hair-pulling incident. Shaw turned to look at him, not with the resentment expected but rather with quizzical amusement. This, wrote McNulty, was the origin of a friendship which was to endure for more than sixty years. Since the lads first met in 1869 and their friendship was to last for at least sixty-one years, it follows that the memoirs (written in 1901) must have been revised in 1930 or later. Both boys were of the same age; therefore, McNulty must have been at least seventy-four at the time of the revision.

Some days after their meeting, McNulty continued, an event occurred which proved almost disastrous to their flowering friendship. Playhour found some of the boys given over to "single-wicket cricket." When it was McNulty's turn to bat, he "swiped" at every ball having been earlier taunted that he had been playing for "safety." Shaw, who had been carefully observing McNulty's mood and style, suddenly asked if he might "bowl." This, said McNulty, was unexpected since Shaw had previously shown no interest in outdoor games. With a malevolent grin, Shaw bowled several unusually soft and slow balls from which McNulty chose a particularly tempting one and gave it a mighty swipe. There was a shattering crash and one of the stained-glass windows of the aforesaid beautiful Catholic church now displayed a huge, jagged gash. For an instant there was a deep silence "then Shaw, with a wild scream of laughter, threw himself on the ground and rolled over and over, shrieking with joy, like an imp from hell." [59] Of course, McNulty was convinced that Shaw had deliberately staged this awful event—that, at least, was as plain as could be—but how could he prove it? He was terror-stricken; how were his parents going to pay for that beautiful window? Then there was another point to be considered. Though the boys were in a Protestant school, they were taught to be respectful and tolerant towards other faiths and to bear them no animosities. What dire punishment would he now receive for the desecration of sacred property? The red-handed McNulty could see no way out but to report to Mr. de Glanville who, mysteriously, had already been informed of the catastrophe. But instead of caning him, Mr. de Glanville was reassuring and promised to see what could be done. Meeting Shaw again, McNulty stormed at him; his parents would have to share half the cost of repairing the window for he well knew that it was his responsibility but Shaw "only smiled sardonically." Some time later, McNulty was summoned to Mr. de Glanville's office from where they both went to visit the Reverend Dr. Spratt.[60] Passing through the church, McNulty glanced fearfully towards the altar where, he had been told by his loyal classmates, that the ball had caused extensive damage, but he could observe nothing unusual. Having never seen Dr. Spratt, McNulty continued, he naturally expected to meet someone of a vindictive and threatening mien; but at the sight of an aged, silver-haired priest with a round, plump face exuding benignity, his spirits rose. Dr. Spratt smiled and put his arm around McNulty's shoulders to allay the agitation evident in his appearance. It was, said Dr. Spratt, of course an accident—there was no need for the dear child to be frightened—everything would be straightened out. Mr. de Glanville and Dr. Spratt then moved out of earshot to discuss the matter while the boy, relieved at the prospect of being absolved, "emerged into the cold street again, feeling that I had been in the presence of an angel." [61]

Of the subjects that may have been taught in the Dublin Commercial, drawing particularly fascinated both boys. Shaw, McNulty wrote, was not the foremost pupil in Mr. Murray's class—this distinction was held by Richard (Monkey) Moynan who, though "crazed" on horses, later achieved eminence, according to the Royal Hibernian Academy of Arts, for his portrayal of street urchins. Mr. Murray himself, McNulty went on, was emaciated to the point of resembling a skeleton. His hands seemed almost transparent and he had a nose whose chief interest was not in its moderate hook but in its hue which was "permanently red." It was rumored that he drank excessively. The most extraordinary feature of Murray was, however, that although his bony hand normally trembled, the instant it took up a pencil it could draw a line straight enough to have pleased Euclid. As to Shaw, McNulty continued that he had almost no interest whatsoever in landscape but was obsessed with the human figure which the future art critic drew with lines "that were painfully precise." The boys often discussed their differences of opinions with respect to art and frequently visited the National Gallery until they came to know every picture there. Shaw adored the work of Michelangelo which, however, did not appeal to his friend because of its "exaggerated muscularity" and they argued the point again and again. In addition Shaw was also taken with Raphael's *Madonna* and, though McNulty thought it insipid, both were deeply impressed with the old masters' flesh tints and treatment of draperies.

Painting and sculpture were not the only arts Shaw and McNulty were interested in, for they had formed, with difficulty, a dramatic club which undertook to produce the Shakespearean masterpieces. McNulty related that the first offering was *Macbeth,* a desperate enterprise which disintegrated into early chaos due to the fact that none of the cast had troubled to memorize their lines. Consequently, the entire burden fell upon the poor prompter who, after twenty valiant minutes, threw up his hands in despair. *Hamlet* was the next to be chosen and McNulty allowed that of this effort, he could remember no one except Shaw who, being the most effeminate-looking boy of the lot, was cast as Ophelia. This attempt likewise collapsed, as Shaw, for some reason McNulty could not fathom, persisted in moving about the stage on tip-toe uttering his lines in a shrill falsetto that turned the tragedy into an uproarious farce. The dramatic club soon expired largely due to the disappearance of enthusiasm on the part of all the actors but McNulty and Shaw.[62]

With regard to matters more directly related to the school curriculum, McNulty recalled that they both were "rotten" at their lessons but that both had the faculty for writing prose compositions. Prior to Shaw's arrival, McNulty was openly acknowledged to be the foremost essayist of the school, and when one of his efforts was read out in class, there would be rivalry amongst the boys for the privilege of reading it—so much so that McNulty was forced to maintain a waiting list. With Shaw's appearance, there was an end to his unchallenged superiority, for Shaw's essays proved to be as popular, and it was only then that McNulty understood what Dunne had in mind when he warned that the new boy would "knock the stuffing" out of him. Shaw, added McNulty, was not equal to this threat, but he nevertheless shared the throne with him thereafter.

While Shaw in his later years somewhat pointedly illustrated his own youthful prodigy by listing his awesomely-mature taste in literature, McNulty's account had it that it was not always so discriminating. They were, he wrote, "not by any means a pair of juvenile prigs" and announced that their favorite reading matter was, in fact, *The Boys of England,* which, he said, was the first paper for boys ever to be published and was founded by one Edwin J. Brett.[63] He remembered the first serial they read which was called *Alone in the Pirates' Lair, or The Adventures of Jack Harkaway.* So enthralled were the lads with these stories that they could hardly wait from week to week for the next installment and would, in the interim, discuss seriously Harkaway's current dilemma and devise schemes for his extrication. They hated the pirates and swore that when they were grown up, they would shoot all pirates on sight. Concluding, McNulty avowed that if it ever was in his power, he would cause to be erected a statue of Edwin J. Brett in the city of his birth.[64]

VII

SOMETIME DURING HIS TERM with the Dublin Commercial (September [?], 1869–October [?], 1871),[65] Sonny was said by GBS to have had his fill of school. "I decided at thirteen or thereabouts," Shaw chronicled, "that for the moment I must go into business and earn some money and begin to be a grown-up man." [66] Ervine appeared to have accepted unreservedly Shaw's claim that Sonny's desire to seek employment was the result of an independent decision. Speaking of the Dublin Commercial, Ervine wrote that GBS was soon to leave this school in order to work for his living. In fact, he added, when Shaw was between thirteen and fourteen he "sought" employment but this was thwarted by the intervention of one of the partners of the prospective firm who advised him against leaving school "as [Sonny] intended to do." [67] Henderson also accepted Shaw literally, saying that about a year before GBS actually left school the boy had "already decided" to quit and to strike out for himself.[68] One half-expected the Harris book to offer a different slant, and one was not disappointed. Sonny, recorded a busy hand, "was sent job-hunting" at fifteen.[69] Pearson seemed to have been privy to confidential information or, what is more likely, had given more than passing attention to Shaw's comments. He must have had some doubts regarding Sonny's intentions, for he put it that the Shaw family, because of George Carr's deteriorating fortunes, was becoming poorer and poorer and that when Sonny was about thirteen "an effort was made to turn him into a source of income." [70] Pearson did not follow up his interesting observation nor did he offer any opinion as to who attempted to send the boy to work.

Identifying the employer as a firm of cloth merchants doing business as Scott, Spain & Rooney, Shaw related that a friend of the family was a friend of Scott and that this friend paved the way for an interview. "I had," added GBS, "the vaguest notion of what would happen: all I knew was that I was 'going into an office.'" [71] Examination of Shaw's treatment of this episode cannot but reinforce the possibility that the decision to abandon school for the commercial world was not made by Sonny. As it was most unlikely that the friend of the family arranged the interview without the knowledge and consent of the family, the responsibility, consequently, probably devolves upon either George Carr or Lucinda Elizabeth for the original decision to send Sonny to work. In the absence of evidence pointing to the identity of the friend or to the particular member of the family sponsoring this move, as well as the reasons for it, I suggest, in accordance with the "reconstruction" aspect of this study, that there were at this time, ominous rustlings from the ambitious and restless Lee. Having just published his successful *The Voice: Its Artistic Production, Development and Preservation,* the Professor dreamed (and talked) of invading London—a contingency which certainly forced the Shaws to reappraise their economic position in the light of this threat. They would have to vacate Hatch Street, since without the comforting security of Mr. Lee, a return to Synge Street or worse seemed certain. In the face of this imminent disaster, I believe Mrs. Shaw consulted with Lee (without, of course, regard to her husband's views) and decided that Sonny should be withdrawn from school while Lee, as a friend of the family, would see what could be done about placing the boy in a position that would at least make him self-supporting.

For reasons which will be discussed later, Lee's Londonward gestures subsided and the emergency passed by, and in the end Sonny returned to school. Further cause to believe that Sonny was innocent of any real intention to leave school for business was given in the conclusion to GBS's account. Sonny, he wrote, kept his appointment with Scott who, after some routine queries, was about to engage him when the senior partner Mr. Rooney appeared. After a short chat with the boy, he stated flatly that the applicant was too young and, further, unsuited to the work. Analyzing his decision, GBS deduced that Mr. Rooney apparently supposed that "my introducer, my parents, and his young partner, had been inconsiderate; and I presently descended the stairs, reprieved and unemployed." Concluding, GBS acknowledged his gratitude to Mr. Rooney and assured him (if he were still alive) that he had not forgotten his thoughtfulness.[72]

At least two of the biographers echoed Shaw's sigh of relief—Harris even echoing one of Shaw's words. Rooney, approved rewrite man Shaw, was a fatherly sort with a conscience to match. He could see that the boy was unsuited "for such common work. Shaw fled, grateful for the reprieve." [73] Henderson had it that GBS was happy to be relieved of the drudgery,[74] and Pearson, in keeping with his air of skepticism, observed wryly that Mr. Rooney's decision did not stimulate the appreciation of the Shaw family.[75] Thus it may be seen that the entire incident is fundamentally contradictory. In the preface to *Immaturity* GBS recalled that he had "decided" to leave school and enter business—indicating an entirely voluntary decision. Yet a friend of the family used his influence to arrange a meeting with an employer, and Sonny's ignorance of the whole affair is implied by the admission that he knew nothing except that he would be "going into an office," thereby quoting, possibly the director of these proceedings. It seems to me that GBS may have been shielding someone who may have been compelled by circumstances to send the fourteen-year-old Sonny to work.

Commercial career temporarily deferred by Rooney, Sonny returned to the Dublin Commercial to serve out the remainder of his sentence. Henderson reported that during 1871 our lad, grown weary of institutions that had no interest for him, withdrew in defeat and resolved to find a job.[76] Winsten had inside information. According to his account, Sonny had ganged together a number of boys whose sworn objective was to torture teachers by deliberately giving the wrong answers to questions and by jockeying for the lowest position in class. One of these teachers, concluded Winsten, was so enraged with Shaw, "this devil incarnate," that he struck him savagely upon the ear causing Sonny to leave school and never return.[77] In 1871 and about three months after he turned fifteen, young Shaw broke with his school prisons forever.

VIII

THE FIRST SIGNS OF A DISINTEGRATING Shaw-Lee household seemed to appear in 1869. The Professor, who had now been continuously and energetically active in Dublin's musical circles for seventeen years had probably become convinced that The Method had some larger destiny than merely to gleam and sparkle under the bushel of Dublin. He was certain that it needed only to be introduced to the outside world for it (and him) to instantly become a huge success. Sensing that the time was rapidly approaching for the release of The Method, he procured, according to Shaw, the services of a ghost writer. The Professor, GBS explained, was so "destitute of any literary bent" that before he offered his *magnum opus* to the publisher, it had to be written for him by an unidentified blackguard of a physician whom Lee had approached for the job exactly as he later approached Shaw during the London years to do his screeds for the press and other purposes.[78] Ervine reported Shaw's opinion of Lee's literary abilities to fall even short of the talent required to compose ordinary handbills and ventured that the roguish doctor might be one Dr. Smyly mentioned by Lee in his preface to *The Voice*.[79] The usually prudent Henderson incautiously referred to the Professor as "the almost illiterate Lee"[80] and elsewhere described the ghost writer as a German and a miserable alcoholic at that.[81]

Shaw's assertion that *The Voice* was not written by Lee was modified some twelve years later. Writing to M. H. Mushlin in connection with Mushlin's discovery of Shaw's 1882-86 new version of *The Voice,* GBS revised his estimate of the Professor's literary faculties. Lee, he now declared, was either unequal or believed himself to be unequal to the requirements of literary composition, and when he produced his book in Dublin, "it was written for him mostly by another hand," thus, for all practical purposes, acknowledging that Lee was responsible for less than half of *The Voice*. After reviewing the history of this new version (he warned that as he was then over ninety-one, he could not guarantee its accuracy), GBS advised one and all to beware the Shaw-worshipping professor of literature announcing the discovery of a hitherto unpublished Shavian gem. True, he added, "The hand is my hand; but the soul of it is Lee. He was a genius in his way; but not in my way." [82] Although Shaw's explanation of his connection with the projected revision of *The Voice* was true as far as it went, it did not, in my opinion, go far enough. The matter will be dealt with in its proper place. For the present, *The Voice* will be examined in an effort to determine Lee's part in it and appraise him as a writer in his own right.

First published in 1869 by the Dublin firm of M'Glashan & Gill then located at 50 Upper Sackville Street,[83] *The Voice: Its Artistic Production, Development and Preservation* by George J. Lee appears to have been completely disposed of by advance subscription.[84] *The Voice* (6″ x 8″, 130 pp., quarto) is encased between heavy dark green covers and elaborately stamped in gold.[85] Cover illustration, according to *The Irish Times,* is Maclise's celebrated drawing, the *Origin of the Harp* while the text's illustrations were from Dr. Mapother's *Manual of Physiology*. With respect to its manufacture, Lee again proved himself a true son of Erin when both *Saunders' News-Letter* and *Freeman's Journal* reported proudly that *The Voice* was from first to last a product of Irish materials and Irish skill.

> The paper [it continued], which is so agreeably tinted, was made in Dublin; the typography is really a praise to our Dublin presses; the woodcuts were executed by Dublin hands, and are perfect specimens of art; and the binding fully equals the best of the London's season's annuals. We congratulate Mr. Lee on having been one of the very few who dare to trust the aesthetic and industrial capabilities of his fellow-townsmen, and we congratulate him and them on the success of the experiment and on the beauty of the execution.[86]

Freeman's Journal was not quite as lavish in its reportage but was similar in content to *Saunders'*.

Henderson offered no opinion on the merits of *The Voice,* literary or otherwise, but in a footnote recommended those interested to examine that engaging and debatable "memoir" *Bernard Shaw:*

His Life, Work and Friends by St. John Ervine for an "analysis" of Lee's work. Thus commended, Ervine's "memoir" was consulted. If Ervine's opinion of *The Voice* was direct and succinct, it was also shallow and sarcastic. In fact there was no indication that he had even read the book, for in a footnote he acknowledged his debt to a well-known Shavian for "information" about *The Voice.* Ervine rendered his opinion of the book's contents by commenting that its author was given to a literary style which might best be described as a "sort of debased Burke." This style, he continued, had remained fashionable in Ireland up to recent times but was still inflicted upon bored audiences by Irish-Americans and opined that Lee would have been wiser to sack the ghost and write it himself, notwithstanding the possible crudity of his own style. The ghost, Ervine continued, obviously padded his preliminary sections with frequent pulls from the nearest reference sources, thus masking his simplicity behind a cloud of ambiguous verbiage all designed to imbue "emotional" women with the higher thought. Part II dealt with the physiology of the throat and it was here that Lee's hand appeared, Ervine thought, where Lee discoursed on the three schools of theories of voice production and rejected the "reed" and "pipe" theories in favor of the "flute" theory upon which his Method was based. Part III—the Practical section—offered advice on how to preserve one's voice to a great age but these instructions, Ervine asserted, were in effect useless, since Lee also warned the reader frequently to take no measures without first consulting a skilled teacher. It was evident to Ervine that the Professor had no real desire to help anyone to a singing voice but that the reader was simply told enough to convince him to enroll in one of the maestro's classes. It was *The Voice,* Ervine concluded, upon which the future music critic Corno di Bassetto based many of his articles on the human voice in song.[87]

Choosing an appropriate excerpt from Pope for an epigraph, Lee sprinkled his text with selections from Greek, Latin, French and Italian sources. In addition to Pope, the Professor supported his theses with quotations from Panofka, Columba, Bunting, Cowper, the "illustrious" Boyle, Carlyle, Plato, Horace, Xenarchus and Sam Slick, a fictional character created by the Canadian humorist Thomas

Chandler Haliburton ("First, be sure you're on the right track, then go a-head!")

The main body of *The Voice* is preceded by a three-and-one-half-page preface wherein Lee defined his objectives; it is particularly noteworthy because of Shaw's equivocal declarations that *The Voice* was not written by Lee or written mostly for him. With the opening paragraph, the author advanced into battle at once. Was the medical profession jealous of its divinely-appointed dominion? Would they denounce, persecute—even prosecute the challenger and truthseeker? No matter, the author would defy them boldly. Was this the work of the one who wrote *The Voice* for Lee—or was it by the hand of the one who was so destitute of literary bent? Could this be the product of that miserable alcoholic of a German—or was it from the pen of the almost illiterate but musical genius?

> It might be deemed [the preface went on] presumptuous in one outside "the Pale" to offer an opinion on the Anatomy and Physiology of the human vocal organs; but it must be borne in mind, that the present is emphatically a day of inquiry, and that nothing is now taken for granted because established, nor deemed right because antiquated . . .[88]

Concluding his preface, the author modestly appraised his own literary talents and expressed the hope that his revolutionary theories and methods would inspire others to carry on the struggle. He noted that the rendering of the art of singing into everyday language had always presented difficulties

> to wiser heads and abler pens; but, if in the little which may be accomplished by these efforts, there will be found sufficient to stimulate society to a taste for these matters, plenty of skilled writers are to be found who may more worthily and satisfactorily carry out the good work.
>
> G. J. Lee
>
> Dublin, 13th December, 1869 [89]

If one takes into consideration the period and locale, examination of *The Voice* will reveal it to be a serious and well-written contribution to music literature in general and vocal instruction in particular. It will also be evident that it could not have been written by anyone without a considerable familiarity with human anatomy, a broad base in classical literature, a knowledge of the legendary and historical evolution of choral music and a technical intimacy with the contemporary musical world. With regard to *The Voice*'s treatment of the physiological aspects, C. A. Erskine, Professor of Anatomy in Trinity's School of Medicine was consulted. In a letter (dated 22 February 1960), he related that he approached the book as if he had stumbled upon it by mere change, that is to say, he read it as though it were a curiosity. Of Lee's eccentric views on alcohol, diet and smoking, Dr. Erskine believed them to be somewhat chaotic and inaccurate, but he reported that many of Lee's opinions were accepted by the majority of physicians today. As to his personal response to the author's description of the physical and functional particularities of the vocal organs, Dr. Erskine was in almost entire agreement. It was, he wrote, "substantially correct for the present day and would serve with some relatively minor modifications as an introductory text for medical auxiliaries." He went on to state that even with the most modern techniques of today, e.g., high-speed cinematography, X-ray and complex electronic technology, the mechanism of voice production was not wholly understood, and he noted that it was interesting to see that Lee's assertion about the ascending and descending larynx in step with the high and low notes had but recently been confirmed through X-ray studies. "I approve," he concluded, "of most of Lee's statements on structure and function and I think that much of it is valid today; I also consider his opinions and theories on voice production quite sensible."

The Voice is divided into three major divisions; subdivided, with Part The First being a short but wide-ranging summary of the origins and history of individual and group singing. It includes a general review of music-making and singing from the pre-Christian era through the early Italian music dramas and up to Lee's time. Emphasizing the Irish contribution, he scolded England and Germany for not acknowleging their debt to Ireland. But perhaps the most interesting paragraph in this section (insofar as this study is concerned) is his reference to the Roman Catholic Church. Lee's gratitude to the source of his best vocalists is suggested in his comments on the period following Ireland's golden age of saints and scholars:

> During the perplexing and seemingly interminable social and political discords of the middle ages, the Church of Rome became the nursing mother of music; and in the quiet seclusion of monasteries and cloisters originated that counterpoint in part singing which is a most essential condition towards effect.[90]

This reference, an indirect influence on both Lucinda and Sonny, is, I think, a reason for the beginning of Shaw's break with religious bigotry.

Part The Second is concerned with the physiology of the chest, throat and head as producing and affecting the voice. Examining the conflicting opinions of authorities as to the principle involved in the production of the voice, Lee reported the three warring factions to be the "reed" school, the "string" school and the "wind" school—adding somewhat contemptuously there were those physiologists who regarded it as a combination of all three "more, perhaps, with a hope of being on the safe side."[91] Lee's gentle warning that the medical fraternity was not above criticism was given further force here. In announcing his intention to question Authority and Orthodoxy, Lee drew up the battle lines:

> And, whilst paying the greatest deference to the expressed opinions of the mighty minds which have gone before us; and feeling deep respect for those of the acknowledged teachers who are contemporaneous with us, we must not hesitate to express our own convictions boldly because of fear of comment or ridicule.[92]

Although expressed in tactful terms, these observations were clearly a statement of principle by a man who seemed intent upon exercising them and, if necessary, to any extremity—a position that foreshadowed Shaw's own fearlessness in public debate and his caustic treatment of pompous authority and false prophets.

Dissatisfied with the disputatious theories put forth as evidence by the authorities, pioneer Lee interested medical acquaintances in the subject[93] and he appears to have spent some time in the Ledwich School of Anatomy, an adjunct of the Adelaide Hospital in Dublin. While Shaw did not identify any of Lee's medical friends it is possible that a Malachy J. Kilgarriff, F.R.C.S.I., L.K.Q.C.P.I., was one of them. Recorded by Thom's as having been the occupant of 47, Harrington Street in 1864 (1863), neighbor Kilgarriff was additionally identified as a Demonstrator of Anatomy at Ledwich. Lee's fanatic search for *bel canto* did not preclude the actual dissection of human as well as animals' throats. Writing in *London Music,* GBS related that in his pursuit for the secret of the voice beautiful, Lee consulted all the singing teachers available to him. Their combined wisdom left him none the wiser. There was, they chorused, a throat voice, a chest voice and a head voice. There was nothing to do but find out for himself. Bird and human corpse alike received his attentions—both were subjected to his dissecting knife. At the conclusion of his studies (Shaw added), Lee was able to inform the teachers that their three voices were entirely mythical and that the voice was actually generated in the larynx.[94]

Part The Third was the "Practical" section in which The Method was discussed at length. Lee offered encouragement to those who had despaired of ever singing properly, declaring that the ability to sing was greater than believed—if one had the proper teacher. Having a disappointing singing voice was not necessarily a sign that the would-be singer should seek other means to express himself for Art

> enables the teacher to make up in a great measure for the shortcomings of nature; and, except in cases of great or hopeless deformity, he can so direct the *will* of the pupil to the placing and sustaining of parts in certain positions, as very often wholly to overcome, or skilfully conceal the want in the vocal instrument.[95]

Addressing himself to the ladies in particular (the married as well as the single), Lee, in an uncanny portent of a future feminist, spoke out boldly against the remaining Victorian restrictions barring them from certain cultural activities. In a manner, he congratulated the ladies on their influence in civilization and noted that this progress could be ascribed to their many virtues and merits and that they had at last affected the rejection of prudery and selfishness as basic elements in their society. As to the then current prejudice against the participation of married ladies in musical affairs outside their own drawing rooms, Lee displayed both erudition and humor delightfully combined. Quoting Xenarchus on his envy of the male grasshopper who was happy because his wife was dumb, Lee asserted that Xenarchus' cricketings were forgotten when the ladies raised their voices in sweet strains. The popular caveat of "Beware, ye young men, of a musical wife," was rapidly being replaced by the much more dulcet and lyrical eloquence of "Her Heart Was in the Song." [96]

The ideological resemblances heretofore noted between Lee and GBS become more evident as *The Voice*'s subsection "Health and General Habits" is examined. Here the Professor offered sensible but revolutionary advice to ladies and gentlemen, whether or not they had vocal ambitions. His advice was, in fact, a frontal attack upon Fashion and, simultaneously, an appeal for sensible dress reform—an appeal which is as applicable today as it was when Lee penned

> It is extravagantly absurd to suppose that a man with a collar fastened round his neck so tight as to call to mind the days of neck-ring torture, can expect to maintain his windpipe, or larynx, in a normal condition; and it is equally preposterous to imagine a lady who tightens herself in stays 'till the vital capacity of her lungs is so diminished as to lose half its resources, can inhale sufficient of the breath of life, or digest enough food to exist in any state other than that of waxy emaciation and hysterical wretchedness. Nothing is more ruinous than the abominable and absurd custom of stays-wearing and tight lacing . . .[97]

Shaw's unconventional attitude towards clothing was well known and up to the time of his marriage, he attracted considerable attention as a dress reformer. Jaegerized, sandaled and linenless, GBS strode the streets of London, a sight to behold. Writing in the third person in *How Frank Ought To Have Done It,* Shaw gave some reasons for these sartorial departures. Imaginative journalists had reported, he wrote, that he wore flannel shirts. Not so, he countered, he never wore a shirt at all—to say nothing of a flannel one. He refused to wear a shirt, he said, because it was improper to engirdle one's torso with two thicknesses of material (that is, an undershirt plus a dress shirt). Consequently he wore something entirely unknown to shirt manufacturers: an undergarment that reached from his feet to his head which I take to mean some sort of cotton or flannel combination of long underwear sewn or attached in some way to a shirt of approved material. Furthermore, wrote Shaw, Mr. Shaw would not wear white collars because the contrast to European skin-tones was offensive to the eye and he therefore wore gray collars later adding others of assorted hues. His jacket, while in the best traditions of quality and workmanship, was left unlined "on principle." [98]

Fresh air and the use of alcohol and tobacco also received their share of attention from the Professor who did not bear his responsibilities lightly. There were a large number of practices, he sermonized, which were detrimental to singers and declared that "it was the sacred duty" of those guardians of the art, the Professors of Music, to warn their pupils and to use every measure at their disposal to eliminate these evils. Mentioning but two of the evils, Lee asserted that intoxicating liquors were not only useless but pernicious into the bargain. He was kinder toward smoking. Tobacco, he said, was a toxic weed—a poisonous narcotic whose effect upon the body was singularly depressing and similar in effect to that of prussic acid. The only good that he could say for it was that it was handy as a last chance remedy in the cases of some diseases.[99] Discoursing at length on the importance of fresh, circulating air day and night, Lee warred on the "Keep-the-windows-closed-and-the-diseases-out" school with a barrage of facts, logic, ridicule and example. Many people, he wrote, believed that pure air—the air suitable for breathing—was synonymous with warm temperatures. To these persons, cold air was always associated with diseases of the lungs such as bronchitis and other respiratory ailments, and, accordingly, they approved of rooms in which the doors and windows were closed. These people, continued Lee, took their outdoor exercises in either a closed carriage or walked about with a respirator covering the mouth and considered this the proper and wholesome way to air the lungs. Of the few who were induced to allow some fresh air into their homes during the hours of daylight most, if not all, would

> carefully choke up every crevice at night, under the impression that it is bad to breathe *night* air, as if any other air could be breathed at night but night air; not thinking that the means by which they exclude the admission of external pure air, also prevents effectually the escape of internal foul air which had been breathed from their lungs, and exhaled from their bodies, and which filling every aperture of their chambers, is breathed over again to poison the blood.[100]

After examining the disadvantages of opening the windows from either the top or the bottom, Lee recommended that the windows be opened both top and bottom and suggested an experiment to prove that with both windows open, fresh air would enter into the room through the lower part and foul air issue forth through the upper part. If, he continued, one held a lit candle in both positions, it would be observed that the candle flame would bend inward at the bottom and outward at the top.[101]

The influence of Lee's views in this and other matters on young Shaw did not come to an end with his departure for London in 1873. McNulty reported that Shaw, at nineteen or so, held similar views. He recalled that their walks together were taken mostly at night. Shaw, he said, "ridiculed the popular idea that 'night air' was unhealthy, and declared it purer than day air." [102] Lee's views on open windows and night air were to crop up again fifteen years later as an amusing incident in Shaw's sixth but strangled-at-birth novel. Untitled and uncompleted, *An Unfinished Novel* (begun in 1887) features the topic in the form of a three-way tug-of-war amongst certain of its characters. Young Dr. Kincaid, recently graduated from medical school, has been employed by "Dr." Maddick (who has learnt his trade as an apprentice to a physician) as "cover" in connection with certain legal formalities. Receiving an urgent call from Lady Laurie, a rich hypochondriac, Maddick sends Dr. Kincaid with the intention of following soon thereafter. Entering Lady Laurie's chamber, Dr.

Kincaid glanced about the room, strode to the window and opened it generously at the top. Lady Laurie is shocked at this inconsiderateness and ignorance. "Oh doctor: how can you? I shall get my death. Please shut the window." This plea brings the maid scurrying to obey, but she is brought up sharply by the doctor who commands her not to touch the window. Turning to his patient, he assures her that he will close the window himself when the temperature of the room becomes more reasonable. This seems to quiet Lady Laurie but only for the few moments during his interrogation at the completion of which she complains crossly that she cannot bear the cold; she must have the window closed. Dr. Kincaid, in an effort to humor her, rises patiently, shuts the window partially and composes the draperies to deflect the draft.[103]

The subject of fresh air was again raised with the sudden arrival of Maddick who, after a brief nod to his assistant, hastened with hushed footsteps and an affected air of anxiety to Lady Laurie's side. "Not fever exactly; but feverish" is Maddick's considered diagnosis to which the patient points out that this explains why she feels so cold and inquires

> "Is it right for me to have the window open?"
> "God bless my soul!" said Maddick, "the window open! Certainly not. You must be very careful, *very* careful. Kincaid: will you be so good as to close the window."

Kincaid replies that he has already closed the window since "Lady Laurie is afraid that she will die in the middle of the night if it is closed altogether." [104] Maddick, scoffing away the notion that she would die during the night, suggests a sleeping draught and promises Lady Laurie that she will be as right as rain in the morning. The patient is so relieved—Dr. Maddick understands her constitution so well. She would prefer to have the window shut tightly, that is, if Dr. Maddick approved. "Of course," he said, hastening to shut it himself. "You should never let in the night air. Now. Shut and bolted." With this, Lady Laurie threw a victorious glance at Dr. Kincaid but felt put out at finding that he appeared only amused.[105]

Although Shaw was acquainted with *The Voice,* he stated that it was from his mother that he received his lessons, and he attributed the success he achieved on the soapbox and lecture platform to her secrets of breathing and so forth.[106] In the account of his attempts to produce a singing voice according to The Method he implied that he had his difficulties. The jaw, he said, had to be totally loose, tongue held flat, larynx and soft palate to be "rounded up," and, while all this was going on, one must exercise diaphragm control. It was, he added, like trying to wiggle one's ears, and at first he could not utter a properly-produced sound. Nevertheless, Shaw concluded, he had confidence and faith in Lee's system and eventually developed an "uninteresting" baritone[107] having a range from B♭ to F with French pitch preferred for the F.[108]

Could the complex and difficult description of The Method be written by any one other than a Professor of Music? In short, could *The Voice* have been inspired, conceived and executed by anyone other than George John Lee? Judging it from its contents, treatment, opinion and spirit, one must inescapably conclude that *The Voice*—apart from its physiological matter—is wholly the work of George John Lee.

In the British Museum there is a series of twenty-five or more letters from Lee to GBS during the London years from 1877 to late August of 1886—just three months before the death of Lee. Examination of these letters with respect to style and characteristics was not particularly revealing, since they were written with that breezy informality of correspondence which did not expect to be studied by strangers and certainly did not expect to be memorialized through publication. But as regards Lee's literacy the letters clearly, finally and forever dispose of the myth that Lee was illiterate, almost illiterate, unable to write a handbill of any worth, destitute of literary bent or that he believed himself to be so destitute. Writing from Scotland in 1881 (where he seems to have gone frequently) Lee had already opened discussions with Shaw on the subject of reviving *The Voice* for a third edition. While this letter raises questions of meanings, they will not be dealt with at this time but be confined to the examination of its present aim: the assessment of Lee's literary talents. In the following, no attempt has been made to delete, supply or correct any real or alleged defect.

> Post Office St Andrew NB
>
> Would it suit your proclivities at present to construct something upon whatever lines of the "Voice" etc you might wish to adopt. Including your own observations? If so, I shd like to make the action of the tongue a salient point. Its injurious influence upon the production of the voice when placed firmly and flat as in sounding A according to the Italian notion tending to rigidity of the Larynx. & thereby causing strain upon the internal mechanism & its absolute utility in reflecting vibration from a widely and steadily distended pharynx into the oral cavity or against the hard palate producing that travelling or penetrating quality born upon a foundation of full sound consequent upon certain positions of Larynx & pharynx. It is really the mechanical consummation of voice production for public singing. Perhaps you might find some good modern monogram in the B.M. that wd be useful— If you take up this subject for me I'm sure you will make a success of it—& it wd be doing good work to open the vials of your wrath upon the Italians—of course I shall be delighted to send you some coin as you will require it for books of reference & etc. I only heard of your illness a couple of days before I left town. I hope that you are feeling all right again. Drop me a line to above address. As I shall be moving about. Fife. Kind regards to Dr. & Mrs. Gurly. Also to yr mother.
>
> Ever yours sincerely
>
> V. L.[109]

Since the letter is wholly concerned with vocal music and a rather technical subdivision at that, such intelligence as it contains becomes intelligible or not to the initiated—of whom GBS was one. While offering little in the way of something one can put one's teeth into, the letter is nevertheless a fair example of Lee's literacy and literary proficiency, especially since it is, so to speak, *ad lib* and not intended for publication. It is reasonable to assume that if Lee had anticipated critical attention, he could have produced a more polished specimen for evaluation as, for instance, correcting born to borne, monogram to monograph and clearer definition between sentences and so forth. Be that as it may, Lee's letter bears the unmistakable marks of an educated and articulate writer whose vocabulary was of sufficient range and flexibility to accommodate the needs of a complex subject.

Conclusion: George John Lee's literary aptitude can be entertained as a factor in the genius of George Bernard Shaw.

IX

HAILED BY THE PRESS, Lee probably considered the reception of *The Voice* by Dubliners to be an augury of a future that would cap his career with glory, honors and wealth. It is quite possible that he now talked of invading London, but his hour had not yet struck. Overwhelmed by the ardor with which the public accepted *The Voice,* Lee pressed for another issue and in the following year, M'Glashan & Gill entered into a cooperative venture with Simpkin, Marshall & Company of London for the simultaneous publication of the second edition. As to the impact of *The Voice* on London, Ervine believed that it was received in such a manner as to raise within Lee visions of a wonderful career ahead, and he "caused consternation in Hatch Street by announcing his intention of migrating." [110] GBS recalled that someone (he did not say who) assured Lee that he would have to start all over again in London and reminded him that perhaps after fifteen years or so he would attain some measure of recognition.[111] Whatever the reasons, Lee dropped his plans—for the time.

X

IT IS DIFFICULT TO DETERMINE the precise circumstances under which Sonny left school, possibly because GBS seems to have deliberately avoided exactitude in this area. Henderson declared that in 1871 Sonny, being bored with school in which he no longer had any interest, "gave up the struggle and decided to go to work for a living,"[112] thus stating, in effect, that Sonny quit school of his own accord to seek employment. Henderson's source for his opinion appears to have been Shaw's 1905 letter. Here GBS stated, "In 1871, I being then fifteen, and there being no money to give me a university education . . . I went into the office of an Irish land agent . . ."[113] If Henderson used this as his source, he certainly interpreted it loosely. Ervine was equally positive in his account. Linking the occasion to Lee's second startling announcement, he asserted that Sonny was *removed* from school. There was, he reported, "much fruitless confabulation" from which issued some fruit: "Sonny was withdrawn from school and put to work."[114] The truth of the matter has yet to be revealed. Shaw's own comment was confined to the merest reference. He reported that about a year after the Scott, Spain & Rooney adventure, his uncle Frederick (an important official with the Valuation Office) used his influence to secure a position for him but did not name the person who asked uncle Frederick to intercede.[115] Ervine's account however, suggested that it was Mrs. Shaw who "settled [Sonny's] immediate career in 1871, while Lee was still in Dublin. Her brother-in-law, Richard Frederick Shaw, was an important official in the Irish Valuation office and influential, therefore, with estate agents. He was able to secure a post for Sonny . . ."[116] Ervine's contention that Sonny was removed from school as a result of Lee's latest restlessness is, in my opinion, quite sound, but I believe it was George Carr who asked brother Frederick to give the lad a push and that this request was made under the urging of Mrs. Shaw who had long since severed relations with the Shaws.

The decision to send Sonny to work seems directly traceable to the publication of the second edition of *The Voice*. Two years had passed since the success of Lee's treatise in 1869, and the apparent success of the London edition may have convinced Lee that the iron was hot enough to be struck and struck hard. Winsten had it that both Queen Victoria and Gladstone expressed their interest in The Method by acknowledgment through their secretaries, but unfortunately he neglected to honor his source.[117] The Professor's reaction to the second edition was more than mere professional gratification. He was right after all. What more proof could anyone ask? London crooked its beckoning finger—could it be prudently denied the second time? He once more announced his determination to embark for England and proceeded to put his affairs in order: disposition of property; legal, financial, social and professional arrangements; discussions with his musical confreres regarding the fate of the Amateur Musical Society and its obligations and, of course, conferences with Lucinda in connection with certain problems that would develop with his departure. It was at one of these conferences, I believe, that the decision was made to withdraw Sonny from school and propel him into a commercial career.

On the first of November, 1871,[118] G. B. Shaw, aged fifteen years and three months, entered the employ of C. Uniacke Townshend & Company of 15 Molesworth Street, Dublin—a firm engaged in estate management and associated matters. In accordance with the customs of the times and place, "apprentices" were engaged at very little or no cost to the employer during the period of their apprenticeship which, not infrequently, extended over a number of years. In the more gentlemanly pursuits, it was common practice for the parents of the boy to pay a large premium for the privilege of having their son attached to a genteel enterprise. As Shaw was recommended to the firm by an important personage and was not accompanied by a premium, he received, accordingly, particularly low wages. Employed in the capacity of an office boy (he was ashamed of the title), he called himself a "junior clerk" and earned either eighteen shillings per month or eighteen pounds per year, depending on where, when and from whom one received one's information. Writing in his preface to *Immaturity,* GBS noted that he received a series of raises in salary as his tenure and importance increased, and that some time between his promotion from office boy to a higher position, he had already been given a salary increase of twelve shillings per month to make a total of eighteen pounds per year, thus supporting the eighteen-shilling salary as more accurate.[119]

Pearson—in disagreement with Ervine—pointed out that Shaw was unhappy in his employment. As a junior clerk to a land agent (Pearson wrote), one of Shaw's most disagreeable tasks was to gather the rents from very poor tenants and he likened it to a visit to Mountjoy Prison which, by comparison, was a merry outing.[120] Objecting specifically, Ervine expressed astonishment with Pearson's "surprising assertion" and argued that the "evidence" showed Shaw to have been relatively more content—even happier—with Townshend & Company than he had been in much of his childhood or, for that matter, happier than he would be in much of his young manhood. He declared that GBS's successful sojourn with Townshend was "sufficient in itself to refute Mr. Pearson's statement; for no man works well in employment which he loathes." [121] Concluding, he generalized, everything that was known of this period in Shaw's life proved without a doubt that GBS was (as far as he could be happy in any office) pleased with his employment. What unhappiness existed, Ervine declared, was not caused by Shaw's occupation but came of his dissatisfaction with the situation in his home.[122]

Ervine's opinion was not shared by his colleagues. Pearson pictured a discontented Shaw who detested his job. The Harris book stated that GBS "loathed his servitude" and impatiently awaited his release.[123] McNulty reported that young Shaw "hated [his] occupation and loathed his employer," giving as the chief reason for his abhorrence of Townshend, his friend's objection to the middle-class snobbery of the "h" in his name.[124] Henderson seemed to believe that Shaw hated his post,[125] possibly because of Shaw's 1905 letter to him. GBS himself could scarcely have made his feelings plainer. To Henderson he wrote that he "hated" his job and the work it entailed.[126] Addressing himself to the unorganized clerks of London through the pages of an organizing pamphlet, GBS wrote that he would have used his experience as a clerk as a steppingstone to a successful business career had clerking interested him to the slightest degree.[127] To his readers of the *Sketches* he confided that his heart was not in the work[128] and in the preface to *Immaturity* he allowed that while it was an excellent opportunity it was utterly wasted on him and considered the position as earning his cordial detestation.[129]

Though unhappy in his employment, young Shaw made the best of it and, apart from the occasional operatic and debating exercises with his fellow clerks during the absence of Mr. Townshend, performed his duties conscientiously and efficiently, so much so that when the firm's regular cashier disappeared about a year later under traditionally suspicious circumstances, office boy Shaw was deposited upon the cashier's stool, whilst the firm sought an experienced and more mature replacement. Actually, he was second choice, as those who have read the *Immaturity* preface will recall. Here GBS remembered that, with the sudden vacancy, one of the older men was pressed into service. Though competent enough in his former capacity, this gentleman was unable to balance the accounts and, after one or two chaotic days, the office boy was thrown into the breach. Considering that the agency was "crowded" with premium-paying apprentices who were for the most part university graduates,[130] the selection of the unlettered office boy for the temporary position of cashier may have reflected Townshend's opinion of his staff rather than the esteem in which he held Shaw. Indeed, Sonny's shady school career seemed to disqualify him automatically. Further, his self-acknowledged clumsiness in mathematics or even arithmetic in any of its more common branches made it highly unlikely that he was spurred to volunteer for the post.[131] His year with Townshend seems to have offered no opportunities to prepare him for the complexities of accounting, for he recorded that up to his promotion to cashier, he ran the errands to the Custom House, filed and found letters, made copies of the outgoing ones, fetched lunches for the staff and, so far as accounts were concerned, was responsible only for the postage account.[132]

Perched upon the cashier's stool, Shaw combined his innate

sense of responsibility with the little arithmetical intelligence he had to produce results which Townshend must have regarded with satisfaction, since the firm's efforts to obtain a professional cashier gradually subsided. GBS's ability to adapt a situation or adjust himself to it is illustrated in his early self-imposed discipline. Observing that his handwriting was boyish, slanting—"even weak-minded," [133] he succeeded in modifying these characteristics to what he described was a reasonably accurate imitation of his predecessor's closely-written style.[134] For executing his new duties so admirably Shaw's thirty shillings per month rocketed to eighty and he now sported a tailed coat which he wore despite the chaffing of the staff. But as his salary spiralled upwards, so did the number of new duties—several of which were distasteful as well as otherwise objectionable—but they all played their part in the forming of George Bernard Shaw. There were rents to be collected, interests to be paid, insurances to be minded, private allowances to be distributed, country clients' shopping accounts to be settled—in short, a mobile bank *en miniature,* bustling and responsible. He was, he said, an astonishingly accurate cashier adding that though he never knew how much money his own pockets held, "I was never a farthing out in my accounts . . ." [135] Yet with all these diversified activities, young Shaw continued apathetic. Subconsciously, he stocked up a large store of impressions which were to remain dormant until their meanings were explained to him by the American economist, Henry George.[136] At a later period, GBS added new details in which he strongly suggested a growing uneasiness that kept pace with his mounting importance to Townshend & Company. He had, he said, succeeded, despite his disinterestedness, and discovered to his alarm that business, instead of ejecting him as the worthless fraud he was in reality, clung to him without the slightest intention of releasing him.[137]

Misalliance, written some thirty-five years later, may have resurrected the teen-aged cashier. In a fury of bitterness, GBS poured his four and one-half years of unhappy servitude out through The Man, a nameless, faceless person who sought to avenge his mother's "shame" of bearing him out of wedlock. Accused by the pistol-toting

Man of being the scoundrel in the case, Tarleton maneuvered the conversation away from the object of his would-be assassin's visit. Perhaps he had been mauled by Society? Certainly he didn't look starved and he was wearing a respectable-looking suit. Forty-two shillings, The Man rejoined, it cost him forty-two shillings. Was it paid for, Tarleton persisted, to which The Man replied in substance, that of course it was paid for—did he think he was a thief?

> Dont flatter yourself [he continued] that I'm a loafer or a criminal. I'm a cashier; and I defy you to say that my cash has ever been a farthing wrong. . . .

Shortly thereafter, The Man was prodded into further details of his employment. Trapped, he declared, trapped for seven hours a day in a musty-aired prison and forced to count someone else's money. Did he not possess a soul, a mind, a brain and an intellect? And all the use that was made of these precious and immortal gifts was to employ them on sixpences, tuppences and four and ha'pennies. For seven hours a day he must enter and enter, add and add; he must take money and give change; write out checks and issue receipts; but not a farthing of all that money was his, and neither he nor anyone else in the world, except his employer, had the slightest interest in these activities. Oh! he concluded, "Of all the damnable waste of human life that ever was invented, clerking is the very worst." [138]

Robert Smith, the central figure in *Immaturity* was also, like his creator, a clerk. Employed in recording transactions in "large ledgers," he was unhappy with the smallness of his emoluments as compared to what he could earn by "condescending to the vulgarity of retail trade." He detested his occupation and loathed his own servitude. Reviewing his situation, Townshend's embezzling cashier appeared for a moment in the discontented Smith's thoughts. He wondered whether there was an occupation anywhere so odious as a clerk's and recalled that his employer's very first cashier had mounted a record of thirteen years of impeccable integrity and honesty before decamping with twelve pounds two and six.[139]

It would be another four years before discontented clerk Shaw would put the counting of other people's money behind him, but not for quite the same reasons biographers have assumed.

XI

THERE CAN BE NO DOUBTS that *The Voice* attracted considerable attention and was well received. The fact that it was republished not only in Dublin but also in London is sufficiently impressive, as no hard-headed businessman would risk capital on such a relatively confined subject, unless there appeared to be a popular demand or it was of extraordinary merit. To Professor Lee the scent of success was in the air and he fixed the date of his departure. Henderson put it in a round figure: 1872.[140] Ervine gave the impression of being informative: Shaw had been in the Townshend office "some months" when Lee left Dublin.[141] Pearson either avoided or overlooked this event, merely relating it to a time in advance of Mrs. Shaw's departure in 1872.[142] Shaw's comments were generally consistent but not specific. Earliest was to Henderson in 1905: Lee went to London in 1872 "or thereabouts." [143] In 1916 he told O'Bolger that he could not remember the exact date of the "debacle" set off by Lee's exodus from Dublin.[144] To Harris in 1930 Shaw wrote that the breakup caused by Lee's emigration "must have been somewhere round about 1871," [145] while the preface to *London Music* (1935) contained the information that Lee departed when Shaw "was fifteen or thereabouts." [146] The precise date of Lee's departure for London could not be ascertained without an effort considerably out of proportion to its importance—yet it may be possible to narrow the period down from published and unpublished material.

The decision was final and irrevocable, Lee was leaving. Since the Professor did not own Number 1 Hatch Street, being merely its tenant, its disposal presented no particular problem. As it affected the Shaws it was, to put it succinctly, the end of the line: they would have to seek other means to maintain themselves in Hatch Street or engage quarters more in keeping with their purse. Torca Cottage, however, was another matter, and there is some question regarding its history. Shaw first alluded to the Cottage in 1916 to O'Bolger. Lee, he said, purchased Torca Cottage and "presented" it to his mother (who I assume "accepted" it) but, continued Shaw, as no deed was made, he sold it as his own property "many years later." [147] In the 1935 preface to *London Music* GBS gave two accounts, one of which was almost identical with that to O'Bolger. Here Lee purchased the cottage, "presented" it to his mother who, because she had no legal claim, received no "benefit" when it was sold "later on." [148] Twelve pages later Shaw again referred to the cottage. When Lee, he wrote, went to Shropshire to conduct some private concerts, he ended his tenancy with Hatch Street and sold Torca Cottage.[149]

The biographers have followed Shaw more or less faithfully. Henderson put it that Lee sold (thus inferring purchase) Torca Cottage which he had presented to Mrs. Shaw.[150] Pearson told his readers that, in addition to sharing the Hatch Street house, Lee also purchased the cottage and conferred it upon Shaw's mother. Ervine, for reasons unstated, reported that when Lee bought the cottage, he "invited" the Shaws to use it whenever they wished but sold it before leaving Dublin. All agreed that Lee bought and sold Torca Cottage. As the manner of its disposition must have been determined by the manner of its acquisition, it seemed appropriate to explore this avenue. As previously noted, inspection of the rates record of the cottage prior to and during its occupancy by the Professor and the Shaws did not lead to any connection with Lee but, in fact, to one Hercules MacDonnell [151] who, according to Dublin's Valuation Office, seemed to own the entire hill of Dalkey. Thom's directories showed Torca Cottage to be tenanted by George Carr Shaw from 1866 until 1875, suggesting that it was not bought by Lee but rented by him from MacDonnell. Although George Carr was listed as being its occupant, there could be no doubt that Lee undertook its legal responsibility. The *Registry of Deeds,* King's Inns, Book 1881-40-12, recited an agreement between Lee and a member of the MacDonnell clan entered into on the 19th day of September 1872 under a "Lease

Hold" (nominal annual rent) arrangement. The copy of the Land Judge's Court Rental appeared as follows:

LOT 11.

The houses and Premises on TORCA HILL, known as TORCA COTTAGE . . . being part of the Commons of Dalkey, situate in the Barony of Rathdown, and County of Dublin—held in fee.

Denominations	Tenants' Names	Gale Days	Yearly Rent			Quantity Statute Measure			Tenure of Tenants
			£	s	d	A.	R.	P.	
Torca Hill-Torca Cottage	George V. Lee, Esq.	1st May, 1st Nov.	8	0	0	0	0	33	Lease dated 19th September, 1872, from Very Rev. J. C. MacDonnell and others to G. V. Lee, for 900 years from 1st May, 1872

Covenant by the lessee to insure and keep insured said premises in the Royal Exchange Insurance Company in the sume of £250 at least, with power for the lessors to insure same on his default; and covenant by lessee not to build between the present front of the dwelling-house and Torca-road.

Further efforts to cast more light on Lee and Torca Cottage succeeded, oddly enough, only in throwing new shadows. Mr. Gilbert Paterson, present (1961) owner of Torca Cottage, inspected the original documents and reported that during the period in question, it was leased to one George Vandeleur Lee for the sum of £30 per annum (adding, incidentally, that there was no mention of Mrs. Shaw). At any rate, the discrepancy between £8 and £30 per year does not affect the principal issue: the nature of Lee's connection with Torca. In my opinion, Lee rented the Cottage on a monthly or annual basis from 1866 to 30 March 1872 when, for reasons unknown, he undertook a long-term lease on the eve of, or soon after, his departure for London. Winsten had an explanation which, it must be admitted, seemed quite reasonable but, unfortunately, lacked support. He reported that Lee's conscience was, in effect, a hindrance to his ambitions. If it had not been for his many fans and his particular obligation to Mrs. "Carr Shaw," he would have long since been on his way to London, but it was now or never, so away with maudlin susceptibilities. Yet he would yearn for Torca Cottage where, when his fortune was made, he hoped some day to return and spend his last years.[152] The lease with MacDonnell demonstrates that Lee never bought the cottage and consequently could not, in the legal sense, present it to Mrs. Shaw. Further, the new lease identified Lee as the "tenant" and came into force four and one-half months before the activating date of 19 September 1872, thus suggesting the expiration of an earlier lease. Whatever this earlier arrangement, the present conditions bound Lee to keep the premises insured and restrained him from erecting any structure between the house and the road (about thirty feet). On the other hand, Lee was free to let, sublet, give, transfer or sell his remaining interest in the cottage, and this he did within two years.

Of most particular interest at this moment was the modification in Lee's name. In place of the familiar G.J. or George John, there now appeared the pretentious G.V. or George Vandeleur. With the exception of Ervine, none of the biographers regarded this as noteworthy, and, excluding Winsten, all of them used "Vandaleur" (as GBS consistently misspelled it) indiscriminately in both the Dublin and London periods. Ervine appreciated the distinction and explained in a footnote that Lee did not seem to have used Vandaleur in Dublin and quoted GBS as reinforcing this belief.[153] In the *Sketches,* GBS told how his mother received singing lessons from "George John Vandaleur Lee" who had, he wrote, already been firmly established professionally in Dublin.[154] The *London Music* preface recorded that when his star was falling in London, the Professor abandoned his principles, altered his facial adornments from the Dundreary "mutton-chop" style to a moustache waxed and pointed—and "became" Vandaleur Lee.[155] O'Bolger was given a rare treat: the life and times of the Professor, including the metamorphosis which came over him after he left Ireland. G. J. Lee of Dublin, Shaw wrote on the second page of his thirty-page letter, was a man of spirit, of energy and a conductor of genius—and he taught singing with integrity and grace as his mother would have affirmed. But in London he turned imposter and swindler. He shaved off his whiskers, grew an imperial in the manner of Napoleon III and called himself Vandaleur Lee.[156] This shift was not, however, Shaw's last word in the matter. On the sixth page of the same letter, GBS summed up the Professor's career.

Lee in Dublin was an active volcano, spewing with energy, but Lee in London was extinct: "His name, by the way," Shaw added, "was really Vandaleur Lee. In Dublin he was G. J. Lee; but we always knew that he was George John Vandaleur." [157] Henderson was informed that the disappointed wife of George Carr Shaw found salvation when she became associated with "an artist, a conductor and a man of quite exceptional temperament and energy, [which] must have had considerable influence on me. This man, by name George John Vandaleur Lee . . ." [158]

Shaw's implication that Lee's Christian names were always George John Vandaleur is not borne out by the public records. Examination of Lee's trail from his earliest traces to the latest through Thom's Registers, the *London Post Office Directories, Saunders' News-Letter,* the *Irish Times,* etc., reveals clearly that Lee adopted Vandeleur in his forty-first year. (See Appendix C for abstract upon which this conclusion is based.)

In these records, from the eight-year-old George in school to a fifty-six-year-old Vandeleur in the morgue, two complementary facts appear. First, that prior to the third of December, 1871, neither V. nor Vandeleur had any discoverable associations with Lee—neither with his schooling, his homes, professional references, news accounts or published work, and he was exclusively referred to as George, George John or G. J. Lee. Second, that after the eighth of December, 1871, Lee's Christian name John had no discoverable associations with him—neither with his homes, professional references, news accounts, legal matters or personal correspondence, and he was exclusively referred to as G. V., George V., George Vandeleur, G. Vandeleur, V.L. or Vandeleur Lee. Subsidiary conclusion: George John substituted Vandeleur for John during the week of December 3-December 9, 1871. It could not be determined whether this substitution took place in Dublin or London, since there is considerable doubt that Lee emigrated to England in 1872. Yet there is the possibility that sometime during that week, Professor Lee left Dublin to keep a private engagement in Shropshire[159] from where he proceeded to London, surveyed the professional situation, jettisoned John for Vandeleur and returned to Dublin to prepare, rehearse and conduct a series of the grandest of the "Grand" concerts of his career. Regarding the selection of a substitute for the provincial John, I believe that the Professor, perhaps mindful of his brother William's preference for Harcourt and Nassau, chose rhythmic, continental and mellifluous Vandeleur as a practical measure. Snobocratic Englishwomen would readily pay that guinea-per-lesson fee for teaching their marriageable daughters vocal glissandi.

XII

UP TO THE TIME OF HIS PROBABLE VISIT TO LONDON in December of 1871, matters had not gone well for Professor G. Vandeleur Lee and his Amateur Musical Society. It seems that Lee had been gradually maneuvering the Society out of its amateur status into the commercial entertainment field, a movement, according to a brief and tactfully-worded news item, to which there was a considerable body of members opposed. The rumbles appeared to have developed at a concert given by the Society on 1 April 1871 in Dublin's largest and most famous theatre and, according to the announcements, not in support of the usual worthy cause. Containing all the signs of a full-fledged commercial performance, the advertisements appeared in *The Irish Times* and other papers from 28 March to and including the opening day:

THEATRE ROYAL, DUBLIN
AMATEUR ITALIAN OPERA
Under the Distinguished Patronage of Their Excellencies The Lord Lieutenant and the Countess Spencer, Lord Sandhurst, Major General Newton C.B. Commander of the Garrison, and General Wardlaw C.B. Commander of the Cavalry in Ireland
On Saturday Evening
April 1, 1871

Will be presented the Gipsy Scene from the 2nd Act of Verdi's Il Trovatore.

Manrico }
Ruiz } .... By Gentlemen amateurs

Azucena .... By a Lady amateur

To Conclude with
Mozart's Grand Opera
Il Don Giovanni
[All members of the cast by
Lady and Gentlemen amateurs]
Conductor
GEORGE J. LEE

Private Boxes 3 guineas, 2½ guineas and 2 guineas
Dress circle 6/, Second circle 4/
Pit 2/6, Lower Gallery 1/6, Upper Gallery 1/
No Free list, the Press excepted. Pass out checks not transferable. Children in arms not admitted.
No money returned.

Concluding the season with one more concert on 21 April, the Society disappeared from the columns of the daily press for the summer holidays and reappeared on 11 November of the same year—rather late in the year, as several other Dublin choral societies were already in full cry. However, in place of the usual advertisement announcing its opening concert, the Society advised its membership that its regular annual meeting which had been adjourned from the previous Saturday, would be held that evening at seven-thirty in the Antient Concert Rooms. Purpose: to receive the past year's reports, statement of accounts and for the selection of officers and committee members for the coming year—duly signed by J. Adair Phillips, Hon. Sec.[160] On the surface all seemed serene, proper, even democratic, despite the absence of announcements of previous "annual" meetings. Fortunately (at least for the purposes of this study), *The Irish Times* had its journalist on the job and its brief paragraph, though couched in soothing syllables, suggested a meeting incipient if not seething with rebellion. The Society, declared Chairman Edward Purdon Esq., was to be congratulated on its increase in membership and on the most satisfactory state of its finances. Commenting editorially, the *Times* added

> We regret to learn from our correspondent that some misunderstanding has arisen as to members of the Society performing in English or other operas at the theatre, and in consequence of which a considerable number of the committee refused to offer themselves for re-election.

Recalling the Society's early days, the *Times* concluded it was regrettable that its existence should be endangered by internal differences and hoped that the "little misunderstanding" would be solved easily.[161] I take it that the reference to "English" opera was one of the issues which divided the Society's membership and developed into the traditional squabble between reactionary "classicists" and progressive "modernists." All the same, whether heterodox English opera or orthodox Italian opera, there appeared to be organized opposition to performances by the Amateur Musical Society in the commercial theatre.

Within three weeks (during which there were rehearsal calls on the 18th and 25th) another announcement appeared notifying all concerned that a "General" meeting would be held 30 November that evening at the Concert Rooms; purpose: the election of a Committee and Officers for the current season, thus indicating that the previous "annual" meeting got no further with its agenda than Old Business. The real purpose of the second general meeting was at least partly disclosed two days later in a press release whose lead ran

> AMATEUR MUSICAL SOCIETY IN CONJUNCTION
> WITH THE OPERATIC AND DRAMATIC SOCIETY

Reporting on the meeting of November 30, the Society announced its amalgamation with what seemed to be a new or, at most, an existing but obscure group, and it named a sixteen-man committee with thirteen members from the military: one Colonel, two Majors and ten Captains. M. P. Healy Esq. was the Leader; J. P. Clarke Esq., the Librarian and G. J. Lee, of course, the Conductor. The release closed with what may have been a sop to the anticommercial members: "One of the objects of this Society is to give an annual performance in aid of the poor of Dublin, irrespective of religious denominations," [162] a laudable object incidentally but perhaps a necessary object, if one wished to grace one's announcements with the names of noble patrons. It seems that the dissension within the Amateur Musical Society had not yet dissolved, as the *Times* had hoped, and was still of a nature serious enough to split the Society organically. It is not known what happened to the body, but its brain and spirit, seeking a new and respectable home, settled restlessly in the Operatic and Dramatic Society.

Driven by its energetic conductor, the new Society soon blossomed into print with a dazzling bouquet of promise that bid fair to please all tastes, for on Saturday, 9 December 1871, the following appeared under Public Announcements of *The Irish Times*:

AMATEUR MUSICAL, OPERATIC AND
DRAMATIC SOCIETY.
Conductor—G. V. LEE, Esq.
A GRAND
MILITARY, DRAMATIC AND OPERATIC PERFORMANCE WILL BE GIVEN AT THE
NEW GAIETY THEATRE
On Friday Evening, the 22nd Instant.
The Programme will include Sheridan Knowles's Celebrated Comedy
"THE HUNCHBACK."
Selections from "IL TROVATORE" Verdi
And the MUSICAL BURLESQUE,
"PATIENT PENELOPE,"
By C. Burnand, Esq.
The following distinguished Amateurs will perform upon this occasion:
Major S. Hall
Captain Vivian.
P.O.R.Butler, Esq, Late 60th Rifles
J. Younger, Esq, R.H.A.

W.F.Way, Esq, 5th Fusiliers
R. Auld, Esq, 5th Fusiliers
Captain M'Calmont, 8th Hussars

The Surplus to be devoted to the relief of the poor of this city, and a special case of distress. Ladies and Gentlemen desirous of becoming members of this Society, will please address communications to the Honorary Secretary, 61 Grafton street. Subscription, one guinea for the season, for which each member will receive two tickets for Dramatic representations, two for Italian Opera, and two for each Concert of the Society free; also admission to the Conversazione.

J.F.Waller, LL.D., Hon. Sec.

After being repeated daily for the next four days, plus one rehearsal call on the 16th, the advertisement ceased and nothing more was heard from the Society until eight days after the promised Grand Performance. Whether the public response was not as expected or Lee was unable to bring the participants up to the level suitable for public performance cannot be determined; but, on the surface, the Society was in default. Thereafter, while Lee continued his connection with it, it was clear that this Irish stew was not to his taste. After a valiant effort with Racine's *Athalie* on 30 March 1872, the Society went down for the second time not to surface again until early the next year. At that time the Society reappeared as the Amateur Musical and Dramatic Society with a reminder from conductor G. V. Lee to the membership that their season's subscriptions were past due and would they remit. He added that their next concert would be held on 24 February 1873 but the 24th came and went without a sign. Quietly, the A.M. & D.S. sank beneath the waves for the third but not the last time.

Yet if this descendant of the Amateur Musical Society did not have the will and stamina to survive, its extinction could in no way reflect on the organizational potency of G. Vandeleur Lee. Indeed, even as the A.M. & D.S. lay expiring, the Professor bent solicitously to the task of bringing his third creation into the world and announced for Friday, 12 January 1872, the birth of the New Philharmonic Society. This Society, he stated, would be established as "A GRAND VOCAL AND INSTRUMENTAL SOCIETY" and offered facilities for the study and practice of oratorios and the opportunity to cultivate the works of the finest composers.[163] Here Conductor Lee came back into his own and on 18 April was billed in the Gaiety Theatre with a production of *Lucrezia Borgia* in full costume, full band and with distinguished Lady and Gentlemen Amateurs—top price for seat three guineas. In June the New Philharmonic Society gave a GRAND CHORAL CONCERT at the Exhibition Palace in connection with the 1872 *Exhibition of Arts, Industries and Manufactures.* Complete with organ and full band accompaniment, Lee directed and conducted five hundred performers through masterpieces of Handel, Mozart, Beethoven, Mendelssohn, Rossini, Gounod, Meyerbeer and Haydn,[164] and in October the Society gave a concert at which G. V. Lee conducted four hundred "members," which, if that number is not exaggerated, must have provided something over operating costs.[165]

The final month of 1872 found Lee engaged in scaling what GBS termed "the summit of a provincial conductor's destiny" in Dublin: a musical festival patterned on the Three Choirs or Handel Festivals. This, said Shaw in his preface to *London Music,* Lee did in collaboration with an Exhibition in Dublin but did not identify the Exhibition or name the year.[166] To Henderson, in a bygone era, GBS disclosed one or two details later omitted in the *London Music* preface. Lee's ambitions, wrote Shaw, drove him irresistibly towards London. He had made himself into a first-class teacher with something original to offer. From there he wished to go on to be a conductor of operas and, when he had achieved this, aspired "to conduct a Handel Festival in Dublin with all the greatest singers of the day—Tietjens, Agnesi & etc. He did it." [167] Judging the occasion by the program, the circumstances and the reviews, one must conclude that the Professor certainly "did it". The announcement as it appeared in the *Irish Times* for Thursday, 12 December 1872:

DUBLIN EXHIBITION PALACE
New Philharmonic Society

The Dublin Music Festival will take place in January next for which the following distinguished artists have been specially engaged:—Mdlle Titiens, Mdme Sinico, Mdlle Justine MacVitz The Celebrated Contralto from St. Petersburgh, Signor Tombesi, Signor Campobello, Signor Borella and Signor Agnesi. Solo Violincello Mons. Albert. Solo Pianoforte Mr. F.G.Cowan. Organ Mr. W.H.Gater.

FIRST PERFORMANCE MONDAY 6TH JANUARY, 1873 AT 8 O'CLOCK

Part I Rossini's Stabat Mater and
Part II Secular Selections

SECOND PERFORMANCE 11 JANUARY 1873

Part I Handel's Messiah and
Part II Secular Selections

BAND AND CHORUS OF 500 PERFORMERS
Musical Director—G. VANDELEUR LEE

Doors open at 7.30 Carriages may be ordered for 10.30
The Dublin Tramways Company have made special arrangements to run special cars up to a late hour each evening for the Convenience of the Public.

First performance to be honoured by the Presence of
Their Excellencies
The Lord Lieutenant and Countess Spencer

If there were any other participants in the Dublin Musical Festival, their contributions were eclipsed by the attention given to Lee and his Society. After a thorough and laudatory review of singers individually and collectively, the *Times* turned to the civic aspects of the concert, revealing, incidentally, some notion of the size of the audience. "The crowds of persons" wrote the reviewer-reporter, "who besieged each portion of the [Exhibition] Hall soon filled to its utmost capacity, every particle of available space obtainable, and the crushing at length became so inconvenient that the large doors leading into the building at the end of the Hall had to be thrown open and numbers were content to obtain standing room in the outer galleries." In view of the high admission prices charged, he added, it would be advisable if the management would consider the comfort and safety of its patrons on the next such occasion.[168] The second performance five days later was equally successful, but this time the reviewer confined himself to the rapport between conductor and musicians. Mr. Lee, he wrote, was to be congratulated on the splendid results achieved in so short a time. His control of the large body of singers and players was evident in his "steadiness, precision and ability" and predicted even greater successes for him: with a little patience he would surely "reap the rewards his energies and abilities deserve." [169] All too plainly, G. Vandeleur Lee had forsaken his genteel "amateur" status and had reached the musical summit in Dublin. Surely, nothing remained but fresh peaks in London.

As might have been predicted, the first perceptible sign of a move in that direction appeared shortly afterward in the form of a "benefit" which, for some reason not revealed, Lee shared with a Mr. [R.M.] Levey known as sometime "leader" or concertmaster in the Lee organization. In view of the scope and vigor of the Professor's activities over twenty years, it is difficult to appreciate his willingness to share the limelight (and the profits) with anyone. I can only speculate that in the course of his activities he, with that inspired contempt for fools and knaves, trod the toes of the academicians and rival professors of music, antagonizing so many that he despaired of his own value at the box office. By pairing with Mr. Levey—a popular and eminently respectable musician—the double benefit might prove more profitable in terms of individual gain. In any event on the 27th, 28th and 31st of March, 1873, the *Irish Times* prominently displayed at the top of its first column, the advertisement that two performances of "Amateur Italian Opera" would be given for Levey and Lee (Levey received the top billing). No explanation was offered in either the advertising or news columns why these gentlemen should receive a benefit, but perhaps that would be asking too much of a time-honored custom. The first performance, consisting of two acts of *La Sonnambula* and a "slightly compressed" production of *Lucrezia Borgia,* elicited the usual compliments from the critics: Mr. G.V.Lee "the talented Conductor and Promoter" was described additionally as "one of Dublin's foremost interpreters of the lyric art." [170] The second program (*Il Trovatore*) was noteworthy because of the critic's reference to its prima donna. "The Lady who sang Azucena," wrote the reviewer, "was exquisite and her acting superb." [171] The Lady: Mrs. Shaw.[172]

If Lee exuded satisfaction with the perfection of harmony upon the stage of the Theatre Royal, he must have winced at the sour notes coming from the box office. The echoes of *Il Trovatore* had barely died away when Levey and Lee repaired to the offices of the *Irish Times* to express their gratitude to certain citizens of Dublin for their unstinting support.

> Theatre Royal Dublin
> THE DEBENTURE HOLDERS
> Messrs Levey and Lee
> Beg to return their grateful thanks (?) to the many debenture holders who honoured their BENEFIT on Monday and Friday Evenings, either by making use of their FREE admissions, or transferring them to others.[173]

'Twas a sorry state indeed when speculating shareholders (and so many of them) chose to exercise their special privilege on these nights of all nights—surely it was an act of meanness calculated to deprive a worthy cause of its rightful due—now London would have to wait. But at least one creditor took umbrage. Signing himself as "One Who Used A Debenture," he resented the sarcasm implied in the (?), and declared that he, for one, had paid for his debenture. Furthermore, he continued, he donated £1 to Mr. Levey's testimonial who was a well-known and honorable figure in the musical world, but what, pray, was G.V.Lee's connection with the benefit other than that of a joint speculator? [174]

On the 28th of April, Lee resuscitated the Amateur Musical and Dramatic Society for the fourth time and offered the third grand concert of the season, but it was not reported by the press. The 14th of May saw another maximum effort by the Professor without, however, a mention of any Society. The powers that were saw fit to reopen the Dublin *Industrial Exhibition of the Arts, Industries and Manufactures* and invited G. V. Lee to conduct the major musical contributions, including a grand performance of Mendelssohn's *Athalie* with a chorus and band totaling more than five hundred members. Soloists included Madame Demeric Lablache of whom GBS was to report later that when, during rehearsal, contralto Lablache refused to sing for some reason or other, Lee unconcernedly requested mezzo-soprano Mrs. Shaw to take her place. Mrs. Shaw, added her son, was so effective in Lablache's role, that Lablache took good care not to give her another opportunity.[175] Of this concert the *Irish Times* reported that perhaps three thousand or more persons attended and who were, for the most part, members of Dublin's *elite.* Of the choruses it was further reported that "they were in perfect unison, and the five hundred voices blended most harmoniously . . ."[176] The 19th of May saw the formation of The National Institute of Music which was incorporated with the New Philharmonic Society (Director G. Vandeleur Lee). Avowed purpose: to bring choral music to a wider audience but it seems to have failed in its object, since it expired with its first breath. On Monday, 26 May, G. Vandeleur Lee exhumed for the last time the name, if not the body, of the Amateur Musical and Dramatic Society in what appears to have been Lee's last publicly-held concert in Ireland. Of this "Grand Charity Concert," the *Irish Times* reported disappointing attendance, despite the presence of the Lord Lieutenant and his amiable Countess.[177] *Freeman's Journal* for the same day had kinder things to say, but what made its review especially interesting was its closing sentence: "Mr. G.V.Lee conducted and presided at the pianoforte with much skill and taste." This observation remains the only evidence that Lee actually played a musical instrument.

This recital of the public history of Conductor and Promoter G. Vandeleur Lee, shows that he had been active on a scale which, by any standard, justified statistically and dramatically Shaw's description of Lee as "energetic." But apart from this aspect of Lee's last days in Dublin, the record of the daily press also shows the biographers and Shaw to have been mistaken with regard to the time of Lee's departure for London. GBS's recollections that Lee left Dublin in 1871-1872 or "thereabouts" must be discounted, for Lee was furiously occupied with his Dublin productions into the last days of May, 1873. Examination of his residential records in both Dublin and London helps to throw further light on the probable time of his emigration:

Actual Year	Residence	Occupant	Source
1871	1 Hatch Street	Lee, J. G. Esq.	Thom's
	13 Park Lane[178]	Riel, Madame	London P. O. D.
1872	1 Hatch Street	Lee, G. V.	Thom's
	13 Park Lane	Marshall, Julian	London P. O. D.
1873	1 Hatch Street	Lee, G. V. Esq.	Thom's
	13 Park Lane	Marshall, Julian	London P. O. D.
1874	1 Hatch Street	Vacant[179]	Thom's
	13 Park Lane	Marshall, Julian	London P. O. D.
	Ebury Street, Pimlico	George Vandeleur Lee	Document of Sale of Torca Cottage to Julian Marshall

Thus it can be seen that there is substantial agreement between the residence records and the reports in the daily press: Professor Lee was in Dublin up to and including some portion of 1873. The residence records further indicate that in 1874, 1 Hatch Street was reported vacant and its former occupant was simultaneously and unmistakably established in London. In the document of sale and transfer of Torca Cottage signed in London on 20 April 1874, Lee declared his place of residence to be Ebury Street, Pimlico, in the County of Middlesex. This does not, of course, necessarily mean that Lee did not go to London until April of 1874; he could have been there since June of 1873.

Because of the foregoing records and for further reasons which will be discussed shortly, I believe that G. Vandeleur Lee left Dublin for London on one of the twenty-one days between 26 May and 17 June 1873.

XIII

WITH LEE GONE FOREVER FROM DUBLIN, Mrs. Lucinda Elizabeth Shaw completed her preparations to follow. I have used the word "completed" intentionally, as there is some evidence that her preparations to leave Ireland were begun prior to Lee's departure. There is, in addition, some difference of opinion as to when, why and how Mrs. Shaw set her course.

Henderson reported in one place that when Lee "sold" Torca Cottage, Mrs. Shaw "then" made her first moves, and in another place he informed his readers that the Hatch Street household fell apart when Lee left for London in 1872.[180] Ervine did not differ in substance. Mrs. Shaw sold her home in 1872, pocketed the proceeds and embarked for London whither Lee had already gone.[181] In his published and unpublished comments, GBS was as vague about his mother's departure from Dublin as he was about Lee's. In 1905 he told Henderson that when Lee migrated in or about 1872, the Hatch Street home disintegrated and his mother went to London "boldly." [182] In 1930 he replied by letter to a direct question from Harris that his mother and Lee could not have left Dublin together, since Lee had to organize his position in London before establishing a "musical setting" suitable to mother and daughter. He further stated that when it became obvious that Lee would not return, his mother then gave up the Hatch Street home. These events, he concluded, must have taken place some time in 1871 or thereabouts.[183] In 1935 he touched upon the subject in the preface to *London Music*; though he made it clear that Lee went first, he did not give the year.[184]

Shaw's 1948 account in the *Sketches* warrants closer attention. Writing to O'Bolger, GBS avoided relating the time of Lee's departure to the time of his mother's, saying, simply, that she "also" went. In his version for the *Sketches,* GBS changed its form in a manner that indicated an earlier reluctance to feed O'Bolger more fuel for his burning curiosity. Comparison of the two treatments illustrates the point. Speaking of the relationship between his mother and Lee in the late London years Shaw phrased it in this fashion:

Original Letter	Revised Letter
My mother, who also came to London, was as available as in Dublin.[185]	My mother, who followed him to London . . . was as available as in Dublin.[186]

In the summer of 1922, the relentless O'Bolger queried: "Does

Mr. Shaw know why Lee so suddenly departed Dublin and forsook his mother, and why his mother decided to go to London only after Lee had gone there?" Although GBS had answered—indeed volunteered such information before to O'Bolger, the tormented playwright obliged once more, but this time he added a refreshing variation. "Demetrius:" GBS wrote, "you are a God-forsaken lunatic." He denied that "forsook" had any relevance in the matter and added that after his emigration, Lee soon achieved some success and "It did not take very long for my mother to make up her mind. She sold up Hatch St. after a reconnaissance in London . . ." and settled in a house in Victoria Grove. Concluding, GBS invited O'Bolger to make his usual inquiries to satisfy himself that Park Lane and Victoria Grove were about two miles apart.[187] Examination of Shaw's patient review to O'Bolger shows the sequence of events: Lee left Dublin, achieved some measure of success, communicated this to Mrs. Shaw who, after a brief period of contemplation, visited London for the express purpose of appraising the situation. Satisfied, she then returned to Dublin, sold the family furniture and once again departed for London. In short, Mrs. Shaw made two trips to London.

Examination of the *Arrivals and Departures* departments of Dublin's daily newspapers, while most unsatisfying and inconclusive, offered some interesting items for speculation. The record of *The Irish Times*:

YEAR OF 1873	DEPARTURES FOR HOLYHEAD PORT OF KINGSTOWN, COUNTY DUBLIN
Friday 16 May	Mrs. Shaw
Wednesday 18 June	Mrs. Shaw, Miss Shaw
Wednesday 27 August	Mrs. Shaw

In view of certain complicating factors in connection with the illness of Elinor Agnes, a projected timetable of the movements of those concerned will be deferred for the present.

Almost as a body, the biographers believe that Mrs. Shaw's decision to leave Dublin was a sudden desire for an economic security unobtainable from her husband and in this belief they were, of course, encouraged by GBS. Thus Henderson allowed that when Lee left Dublin the Shaws were deprived of his share in the cost of Hatch Street and George Carr was, consequently, unable to maintain the establishment. Mrs. Shaw, Henderson implied, grasped the situation and provided the solution: "With characteristic energy and decisiveness, Mrs. Shaw went to London to become a professional teacher of singing." [188] Later, Henderson reinforced the economic aspects of her move by observing that when Lee "sold" Torca Cottage which he had given to Mrs. Shaw, she received nothing from the transaction and only then became aware of the seriousness of "their" situation. She proceeded forthwith with the sale of the household furniture prior to leaving for London.[189] According to this account, it is almost impossible not to conclude that Mrs. Shaw's departure for London was an act of despair growing out of the insufficiency of her husband's income to maintain Hatch Street and her disappointment in not receiving the proceeds from the sale of Torca Cottage. Other than this, one may rightly puzzle how biographers could be taken in by Lee's flimsy pretext of "giving" the cottage to Lucinda since he could hardly have sold her property without her cooperation. Then, of course, there is the minor matter that the cottage was not disposed of until September of 1874 when both the Professor *and* Mrs. Shaw had already been in London for more than a year.

The Harris book took up where Henderson left off. Lee's departure left the Shaws without their star lodger and in a house too expensive for them. Lucy, Shaw's elder sister, had been brought up on The Method, and, "Harris" asserted, the most sensible thing to do was for her and her mother to follow Lee—particularly as there was some possibility of Lucy's professional debut under Lee's management. The author further implied that George Carr, sinking lower and lower into financial distress, was of no service to his family; consequently, "Left with no one to lean on," mother and daughter followed Lee to London.[190] Thus the writer of these lines put it that Mrs. Shaw's departure had two objectives: Lucy's career and their own economic welfare. Pearson confined the professional intentions to Mrs. Shaw who, he said, dissolved her home as she was "anxious" to become a commercial teacher of singing in London.[191]

Ervine offered no real conflict with the biographers who went before him. The Shaws, he wrote, were in difficulties—Lee had flown. No longer able to keep Hatch Street without his contribution, they were also beset by the specter of George Carr's imminent bankruptcy. Mrs. Shaw, continued Ervine, "who now made all the family decisions, solved their urgent problem abruptly and drastically"—she closed out Hatch Street and, in what was tantamount to desertion, abandoned her husband and son to follow Lee with whom she believed her professional future to be linked.[192]

Examination of Shaw's expressions in this matter shows the biographers' source and guide for their treatment. Shaw's versions, incidentally, offer further examples of his tactical use of language. Earliest view was to Henderson. When Lee put Dublin behind him, Hatch Street collapsed. Since

> My father's affairs were as unprosperous as ever; the return to a single household on his income was almost impossible; and there was some question of my two sisters becoming professional singers. So my mother boldly went to London too, and became a professional teacher of singing.[193]

Here Shaw gave three reasons for his mother's decision each of which, however, was couched so as to convey impressions without being specific. (1) George Carr's business was bad (but no worse than it ever was); ergo, a return to a *ménage à deux* on his earnings was nearly (but not) impossible. (2) There were vague or unresolved ruminations as to the musical future of Lucy and Yuppy, and (3) the urgency of these two conditions convinced Mrs. Shaw that she should go to London where she took up the occupation of singing teacher.

O'Bolger was the next to receive the tale. GBS warned the Professor from Pennsylvania not to be, like the Professor from North Carolina, carried away by his romantic imagination and regard the Mrs. Shaw-Lee departures as an elopement. It was, he advised, "practically a pecuniary necessity; for my father's resources were always shrinking, and something energetic had to be done when we no longer had Lee to pay the rent and rates of a sufficient house." [194] In substance, O'Bolger was informed that the withdrawal of Lee's support to the Shaws forced Mrs. Shaw, who had become accustomed to living on the scale of Hatch Street, to make up the difference by going to London.

In his Parknasilla letter to O'Bolger, Shaw offered variations on this theme—the differences again inviting attention. As published in the *Sketches,* Shaw had it that his father was "left alone" by his family because of the hard fact that he was unable to provide for them.[195] In his original letter, the fact was a hard as ever: "he could not support them" and "He was, poor man, abandoned by his family . . ." Common to both original and revised letters, Shaw further stated that for the family to remain with him held no future for them whatsoever.[196] In still another portion of the same letter as it appeared in the *Sketches* version, GBS inserted information too late to be of use to O'Bolger: his mother followed Lee to take up the profession of music and to embark daughter Lucy upon a career of professional singing.[197] Harris was told that the splitting of the family was imperative since Lee's emigration left them in a house they could ill afford, but GBS implied that there was a possibility that Lee might return to Dublin. When it became clear that Lee would stay in London, Hatch Street was vacated.[198]

To the readers of the *London Music* preface, GBS went into further details of this difficult period. His father's ailing business was sicker than ever. Further, Yuppy was seriously ill of tuberculosis—she was going to die and all that could be recommended was a removal to a kindlier clime. Shaw went on in a manner to indicate his mother believed that after a rehearsal or two she would be quite ready to replace Adelina Patti or Christine Nilsson on the operatic stage in London. In this connection, Lee would prove to be invaluable, since, being in the midst of his first successes in Park Lane, it would be a simple matter for him to provide such an opportunity. Finally, Shaw concluded, his mother (whom he described as "now elderly") was convinced that she would, if it became necessary, relinquish her amateur respectability and earn her living as a singing teacher. After all, had she not The Method to offer? That settled it—she sold a small parcel of property Aunt Ellen had been unable to take from her, disposed of the Hatch Street furnishings and departed.[199] Thus, to the reasons given earlier in justifying his mother's following Lee to London, GBS added the need for removing Yuppy from the rigors of Irish weather and his mother's aspirations to the professional opera stage. Skillful touch was the reference to his "elderly" mother (then a forty-three-year-old dodderer), perhaps with the intention of discouraging "romantic" connotations.

Shaw's explanations for his mother's decision seem, on the surface at least, to be fairly consistent and even reasonable. When the Professor departed for greener fields than Ireland's, he terminated his responsibilities to the Shaws; consequently, George Carr's income was insufficient to bear the burden of the Hatch Street establishment or its equivalent. Whereupon Mrs. Shaw deemed it necessary to seek means to support herself and, presumably, her two daughters. In the belief that London offered opportunities superior to those of Dublin, she sold the Hatch Street furniture and went to London, where (a) she would sing in grand opera or (b) descend to the teaching of singing and, with Lee's help, launch one or both daughters in a singing career.

Without denying the consistency or the reasonableness of Mrs. Shaw's motivating forces as outlined by her son, I suggest that GBS's excellent array of cause and effect was developed to draw attention from other matters, particularly the eyebrow-raising sequence of desertion in Dublin and conjunction in London. I think Shaw was sensible of the risks involved in allowing free speculation in this area which, if not halted or diverted, might lead to closer examinations by a host of O'Bolgers. Therefore, the departure of Mrs. Shaw in the wake of Professor Lee must have—for the public—reasonable, sensible and acceptable motivations.

It is difficult to accept the overnight metamorphosis of an Irish gentlewoman into breadwinner, and I regard the job-hunting Lucinda Elizabeth to be utterly at odds with her son's description of her as a carriage lady. Brought up in iron-handed severity to be a model of perfect breeding, Mrs. Shaw had, up to this time, never lifted her hand in an act of housework—let alone an act in her own support—nor was there any real urgency for this pattern to change. Other than a natural desire to rise out of unfashionable, plebeian Synge Street, there are no indications that Mrs. Shaw had extravagant tastes, and a review of the economic picture as a whole shows no need for drastic measures. The combined incomes of her husband and son, income from the parcel of property referred to earlier and the interest on the £1500 Whitcroft bequest would have been sufficient to keep her comfortably and respectably content in Dublin. Further, if Mrs. Shaw's principal reason for going to London was to make up the deficit caused by the loss of Lee's contributions, Dublin had a ready-made and waiting opportunity: Lee's musical enterprises, the most important and genteel of which (and at the same time satisfying her need for artistic expression) was the Professor's voice pupils eager to be taught The Method. And who was better qualified to succeed the Master and inherit his Dublin practice?

There was an additional incentive for Mrs. Shaw to remain in Dublin: a miracle had occurred. Her husband had seen the error of his ways and taken the pledge. Yes, George Carr Shaw, the King Cockatoo of the Convivial Cockatoos, the teetotaler in principle, had at last become the teetotaler in fact. Writing to Cousin Charles MacMahon, GBS informed him that it happened quite suddenly one Sunday morning when Mr. Shaw collapsed on their doorstep in the throes of a fit; the effect of which was to terrify him into teetotalism.[200] In the *London Music* preface he put it, in respect to the Hatch Street smashup, that his father finally realized his wish to become an honest teetotaler and "was now as inoffensive an old [59] gentleman as any elderly [43] wife could desire."[201] The time of this conversion to practical sobriety has been put in or about 1871 and so GBS told O'Bolger. He added that towards the end of his life, he was not sure that his father did not take a nip now and then but that it was a respectable nip so often indulged in by older people.[202] But if George Carr held any hopes that his embrace of temperance would eventually be followed by an embrace from his wife, they were quickly dispelled by her converting the Hatch Street furnishings into cash.

The statements of GBS and the beliefs of the biographers that Mrs. Shaw went to London *because* she found it necessary to earn her own living are, in my opinion, not justifiable within the framework of all available information. Mrs. Shaw went to London principally because she believed that a Dublin without the energetic, talented and enterprising Lee would be a Dublin without the joy of accomplishment, without music and without purpose—in short, without life. Notwithstanding the whispers and frowns of conventional disapproval, Mrs. Shaw preferred to follow George Vandeleur Lee who, in the fullest symbolic sense, had supplanted her husband. Could twenty years of close association—successful, happy and creative years—be swept away because of the ridiculous demands of a hypocritical society? I think not. I believe Mrs. Shaw followed Lee because she hoped their occupational relationship would continue to the cultural and professional advantage of herself and her daughter. For these reasons she would abandon her home, abandon her husband, abandon her son and, if need be, abandon her genteel amateur status.

How Mrs. Shaw left Dublin is likewise obscured within a confusion of statements and opinions. Henderson said that Mrs. Shaw and her two daughters embarked for London but, while not specifically relating it to the moment, added that the ailing Agnes unexpectedly took a turn for the worse and was sent off in the charge of Lucy to be placed in a sanatorium on the Isle of Wight. He did not make it clear whether Agnes' sudden turn occurred during the trip to or after their arrival at their new home in Victoria Grove.[203] Ervine's account ran parallel to Henderson's but could be construed to suggest that Agnes' illness developed en route. Sisters Lucy and Agnes, he wrote, accompanied their mother. The younger one, he continued, was obviously "doomed"; so Mrs. Shaw sent her in Lucy's custody to Wight "while she settled herself in [Victoria Grove.]" [204] Pearson shied clear of controversy, merely reporting that Mrs. Shaw left Dublin with her two daughters.[205] The Harris work seemed to differ from the assertions in its fellow volumes. As touched upon earlier in this section, "Harris" wrote that when Lee left for London, Lucy and her mother decided it would be the sensible thing to do if the two of them would also go.[206] McNulty's account was one based entirely on first-hand knowledge. Shaw, he wrote, grew up in an atmosphere of domestic discord. There finally came a day when his parents agreed to an amicable separation whereupon Mrs. Shaw chose to go to London whilst Mr. Shaw seemed content to remain in Dublin. Agnes, McNulty recalled, being the younger and most frail of the two girls, was the first to go with her mother—Lucy and George staying behind with their father until Mrs. Shaw had established a home for them.[207]

Shaw's own pronouncements were few, far apart and as full of conflicts as those of his biographers. Undoubtedly the earliest reference was contained in an extraordinary letter to Arnold White, General Manager of the Edison Telephone Company of London. On 5 October 1879, from 13 Victoria Grove, Shaw wrote White that he had come to London in 1876 "where my mother & sisters had been for some time." He offered no hint as to the length of their stay in Victoria Grove before Agnes' departure for Ventnor in the Isle of Wight where she eventually died.[208] The next time Shaw discussed this question was in 1922. In a letter to O'Bolger which agreed substantially with his account to White, GBS wrote that after his mother sold the Hatch Street furniture and saw to it that her husband and son were comfortably placed, "she took a house for herself and her two daughters in Victoria Grove . . ." [209] In one of his 1930 letters to Harris GBS reduced the number of departing Shaws to his mother and one daughter: Lee, he said, went first in order to prepare a suitable musical background for "my mother and sister." In the closing paragraph of the same letter, Shaw perversely increased the travellers to three and put them all into Victoria Grove. When, concluded GBS, the Shaws were certain that Lee had no intention of returning to Dublin, his mother secured a house in London "and settled there with her two daughters . . ." [210] In the preface to *London Music,* Shaw delivered an account which collided clangorously with his previous utterances. Here his "elderly" mother turned the Hatch Street furnishings into cash, moved her husband and son into agreeable quarters "and took my sisters to the Isle of Wight, where [later] the younger one died. She then took a semi-detached villa in [Victoria Grove]." [211]

Considering the accounts by Shaw and McNulty, with due regard to the public record of Lee's last days in Dublin, and bearing in mind the press reports of the departures of "Mrs. Shaw" from Kingstown—unsatisfactory though they may be, the following timetable is offered as a possible sequence of events:

DATE	EVENT
Period: Sunday 3 December Saturday 9 December 1871.	G.J.Lee becomes G.V.Lee; result of a possible visit to London.
Friday 15 May 1873	Mrs. Shaw leaves for "reconnaissance" of London.
Period: Monday 26 May to Tuesday 17 June 1873	G.V.Lee leaves Dublin for London.
Wednesday 17 June 1873 (*Twenty-first anniversary of the marriage of George Carr and Lucinda Elizabeth*)	Mrs. Shaw and Agnes depart for Isle of Wight. Agnes is admitted to Sanatorium.[212] Mrs. Shaw continues to London, engages 13 Victoria Grove and returns to Dublin.
Wednesday 26 August 1873	Mrs. Shaw and Lucy leave Dublin.

XIV

Writing in the preface to *London Music,* GBS told his readers that when his mother left Dublin neither she nor any member of the little Shaw family realized that she would never return, and he so connected his sentences as to convey the impression that her refusal to sell the piano (neither he nor his father could play it, he said) was evidence of her desire or expectancy to return.[213] But—bridges burnt—Mrs. Lucinda Elizabeth Shaw gathered her belongings, her daughters, said her goodbyes and shook the dust of Ireland forever. Behind her, if we may put Lucy aside for the moment, she left a sober, possibly frightened and certainly bewildered fifty-nine-year-old husband and a thoughtful, haughty and perhaps sardonic seventeen-year-old son. According to that son, his mother sold all the furniture but the piano and removed both him and his father (and the piano, one supposes) to a lodginghouse about midway between Hatch and Synge Streets. The biographers' accounts were, in the main, fairly uniform, but they contained conflicting variations. Pearson was prudence itself; no hint of the year or Mrs. Shaw's part in the proceedings. The Shaws, he wrote, senior and junior, moved to lodgings in 61 Harcourt Street.[214] Winsten reported the sale of the Hatch Street furniture and the subsequent removal of father and son to "humble" lodgings.[215] Rattray went one better. The Hatch Street furnishings *and* Torca Cottage were sold in 1872 and the two Shaws went into Harcourt Street.[216] Hamon's facts were badly mangled—perhaps in the machinery of translating from French to English—and he told his English readers that when George Carr died [1885], Mrs. Shaw took her two daughters to London where they were joined four years later by her son.[217] Henderson's earliest work put father and son into Harcourt Street from 1871 to 1876 and in his subsequent works, repeated this virtually word for word.[218] Ervine marched off boldly in new directions. He declared that George Carr took the initiative in finding a place for himself and son. Mr. Shaw, he wrote, "removed himself and his son to lodgings at 61 Harcourt . . ." [219] and in another place had them there from 1870.[220]

Shaw's published treatment of this aspect of the Hatch Street breakup was not entirely in harmony with his unpublished views. Thus in his 1905 letter to Henderson, GBS informed him that he lived with his father in a Dublin lodginghouse for five years from 1871 to 1876 and made no mention of his mother's role in this connection.[221] In 1930 he told Harris that when his mother took a house in London he and his father moved into lodgings in Harcourt Street. While implying simultaneous movements he still avoided any reference to his mother's concern, if any, in their welfare.[222] In 1935 he suggested a solicitous wife and mother who, prior to her departure, was sufficiently interested in their behalf to see that they were comfortably relocated in the Harcourt rooming house.[223] But to O'Bolger he presented the episode in a somewhat different light. Making no reference to the time or place of removal, he recalled dryly that when Lee left Dublin "my mother calmly went too, leaving my father and me behind exactly as she left the furniture behind, without troubling herself for a moment as to what anybody might think of the transaction." [224] From this one may glean the following possibles: (a) Mrs. Shaw left Dublin without regard to human compassion or the ordinary proprieties, (b) the welfare of husband and son was of no concern to her, (c) father and son remained in Hatch Street and (d) the furniture was not sold.

The version given to O'Bolger may be closer to the whole truth than any of Shaw's published accounts. Examination of sources shows that George Carr and son remained in Number 1 Hatch Street until at least 1874 when they then or thereafter removed to 61 Harcourt Street. This does not mean that after Mrs. Shaw's departure they continued to occupy the whole of the Hatch Street house. Mrs. Shaw may have sold most of the furniture, leaving only the essentials for her husband and son, who were then confined to one or two of its rooms —the remainder being let out to lodgers by the owner. The following extracts from official publications[225] are presented to support the opinions expressed.

	DUBLIN STREET DIRECTORY		MERCHANTS, TRADERS AND GENTRY
Year	Occupant [1 Hatch Street]	Occupant [61 Harcourt Street]	Residence [Shaw, George Carr]
1873	Lee, G. V. Esq.	Morgan, R. W. Esq.	1 Hatch Street
1874	Vacant	Morgan, R. W. Esq.	1 Hatch Street
1875	Fraser, Mrs. Anna F.	Higginbotham, Miss	1 Hatch Street
1876	Fraser, Mrs. Anna F.	Higginbotham, Miss	1 Hatch Street
1877	Vacant	Higginbotham, Miss	No entry

While Thom's is quite in error as to the number of years George Carr spent in Hatch Street, the record cannot be ignored. Reduced further, the table shows that in 1874 Lee was gone and the Hatch Street home apparently vacated, with nothing to disturb its silence but the ghostly strains of the Professor's music. It is, however, certain that the house still harbored the father, the son and the sacrosanct piano. It may be noted that though Thom's had never reported Mr. Shaw as a tenant in Hatch Street (it recognized Lee as the principal occupant), Thom's readily accepted Merchant Shaw's personal acknowledgment that his residence was there. The year 1875 saw the occupation of 1 Hatch Street by Mrs. Fraser who, according to the Valuation Office, was its owner, and I believe that this was the year when the two Shaws and their piano left for Harcourt Street.

Winsten seems to have been the only biographer to pay some attention to this brief period. Whether it was because of his talent for dramatizing biography or because he snapped up the unconsidered trifles of an octogenarian's dozing reminiscences, I cannot say, but his comments bear some notice. "George," he said, wrote long letters to Agnes and his mother, reporting, for example, that since papa had his fit on the doorstep, his consumption of alcoholic beverages had been considerably reduced, forgetting that Mr. Shaw's fit had taken place two years before the departure of his wife and that it had the effect of making him a practical as well as theoretical total abstainer for more than ten years.[226] At any rate, the main point of Winsten's account is that Shaw maintained correspondence with London during this period—an assertion which has been confirmed. Excavations at the British Museum brought to light letters from GBS to both his mother and sister Lucy. The bushels of Shaviana still to be categorized, released and examined will, in all probability, contain many details of the life of father and son in Dublin from 1873 to 1876. But for the present purposes, it was reported[227] that there were at least three letters establishing the whereabouts of George Carr and George Bernard after the departure of Mrs. Shaw. On 4 March 1874 the eighteen-year-old Shaw wrote from 1 Hatch Street to his sister in London addressing her affectionately as "Cara Lucia." On 24 February 1875 he saluted her with "My dear Lucy," giving 61 Harcourt Street as the return address and on the same day or the next wrote to his mother greeting her as "My respected Parent"—a salutation which could be construed as either priggishly courteous or caustically sardonic.

General conclusion: Immediately prior to her embarkation for

London Mrs. Shaw probably sold most of the furniture in Hatch Street, leaving only enough to give husband and son the basic comforts. After she left, they remained in Hatch Street until sometime between 4 March 1874 and 24 February 1875, when they moved to 61 Harcourt Street.

In attempting to account for the differences among Shaw's published accounts and his explanation to O'Bolger, the public registers and his correspondence between Hatch Street and London, I can only suggest that GBS found the differences unavoidable. To report that he and his father remained in Hatch Street after his mother left would, he perhaps believed, cancel the effectiveness of his contention that with Lee's flight, the Shaws could no longer afford to remain in Hatch Street. At worst, it was an easy matter to tailor an explanation to fit the truth without actually revealing unnecessary and complicating facts.

XV

FOR ALMOST THREE YEARS THE TWO SHAWS lived together, first in Hatch Street and then in the Harcourt lodginghouse, now known as the Rosslare Hotel. According to the present (1959) proprietor, who was so informed by the previous owner, the Shaws occupied Room 20. Formerly a large and cheerful room, first floor rear, it is now divided into three small rooms. Inspection of these rooms indicated ample space for a large piano as well as the accommodations for two or even three persons.

Though Mr. Shaw had at last effected sobriety, this herculean achievement could not have increased his desirability as a roommate. Discouraged by his faltering business, troubled with the knowledge that his wife had run after a musical mountebank (and a hell-bound Papist at that), deprived of the protective insulation of whiskey, he was hardly company for anyone—certainly not for the young Bernard

Shaw. Writing to O'Bolger in 1916, GBS recalled that his life with him during these years in Dublin was unmarked by his father's concessions to the demon Rum and that he often looked at him in Harcourt Street and found it a little difficult to believe that this upright and friendly old teetotaler was the same person he had known as an incorrigible drunkard.[228]

Ervine's attention to this period was, by comparison with other biographers, copiously detailed, and apart from insisting that the two Shaws lived together in Harcourt Street from 1870 to 1876 [229] offered a credible account based on equal parts of McNulty, Shaw's diaries and his own biographical talent. He told his readers that father and son had little if anything in common, and such conversation as passed between them was inconsequential. They would meet for their meals and separate for the evening—Mr. Shaw to struggle over his account books (he was too proud to ask his cashier son for help) while GBS sought the company of McNulty or Chichester Bell, a fellow lodger. Sometimes he would stay at home where he would labor away awkwardly at the piano over a musical score. In general, Ervine had it, Shaw could be said to have had a fairly satisfactory intellectual existence but practically no contact with the social body of Dublin. There was, however, some discrepancy between his literary comments and his oral comments. In connection with the time prior to Lee's emigration, Ervine reported that as the result of a fit one Sunday afternoon, George Carr was terrified into teetotalism. In a subsequent reference to this subject, Ervine was consistent in his reportage: George Carr had taken the pledge. When Mr. Shaw and his son (wrote Ervine) lived in Harcourt Street, the elder man deteriorated considerably. His conversion to total abstinence had not increased his ability as a business man—in fact it contributed to his deterioration, since he now denied himself the whiskey which formerly braced him for the problems of the day. Not so was Ervine's opinion on the occasion of the publication of his centenary biography of GBS. George Carr's determination to put whiskey behind him, Ervine implied, was a failure. Speaking on a transatlantic broadcast to an American audience, the author declared that Mrs. Shaw "left her son alone in lodgings with this drunken, feckless old father. Now this seems to me to be a terrible thing for a mother to do to her only son . . ." [230] From this it would appear that Ervine had forgotten that he had once scouted the seriousness of Mr. Shaw's drinking and forgotten that he had recorded in his book (the subject of the broadcast) the tale of George Carr's headlong flight into teetotalism. He did not, however, forget to take a cut at Mrs. Shaw in passing.

McNulty's reminiscences of the Shaws during this period were, in the main, confined to his observations of and relations with GBS and Lucy. He recorded that about the time Shaw went into the Townshend land agency he (McNulty) received an appointment with the Bank of Ireland and, after three months in the Dublin office, was transferred to the Newry branch in County Down some sixty miles to the north. In this little town McNulty could find no companions with whom he could establish rapport and he entered into a daily correspondence with Shaw in Dublin. GBS, referring to it in the *Sketches,* described the correspondence as consisting of enormous letters, containing rough sketches in illustration of their contents, which were brightened by farcical dramas. The two friends agreed, said Shaw, to destroy the other's letters immediately they were replied to, as neither of them took kindly to the prospect of these highly personal exchanges coming under alien eyes. After McNulty was transferred to the north, they never saw one another again.[231] McNulty's recollections were, by and large, in agreement with Shaw's but they contained some serious differences. He remembered that Shaw spent his holidays with him during the summer of his second year in Newry (1874) and that they made the most of those two or three weeks. As McNulty was occupied with his duties at the bank during the day, Shaw—who always loved to walk—roamed about the town, but in the evening the two would devote themselves to their literary interests. Comedy, burlesque, tragedy and the short story would each in turn receive their attention, their greatest pleasure being, McNulty continued, in reading the other's work and in subjecting it to "forcible" criticism. In addition to initiating what they called "The Newry Nights' Entertainment," the two lads also drew up a formal pact of "Eternal Friendship" consisting of a number of clauses having among them, McNulty recalled, the following conditions:

> Their fortunes—good or bad—were to be shared between them.
> Utter frankness was to be the keynote in writing or speaking to each other.
> Regardless of the provocation, neither was to become offended with the other.
> If there was life after death, the first to die was to appear to the other.

They then solemnized the declaration by pricking their arms with a pin, drawing blood and affixing their signatures to the document with their respective blood.[232] And all this, said Shaw (but not McNulty), was destroyed. Yet, Shaw's contributions may have been in existence up to 1957 when, descendants of McNulty informed me, a trunkful of old papers belonging to him were burnt. McNulty's part in these proceedings may still come to light in the mass of Shaviana in private hands and in the British Museum, but I assume that young Shaw fulfilled his part of the pact and destroyed them.

The attention of the biographer is particularly drawn to a photograph which seemed to belie Shaw's statement that with McNulty's transfer to the north, they never saw each other again. According to McNulty, the two posed together for a picture on the second day of Shaw's holidays in Newry, that is, sometime during the summer of 1874 and two years after McNulty's appointment to the branch office. Reference to *Bernard Shaw Through the Camera* readily confirmed McNulty's statement. Appearing on page twenty-one of that fascinating collection was a reproduction of the print and a caption authorized by GBS:

> Matthew Edward McNulty and G.B.S. (1874) (the earliest photograph of Shaw).

McNulty reported Shaw's reaction to his examination of the print: "Stupefaction" was the word he used to describe his friend's aspect.

"I say", McNulty quoted Shaw, "you look like a man and I look a nonentity!" Of course, McNulty disagreed and tried to assure him that he was quite mistaken but Shaw would not be consoled.[233]

In 1876 McNulty was transferred back to Dublin and, as he put it, was overjoyed to be back in the city he loved. His friendship with Shaw had held fast and, with developing manhood, love had come—the object of his passion being none other than Lucy Shaw, who, sad to relate, would not encourage him because he was five years (actually only three) younger than she. McNulty quoted Lucy's feminine logic in rejecting his suit: when he would be forty-five, she would be "a white-haired old woman of fifty," thus perhaps providing GBS with one of Candida's memorable lines to the poet Marchbanks (end of *Candida*). Continuing, McNulty recalled that Mr. Shaw, his son and daughter Lucy lived at 61 Harcourt Street after Mrs. Shaw and Yuppy left. Here he would come to goggle at Lucy and "stagger" through piano duets with GBS. Examining the little Shaw circle more closely, McNulty observed that his friend paid little if any attention to his father who, he added, spent his evenings struggling over the account books which he brought with him from the office.

Appreciating the community of interests between them, the two young men explored, examined, criticized, debated and enjoyed their excursions into painting, sculpture, music, science and roamed through literature in general. Caught up in that "damned century's" speculations of evolutionists, physicists and hell-fire salvationists, they delved into texts on heat, light, electricity and spectrum analysis, of which Huxley and Tyndall were then the high priests. McNulty was especially fascinated with the rubbish put forth by Scottish metaphysicians (as in all ages and all climes) under such pompous phrases as "double consciousness" and "Sense of the Cosmos." He tried to interest Shaw in these matters but succeeded only in arousing his derision, though Shaw reluctantly joined with him in one experiment —possibly to humor him or to expose the nonsense.

They now seldom visited the National Gallery since Shaw had given up his ambition to become an artist, because, as McNulty quoted him, "My people cannot afford to send me to Italy, and it is necessary for an artist to study there." This decision was to McNulty's satisfaction, for he had already decided that literature was the field for himself. But as a profession, literature had no particular attractions at this time for Shaw. During one of their strolls in the Dublin of 1876, McNulty was astonished by Shaw's announcement that he had no intention of becoming a literary man and would, instead, found a new but otherwise unidentified religion. Dismayed, McNulty turned to the attack with spirit. There were already too many religions, he pointed out, and implored Shaw to reconsider. Thus appealed to, Shaw relented and agreed to become a man of letters too. In connection with music, McNulty reported that Shaw's entreaties to his mother and Lucy for piano instruction had been unsuccessful and he had to teach himself. (McNulty's parents, on the other hand, were more sympathetic to their son's yearnings and after a few lessons at home, he was enrolled in the Royal Irish Academy of Music.) Nevertheless, wrote McNulty, Shaw was more familiar by far with orchestral and operatic music than he and attributed it to his musical environment and to the fact that Mrs. Shaw was the most prominent amateur singer in Dublin. Gounod's *Faust,* he said was Shaw's favorite and he knew its every note before he could execute a five-finger piano exercise. Faust, he believed, influenced Shaw in his literary work, while Mephistopheles especially attracted both of them, and they often introduced ironic witticisms with "As Meffie would say—." [234]

The friendship of Matthew Edward McNulty and George Bernard Shaw endured until the death of McNulty seventy-four years after their first meeting in the Dublin English, Scientific and Commercial Day School. Shaw's thundering success in the world in comparison with McNulty's modest accomplishments[235] aroused neither gloating in Shaw nor envy in McNulty. Summing up quietly and simply, the retired bank official related that from their earliest childhood, he and Shaw had what Locke would term "the innate idea"—the settled conviction of their destiny to become famous men. It was not, he continued, a consequence of vanity but rather it seemed to be something born within them—a sort of natural and foreordained conclusion. Youthlike, they expected to reach their goal before their thirtieth birthdays but, alas "Such are the illusions of the young!

Fame did not come to Shaw until he was fifty or more. To me it never came."[236] Some estimate of Shaw's attachement to McNulty and, incidentally, a rare view into Shaw's generous but well-hidden heart, may be discerned in an exchange between them concerning a loan made by the successful and wealthy Shaw to the Dublin-bound McNulty. Asked for £200, GBS sent £250 and on 7 June 1914, acknowledged the receipt of a check for £50 returned as being over and above the amount requested which McNulty did not require. With pseudoformality, Shaw added that the debtor was to take notice that his Trustee-Executor had been instructed that in the event of his death, the £200 was to be regarded as one of those debts to be written off; and he advised McNulty to put the letter in safekeeping against that contingency.[237] The passage of twenty-five years had its effect upon the memory of GBS—or at least he would have it so believed. On 3 March 1939 Shaw sent McNulty a receipt for £100 "alleged" to have been in payment of a loan and enclosed a personal note to "My Dear Mac." Mac must be mad—Shaw had not the slightest recollection of such a loan and could not believe that it had ever taken place. However, if Mac could afford to throw £100 checks about so unconcernedly, he (Shaw) was more than delighted to be one of the recipients. Still, his acceptance of the check gave him the right to do with it as he wished, so (if Mac didn't mind) he would throw it into the fire.[238] Exasperated but touched, the eighty-three-year-old McNulty replied:

> My dear Shaw,
>
> Although you have been such a blazing devil of a success there is something angelic lurking somewhere in you. (Always I have known it). I am not any more crazy than I have always been. As for having hundreds to fling about, that cheque which you so sweetly incinerated took 20 years to save.
>
> And now, listen—
>
> Keep keeping young. Old age a myth!
>
> E. McN.

The twelfth of May, 1943, saw an end to their comradeship,

for this was the day that Matthew Edward McNulty, aged eighty-seven, widower, bank official of 32 Cowper Road Rathmines, died of cardiac failure arising out of myocarditis. From 4 Whitehall Court went the reply to a telegram from "————" of Dublin. Shaw was grateful to be informed. He was sorry he could not understand the telephoned message that preceded it, since, being deaf and very old, he could make nothing of the caller's name. Whatever Shaw's private reactions were, one of those reactions expressed itself in the characteristic Shavian attempt to take the sting from death. McNulty, wrote Shaw to his Dublin informant, was like himself near ninety: not a time for sadness but a time for resting. Was there a photograph of him in his final years and would it be possible for him to see it? If there was anything he could do—. Faithfully, G. Bernard Shaw.

XVI

THE EVENTS LEADING UP TO SHAW'S DECISION to go to London may said to have been ignited by a blazing debate on religious matters among the clerks in Townshend's office. His own position on this fascinating topic had already been formed as far back as Synge Street in 1862. To MacMahon Shaw, GBS noted that he was reared in a setting of anarchism, that is to say, there were no prescribed social, moral or ethical codes of conduct.[239] In reply to Harris' request for a contribution to his *Contemporary Portraits* (1919, Second Series), Shaw obliged with something from his childhood. Before his tenth birthday (he wrote), he had been immersed in an atmosphere of free thought and discussion directed against prevailing conventions and that one of those who contributed to this environment was that blasphemous and obscene but educated and witty uncle Walter.[240] To Winston Churchill, Shaw remonstrated that the Right Honorable was mistaken. As a child he was *not* forced to go to both Protestant and Catholic churches. On the contrary—the family circle was dominated by scoffing heresies and that his parents had dropped even the appearance of conventional church attendance. As to himself, he ceased, after a critical self-examination, to say his prayers because he had become an atheist. All this, he said, occurred by the time he was ten.[241] O'Bolger was informed that when Shaw was between six and thirteen years of age (apparently coincident with the appearance of Lee in Synge Street), he was subjected to influences and experiences which had made him much more of a "freethinker" than any of his teachers, any of the average people within his reach or any of his conformist relatives. His father, he added, was one of them and he described him as a "stickler for conventionality." [242]

Henderson reported that as a boy, Shaw acquired a skeptical outlook towards religion and described a typical gathering in the Shaw home to illustrate the environment in which Sonny developed his skepticism. Dealt with in all three major works, the earliest exhibited a conspicuous reluctance to name one of the principals—possibly because of Shaw's refusal to give his biographer a free hand. Here Henderson told his readers that on one occasion George Carr, Sonny's maternal uncle Walter and a "visitor" engaged in an exchange of views with respect to Jesus' reversal of Death's untimely call to Lazarus. Mr. Shaw, wrote Henderson, took the orthodox position: it was the gospel truth. The boy's uncle delivered the scoffer's attitude: it was a plain case of collusion—while the "visitor" presented the skeptic's view: the affair was rejected as being implausible and plainly contrary to reason.[243] In his second major effort, Henderson became bolder (perhaps because his subject's attention was engaged elsewhere)—he named the visitor as Lee.[244] In his final work, Henderson dispensed with caution. Attending the three-cornered debate on the risen Lazarus were "His father, his uncle and G. J. V. Lee. . . ." Ridiculing Chesterton's view that ascetic Shaw was the product of his "narrow, Puritan home," Henderson repeated that George Carr believed the story to have happened precisely as stated, that it was skeptically brushed aside by the musician as utterly impossible and jeered at by uncle Walter as having been a bargain between Jesus and Lazarus whereby the latter would pretend he was dead.[245]

The New Theology by R. J. Campbell contains confirmation

of these debates and, for all practical purposes, effectively identifies the contenders. Campbell's sermons went into two editions of which only the "Popular" contained Henderson's material. Principally concerned with proving "logically" certain scriptural allegations, some parts of the book were given over to those who had been invited to address the congregation. Being the advocate of a new theology, Campbell encouraged the use of his church, "The City Temple," for the discussion of topical as well as inspirational questions and, in the course of events, offered his pulpit to G. Bernard Shaw. Addressing the body on "The Ideal of Citizenship," GBS, by way of linking up his immediate surroundings to the subject of his discourse, reminisced on the days of his childhood.

With typical charm, GBS warmed up the congregation by warning them that finding himself in church he could not resist the temptation to deliver himself of a profane but true story. He asked his listeners to imagine him as a "very small boy" in what Chesterton called his "narrow, Puritan home" [246] and told them of three gentlemen he remembered who were excitedly exchanging their views on the return of Lazarus from the Dead. One of these gentlemen, GBS said, was his father, the second a "visitor" and the third his maternal uncle. Of these three (he did not say which), one took the evangelical view—that is, it was a genuine and authentic account. The second of these gentlemen—the visitor—held a totally skeptical position: he denied that it ever took place, that such tales were part of the fables attributed to every great teacher and that it was more likely that the person responsible for the story was a liar than that anyone could be redeemed from death. The last member was his uncle who differed completely with the other two: he declared the miracle was nothing more than a fraud and explained that Jesus and Lazarus entered into a contract wherein Lazarus agreed to play "possum." Concluding, GBS told his audience that he listened to these views with considerable interest and admitted that it was the view of his uncle which appealed most to him. His audience would, he thought, on reflection agree that this was the best balanced and most correct view for a boy since it engaged the sense of humor—a very human and laudable thing too—compared with which the other two offered, respectively, mere faith on the one hand and mere incredulity on the other and, consequently, did not appeal in the least to anything that had real religious merit.[247] As George Carr was named one of the trio, his must have been the evangelical position, since the visitor was the skeptic and uncle Walter the scoffer. As to the identity of the visitor, only O'Bolger received the facts. "When my father," GBS wrote, "Lee and Uncle Walter got into an argument on religion or anything else, it was such an argument as no other child in Ireland, probably, would have been allowed to listen to." [248]

Shaw's deep and continuous interest in religion (infallible hallmark of the secularist) was construed by O'Bolger, if I may put it so, to be the gropings of a white boy in search of God, and he wondered aloud why Shaw never sought the comfort offered by Roman Catholicism which, he was certain, would have satisfied his spiritual yearnings.[249]

The forces of the conflicting opinions as expressed through George Carr, uncle Walter and Professor Lee, dramatized by their own contrasting personalities and enacted in a theatrelike setting, could not have failed to make a vivid impression on the young Shaw. Some fifty years after these scenes, GBS recalled them to provide the background for aviator Joey Percival, the romantic hero of *Misalliance*. Joey's appearance in the play is somewhat delayed, but he more than makes up for his tardiness by the originality of his entrance—the airplane he arrives in crashes into the greenhouse of his host. Prior to his descent from heaven, his friend Bentley has described Joey to an attentive Hypatia. Joey, declares Bentley, is a remarkably clever chap; when he was once asked why he was so different from his schoolfellows at Oxford, Joey replied: Easily explained; they had only one father each, while he had no less than three. Number one was the official father who maintained in his home father number two: a "tame" philosopher of the Spencer and Coleridge stripe. His mother, continued Joey, was an Italian princess. Her inseparable companion was an Italian priest (father number three) whose chief function was to keep watch over her conscience but, as far as Joey could see, it was the other way about. These three, said Joey, took on the responsibility for his own conscience. He used to hear them, he told Bentley, quarrelling like mad over every subject. The philosopher, being a freethinker, would always believe the latest theories. The priest would believe nothing because it was certain that no matter which way he faced, he'd be sure to be in difficulties with someone. As to his regulation natural father, he kept his mind open and believed whatever was to his profit. From this trio Joey received no end of cultivation and concluded that if he had been blessed with three mothers as well, he would have faced Napoleon himself. Fascinated, Hypatia inquires whether Bentley can prevail on Mr. Percival to visit them, but Bentley, being enamored of Hypatia, objects on the ground that she would throw him over the moment she clapped eyes on Joey.

In connection with this abstract from *Misalliance,* it will be seen that character inversion is clearly evident—each borrowing something from his neighbors, so that no single portrait can be conclusively recognized. Precise identification of the three fathers is a hopeless task, as they melt and flow fantastically into one another. Since Mrs. Shaw was still alive at the time, GBS may have felt a certain amount of concealment to be necessary, and he may have distorted or shifted characteristics about for maximum obscuration. In any case, exact identification was quite unnecessary to the play's structure, since the three-fathers theme was sufficient for his purpose. Clearly demonstrated, however, was GBS's identification with Joey Percival—that remarkably clever chap, the lad with three fathers and a devil with the ladies.[250]

Shaw himself seemed to have little if any reticence in acknowledging the umbilical link from *Misalliance* to Dublin. He wrote to Harris in March of 1930 and told him that his leading young gentleman in that play had three fathers and that he could not have conceived this without the inspiration of his own life—for he too had had three fathers: Lee, uncle Walter and the "official" one.[251] As one examines the "Harris" treatment in the text, one may detect its guiding spirit. Shaw, the text read, "confessed" to having three fathers; Mr. Shaw, Professor Lee and uncle Walter but "Only George Carr Shaw, however, had anything to do with his presence on earth. The others contributed their parentage after birth." [252]

Though often a witness to the trio's controversial combat, young Shaw lacked the experience of participation, and in his theological engagements with the apprentices in Molesworth Street he suffered severely at their hands. Shaw recalled an occasion a short time after he entered Townshend's when he was discovered to be what was then known as an "infidel." In defending his position against the solid God-fearing bloc, Shaw was unable to sustain his views. Humphrey Lloyd, probably one of the university apprentices, taunted him with being even ignorant of how to present his arguments syllogistically. The chastened Shaw went to the dictionary only to find that he had been syllogizing all his life without being aware of it. That the future polemicist retreated in embarrassment is incidental to the point. What mattered was that Townshend (an important member of the Protestant respectables) somehow got wind that his office was being used as a forum for debates on religion and summoned his office boy for censure. While Townshend made no effort to influence him one way or the other he "demanded" that Shaw give his word never again to raise the subject while on the premises of Townshend & Company. Humiliated, Shaw accepted Townshend's command but in the act of accepting knew that if he had ever entertained notions of a career in land agency, they were now dismissed forever.[253]

Henderson asserted that it was not until four years before GBS's death that the truth came out regarding the circumstances of Shaw's decision to resign. Up to that time it was generally believed that GBS threw up his job with Townshend in order to embark on a professional career suitable to a growing genius[254] and in this respect Shaw issued communiqués to support these beliefs. In the 1921 preface to *Immaturity* he invited his readers to behold him in his twentieth year: trained to business and trapped in a hated occupation from which he could not escape. But in March of 1876, he seized at freedom by giving his employers a month's notice. They, thinking that he was dissatisfied with his £84 per annum, offered to make the position more attractive. His only fear now, GBS continued, was that if they implemented their offer his excuse for leaving would disappear. He declined the overture with thanks and replied that he was determined to go though "I had, of course, no reason in the world to give them for my resolution." [255] At another place in this autobiographical warehouse, Shaw revealed to the readers what he was perhaps unwilling to admit to his principal—that he had ambitions in matters far removed from Townshend's ledgers. Dublin, he wrote, was not the city where his appointment with destiny was scheduled, and he offered an apt illustration. Just as his father had to go to the Dublin Corn Exchange in the course of his business in life, so his son had to go to London for *his* business in life. London, he said in effect, was the Mecca of the English-speaking and English-writing world, and since he intended to become the crowned head in that world, it was to Mecca that he had to go. He supported his view with a further illustration. Any Irishman who had something more to do in life than that which could be done in Ireland had to put her behind him and seek an intellectual or artistic climate better suited to his free and healthy growth. As for London itself or, for that matter England, he had not the slightest interest. If his ambitions were in science or music, he would set his course for Berlin or Leipzig; if he had inner stirrings to paint, it would have been for Paris; Rome for theology or Weimar for the Protestant philosophy. "But as the English language was my weapon, there was nothing for it but London." [256] Certainly, if GBS wished to establish a motive for breaking loose from his cashier's desk, he could hardly have expressed his intentions more clearly had he portrayed himself actually charging upon London with his pen lowered lance-fashion.

Yet the record is not always consistent in its support of Shaw's intentions. For example, the *Immaturity* preface contained the admission (reported earlier by McNulty and by Shaw himself) that when GBS was a boy, he never wanted to be a writer: it was his wish to be a painter.[257]

Ervine did not regard Townshend's reprimand to Shaw (in connection with the debates on religion) as a major contributing factor in Shaw's decision to leave Dublin. This decision, he believed, was due to a combination of circumstances. He held it to be a fact that GBS was "restive" in the land agency and further asserted that Shaw was tortured by some unspecified adolescent complaint, offended by his supersession as cashier by a nephew of Townshend and, lastly, that he was in the grip of a mystical force which impelled him to seek self-expression through literary composition. "The itch to write," continued Ervine, "was about to drive him out of Dublin, though he did not realise then that he had the itch." Shaw's replacement by Townshend's nephew, Ervine added, was the immediate reason for submitting his notice and Ervine exhibited the letter of resignation itself as recovered by Loewenstein and published by him in *Adam* of August 1946. Reported to have been written 29 February 1876, its writer begged to give notice that at the end of March he would leave the office. In justification whereof, he explained that he arrived at this decision through expecting a salary not warranted by the services he performed. Having so little to do (he continued), it followed that what he had done was done poorly, but he had foreseen this situation when he no longer acted as cashier. Circumstances being so, he preferred to sever his connections entirely, very truly yours, G. B. Shaw. Summing up, Ervine judged the letter to be "singular"—even "incoherent"—and attributed those alleged properties to Shaw's humiliation in being replaced as cashier. Ervine did not explain how he learned that Shaw's successor was a nephew of Townshend.[258]

Henderson's acknowledgment that the truth regarding Shaw's resignation was revealed only four years before Shaw's death likewise attracts some attention because he offered the same letter (containing minor differences) without crediting its origins. He reported that GBS was greatly pleased with his successful career in Townshend's office but one day, much to his vexation, found himself "supplanted as cashier by a nephew of a member of the firm." [259] Dr. Loewenstein's "Do You Remember, Mr. Shaw?" [260] also mentioned the nephew. Although Loewenstein failed to give his source, it was undoubtedly a then unpublished letter from Shaw to prospective employer Arnold White, manager of the Edison Telephone Company of London, since the letter in rough draft was in Shaw's files, to which Loewenstein had access. The White letter[261] appears to be more in the nature of a confession than a résumé for employment. Possibly intended originally for some other use, it alternatively could have been an early autobiographical sketch. At any rate, before he sent it to White, Shaw made several deletions, additions and corrections. He told White something of his history with Townshend—that, satisfied with his importance as the most active figure in the office, he had not encouraged hints to promote him out of the cashier's post: "However, the firm desired to place a relative of theirs at the cash desk" and consequently, he was shifted into a sort of clerk-at-large. In effect, added GBS, he had no duties and received a higher rate of pay for doing them.

Shaw's discontent with his altered circumstances was mirrored in his wry account of his rise, and there can be little doubt that he had been offended by the firm's nepotism. Had he not assumed a difficult post bearing heavy responsibilities during a crucial period? Had not his abilities over the last three years been proven? Had not Townshend acknowledged appreciation of his cashier by increasing his salary to £84 and had he not underscored that appreciation by offering additional emolument as an incentive for him to withdraw his resignation? Though GBS had no love for his duties, there was little reason to believe him to be dissatisfied with his conditions. The land agency itself offered a dignified, genteel occupation—a condition essential to a Shaw. Townshend & Company, GBS noted, was a "terribly respectable" [262] and "highly genteel" enterprise.[263] He maintained friendly relations with congenial colleagues of approved social and cultural position[264] and, being free from parental supervision, enjoyed unlimited social independence. Nevertheless, Shaw's basic discontent with his onerous duties and his resolve to put land agency out of his head as the result of Townshend's dictum on religious discussion made his supersession as cashier merely the final blow. Thus we may dispose of the impression—sometimes fostered and sometimes denied by GBS—that he was conscious of Destiny's beckoning finger. After licking his wounds for some period—possibly in the hope that his successor would snarl the accounts—Shaw resigned.

Townshend's reaction to his ex-cashier's resignation may have been an interesting study in guilt. Quite aware that he had treated young Shaw shabbily, he could have been fearful of incurring the displeasure of the lad's uncle Richard Frederick Shaw, chief of the Valuation Office who had originally recommended Sonny to the firm. With the event still fresh in his mind, GBS advised Arnold White three and one half years later that an offer of reinstatement was made but that he rejected it.

About this time the Shaws in Harcourt Street may have received a letter or a telegram from either London or Ventnor advising that Agnes was dead or dying and that the presence of a member of the family was essential. Although there is no evidence of such a communication being sent or received, it appears likely. Ervine suggested the existence of such a message in a reference to GBS's alleged vacillation concerning his future—that Shaw's uncertainty in this area vanished with the death of Agnes on 31 March 1876 and coincident with the termination of his employment with Townshend.[265] Henderson disagreed: Agnes died on the third of March with GBS leaving a few weeks later.[266] The well-informed Loewenstein disagreed—Agnes died on March 23.[267] The record shows Agnes to have died on 27 March 1876 (see Section VI).

Resignation impulsively tendered and regretfully accepted, the not quite twenty-year-old GBS finished his term of notice to Friday 31 March and, since nothing could be gained by hurrying to Ventnor, leisurely concluded his preparations to leave the land of his birth. Having reached his decision to be quit of Dublin, GBS moved rapidly. Since he had few possessions, there remained little to pack except for his clothing. Bidding farewell to his friends, Shaw posed for photographs with Gibbings and Fishbourne and took himself and his carpetbag to the North Wall.[268] Shaw's personal account was, for once, in happy accord with his biographers. But he did recall an incident unreported by them. Probably to say farewell, he visited his aunt Cecilia, and when he was invited to sit down, he did so with such force that the back of the chair broke off with a loud and nerve-splintering crash. "And that, I imagine, was her main recollection of her freethinker nephew, the son of the Gurly woman." [269]

After savoring a few days of freedom and idleness (during which he was, if not master of himself, then at least no one's slave), he packed his carpetbag, went to the North Wall of the Liffey and there boarded the ship which, whether he willed it or no, would take him towards Mecca.[270]

VI / London

I

THE ARRIVAL OF GEORGE VANDELEUR LEE in England during the late spring of 1873 has been uniformly treated by the biographers—that is to say, they followed their subject's advices with little variation. In substance, Shaw's infrequent accounts through the years told a consistent story. Having exhausted Dublin's opportunities, Lee set his course for London where, he had often declared, he would obtain a house in that street restricted to patricians and plutocrats: Park Lane—and this he did: Number 13.[1] There was nothing in any of Shaw's comments to indicate when Lee actually occupied the house and it appears that biographers assumed that, after perching briefly in Shropshire whither he had been invited to conduct a private recital, the Professor moved directly into Park Lane. This is at odds with the record. According to the sources credited below, the following premises were occupied as indicated:

Actual Year	1 Hatch Street	Ebury Street	13 Park Lane
1871	Lee, G. J. (T)	—	Riel, Madame (P)
1872	Lee, G. V. (T)	—	Riel, Madame (LT)
			Marshall, Julian (P)
1873	Lee, G. V. (T)	—	Marshall, Julian (P)
1874	Vacant (T)	Lee, George Vandeleur (S)	Marshall, Julian (S)
			Lee, George Bilton (P)
1875	Fraser, Mrs. Anna (T)	—	Lee, George Bilton (P)

(T) Thom's Registers (S) Document of Sale, Torca Cottage (LT) London *Times*
(P) *London Post Office Directories*

Since Lee departed from Dublin about the first of June, 1873, the foregoing table suggests that when he arrived in London, he settled in Ebury Street—then a London quarter swarming with writers and musicians. He appears to have remained there until some time in 1874 when he replaced Julian Marshall as the occupant of 13 Park Lane. What complicates a comparatively straightforward series of movements is the baffling introduction of George "Bilton" Lee. Tracing the residential history of 13 Park Lane to the death of Lee in 1886, we find that the *London Post Office Directories* list Bilton through 1885 when, for the first time, Vandeleur is recorded. Perhaps Lee wished to separate his professional musical interests from his less artistic engagements and adopted Bilton to help maintain the division. Bilton itself suggests its selection by Lee who may have remembered it as the name of a hotel (now long extinct) in Dublin's main thoroughfare of that time, Sackville (now O'Connell) Street. It is not difficult to see how 13 Park Lane passed into the hands of Professor Lee after its occupancy by Madame Riel and Julian Marshall.

MURDER IN PARK LANE was a headline in the London *Times* of 9 April 1872. With robbery the apparent motive, the body of Madame Riel, a widow of 13 Park Lane, was discovered by the victim's daughter. As reconstructed by the police, death was caused by strangulation with the corpse exhibiting sundry other marks of violence. Suspicion immediately centered upon the victim's cook Marguerite Dixblanc who was described by the *Times* as an exceedingly powerful woman. She was also said to have been in the siege of Paris during the Franco-Prussian War and to have been numbered among the Communists in the civil fighting that took place after the German occupation. Up to a late hour that night Dixblanc was still missing along with a quantity of French bonds, banknotes and railway shares.

Number 13 Park Lane was then acquired by Julian Marshall, who lived in it for part of 1872, all of 1873 and part of 1874.

How Lee and Marshall came to meet is another one of the minor mysteries, yet it is not impossible that they met through their common interest in musical affairs. Marshall's wife appears to have written a book on Handel,[2] and Marshall himself, according to some references in Lee's letters to GBS, may have been a performer in one or more of Lee's own productions. In any event, they met and after a suitable period of negotiations entered into an agreement whereby Marshall secured a simple Irish cottage nestling in the hills of Dalkey and Lee a sum of money sufficient to ensure his entry into the street of his dreams:

> REGISTRY OF DEEDS
> King's Inn—Dublin
> Book 1874—36—82
>
> A MEMORIAL OF AN Indenture of Assignment bearing date of the 20th day of April 1874 and made between George Vandeleur Lee late of No. 1 Hatch St. in the city of Dublin and [now] of Ebury Street Pimlico in the County of Middlesex Esquire of the one part and Julian Marshall of 13 Park Lane in the County of Middlesex of the other part. [Here followed a recital of indenture of lease bearing date 19 September 1872 being proof of Lee's right to dispose.] It was witnessed that in consideration of the sum of £300 the said George Vandeleur Lee granted bargained sold assigned transferred and set over unto the said Julian Marshall his executors administrators and assigns all that and those that piece or parcel of land with the dwelling house thereon therebefore described as being in the Torca Road . . . Execution thereof by the said George Vandeleur Lee is duly witnessed by Andrew Kelly of 60 Russell Square in County of Middlesex Solicitor . . . (&c)
>
> (Sign) George Vandeleur Lee (Seal)

Thus the history of 13 Park Lane strongly suggests that if it had not been the scene of a sensational police matter, Professor Lee's dream of a castle in Park Lane might never have materialized.

There seem to be fewer mysteries regarding Mrs. Shaw's London residence, although the entire record is far from clear. The biographers agree that upon her arrival she promptly settled in a semidetached house in Victoria Grove. The *London Post Office Directories* show that 13 Victoria Grove was occupied by a Mrs. Parker from 1872 to 1875 and by "George Shaw" from 1876 to 1880, when Mrs. Shaw and her son removed to 37 Fitzroy Street. In explanation of the above I may offer that Mrs. Parker shared the house as senior occupant, but with the arrival of GBS in 1876, recognition as principal householder passed to its only male tenant. Writing to O'Bolger in 1916, GBS volunteered an opinion. Mrs. Shaw's acquisition of a separate house for herself and her daughters should not be construed as evidence of any concession to Mrs. Grundy. She would not have hesitated for one moment in sharing 13 Park Lane with Lee if the economics had permitted. Park Lane, said Shaw, was very expensive to maintain, and Lee found it essential to let rooms out to lodgers in order to make up the overhead while he confined himself to a bedroom and the music room.[3] The effect of Shaw's illuminating contributions to O'Bolger must have shown itself in a future set of questions he fired at the hapless GBS. In 1922 he was again harping on the same themes (reported earlier) and again GBS obliged. Yes, Lee went to London. Yes, his mother followed him and now, he parenthesized, O'Bolger could make his usual inquiries to assure himself that Park Lane and Victoria Grove were two or so miles apart.[4]

The relations between Mrs. Shaw and Lee under these new circumstances have not received the attention merited. Henderson had observed the identical numbers of the two homes and allowed that "numerologically" speaking, the resumption of their "business relations" took place under an unlucky star. Mrs. Shaw once again assisted Lee with his concerts and musicales and in furtherance of this went to Park Lane.[5] Ervine ignored the area altogether. Winsten reported that when Mrs. Carr Shaw arrived in London, she tried in every way to resume their Dublin relationship, but Lee would have none of it. He was bent upon living "his own life" and reluctant to be the target of her bad-tempered daughter Lucy's rudenesses. Nevertheless, continued Winsten, the Professor invited Mrs. Carr Shaw to help him with his students and for her special assistance in connection with his musical At Homes paid her handsomely. All the same, Winsten insisted that Lee was determined to keep the relations between himself and Mrs. Shaw scrupulously impersonal and, possibly to discourage emotional episodes, reduced his visits to Victoria Grove, but Lucy eventually put an end to even them.[6]

Though young Shaw was not in London during 1873-1876 he has, notwithstanding, given one or two very brief accounts of the early London association between his mother and Lee. In 1916 he told O'Bolger that by the time he had arrived on the scene Lee was coming and going to Victoria Grove very much as he formerly had and was as much a part of the house as the hat rack, though he slept elsewhere, of course. Further, his mother and sister were active in Lee's affairs—Mrs. Shaw by singing for him as she had always done and Lucy, who had now grown into an alluring and musically-talented young lady, by taking an active part in his At Homes.[7] Twenty years later GBS again directed his attention to this subject and offered what was substantially repetitive matter. At first (Shaw reported) Mrs. Shaw came and went at Park Lane and he went and came at Victoria Grove. Whatever it was that required Lee's presence in Victoria Grove, GBS did not dwell on, but Lee's At Homes had the advice and assistance of Mrs. Shaw who even sang the role of Donna Anna in one of Lee's amateur productions.[8]

Henderson's representation of Mrs. Shaw as resuming her business relations with the Professor seems not to be warranted, since their Dublin alliance was principally a cultural one and, in the strictest sense, nonprofessional. It would perhaps be more accurate to say that business relations were inaugurated, but, if so, they existed in the loosest manner—that is to say, such "business" as she received from her partnership with Lee consisted of the overflow, if any, from his own classes. Winsten believed that Mrs. Carr Shaw had difficulty in making ends meet. Lucy, he said, refused to seek employment, and, above the usual expenses, there was Agnes to think about. Agnes was very ill and was receiving special treatment in the Isle of Wight. Fortunately, Winsten reminded his readers, there was the Whitcroft legacy and the pound a week from Mr. Carr Shaw in Dublin, and these made the difference. Now and then uncle Walter would contribute sums but these offerings, concluded Winsten, were always returned by the proud Mrs. Shaw.[9]

Ervine saw the period as one of comfort, if not of prosperity. According to his calculations Mrs. Shaw received not less than £300 per year from the following sources exclusive of earnings through teaching: 1. Interest of £40 per year on a property in Cork. 2. Interest on the £4000 Whitcroft bequest. 3. Contribtuion of £1 per week from George Carr.[10]

Under examination, the impressive income loses some of its glitter. There were no properties in Cork that could have any connection to Mrs. Shaw. (There was a parcel of property, but she disposed of it prior to her departure from Dublin.) Beyond this Mrs. Shaw's remaining property (acquired on the death of her father in 1885) was located in Co. Carlow, ancestral seat of the Gurlys and Bagenals. As reported by GBS's confidential Irish land agent,[11] the Carlow property, before passing to Shaw on the death of his mother, produced a gross annual rental of £28. 5/ 2d and, consequently, earned interest of between one and two pounds annually. Presuming the Whitcroft bequest to Mrs. Shaw (actually £1500) was still intact at the time, the interest on it could not have exceeded £30 per annum. Also, George Carr's generosities to his London brood have yet to be appreciated. As to Mrs. Shaw's earnings through her efforts as a teacher, Ervine asserted that they were "moderate," [12] but what evidence there is suggests something closer to zero. Reassessment of all sources indicates that Mrs. Shaw's annual income during the early London years (it was to become worse before it got better) probably did not amount to more than £100.

Henderson offered no opinion of Mrs. Shaw's economic position in Victoria Grove. He summarized Shaw's accounts accurately but all too briefly. During her earlier years in London, Henderson wrote, singing pupils did not come to her in large numbers. He implied that as Lee was engaged in the same business, Mrs. Shaw could have only those students whom Lee regarded as being best taught by Mrs. Shaw who, Henderson concluded, "was [more] rigorous in her requirements." [13] Henderson here may have meant that Lee had already embarked on his betrayal of principles and was by now turning out divas after a dozen lessons. Although the moment of Lee's metamorphosis has yet to be established in time, it is certain that for at least two or three years he sincerely attempted to give honest measure in The Method, according to his Dublin lights.

Shaw's own comments point up the difficult times. In 1905 he told Henderson that when his mother took up the profession of teacher of singing, she taught according to The Method, refused to deviate in the smallest degree from its principles, tolerated no exceptions from fashion, conducted herself with the independent air of an Irish lady and, as a result, "had a very bad time of it." [14] In the same year, he completed the preface to the first edition of *The Irrational Knot* and in it he remembered that during this period he threw himself as a burden upon his family then "heavily embarrassed." [15] In the preface to *London Music* he recalled that his mother's plans to teach Englishwomen to sing according to The Method was almost a total failure for several years and her occupation with private students "negligible." [16] Such were the circumstances in Victoria Grove during April 1876.

II

G. B. SHAW, ESQ., LATE OF DUBLIN, smooth-chinned when other young gentlemen of twenty exhibited splendid beards, descended from the Holyhead train at London's Euston Station to be saluted by a porter whose cockney query "Ensm' faw weel?" has been imperishably preserved.[17] Deciding against a hazardous leap into what appeared to be a stepless carriage, Shaw chose the four-wheeler, whose driver coolly palmed four shillings as a reasonable fare to 13 Victoria Grove. The lapse of three years since Mrs. Shaw's goodbye to her seventeen-year-old son and his reappearance as a twenty-year-old young man did not seem to animate maternal or sisterly affections. Henderson believed Mrs. Shaw's dissatisfaction with her son's materialization was economic in nature; he had thrown up a first-class position and by coming to London had worsened her already difficult situation.[18] Ervine offered that after the passage of five years, Mrs. Shaw regarded her son with something akin to apathy but yet held that his presence was "disturbing" to both his sister and mother. In explanation he suggested that since Agnes died two weeks earlier, sister and mother were still in mourning.[19]

Preliminary civilities dispensed with (such as they were), the conversation must have shifted to a most unhappy event: the death of Yuppy. Winsten—ignoring the medical diagnosis—reported that Agnes' fatal illness had developed out of a passion for the only man she had ever loved: could it have been that mesmeric conductor L--? [20] Shaw, on the other hand, insisted unromantically that Agnes had contracted tuberculosis from a housemaid and, after a "rapid decline," died in a private rest home in the Isle of Wight.[21] Dead less than two weeks before her brother's departure from Dublin, Agnes may have received some of the love in her illness denied to her during healthier days. Winsten quoted GBS as saying his mother had the "most" affection for Lucy and Agnes but had a special fondness for Agnes of the pale, red hair. When the younger girl became tragically ill, Winsten continued, Mrs. Shaw devoted herself entirely to the task of returning her to health. Henderson declared that Yuppy was "adored" by her mother and, when it was discovered that the girl had fallen a victim to tuberculosis, "cherished her tenderly." [22] Although McNulty did not remark on the relations between mother and her daughters, he did note the affection of Lucy for her sister. Agnes, he wrote, was "a lovely, sweet-tempered girl with large hazel eyes, and superb reddish-gold hair, which could be combed almost to her heels." Agnes, he went on, had fallen victim to dreaded phthisis and had been rushed to Ventnor as a last measure. But alas, it was too late and Lucy, who loved her dearly, was inconsolable for a very long time.[23]

Unattended by mother, father, sister or brother, Elinor Agnes Shaw, second child of Lucinda Elizabeth, had succumbed in her twenty-first year. If one were to be guided by the biographers there seemed to be almost as much difficulty in establishing the date of

Agnes' passing as there was in fixing her birth, but in this matter, at least, the record was clear—and available:

HB 216843 *CERTIFIED COPY OF AN ENTRY OF DEATH*[24]

1876 Death in the Sub-district of Godshill in the County of Wight

No.	When and where died	Name and Surname	Sex	Age	Occupation	Cause of Death	Signature, description, and residence of informant
441	27th March 1876 Balmoral House Ventnor	Agnes Shaw	Female	21 Years	Daughter of George Carr Shaw Corn Merchant	Phthisis Some months Certified by Arthur H. Hassall, MD	E. H. Sarl present at the death Balmoral House

Registered 31 March 1876 *Registrar:* Alfred Cole

Agnes was buried on the 30th of March in Grave Number 1046—a consecrated plot—and her commitment therein duly observed by officiating minister Reverend W. W. Wellan. There was no mention of any relative or of any authorizing source, and apparently those engaged in such matters seemed assured that final expenses incurred would be honored—possibly because of the regularity of payments to Balmoral House.

Since Mrs. Shaw must have received notification of her daughter's death from the Isle of Wight authorities, it follows that the notification may have contained a request for instructions with respect to the disposition of the deceased and related problems. Unable or unwilling to go herself at the time of the receipt of the news, and perhaps reluctant to send Lucy alone, the arrival of her son from Dublin seemed to settle the matter, for both Lucy and George were dispatched to Ventnor. Inquiries amongst secular and clerical authorities in Ventnor regarding the probable duties of the pair found general agreement centering around the following: formal "receipt" of the deceased; examination and acceptance of the burial site; selection of headstone and composition of epitaph.

The headstone was the simplest of grave markers, which, after some eighty-three years of exposure to the elements, has become somewhat eroded and tipped a few degrees from the perpendicular. The grave itself is neatly kept (as were all the graves) and rests on a gentle slope in the cemetery of St. Catherine's Church, Ventnor.

Responsibility for the wording of the epitaph cannot be finally determined as the executing stone mason has long since gone to his own reward and, so far as his vanished records were concerned, might have had them buried with him. Ervine was the only one to take the trouble to gaze in this direction and thoughtfully he did so. He noted that the stone's inscription which he quoted as "With Christ which is far better" hardly suggested that the one who chose it was an atheist or a backslider. Could it, he pondered, have been Mrs. Shaw? Her position was difficult to ascertain. He recalled her "declaration" of conversion to atheism[25] but shrewdly observed that this conversion did not deter her from having the children baptized, though he was inclined to think it more of a gesture to convention. Transferring his attention to George Carr, Ervine allowed that *he* may have had the stone erected but, on reflection, dismissed the possibility as unlikely in that Mr. Shaw had never been to Ventnor, did not attend the funeral of Agnes and, finally, was not what one would call a man of piety. Concluding, Ervine returned to the theory that Agnes' death may have revived Mrs. Shaw's dormant religiousness but it was all conjectural and impossible to prove.[26]

Agnes formally receipted for, brother and sister visited the grave, selected the headstone and (in my opinion) composed and authorized its inscription which is, in itself, curious enough to warrant further attention. As may be noted in the photograph of the stone, the epitaph reads "TO BE WITH CHRIST WHICH IS FAR BETTER" and which was plucked, albeit carelessly, from 1:23 of Paul's Epistle to the Philippians wherein Paul discourses on the folly of living and the wisdom of dying. From Paul's point of view, to be alive is to be really dead and to die is to really become alive. In effect to be without Christ is to be dead, therefore to die is to *live* with Him. While Paul commends others to remain in the flesh—for himself there was little doubt:

> For I am in a strait betwixt two, having a desire to depart, and to be with Christ; which is far better:[27]

Without descending further into the bottomless pit which is scriptural interpretation, I suggest that the selection by this twenty-year-old atheist of that particular sentiment from the Paulist precepts is one of the earliest "published" Shavian comments and is as deft a piece of tongue-in-cheek business as was ever perpetrated by him.[28] In a sardonic comparison of Agnes' future to her twenty-one pathetic years, the unhappy, hopeless years, did he who chose this inscription stop to inquire whether she was not better off with Christ? It is highly unlikely that either George Carr or Lucinda Elizabeth would seriously or otherwise offer any scriptural suggestions for Agnes' headstone. Shaw's presence in Ventnor, his familiarity with the Epistles of Paul and the particularly flexibility of 1:23 all combine to point to GBS as the responsible agent.

In any event, thus ended the brief history of Elinor Agnes Shaw —Agnes of the reddish-gold hair, the lovely and sweet-tempered Agnes. Dying among strangers, her unhappy life was capped in death by the certifying physician's compression of three years suffering into a laconic "some" months.

III

SHAW'S AVIDITY IN CONFESSING to his flint-hearted exploitation of his mother during his earliest post-Dublin years merits the closest examination. As in many another area the biographers, with one exception, dutifully quote, paraphrase or otherwise perpetuate the GBS-inspired picture of a young man descending on his mother determined to achieve literary success at the expense of her purse and her health. Shaw asserted, in almost as many words, that he, like Tanner's artist (*Man and Superman*: Act I), would see his mother work her fingers to the bone before he would employ his own in anything but what he called his art; and this, according to Shaw, was true insofar as he and his mother were concerned. In illustration of which, his readers were given to understand that with his mother and sister in straitened circumstances, he, though of sound mind, wind and limb, rejected his plain duty and chose to be a burden instead. Recognizing this as wicked according to the conventional prescription, he declared that he nevertheless seized upon that wickedness without hesitation: "I did not throw myself into the struggle for life: I threw my mother into it. I was not a staff to my father's old age: I hung on to his coat tails." Huneker, dean of American critics in the earlier decades of this century, had long observed Shaw both as a creative artist and as an interesting biographical personality. Usually percipient, Huneker had described Shaw as a model of filial devotion. Shaw protested that he could not allow Huneker or any similarly romantic-minded person to pass him off as a praiseworthy son maintaining an infirm or superannuated mother. On the contrary, Shaw insisted that he was a singularly egotistical artist who had fastened himself upon a capable and energetic mother. He advised Huneker that his mother struggled to provide him with his material necessities and did not grumble or nag about his obligations to her; therefore, it would be well for Huneker to doff his hat to his mother in token apology. "Callous as Comus to moral babble," ran Shaw's familiar boast, "I steadily wrote my five pages a day and made a man of myself (at my mother's expense) instead of a slave." [29]

Ervine refused to be taken in by what he called the "romantic nonsense" of artists who sacrifice everyone and everything to their art and asserted that there was barely a word of truth in Shaw's unbosomings. He argued, quite reasonably, that it was impossible to believe that when Shaw crossed the Irish Sea his nature changed from that of an ambitious and conscientious young man to that of a parasite and a conscienceless blackguard. It was not true, he continued, that GBS preyed on his parents. As a matter of fact, it was his mother who played the parasite of the family by her acceptance of a pound a week from her unfortunate husband. In support of his belief that Shaw was not an idler and leech, Ervine took note that he had been employed for three of his nine lean years, laid low by smallpox for one and, for the remainder of the period, occupied with the writing of his novels. He further declared that the cost of Shaw's maintenance was "trivial" in comparison with the cost of keeping Agnes domiciled in Balmoral House but added somewhat contradictorily that the children's upkeep did not cost Mrs. Shaw one penny. On the contrary, he said, she profited handsomely through the Whitcroft bequests. He explained that as each child came of age, Mrs. Shaw was able, with their consent, to make use of a total of £3,900 plus accumulated interest. Lucy's share was "presumably" expended in her maintenance and musical education. Agnes' division, he continued, could be considered as "pure profit" to Mrs. Shaw since the girl died before it came due and consequently, the entire share of £1,300 dropped into her lap. As to GBS's portion, it matured during his second year in London. This was also commandeered by Mrs. Shaw and surely, Ervine supposed, GBS had the right to expect that in handing £1,300 over to his mother it would cover the cost of his maintenance during his literary apprenticeship.[30]

Ervine believed (with much justification) that Shaw, contrary to his claims of having lived off his mother, was actually engaged in commercial employments for one-third of the nine years and for the remaining six (except for the smallpox period) was occupied in writing what he hoped were publishable, income-producing novels. However, I cannot agree with Ervine's characterization of Mrs. Shaw as a sponger. Contrary to GBS's oft-repeated assertion that this was a difficult economic period for his mother, Ervine insisted that Mrs. Shaw was comfortably placed, since she had George Carr's contribution of £1 per week and the Whitcroft inheritance of £1,500—which had no connection whatever with Lucy, Agnes or George Bernard and was bequeathed exclusively to Lucinda Elizabeth Shaw to use as she saw fit.

Henderson's comments were brief but hewed to the Shavian line. Mrs. Shaw's economic circumstances were unenviable and the arrival of her son did not render them better. George Carr sent a pound a week and, from time to time, Mrs. Shaw was forced to draw upon the four thousand pound inheritance. GBS's "momentous decision" to refuse to support himself and add to his mother's burdens may seem, Henderson opined, like the basest selfishness but the judgment of modern letters confirms the wisdom of Shaw's "strange" resolve.[31] Pearson likewise reported the approved Shavian view and reinforced it with his own opinion. Shaw, he said, had not the slightest intention of contributing to the support of the little household.[32]

GBS's flaunty exhibit of his parasitism is—especially considering its ostentation—difficult to accept, and it is incumbent upon the biographer to seek its cause. Examination of GBS's activities in his early London years helps to round out the picture. Loewenstein's comments were based largely on his inspection of the White letter. Shaw, he said, wandered happily about London for three months, enjoying its music, art and the British Museum. Money, Loewenstein added, being in short supply in the Shaw household, GBS applied to the Excise Department of the Civil Service in July.[33] Ervine's report had a familiar ring. Shaw's first three months in London, he wrote, were something in the nature of a prolonged vacation as he occupied himself with its general exploration. Concerts, art galleries and the British Museum received his close attention, but at the end of this period his dwindling resources and the goadings of Lucy forced him into an unsuccessful effort to seek employment in early July with H.M. Excise and Inland Revenue.[34] For most of his first two years in London, Ervine added, GBS spent his time in casual and aimless employments including some ghosting for Lee on *The Hornet* and assisting him in Park Lane.[35] Henderson made little if any effort to trace the history of his subject from 1876 to 1879. He dismissed these years in the first half of a short sentence: after a few years of "casual and desultory activities," GBS, in 1879, got down to the difficult task of writing his novels.[36] Elsewhere, Henderson referred to Lee's assistance to Shaw through the offer of an opportunity to ghost but failed to relate it to any particular year. Pearson also neglected to place his remarks within a time reference. Reporting that Shaw refused to entertain notions of remunerative employment, he related that the first to "force" GBS's hand was Lee who turned over to Shaw his own duties as music critic on *The Hornet*.[37] McNulty's account did not help specifically, but it did lend some fresh color to an otherwise monotonous canvas. While Mrs. Shaw attended to the teaching of her music, Lucy busied herself with the housework. As to G.B., he appeared to be idle—that is to say, he did nothing to earn some money. But, McNulty continued, appearances were misleading; Shaw was writing continuously. He recalled that Lucy had written to him frequently—principally at the request of her mother—complaining of her brother's idleness, and would McNulty, as the only person who had any influence with him, write and urge him to find work? McNulty confessed that he was loath to do so, but at length he did, merely to please Lucy. He remembered that Shaw took his advice, though unwillingly, and succeeded in obtaining a job with an American telephone company doing pioneer installations in London.[38] In the Harris book, one of its writers offered authoritatively that Shaw was resolved not to return to cashiering, but as he could neither play a musical instrument nor paint, nothing remained for him but to write. However, on his arrival in London, he permitted himself to be propelled into his last commercial association: the Edison Telephone Company. (The author also added that Shaw received some help from Lee who undertook for his sake, the responsibility of writing music criticism for *The Hornet* with Shaw doing the actual writing.[39])

Shaw's own history of the first post-Dublin years is scanty and difficult to piece together. The earliest reference was given in the White letter and first revealed by Loewenstein when he published some fragments of it in *Adam*.[40] When he came to London (Shaw wrote White), he first planned to join the civil service, but as he was not versed in mathematics or languages he was forced to prepare for a lower-grade appointment. During the course of being tutored for this position by a crammer, a friend of his who was employed as a music critic on a weekly paper suggested that if he (Shaw) would do the work, he (the critic) would hand over the payments. He accepted "& set to work to reform the musical profession." As a consequence of his painful criticisms the weekly found itself in difficult straits and his friend "one of the most unpopular men in London." Upshot was that although he relinquished the post, the owner was ruined and the weekly sank from sight. Shaw further told White that in the previous two years (October 1877-October 1879), he had been unemployed and had done nothing during that period which could be recognized as preparation for any sort of commercial position. From October 1877 to October 1878 his intentions and plans had not yet taken form, and much in the manner of visionary romantics, he prowled about London after dark absorbed with Shelley, social reform and the search for truth. He also wrote a few articles which were unsaleable, studied music (harmony and counterpoint) and finished a novel then being revised. The novel represented five months of work already, but Shaw admitted that he was at a loss as to how to get it published.

Notable omissions in the letter to Arnold White were the name of his musical friend and the name of the weekly which had provided almost all of his small earnings after his arrival from Dublin. It was not until after Lee's death that he made the identification public. In an article GBS published in the *Scottish Musical Monthly* (December, 1894), he attributed to Lee sufficient interest in his young friend's welfare to accept on his behalf the position the inexperienced GBS could never have acquired on his own, that of musical critic for *The Hornet*. Shaw wrote the reviews and Lee neither changed a word nor deducted any commission from his critic's fee, accepting merely the faintly reflected glory of being thought a musical journalist by his friends and pupils. Shaw's chief complaint was having no chance to proofread his "critical crimes"; nevertheless he preserved the cuttings among his papers all his life, and it was from this set that Professor Dan Laurence was able to extract passages for his *How To Become a Musical Critic* (1961).[41]

Shaw's first contribution was a review of an opera entitled *Pauline,* by Frederick Cowen, and appeared in *The Hornet* for 29 November 1876 under the department "Musical Notes"—the credit, of course, going to Lee. According to Laurence, Shaw continued to ghost for Lee until 26 September 1877 on a variety of topics which, in addition to criticism of contemporary events in the music and drama worlds, included miniature biographies, news items and, now and then, leading articles requested by editor Donald Shaw—no relation of his unknown employee.[42]

Also in the Shaw papers in the British Museum, along with the *Hornet* clippings, are letters from Lee to the editor of *The Hornet,* such as the following, in Lee's hand and written on the verso sides of editor Shaw's letter to Lee:

13 Park Lane
1st June 1877

Dear Mr. Donald Shaw,

I shall be happy to avail of yr kind invitation for Saturday. I wd suggest that the portrait and article upon [Christine?] Nielsen [be] this week so as to make a simpler sequence of artists. Same to [ ] in 1st of the Bautines. I think you will find this the correct mode— Hope you are better today.

Sincerely yours,
[Signed] Vandeleur Lee[43]

The puzzle of how letters from Lee to editor Shaw came to be found in the Bernard Shaw collection at the British Museum is, I think, easily explained. Since it was GBS who actually wrote the articles for *The Hornet,* it was of course, necessary for Lee to pass the editor's letters and copies of his own replies to GBS, so that he might tailor his material to the editor's measure. Of incidental interest is the date showing Lee (and GBS) to be still engaged with *The Hornet,* thus lending support to Laurence's statement that GBS was ghosting for Lee up to September, 1877. However, there may be some doubt about this being the *last* of the Lee-Shaw alliance with respect to *The Hornet.* Letter number two from Lee to Donald Shaw is dated almost a year later and, judging by its tenor and contents, their business relations were as active as ever.

13 Park Lane
3 May 1878

Dear Mr. Donald Shaw,

In the absence of arguement [sic] and with the style in which the Biography is written, I believe that it wd be impossible to incorporate successfully any musical matter. I imagine that a biography of Wagner ought to be chiefly a musical article. If you wish I cd give you an article of that kind in yr next issue?—I hope that you are much better. I shall go to opera tonight.

Sincerely yours,
[Signed] Vandeleur Lee[44]

The letter is weighty evidence that Lee continued in the employ of Donald Shaw and, as the letter was passed on to GBS, it may be safely presumed that Shaw continued to ghost for Lee at least into May of 1878. It may be that still more early Shaw will turn up.

How much GBS earned by ghosting for *The Hornet*'s music critic has still to be determined. Yet the biographers professed to some knowledge on this score—at least as to the division of the compensation. Rattray's comment could be construed to mean that Lee was actually music critic but offered to hand over the earnings to Shaw if he would write the articles.[45] Pearson saw a *quid pro quo* agreement between Lee and Shaw. He held that in return for Shaw's piano accompaniment at his At Homes, Lee undertook the music critic's job on *The Hornet* and passed on both the work and pay to GBS.[46] Ervine's account could not have been based on generally available sources. He asserted that Lee suggested to Shaw that he take the duties of music critic to *The Hornet* and perform "general utility" jobs in the Park Lane studio. Lee, according to Ervine, struck a hard bargain. Not only did he take all the credit, but half the proceeds as well.[47] Henderson refused to admit of any bargaining and declared flatly that Lee, in order to help Shaw, agreed to become music critic to *The Hornet*. Shaw, Henderson added, was to do all the work and take all the pay.[48]

Shaw's comments, or, rather, the lack of them, may account for the divergent views of the biographers. In 1947, Shaw, speaking of Mushlin's discovery of his manuscript notes on a projected third edition of *The Voice,* informed him that when he "grew up" he became a sort of literary secretary to Lee. In the course of his activities, Shaw continued, Lee was offered the post of music critic to a paper known as *The Hornet* but the actual writing was handed over to Shaw. There was no mention of any business arrangements.[49] Sixty-eight years earlier, job-applicant G. B. Shaw told telephone company executive Arnold White that a music critic who was a friend of his offered him the remuneration of that berth if he would undertake its duties, thus suggesting, if not establishing, as in the *Scottish Musical Monthly* article mentioned earlier, that Shaw performed the tasks and pocketed the payments.

Shaw reported other earnings of a minor nature. Two items, unrelated to any time, were: five shillings for some verses in connection with a prize for school children and five pounds for a medical essay commissioned by a friendly legal gentleman for use in an "agitation" with patent medicines (probably a preparation of an opinion in an action of law).[50] Henderson reported it to be an advertisement specifically for a patent remedy "which may give some color" to the frequently expressed assertion that GBS was a pretender to the noble throne of letters.[51] Howsoever that may be, neither of these trifles has as yet been turned up. Completed in 1878 (before his first novel) was "My Dear Dorothea," an early appeal to children of the world to unite against their oppressors; they had nothing to lose in the movement but their parents. It was not published until after his death. In October of 1879, while GBS was still occupied with the revision of *Immaturity,* he contributed to the family journal *One And All* a pompously satirical article on "Christian Names," dealing with the inconsiderate saddling of children with resounding or famous names. For it he received fifteen shillings.[52]

November of the same year brought a fresh opportunity. Possibly at the behest of McNulty and through cousin Mrs. Cashel Hoey, daughter of his aunt Charlotte, GBS applied to Arnold White, Secretary of the Edison Telephone Company of London. Henderson implied that Shaw grudgingly accepted White's offer of a position in the Way-Leave Department,[53] and Ervine reported the facts as he believed them without commenting on Shaw's readiness or reluctance. Introduced to White (Ervine wrote) by novelist-cousin Fanny Johnstone (pen name of Mrs. Hoey), GBS then sent what is called here the "White" letter together with a copy of a testimonial from Townshend & Company, secured by his father without his knowledge. The testimonial as reprinted by Ervine:

> 15, Molesworth Street
> Dublin,
> 9th August, 1878.
>
> Mr George Shaw served in our office from 1st November, 1871, to 31st March, 1876, when he left at his own desire. He entered as a youth and left us having attained the position of Cashier. He is a young man of great business capacity, strict accuracy, and was thoroughly reliable and trustworthy. Anything given to him to do was always accurately and well done. We parted from him with regrets and shall always be glad to hear of his welfare.
>
> Uniacke Townshend & Co.
> Land Agents[54]

Ervine reported that Shaw started with the Telephone Company on 14 November 1879, and (though he did not give the source) stated his annual wages were £48 plus commission to be earned by convincing unwilling property owners to allow his Company to raise poles and so forth on their buildings. So satisfactory was Shaw, Ervine concluded, that in six months he received two salary increases and was promoted to manager of the department. But all this came to an end on 1 June 1880 when his company was absorbed into a competing system. Offered an opportunity to remain with the new combine, Shaw refused.[55]

Shaw's account in the prefaces to *Immaturity* and *The Irrational Knot*—brimming with interesting reminiscences delightfully rendered—ignored the areas of dates, wages and commissions. The Edison Company, wrote GBS, after unwittingly achieving literary immortality through its employment of George Bernard Shaw, expired in the embrace of the National Telephone Company. (The *London Post Office Directory* 1881 (1880) located the United Telephone Company Limited at 36 Coleman Street, E.C., Arnold White, General Manager and Secretary.)

It was Shaw's "Bibliographer and Remembrancer" who put the

record straight. Writing in his *Adam* article "Do You Remember, Mr. Shaw?" Dr. Loewenstein examined and displayed some scraps of history. It appeared, according to him, that in their first meeting White offered Shaw an opportunity to be trained as a "Telephonic Engineer" and, probably at White's invitation, Shaw prepared and sent his letter of 5 October. On 6 October, the Company acknowledged receipt, returned the Townshend testimonial and promised consideration of his application. Five weeks later (the letter was dated 10 November but postmarked one day later), Shaw was requested to present himself to be interviewed by a Mr. Dauglish, manager of the Way-Leave Department and, as a consequence, Shaw was appointed Friday, 14 November. At first, Loewenstein surmised, Shaw was put to doing "odd jobs," but when the department was organized, he was assigned to the task of procuring right-of-ways for the Company's wires. The principal advantage of Shaw's arrangement with the Company, Loewenstein added, was that he could devote whatever part or parts of the day he wished to Company business, since he was retained on a commission base only. Thus he was relatively free for his literary pursuits. By the end of the year however, Shaw found his earnings somewhat less than his expectations, for on 31 December he advised the Way-Leave Department by letter (reprinted in part) that he was "under absolute necessity to discontinue my services forthwith." He further stated that notwithstanding the generous commission rate, he had during the six weeks he had been with the Company, earned a total of two shillings and sixpence, and during the same time he had expended forty-two shillings on personal expenses. He admitted that the commission basis, because it allowed him wide latitude in the time he could give to it, was satisfactory but thereby acknowledged his dilemma, for, though he found the commission arrangement unworkable, he was unwilling to be employed under any other conditions. Loewenstein concluded, quite logically, that the resignation letter thus established the commission rate at two shillings and sixpence for each permission of which Shaw had a grand total of one. Loewenstein further reported (though in this case without documentation) that the letter had the practical effect of raising the commission rate sixpence to three shillings, whereupon Shaw agreed to continue.

Included in Dr. Loewenstein's invaluable article were reproductions of two items, one of which is of special interest here. The first was a facsimile of Shaw's identification card with the Edison Company and is mentioned only in passing. The second is that of a report made on 17 February 1880 by Agent G. B. Shaw to his manager. (See photographic section.) It showed that for an indeterminate period of time, Shaw obtained twenty-one consents having, consequently, a commission value of £3 and three shillings. As the report did not specify whether it was daily, weekly, fortnightly or monthly, there is no way of gauging over-all earnings, but it does, I think, tend to show an energetic effort to produce some income.

Commenting on the rival Bell Telephone Company, Loewenstein briefly described their advantages over the Edison method. Eventually, he said, they decided to amalgamate and on 1 June 1880 they combined under the name of the United Telephone Company with main offices at 36 Coleman Street. On 5 June the Edison employees received dismissal notices effective as of 5 July with an opportunity for re-employment with the new company if they would complete and submit the enclosed application. Shaw, wrote Loewenstein, did not avail himself of this offer and at the expiration of the notice was once more unemployed. On his last day in office, Agent Shaw returned to the cashier stamps in the value of two shillings and fourpence. He then returned home and wrote a letter to his former employers calling their attention to the fact that there was due to him "about one guinea, being the proportion of my salary from the 1st inst. to the expiry of my engagement today." He also noted that he advanced out of his own pocket six shillings to Way-Leave Agent C. Knibb for two consents on the East India Dock. Would the Company please remit? If, however, the last request was not acceptable because of its unofficial character, "pray suppress it and excuse my troubling you with it." The reply was prompt:

7 July 1880

Dear Mr. Shaw,

I beg to enclose P.O.O. for 27/- the amount due to you by the Company, kindly let me have your receipt for the same.

Do not let me lose quite sight of you and if possible call upon me, will you. We will arrange to spend some afternoon together in Tottenham.

Ever yours very sincerely,
Rudolph H. Krause.[56]

Shaw's energies did not seem to have been exclusively devoted to the Telephone Company during his six and one-half months with them, for there is some evidence that he was simultaneously engaged in literary matters other than *Immaturity*. In an undated letter for 1880, Lee wrote to his young friend,

1880

Your ms and corrections are admirable—my proof will be returned to you. The enclosed is to pay for subscriptions to libraries and books that you may require to work on & the result that will regenerate the musical world.

When more coin is wanted I shall be glad to send it. Hope to see you soon for a chat.

Sincerely,
V.L.

[Noted by GBS in red ink:] Retained £5 27/1/80[57]

Other than its connection to music, there was nothing to identify its specific intention or the manuscript's ultimate fate.

The years from 1880 to 1885 should, I think, be separated from the previous four because of the business paralysis which crept over the British Isles. On the arrival of GBS, England was on the threshold of one of its periodic economic earthquakes. "In 1879," Rattray noted, "London was hit by an economic depression such as it was not to experience again until 1931" and reported general consternation existing over wide areas. Ervine (1956) allowed that "a tremendous slump in trade had hit Great Britain in 1879, one of the worst in its history and not to be surpassed in severity until 1931 . . ." The Harris book (1931) went into considerable detail to show the state of affairs which confronted GBS, pointing out that Shaw's move from Dublin to London exploded Emerson's theory that the lot of an Englishman was the best in the world, "because a depression had hit London in 1879 such as it was not to see again until the year 1931. Unemployment was mowing men into idleness like harvested wheat." Business was near collapse and shopkeepers, whose windows were usually bursting with wares, stared through them in an unobstructed view of the street. Large-scale labor unrest buffeted industry, banks closed their doors, entertainment of every sort felt the pinch and pubs teemed with those who could not pay for their refreshments. Weintraub, in his introduction to Shaw's sixth but stillborn *An Unfinished Novel,* marked the widespread joblessness as something of a disguised blessing. The scarcity of work, he concluded, offered GBS unlimited time for his literary interests, and he expended the major part of it in the recently electrified reading room of the British Museum.

Shaw's references to these years were largely (and logically) confined to the prefaces of his five novels which were produced, one a year, from 1879 to 1883. Apropos of Edward Conolly, the electrical engineer of *The Irrational Knot,* GBS pointed out that his hero's occupation was in no sense an invention, and he advised the reader that he should not infer because he was a literary man that he had never worked for a living. He was fifteen, he went on, when he first perpetrated that "sin" against his soul: the act of earning an "honest living"—a sin which he, being shy and wanting in confidence, continued to commit until his twenty-third year. But, he concluded, his last effort in that direction was with the Edison Telephone Company.[58] These notes, written in 1905, insisted that after his refusal to return to the telephone company, he never again lifted his hand in the unnatural act of honest labor. This, of course, was a compound of Shavian impishness and artifice. Like all of Shaw's apparent flippancies this contained a bright core of realism for it would have indeed been a sin had Bernard Shaw been forced to dig or weave for an honest living.

While it is substantially true that he thereafter never again worked outside the profession of letters,[59] it was not for the want of seeking such employment, despite his claimed half-heartedness in the attempts. Quoting GBS as writing that he occupied himself with novels because no one would engage him in any other form of writing, Weintraub was inclined to believe that Shaw was referring to employment outside the fields of journalism or critical writing. He added that while GBS knew he was not too efficient in Pitman shorthand, in his distress he nevertheless replied to help-wanted advertisements for shorthand clerk; but even these particularly abhorred occupations were denied to him.[60] If, in *The Irrational Knot* preface Shaw represented the telephone company as his last "attempt" to work in matters other than literature, his preface to *Immaturity* rises in mild amendment. He declared therein that with respect to the few offers and possible offers of jobs that came his way, it was his belief that they could only lead to what he did not want: he had had his fill of commercial employment. He was, he declared, "an incorrigible Unemployable," keeping up the formality (to himself as well as to others) of seeking employment by answering help-wanted advertisements "not too offensively." [61]

That this state of affairs applied also to the post-Edison period is confirmed by the existence of the methodical Shaw's copies of dated correspondence in the Hanley Collection.[62] Noticeably lacking in enthusiasm, most of the letters were plainly not written in a spirit which would favorably impress employers—in fact they seemed to suggest to the recipient that he would do well to file the application in the nearest fireplace. To a G. B. Woodruff of Brighton, Shaw sent a petition dated 12 April 1883 applying for a position calling for sympathy and friendship: companion to a young boy. The applicant, explained GBS, had been informed of the requirements by a mutual acquaintance, Dr. Saville. It was possible, Shaw thought, that he might be able to perform the acquired duties and perhaps if Mr. Woodruff would be so good as to record his address in case he was dissatisfied with other candidates, he was, Sir, &c., G. B. Shaw. The passage of four months did not seem to increase the job appetite of this harried young man. One "H.C.B." of Street & Company, 30 Cornhill, E.C. received a typical composition "not too offensively" drafted by the author of four novels and a fifth in preparation and is reprinted here so that one may savor the temper of a budding genius.

Tuesday 21.8.83

Sir,

I am willing to act as Private Secretary for £105 a year, am 27, have not had a university education, have 5 years experience of business (dating from 1871), and some literary practice. I am no mathematician nor linguist, nor have I ever acted as Secretary; but as far as I can judge from the terms in your advertisement, you might find my application worth considering if the more promising ones come to nothing.

I am, &c.
G. B. Shaw

Other letters exhibiting refreshing variations but in the same mood were dispatched during the eight years following his *Hornet* adventure. Not all were of the take-it-or-leave-it variety (the White letter, for example, where Shaw poured out some of his history and admitted quite candidly that he had literary aspirations to which all other considerations of a commercial nature were merely a means to an end). Still, he had shown some interest in the telephone enterprise. He expressed his belief that it, unlike estate agency, was at least related to the useful society and working for it would not be wasting one's time. He was most reluctant, he concluded, to ask for employment in any capacity for which he had little or no aptitude and expressed the wish that if Mr. White could offer some suggestions as to what he might do somewhere else, he would be quite content.

It was William Archer who delivered Shaw from the sinful paths of honest toil when, in 1885, he insinuated his "tawny complexioned" friend into the *Pall Mall Review* as one of its book reviewers and into *The World* as its art critic. According to Henderson, Shaw received two pounds two shillings per thousand words, thus heralding the end of his apprenticeship. In the preface to *Immaturity,* Shaw marked 1885 as the turning point. In that year he earned £112 through his pen, a sum that was sufficient to accommodate his needs for the first time. As he put it, "My penury phase was over." [63] Nevertheless, it is clear that GBS did not leave Ireland under a conscious, compelling drive for self-fulfillment in literature: he left his homeland not because of any ambition or objective but because Ireland had, as far as he could see, nothing of interest for him—then or in the future. Writing of the late Dublin and early London periods in the *London Music* preface, GBS reminisced that he had, at one time, an ambition to be another Michelangelo, but if that was denied to him, his second choice would have been to become an opera singer—no less than Badiali—and he parenthesized that so far as literature was concerned, he had no ambitions whatever—meaning, of course, that he was entirely unaware of any literary talent.[64] London-based, Shaw was still unconscious of literary genius, though its stimulus seems to have come through Lee and *The Hornet*.

Review of the years from 1876 to 1885 (as reconstructed here) refutes Shaw's contention that he refused to seek and secure employment, flung his mother into the breach or that he was as a barnacle to her until he had gained his goal. Taking into consideration the adjustments of a Dublin provincial to the measure of a roaring, sophisticated London and the general instability of the times, it may be agreed that Shaw's record of activities does not support his oft-painted self-portrait as a parasite. With an income which was irregular and small during these years in London (in practice, of course, there was many a time when Shaw had not a penny),[65] it follows that Shaw was entirely dependent on his mother for lodging and food—not to mention the sundry essentials of daily life. That this was also true of Lucy, as Ervine observed, is quite beside the point. Both Lucy and GBS—each of age—were supported in part through the charity and grace of their mother whose income from the Whitcroft inheritance (somewhat depleted by the ravages of the four income-less years of 1872-1876) and the pound a week sent by her husband was supplemented by such fees earned in teaching a "negligible" number of pupils. GBS's obsessive, almost fanatic adherence to personal honor demanded purging of the sin of parasitism in the confessional. In an effort to remove that stain of eight years, Shaw boldly and dramatically confessed that he did deliberately attach himself to his mother to draw sustenance from her while he laid the foundations for his literary career. Ambitions ultimately achieved, Shaw could look back upon those eight years of dependence on his mother with new perspectives and he believed them to be eight years of degradation, demoralization and dishonor. In avowing this shame to the world he did not, in my opinion, do so because of any regard or affection for his mother but because of that inner fastidiousness, that worship of truth for truth itself. But of the bread of idleness, George Bernard Shaw did not eat.

IV

COINCIDENT WITH THE RISE of Shaw's star in London, another star began its fall in Dublin. At sixty-two, George Carr Shaw was alone. Sometime after this happy event (as GBS would have it), he left his lodgings in Harcourt Street and moved to Rathmines, then a suburb of Dublin. Happily, a vignette of George Carr in his last years was made and it has been preserved. McNulty recorded that when GBS departed for London, his father at first remained in Harcourt Street and it was here that McNulty visited him twice weekly. Mr. Shaw was not (he wrote with that Anglo-Irish reserve) quite up to his son's mental level. He had no interest in scientific, artistic or literary matters but was fairly up-to-date on current affairs. He was always ready to talk about his family in London, for, in truth, they both missed the absent members keenly. He would always greet one with a smile, McNulty went on, and when they met in the street, they would stop to shake hands and pass the time of day. Frequently, when passing the Chamber of Commerce in Dame Street, (of which Mr. Shaw was a member), McNulty would see him seated at the window reading the financial news. He wore his glasses, characteristically, far down his nose and, in order to get proper focus, had to cant his head backwards. He had, continued McNulty, two habits which were somewhat curious. He would smoke only once during the day just before retiring and when he had finished, he would snap the clap pipe (which he purchased by the gross) and fling the pieces into the fire. His second eccentricity was, when walking with a friend, to suddenly run ahead briskly, stop abruptly and stand there until his companion came up to him. He would then take up the conversation as if nothing out of the ordinary had happened. By and large, concluded the boyhood friend of GBS, Mr. Shaw was "a lonely, sad little man" and he dubbed him "The Hermit" —the name by which he was known in his lodgings.[66]

Ervine had exclusive use of the McNulty manuscript and, though doubting its accuracy at times, placed some value on it. His treatment of McNulty's recollections was, in this instance, sufficiently faithful to make particular attention unnecessary—but there was one trifling difference. Speaking of George Carr's reference to his family, he reported that this "lonely, sad little man" enjoyed talking about his truant family *in extenso* but (and here Ervine was presumably still reflecting McNulty's notes) did not seem to have wished for their return—an opinion which I cannot locate in the memoirs. Noting McNulty's significant reference to Mr. Shaw's physical size, Ervine further offered that the "small eccentric man" who had so little happiness in life was somehow gifted by nature to father a genius.[67] Elsewhere, Ervine reported, from unrevealed sources, a remarkably accurate *miniatura* of George Carr under the weather. Perfectly friendly when sober, the corn merchant's temper flared if anyone disagreed with him while in his cups, and a query was sufficient to make him seize any fragile object and dash it to the ground.[68]

Among abundant materials released from the Shaw collection at the British Museum were a number of Shaw's notebooks, one of which contained matter that appeared to be an early Shavian exercise in autobiography. Reported to be undated, it must have been written sometime before 1885, since his father, being the subject of these notes, was dealt with in the sense that he was still alive. Additionally, as GBS probably never again saw his father, his observations were probably recalled from his days with him in Harcourt Street. Speaking of the time before his conversion to practical teetotalism, GBS said that his father had a good appetite, but he was now and then plagued with diarrhea. With regard to smoking, he was a moderate though regular smoker, but after he had taken the pledge, he increased his smoking slightly. GBS also remembered having seen him, while intoxicated, snatch some knickknack from a shelf and hurl it to the floor. In his rage he would sometimes fetch his newspaper a kick that would send it high into the air but, though easily irritated, he never exercised his anger physically against any person. Ordinarily, Shaw's father, to whom GBS referred in one place as "The Hermit," was a well-mannered man whose very timidity made him unlikely to commit an act of violence to any person. The son added that, like several other members of his family, his father was "eccentric" in his behavior and GBS gave an example. If, for instance, some disagreeable thought crossed his mind, he would (if indoors) grind his teeth and rub the palms of his hands together briskly, but if he happened at the time to be in the street, he would sprint a short distance. Some thirty years later, GBS gave O'Bolger additional details. Mr. Shaw, he wrote, after a day in his Jervis Street office, would come home for his dinner and always take a nap on the sofa afterwards. When he awakened, he would smoke a clay pipe near the chimney or in the garden. This routine was a daily one and, in the days before taking the pledge, broken only by surreptitious trips to the spirits shop.[69] One may assume these scenes took place in Synge Street, since there was no garden in the Hatch Street home. In another part of the thirty-page letter to O'Bolger, GBS expressed the possibility that near the end of his days, the reformed Mr. Shaw resumed his acquaintance with the demon rum but at a considerable reduction in volume.[70]

To MacMahon Shaw, in connection with the publication of *Bernard's Brethren,* GBS had a few words to offer respecting the reactions of Mr. Shaw to his disappearing tribe. He told his cousin that the desertions were, in fact, a heaven-sent blessing. O'Bolger had earlier received a similar account. It was, said Shaw, "the happiest time of his life. No more Lee, no more wife, no more son . . ." [71]

Ervine intimated that George Carr, on the occasion of GBS's departure for London, regarded his son's exit with relief in that he "no longer felt any wish to have his family near him." [72] Ervine's disposition to believe that George Carr would have been dismayed had his wife returned could not have been strengthened by his belief elsewhere that Mr. Shaw travelled to London for the purpose of visiting her. Speaking of Mrs. Shaw's arrival in London, Ervine, in an exclusive report, stated that as she thereafter never lived in Ireland, she would never again have seen her husband had he not journeyed to London some seven or eight years later on a visit to her for a week.[73] Usually ready with an opinion, if not a fact, Ervine did not examine this event further, nor did he say from where he received his highly interesting information. One might be inclined to be skeptical regarding this matter, particularly after inspection of the preface to *Immaturity*. Here, speaking of the fortunes of Clibborn & Shaw, GBS recorded that the business, never flourishing, somehow continued to sustain his father until his death—it even permitted him to send assistance to his family in London—and added that Mr. Shaw "never, as far as I know, made the slightest movement towards a reunion . . ." [74] Further search in Shaw's autobiographical estate, however, brought to light one reference to a pilgrimage by George Carr to London and thereby earned new merit for the Argus-eyed Ervine. Recalling his mother's departure for London, GBS asserted that they (meaning his mother as well as his father and himself) did not then realize that Dublin had seen the last of her and that she would never see her husband again if he had not, for the first time to GBS's knowledge, journeyed to London on a visit to his family for "a few days." [75] While it is reasonable to accept "a few days" as approximating a week, there was nothing to indicate that George Carr made the trip in 1879 or 1880, as Ervine estimated.

At any rate, Ervine further stated, in connection with the separation of Mr. and Mrs. Shaw, that it had been obvious for a considerable time that Lucinda was in London for good. He quoted McNulty to the effect that this so irritated her husband that he considered pressing an action in divorce, naming Professor Lee as "co-respondent." Seemingly still quoting McNulty, Ervine added that the project was abandoned because Mr. Shaw realized that "no one in Dublin believed for a moment that she was Lee's mistress."[76] Apparently Ervine, despite his rather indecorous paraphrasing, did not think McNulty's startling revelation to be of sufficient interest or importance, for he proceeded to different matters.

Examination of McNulty's manuscript incidentally illustrated the manner of Ervine's handling of his source materials. McNulty wrote:

> Eventually, matters in the unhappy Shaw household reached a climax, and his parents decided to separate. There were, indeed Court proceedings, initiated by Mr. Shaw, in which figured a certain Professor Lee, not as a criminal offender against the sacredness of holy matrimony, but rather as an object of jealousy to the petitioner . . . [But] Apart from Mr. Shaw, no one in Dublin believed that Mrs. Shaw had any more feeling towards this strange being save that of friendship.

Mrs. Shaw, continued McNulty, made the first move—she went to London with the children and left Mr. Shaw to his own devices. Lest anyone should think that there was any rancor between the principals, McNulty carefully pointed out that Mr. and Mrs. Shaw parted amicably and remained good friends until Mr. Shaw died, and here McNulty dismissed the subject.[77] However, Shaw, in his eighty-eighth year, speaking of the responsibility of the State to its children, owned that he himself was the child of a misalliance. His parents, he said, were naturally affable people but who "separated in the friendliest fashion" and thereafter saw no more of each other, after living together for years with no interest in common of any sort.[78]

The Shaws, McNulty had written,[79] were unhappy together and they agreed to separate, yet they were also, he said, well-disposed to one another at the time of separation and thereafter until the death of George Carr. I believe McNulty, out of his regard for GBS, glossed over the real cause for the wretchedness of the Shaw household and consequently made it appear that the separation was a mutual agreement amicably arrived at, for Mrs. Shaw would not and did not consult her husband in the matter of separating. As to their amity after separation, there is nothing necessarily contradictory here, particularly if one takes into consideration the fact that George Carr sent a pound a week—if no more—to his wife. With regard to Mrs. Shaw's role, her personality did not admit of hate. She expressed her opinion of objectionable persons by tolerating them in circles far removed from those she approved and accepted.[80] Further, it does not follow that unfriendliness is always a cause or a product of a broken marriage. Those who cannot bear one another within marriage are quite frequently pleasantly suited outside that respectable institution (to which many a separated or divorced couple can testify).

McNulty's odd phrasing in connection with Professor Lee's part in the affair has its own significance. Again I suggest that McNulty's loyalty to his friend was uppermost in his mind—hence its ambiguity. Lee, said McNulty, was not accused of violating a husband's exclusive right to his wife's sexual services. He was charged with being responsible for George Carr's "jealousy"—hardly grounds for divorce even within the liberalized English divorce laws of the time. McNulty's final comments are even more interesting and considerably clearer. He declared that all Dublin would have scoffed at the notion of an adulterous relation between Mrs. Shaw and her singing teacher, but, McNulty unwittingly disclosed, Mr. Shaw had other views.

Possibly sometime during the 1870's, Mr. Shaw actually considered a divorce action but, perhaps after consulting with his brothers and sisters, dropped the matter—not because he would have any difficulty in convincing doubting Dubliners—but, on the contrary, because they might be convinced too easily, thus openly exposing him as a cuckold and bringing unfavorable attention to the honored name of Shaw. As for George Carr's visit to London, I think this took place when he learned that the Professor was *persona non grata* in Victoria Grove and does not, in my opinion, present a husband eager to cast off a wife. With Lee gone forever (or so he believed), Mr. Shaw was convinced that he and his wife could at last find some peace and happiness. But he returned to Dublin alone —his mission a failure.

V

SHAW'S "DISQUISITORY" COMEDY *Getting Married* (1908) contains, in my opinion, his major autobiographical contribution entombed within a play. Queried by a reporter from the *Daily* [London] *Telegraph* as to the plot of this play, GBS snorted that he was a playwright—not a plot-monger and that *his* plays needed no plots. Hence, critics and biographers alike have mourned their absence. But had they a vision of the Shaws of Dublin, they might have perceived beneath the façade of edifying discourse and amusing banter, the framework of the Shaw-Lee Hatch Street home. Henderson's opinion of *Getting Married* agreed with the playwright's disavowal of plot-mongering. This play, said Henderson, was exclusively concerned with the institution of marriage "and about nothing else" and that not even Shakespeare himself could squeeze a plot out of it.[81] *Getting Married* does lack the traditional plot form but it is also a play about divorce, a play about a *ménage à trois* and, like all of the plays of GBS, has something more to offer than amusement. Basically, it is concerned with twin explorations of (a) safeguards protecting the rights of the individual within the marriage contract and (b) the then prevailing (and still current) archaisms blocking the dissolution of misalliances. It is preceded with the usual preface in which GBS discoursed both brilliantly and wisely on the origins and evolution of marriage in general and the state of the modern marriage in particular. Monogamy, polygyny and polyandry are subjected to Shavian examination along with a diverting but informative excursion into the *ménage à trois*. Monogamous marriage, he wrote, if entered into on a genuinely tender and romantic basis, would have no room for an additional husband or wife because of one's total absorption with and of the other. He added that such a relationship had never, within his knowledge, been shared by three persons except when they were singularly attached to one another and he cited the case of Nelson and Sir William and Lady Hamilton. The typical triangular household, he continued, could not exist except under certain conditions, which, as Shaw outlined them, seemed similar to those of Number 1

Hatch Street. Every such trio that he was aware of, whether from his own observation or from available histories, was a fiasco in that one of the two candidates for the deepest intimacies of the third was eventually expelled by the other. To put it another way, if A vied with B for the affections of C and succeeded, B would have to go. B, continued Shaw, had an alternative: he could admit his defeat and stay as a friendly gesture to keep up appearances, or for the children's benefit or for reasons of economy; but, GBS concluded, this exception could exist only if B is no longer interested in C.[82] This study suggests that Shaw consciously used his mother as C, his father as B and George John Lee as A for three of the principal figures in *Getting Married.*

The question of whether Shaw used actual persons for any of his approximately six hundred dramatic characterizations has been the subject of some comments. Critics by the score have and still do declare that the dramatic creations of GBS never did and could not live, breathe or even occupy space. Thus Duffin, like many another, asserted that Shaw's characters were unreal, nonexistent, lacking in form, body, etc. To him (and to others who shared his views), Shaw replied that Duffin's opinions made it appear that the characters he created were allegorical figures instead of human beings. Several of his characters, he said, were "close portraits," but for others he used people as painters used models.[83] In the preface to *Immaturity*, Shaw, in reference to the characters in that novel, went to some length to describe how he used living persons by borrowing their physical and personality characteristics, as painters did with models. Sometimes, he admitted, he drew rather close portraits based on a personal, intimate knowledge, but he copied nature with varying degrees of truthfulness. Quite a few of the characters in *Immaturity,* he concluded, had details taken from people he had met, "including members of my family (not to mention myself)"—however, not one of them was a portrait.[84] Henderson, who had several conversations with Shaw, touched upon the subject in a question-and-answer-style article:

> Henderson: . . . [do] you draw many of your characters from real life, at least in their dominant traits?

> Shaw: (meditatively) Sometimes. (pause) But the use one makes of the living models varies from recognizable portraiture to suggestions so overloaded with fiction that the most ingenious detective could not penetrate the disguise . . .[85]

But, according to Shaw, there was one member of his family he did not portray in any of his plays. In response to an inquiry from O'Bolger, Shaw replied, "I have never put my father, or anyone like him, in a play." [86]

As *Getting Married* opens, all concerned gather together, as required, in the kitchen of the palace of the Bishop of Chelsea. The occasion is the imminent marriage of the Bishop's daughter Edith to Cecil Sykes. Before this event finally takes place, the participants proceed to a discussion of the failing marriage of Reginald Bridgenorth (brother of the Bishop) and his wife Leo. Reginald, who might be identified with George Carr Shaw, is described as physically hard and tough, impulsive and immature in both behavior and address. He is a member of that sizeable class of property-owning Englishmen (managed for them by agents) "who have never developed intellectually since their schooldays." He is, continued the playwright, a confused, defiant, impetuous, slovenly, absent-minded kind of a man always late for something or other and who obviously needs the attention of an efficient woman but who "had never been lucky or attractive enough to get it. All the same, a likeable man, from whom nobody apprehends any malice nor expects any achievement . . ." From this description, it may be reasonable to conclude that Reginald Bridgenorth was not one who could be described as a contributing member of society. He seems to have no responsibilities and one could predict that if he did have them, he would not have the character to discharge them effectively. By providing Reginald with an undeveloped intellect, I presume GBS did not mean Reginald was feeble-minded but that he showed no interest in any branch of the cultures in his society after he left schools behind him.

Both Reginald and George Carr belong to what could be considered the socially useless classes. Mr. Shaw, according to his son, had no vocation, no trade and no knack or capacity for any specific social ceremony. As a property owner, Reginald has a weak but familiar echo in George Carr who, while owning nothing, aspired to the propertied class. Writing in his *Intelligent Woman's Guide to Socialism and Capitalism,* GBS placed his father in the middle class but reported that he resented this classification and insisted that as a younger son of many other younger sons, he belonged to the "propertied class." [87]

The "likeable" Reginald has—also in George Carr Shaw—his likeable model. Mr. Shaw was, as GBS told O'Bolger in the *Sketches* version, "really, as men go, humane and likeable." [88] In the original text Shaw put it "really, as men go, an amiable man." [89] McNulty remembered George Carr as an agreeable person who, when meeting a friend, would always smile, shake hands and exchange a few words, and still another direct observer, MacMahon Shaw, regarded his uncle George as "a dear old courteous and charming gentleman." [90]

Reginald seems incapable of harboring malice or, at any rate, he is one from whom no one expects maliciousness. George Carr is similarly spite-free. He has been described by his son as being "nobody's enemy but his own" and hated by no one because no one had anything to fear from him.[91] In yet another place he is "the least formidable of men" because of his kindliness and inoffensiveness.[92] However, it will be seen that GBS deprived Reginald of his amiability when it concerned the intruder in his home even as George Carr may have felt towards the intruder in *his* home. As stated by GBS, Mr. Shaw "certainly did not like Lee" and, further, Mr. Shaw could not have been pleased with the prospect of living in the same house with Lee.

Nor does anyone expect Reginald to "achieve" anything. Being a muddled, hasty, immature, intellectually retarded and forgetful gentleman, he could hardly have been expected to succeed in anything—and the same could be said about Mr. Shaw. He has been described by GBS as being timid, futile, a liar, a hypocrite and a drunkard. In addition to these distinguishing qualities he had, as previously noted, no profession or trade, nor was he equal to the requirements of any social occasion. With these qualifications he could hardly be expected to achieve anything—and he did not.

Additional evidence of similar or duplicated characteristics may have been expressed in the play through Lesbia Grantham, sister-in-law of the Bishop. She advised Shaw's audience that Reginald was "weak" and always had been. Further, when he inherited the family property, it was completely covered with mortgages and he, consequently, was in constant money trouble. It was not until the mortgages were paid off, added Lesbia, that he could afford to marry, and by that time he was over fifty. Though the play did not reveal the nature of Reginald's weakness, it is possible, in creating the character of Reginald Bridgenorth on the model of George Carr, that his weakness was Shaw's allegorical substitute for his father's general impotence or, perhaps, his specific weakness for whiskey.

According to Lesbia's apologies for her brother-in-law, Reginald seems to have had a background of economic distress. While it was true that it was GBS's maternal grandfather who had the long history of mortgages, it was also true that George Carr fared poorly at every time of his life. Recorded here earlier was Shaw's report that it was a difficult struggle for the widow of Bernard Shaw and her eleven children who not infrequently went hungry. MacMahon Shaw's manuscript was favored with a Shavian notation. His father, GBS interpolated, had left him under a strong impression that there were "some terribly lean years" before his brothers and sisters were finally able to stand on their own legs.[93]

Finally, both Reginald and George Carr have married women considerably younger than themselves. It may be well to note, before passing to the examination of the remaining figures of this *ménage à trois,* the relative ages of the members of the two trios. In the following table it will be understood that the ages of the Shaw-Lee group are fixed at the time of Lucinda's marriage while the ages of the Bridgenorth-Hotchkiss entanglement are some years after the date of Leo's marriage.

Dublin—1852	Years	Chelsea—1908	Years
George Carr Shaw	38	Reginald Bridgenorth	(over) 50
Lucinda Elizabeth Shaw	22	Leo Bridgenorth	(over) 20
George John Lee	22	St. John Hotchkiss	29

In proceeding to Leo Bridgenorth, it may also be borne in mind that at the time *Getting Married* was presented to a London audience,[94] Mrs. Shaw, still mentally alert and physically vigorous at seventy-eight was, to use an apt phrase, not more than a stone's throw from her son's residence at 10 Adelphi Terrace. The existence of his mother and her proximity must have, I think, called for some skillful camouflage since Mrs. Shaw sometimes went to see her son's plays.

As Reginald seems modelled, in the main, upon George Carr, so Leo, it follows, is basically patterned after Lucinda Elizabeth. Leo was exceptionally pretty, exceptionally youthful, exceptionally restless and therefore, exceptionally attractive to those who were affected by these qualities and especially so to those who looked upon young ladies as "appetizing lollipops." Objectively viewed, continued Shaw, Leo's restlessness is not as attractive as the "kittenishness" that is released "from a rich and fresh vitality." A natural "fusser," she fusses over herself as well as anyone for whom she feels responsible, and her vanity obliges her to magnify her responsibility with ostentatious display. Leo's fussing, GBS went on, was over matters of little importance, but she frequently referred to them under pretentious designations as, for example: the Universe, Art, good breeding, the Creator, motherhood, the world, the Divine Spark or any other matter which struck her fancy as being intellectually impressive. She had, moreover, an uncommon imagination but, withal, no more than ordinary creative power and no more than ordinary discernment—the end effect being that she was perpetually in the clouds about words and perpetually in the cradle about things. Further, she regarded herself as nimble-witted, contemplative and "superior to ordinary weaknesses and prejudices." Thus convinced, she threw herself rashly at witty and cultured men who were, at first, pleased and flattered, then annoyed and finally bored.

Here, necessarily, the dramatist-painter mixed his paints with masterly skill, making it almost impossible to distinguish figures from the fictions. Nevertheless, familiar colors are discernible despite GBS's efforts to neutralize them. Was Leo Bridgenorth "exceptionally youthful" and did she have a "rich and fresh vitality"? According to GBS, his mother had a "youthfulness" worthy of note.[95] An equally authoritative commentator was GBS's sister Lucy. Writing to her friend Janey Crichton, Lucy marvelled at her mother's extraordinary vitality in her eightieth year—"more juvenile and healthy and energetic than any of us." [96] One year later, Lucy again reported her astonishment to her friend. "My mother," she wrote, "is brilliant; she seems to grow younger and more alert all the time" and described how she pranced off to the theatres and concerts as if she were not eighty-one but eighteen.[97]

Leo's love for the pompous phrase finds an astonishingly strong echo in Lucy Shaw. In addition to having written a "tiny playlet" which reached production in Germany, Lucy authored two opuscules[98] in the way of being a series of letters from "The Lady Theodosia Alexandra Kildonnel" of Kildonnel Castle, Ballymoire, County Derry to her infant goddaughter-grandniece "The Honourable Theodosia Carmelita Kildonnel."

Uncomfortably similar to her brother's earlier *My Dear Dorothea* (1878), Lucy's letters of Lady Theodosia encouraged her goddaughter to question the authority of her mother and father and to beware of their advice or rules and subject them to a clever control system—in short, how to bring up the parents. Her final counsel to the little girl was to marry a millionaire—preferably an American Railway King, Coal Oil Emperor or Canned Meat Monarch—and, after obtaining to this happy estate she could then face the dangers of Life as the Honourable Mrs. Kildonnel B. Perkins. But to return to a less fascinating topic, both of Lucy's books are sprinkled with phrases no less pompous than Leo's. In her last letter to Theodosia they hurtle through the pages like hail. Examples: Divine Spark, Universal Riddles, Cosmos, Realms of Thought, Eternal Secret, Absolute Knowledge, Omniscience and Free Will.[99] As Mrs. Shaw has never been quoted at length, it cannot be said that she had a penchant for pear-shaped profundities, but the possibility exists that Lucy may have received this gift from her mother.

Leo's "more than common imagination" strikes somewhat closer to home. Henderson reported that Mrs. Shaw was purported to be the first person in Dublin to own a "planchette" (a sort of ancestor to the ouija board) and that Sonny was a witness to séances in Synge

Street.[100] She seems to have lost interest in these psychic adventures for some years, but when her daughter died, she returned to the planchette, increased its versatility (if not range) by adding a ouija board and established communications with Yuppy in the world beyond. Henderson reported a personal conversation he had with Mrs. Shaw wherein she gave him, "with the most infectious laugh," the essence of one of these contacts. She "called up" Yuppy one day and asked for her views with respect to her brother George's position in the world as a man of prominence. According to Henderson's account, GBS's earthly eminence was a surprise to her. "But," insisted Mrs. Shaw, "aren't you very proud of George?" "Oh, yes," came the reply from the celestial regions, "it's all very well in its way. But that sort of thing doesn't count for much up here." This episode, continued Henderson perceptively, illustrated Mrs. Shaw's views rather than those of Yuppy's spirit. He also recalled that "George" reported a later exchange in which Yuppy gave notice through spirit-writing that the time had come to separate whereupon she was replaced by what Henderson termed "an entirely imaginary" Christian monk called Father John who preceded Christ by six thousand years. Continuing, Henderson channeled the subject into a tentative probe of the sources for Shaw's genius. He seriously attributed his subject's "remarkable imaginative and creative literary powers" to Mrs. Shaw's fascination with spiritualism and he stated that GBS had frequently asserted to him personally "that his mother was highly endowed with powers of imagination; and he has placed on record his conviction that she 'really lived in it and on it.' "[101] Shaw's version of part of the above was in practical agreement with Henderson and may be seen in the Harris book. His mother, he wrote to Harris, dabbled with spiritualism in her later years enabling her to "play" at conversing with Yuppy. However, she was soon bored with this, and when Yuppy conveniently announced that she must break off permanently, made the spiritual acquaintance of "a certain entirely imaginary Father John, described by himself as 'a Cistercian monk who lived six thousand years before Christ!' "[102] Pearson received an especially interesting contribution. When his mother lost interest in Agnes' communiqués, Shaw said, she then tried to tune in her husband. Failing in this, she rang up Lee, "who was really her man, with little more success . . ." [103] Elsewhere, Shaw said his mother continued her interest in spiritualism until *he* was an "elderly man" (GBS was fifty-seven at the time of his mother's death); the screeds, he added, produced by her exercises "might have been called wishful writings (like wishful thinkings) so clearly were they as much her own story-telling inventions . . ." [104]

A final note of interest regarding the similarity of Leo's traits to Lucinda is in Shaw's depiction of her husband Reginald as one who plainly requires the services of a capable woman and never got one because he was either unlucky or unattractive. The parallel to George Carr and Lucinda Elizabeth is self-evident: Mr. Shaw also needed the services of a capable woman and never got one.

According to his military experience—not to mention his seven duels with the sabre and one with pistols—it would seem that St. John Hotchkiss, who may be identified with George John Lee, is a strong, active and well-built man, though this is not so stated. Notwithstanding Shaw's description of Reginald as physically hard and tough, the play's dialogue makes it unmistakeably clear that St. John is Reginald's physical as well as mental superior, reminiscent of George Carr's total eclipse by Professor Lee. Hotchkiss was, described Shaw, about twenty-nine, very smart, "correct in dress to the last thread of his collar," but this fastidiousness was not to suggest that he was more than ordinarily concerned with his appearance, since he was far more engrossed with "ideas" than with his attire. He spoke about himself, GBS continued, with an "energetic gaiety" and when talking to others, exhibited a gentle indulgence as if out of a good-natured deference to their intellectual poverty. Those who were not amused by this condescension became irritated and either flew into a rage or tried vainly to ignore him.

In contrast to Reginald's prosaic personality, Hotchkiss is a dashing and romantic figure; his charm and wit fascinate the ladies who seek (and receive) his ardent but shallow attentions. Though GBS was not precise with respect to St. John's source of income, he seems to have supported himself and his fashionable apparel from his occupation as a "public trustee." Examination and comparison of Hotchkiss and Lee reveal elements too uniform to be dismissed as accidental resemblances. Both are more suited (chronologically speaking at least), to the ladies concerned, both are the intruding elements of a *ménage à trois* and both have contrasting personalities even as George Carr and George John. Hotchkiss' impeccable habiliments may be likened to Lee's own sartorial refinements. "Harris" reported that "Lee was never carelessly or ill-dressed" [105] and it may be regarded as a certainty that Shaw would have corrected or purged this comment had it been slightly, not to say grossly, inaccurate. Visual evidence of Lee's impeccable haberdashery is available in the Pigott Photograph. Hotchkiss' smart appearance seems to be an inheritance from Lee.

St. John's preoccupation with his "ideas" (unspecified in the play), recalls Lee's own quota of ideas (clearly specified). The Professor's ideas, wrote GBS, amazed the Shaw family. Last, and perhaps least, St. John's "energetic gaiety" in conversation strongly reminds one of GBS's repeated (and justifiable) use of "energetic" to describe Lee.

Additional intellectual resemblances of singular uniformity exist between Lee and Hotchkiss. They are revealed in exchanges between St. John and the Bishop's assistant, Father Anthony Soames—a fascinating Shavian creation in his own right. Here, Lee—skeptic of the Synge-Hatch Street debates is re-created as Hotchkiss, skeptic of the Chelsea debates. It was the "visitor," it will be recalled, who held the skeptical view with respect to the raising of Lazarus. With an insolence perhaps borrowed from Lee, St. John disposes of Father Soames's frequent allusions to the Bible when supporting his assertive views.

HOTCHKISS

[impatiently]

My dear Anthony: I find you merely ridiculous as a preacher, because you keep referring me to places and documents and alleged occurrences in which, as a matter of fact, I dont believe. I dont believe in anything but my own will and my own pride and honor. Your [draught of] fishes

> and your catechisms and all the rest of it make a charming poem . . .

On the subject of marriage, bachelor Lee breathes again in bachelor Hotchkiss who had fixed ideas in this field. Father Soames had, with his earnest preaching, taken Hotchkiss to task for his intentions toward Mrs. Zenobia Alexandria George, bewitching wife of a coal merchant. Hotchkiss is exhorted to give up his sinful way of life and take the vows. If, Father Soames continued, he did not feel up to renouncing the world and its pleasures, would he not at least renounce this woman? Did he not believe in the sanctity of marriage?

HOTCHKISS

> My soul is utterly free from any such superstition . . . I loathe the whole marriage morality of the middle classes with all my instincts . . . I despise all this domestic purity business as the lowest depth of narrow, selfish, sensual, wife-grabbing vulgarity.

The tie of bachelorhood from Hotchkiss to Lee is given elsewhere in the play when it is disclosed that prior to his service with Leo, St. John has had a romance with Mrs. George. At an early opportunity he presses for its resumption vowing that he loved her still. Not unreceptive, Mrs. George agrees but with the stipulation that he must first give up Leo. St. John is quite willing—even anxious to drop her. "But," he lamented, "she wont drop me. Do you suppose I ever wanted to marry her? I was a homeless bachelor . . ." Hotchkiss as a homeless bachelor corresponds more or less with Lee's history in Harrington Street.

As *Getting Married* gets into its stage stride, the author led the dialogue towards the Reginald-Leo-St. John affair. Reginald and Leo have been divorced, but their final decree has not yet been made absolute. On stage are Leo, Reginald, Hotchkiss, the Bishop and Reginald's brother General Bridgenorth—dignified, unintelligent, dull and biased—the product of his training. They are discussing the Church and the State views on marriage and the Bishop is pointing out that at present the relationships between Leo, Reginald and St.

John are thoroughly legal as far as the State is concerned, but could he as Bishop be expected to approve? By George, sputtered the General and, turning towards Hotchkiss, fulminated that Reginald ought to have booted Hotchkiss out of the house.

REGINALD
[rising]

> How could I kick him out of the house? He's stronger than me: he could have kicked me out if it came to that. He did kick me out: what else was it but kicking out, to take my wife's affections from me and establish himself in my place?

Further examination of Reginald's response to the General discloses a triangular relationship comparable enough to the Hatch Street house to be based upon it. Although Shaw avoided outright recognition of a *ménage à trois* in *Getting Married,* its existence is strongly implied if not actually stated by both Reginald and Hotchkiss with Leo modestly holding her tongue. He could do nothing, said Reginald plaintively, to prevent St. John from consolidating his position in his home—he not only appropriated the affections of his wife but he also usurped his position.

In another place, Reginald gave further details of St. John's capture of Leo and his assumption of the practical headship of the Bridgenorth home. In response to Reginald's charge that he had stolen the love of his wife, St. John broke in to protest that he had left no stone unturned to prevent the collapse. Quite true, replied Reginald, St. John could not really be blamed—it was fated—people just didn't do these things to one another. But, he continued to his listeners, what could *he* have done?

> I was old: she was young. I was dull: he was brilliant. I had a face like a walnut: he had a face like a mushroom. I was as glad to have him in the house as she was: he gave us good advice—told us what to do when we didnt know. She found out that I wasnt any use to her and he was; so she nabbed him and gave me the chuck.

Reginald was said to have been as pleased about the presence of Hotchkiss in his home as Leo. St. John himself was quite content with his connection with them and added his voice harmoniously to his two housemates. He admitted to Mrs. George, in justification of his alliance with Leo, that as a bachelor without a home, he was "quite happy at their house as their friend." While it is conceded that both Leo and St. John could be reasonably gay under the roof of a *ménage à trois,* Reginald's satisfaction does not ring true and seems out of place on the stage, in actual practice or in the face of his own general disgruntlement. What Shaw allowed in the play, he disallowed in the prose and (as reported here earlier) pointed out in his preface to *Getting Married* that he did not know of a single instance, with the exception of the Nelson-Hamilton affair, where all three regarded each other affectionately.

Reginald's explanation to his audience that St. John was a useful if not essential addition to his home is raised in his next remark. Hotchkiss, he said, was wiser than the two of them—at least in some respects. When they were at a loss for what to do in a given situation or where they continued doing the wrong things (for that is what Reginald could mean), it was Hotchkiss who advised and guided them and here the parallel to Shaw's parents becomes apparent at once. Apropos of Leo's fitness for marriage, Lesbia Grantham's apologies for brother-in-law Reginald included an oblique view of his wife. Lesbia reminded her listeners that, after all, allowances must be made for Reginald—he didn't marry until he was over fifty and then, naturally, "he made a fool of himself marrying a child like Leo."

According to GBS, his mother was, at the time of her marriage, no more than a child herself. As a tribute to Aunt Ellen's conception of how an Irish lady should be brought up, Lucinda entered into marriage knowing nothing of the world around her. She had no idea of elementary sanitation or hygiene, no idea of diet, preparation or supervision of food, no idea of parenthood or child care, no idea of the value of money or, for that matter, no idea on any subject connected with anything customarily served by solicitors, nurses, servants and parents. With neither George Carr nor Lucinda Elizabeth qualified for the serious business of marriage, Professor Lee's advice and counsel were offered and accepted in Dublin even as St. John Hotchkiss' advice would be accepted in Chelsea.

That the Professor offered advice which was accepted is clear and undeniable though the range of that advice and by whom it was accepted is far from clear. In the preface to *London Music,* Shaw reported on two of Lee's recommendations that "astonished" the family. The Professor, recalled GBS, said that people should leave their windows open at night when sleeping and the audacity of this breath-taking proposal so appealed to Sonny that he was still doing it in his seventy-ninth year. The second break with tradition concerned food. The Professor, continued Shaw, would not eat white bread—only brown would do—a staggering departure from custom but one which he did not report as adopting himself.[106] In the *Sketches,* Shaw repeated the night-air and brown-bread items, and added that he also took up the brown bread—both of which habits he continued to practise into his ninety-third year. Lee's influence in his home, Shaw concluded, also fixed in him the doubts concerning academic authority that he was to retain to the end of his life.[107] As might be expected, O'Bolger received fresh details on the seditious Professor. Lee, he was told, was a skeptic, not only of religion but of lawyers, doctors and the professions in general and Shaw added, "I was thus brought up to regard a doctor as a humbug, a clergyman as a hypocrite, and a lawyer as a vampire. My opinions of schoolmasters I formed for myself." [108]

Although all this shows the influence on and the adoption by GBS of some of Lee's counsels, there is no evidence that any other member of his family accepted these or similar advice. Yet there was one example which illustrated the Professor's influential—even supreme—position in the Shaw family. Lee, continued Shaw in the *London Music* preface, did not have a very high opinion of the medical fraternity and would not even permit an apothecary and his preparations to enter the house. When, on a certain occasion, Shaw's mother fell seriously ill [109] the Professor "took her case in hand unhesitatingly and at the end of a week or so gave my trembling father leave to call in a leading Dublin doctor, who simply said 'My work is done' and took his hat." [110] Shaw's earlier version to O'Bolger had minor but noteworthy variations. Although the Professor had little or no respect for doctors, Shaw believed Lee would have made an excellent doctor himself and seemed to have this opinion because of Lee's success in treating his ailing prima donna. When, Shaw continued, Mrs. Shaw contracted an unnamed illness, the Professor "threw himself into the case with ardor, and would not let my father call in a doctor until he pulled her through it. When the doctor came, he stared, and said, 'My work is done: the patient is convalescent.' " [111] Thus Lee's authority and his advice and counsel in the Shaw household is clearly demonstrated. Brushing aside conventional medical attendance (and, incidentally, Mr. Shaw) the dynamic, confident and inspired Lee took full charge of the wife of George Carr Shaw. Conclusion: Hotchkiss and his advice to the Bridgenorths is biographically parallel to Lee and his advice to the Shaws. George Carr and Reginald, being equally useless to their respective spouses, were given the chuck for their younger, handsomer and more brilliant replacements.

Though all of the autobiographical elements in *Getting Married* have not been sifted, attention should be drawn to a general exchange irresistibly intimating an extraordinary Dublin scene of which GBS may have learned. As explained earlier in this section, the ostensible purpose for bringing thirteen persons together in the Bishop's palace is that they may attend the marriage of Edith Bridgenorth and Cecil Sykes. Just as the members of the cast have exhausted themselves of conversation, it is discovered that Edith has refused to proceed with the ceremony as the result of reading a pamphlet entitled

DO YOU KNOW WHAT YOU ARE DOING?
BY A WOMAN WHO HAS DONE IT [112]

in which the authoress told how her husband (a) committed murder, (b) attempted suicide and (c) was condemned to death but (for his children's sake) snatched from the gallows and given life imprisonment instead. Unable to obtain a divorce, the unfortunate woman published her story, and Edith, having read it, now objects to the marriage, unless the Church, the Law and the principals agree in advance upon certain "escape" clauses in the marriage contract. Is she to understand, Edith demands, that if Cecil becomes a murderer or a forger or a thief or turns atheist, she would be unable to divorce him? Quite so, answered the Bishop, quite so—he must be taken for better for worse. Then, retorted Edith, send the wedding cake back; the performance is off. She cannot and will not agree to such a wicked stipulation and argues, with that superb Shavian logic normally available, that it would be a sorry world indeed if we took our servants, our friends and our Prime Ministers for better for worse forever and that if she had known what she had let herself in for she would never have agreed. But, protested Cecil,

I'm not going to commit murder.

EDITH

How do you know? Ive sometimes wanted to murder Slattox.[113] Have you never wanted to murder somebody, Uncle Rejjy?

REGINALD

[at Hotchkiss, with intense expression]

Yes.

LEO

Rejjy!

REGINALD

I said yes; and I mean yes. There was one night, Hotchkiss, when I jolly nearly shot you and Leo and finished up with myself; and thats the truth.

In support of the suggestion that Reginald's confession of murderous intentions may have had its roots in Dublin, I would like to draw attention to the stage situation. Edith has been on for about ten minutes and has not up to that moment spoken to Reginald. On stage at the same time, besides Edith and Reginald are Cecil, Leo, the Bishop, the Bishop's wife, Hotchkiss, General Bridgenorth and Lesbia Grantham. Despite the unique, ready-to-hand dramatic thrill and tempting humor in asking a Bishop if he had ever felt like murdering someone, master playwright Bernard Shaw rejected the opportunity and, skipping over a bridegroom, a divorcee, a Bishop's lady, a philanderer, a soldier and a spinster, settled upon Reginald. I hold it likely that GBS deliberately contrived this situation with the intention of choosing Reginald as the target for the question possibly because the scene was drawn from life and may have been told to him by the senior member of the original cast, perhaps when the two male Shaws were left alone in Dublin.

Summarizing briefly, I suggest that the dramatist within Bernard Shaw possessed him of an extraordinary compulsion to reveal the drama of Hatch Street, and that *Getting Married* represents Shaw's compromise with that compulsion by being, at least in broad outline, the re-creation of the Shaw-Lee *ménage à trois*.

VI

ACCORDING TO SHAW, the transformation of Lee from musical hero in Dublin to musical humbug in London marked the beginning of the end of his mother's association with him, but a study of the circumstances leading up to their final parting suggested quite another cause. Reviewing the difficult early London years for Mrs. Shaw, it will be seen that her refusal to compromise artistic integrity combined with other matters to contribute to her adversity. In particular, GBS's reluctance to aggressively seek employment outside the arts, the general economic instability of the period and, more significantly, Mrs. Shaw's own innocence of worldly matters and ignorance of elementary business practices, all conspired to keep musical clients from 13 Victoria Grove.

Not so with Professor Vandeleur Lee of 13 Park Lane. As he had predicted in Dublin, London ladies actually paid him a guinea a lesson (or twelve lessons for the price of ten) to teach them how to sing. Unfortunately for the Professor, the ladies did not regard the expenditure of guineas over two or more years with enthusiasm; they expected and demanded miracles from him and his marvelous Method, and the Professor had to supply the miracles or starve. Lee himself had given the account of this experience to GBS who made it the subject of an article four years after Lee's death. Speaking on professors of music, GBS recalled one who was an excellent teacher —until he arrived in London. Subsequently identifying the teacher as George John Vandaleur Lee, Shaw told his readers Lee discovered that first-class teaching was third-class business, since those who could afford the steep fees stubbornly refused to take more than twelve lessons. Seeing which way the wind blew, Lee trimmed his sails accordingly. The ladies, he promised, would sing like Pattis in six weeks if they took his training. They did—and he made certain that at the end of their six weeks they could produce a louder "noise" than they did in their first week, thus impressing their friends with their extraordinary progress. The day came, Shaw continued, when he asked Lee how he came by The Method which he had discarded. Concluded Lee: "The plan [Badiali Method] answered perfectly—except in London, where they dont like it and wont do it, and expect to learn in a month what takes four or five years' hard work." [114] Lee did not reveal how long it took him to realize that it would be impossible to continue to teach singing by the tried and true years-long Method and neither Shaw's nor his biographers' few published comments throughout the years have clarified matters.

"When," GBS advised O'Bolger, "I joined my mother in London [in 1876], Lee was still in and out of our house very much in his old fashion . . ." And again: "When I got to London" wrote Shaw on the bottom of the same page, "she despised him and was going her own way with the great singing method which he was no longer able to teach honestly." The Professor, continued GBS, would have starved, had he not sold the London ladies a bill of goods; but his mother would not hear of such trickery and refused to allow for the pressures of survival. She knew, her son concluded, that it took at least two years to sing according to The Method, that the six-weeks offer was a swindle.[115] Of course it was quite possible for Mrs. Shaw to continue teaching according to The Method, while despising Lee, and permit him to frequent 13 Victoria Grove but it is not in keeping with the spirit and content of Shaw's reflections elsewhere. For example, he wrote to Harris that when Lee turned his coat, his mother "dropped him as unhesitatingly, as her father used to shoot a sporting dog at its first mistake." [116] GBS did not say whether she dropped the turncoat socially or professionally or both. For the readers of the *London Music* preface, Mrs. Shaw's reaction to the double-dealing Professor was given a dramatic flourish. The dynamic Lee—before whom everybody and everything would give way—this genius who created his own realm of music, wherein he reigned supreme, was no more:

> G. J. Lee, with the black whiskers and the clean shaven resolute lip and chin, became Vandaleur Lee, whiskerless, but with a waxed and pointed moustache and an obsequious attitude.

To his mother, GBS went on, this metamorphosis was nearly as great a shock to her as her disillusioning marriage to George Carr. At least that had been remedied by the music of Lee. But that Lee himself should now turn traitor! Throw over The Method! That the only real teacher in the midst of so many swindlers should now turn swindler and out-swindle them all! "This," said Shaw, "was the end of all things; and she never forgave it." [117] Though Mrs. Shaw never forgave her late exemplar, it was not yet the end of all things.

Recapitulating from all sources, it would seem that Lee's scuttling of The Method and the resultant strain of relations with Mrs. Shaw took place within a few months of his move from Ebury Street to Park Lane or probably in the latter half of 1874. As to the changed nature of the relations between Mrs. Shaw and Lee, GBS has, despite what he told Harris, described them as at least cooperative if nothing else. To O'Bolger he said that at first his mother sang for him a good deal, as in the past, and Lucy, who had a beautiful singing voice and was by now most attractive, participated in Lee's At Homes.[118] He confirmed this nearly twenty years later and with a fresh addition. With his charlatanry exposed, Mrs. Shaw seemed unwilling to cast him out forthwith and tolerated Lee the quack even as she once tolerated Shaw the drunkard. Lee, added GBS, was gently dropped—how, he did not say. Still, Mrs. Shaw continued to visit him in Park Lane to assist him with the musical aspects of his At Homes, and he continued to visit her in Victoria Grove, though GBS gave no reasons for these visits. At this point, the reader of Shaw's preface to *London Music* was also gently dropped, for, naturally, one expected to learn that the Professor's final exit from Victoria Grove had been eventually facilitated by the disenchanted but good-natured Mrs. Shaw. Not so. Examination of Shaw's conclusion revealed that Lee's departure was pressed not by Mrs. Shaw but from an unexpected quarter: daughter Lucy. According to Shaw's concluding remarks Lucy, who as a child had "quarrelled" with Lee in the course of being taught how to play piano and who had never thought well of him, now found him intolerable in his new role as musical mentor of impatient Pattis. When, Shaw added, Lucy discovered that Lee had no power or influence to assist her professionally, she cut him entirely "and made it difficult for him to continue his visits." [119] It may be deduced from these comments that if it had not been for Lucy's ambitions, Lee might have continued visiting Mrs. Shaw, notwithstanding her disapproval of his perfidy. There was no indication as to when the rupture finally occurred but I would venture to put it sometime after GBS's arrival and before Lucy's professional stage debut, or between 1876 and 1881.[120]

The biographers' views of the Lee-Lucy discord are of particular interest at this time. They differ with their subject as to the cause for the friction between Lee and Lucy and at the same time coyly ignoring their sources. Ervine, for example, declared that Lucy had a "deep aversion from" Lee but offered no documentation.[121] His statement echoes an earlier reference in the same work. Here, Lucy's disaffection for the Professor received its own warrant as Ervine recounted that Lee had gone to considerable pains to develop her voice but added that Lucy

> detested Lee, who had fallen in love with her and was ardent in his attentions, all of which, except for his singing lessons, she disliked.[122]

Henderson's treatment was not substantially different from Ervine's and was also, with respect to documentation, similarly disappointing. He reported that "An intolerable situation had arisen when Lee turned his amoristic charm upon Lucy. Susceptibility to Lucy's personality and radiant appeal was understandable, although Lee was more than twice her age. Fortunately no harm was done." [123] Further, he reported that Lucy had earlier squabbled with Lee in Dublin and now could not bear him at all. Despite the primness of his prose, Henderson's meaning was clear, although it is not quite certain for whom the situation was intolerable. It becomes more clear in *Bernard Shaw* by "Frank Harris." Written twenty-five years before the centenary biographies, it contained some remarkable odds and ends of intelligence. In the chapter dealing with "The Innocent Triangle" for instance, the author dwelt at some length on the fortunes of Professor Lee. His Method could only fail in London, he wrote, as it required three years training, while the London *dilettanti* insisted that a dozen lessons should be sufficient. The Professor, noting the trend,

> dropped the "G.J." initials and became "Vandaleur Lee." That only raised his fee to five dollars a lesson. He shaved off his black whiskers and grew a moustache. He waxed this and his days of honest toil were over.
>
> Mrs. Shaw, observing that he was developing into a charlatan, would have none of him after that. This was particularly settled in her mind when he became susceptible to Lucy's adolescent sex appeal. No harm came of this because Lucy could not tolerate him.[124]

This extract is very likely the source of the Ervine and Henderson accounts, and although GBS may not have been responsible for its composition, he was certainly the reviser and authorizer of the statement. The publisher of the "Harris" book, being a person sensible of business, sent the manuscript to Shaw for his approval, and GBS has affirmed his intimacy with and influence upon this document. Prefacing his *How Frank Ought To Have Done It,* Shaw stated that when Harris was in the illness that led to his death, a New York publisher engaged him to do a biography and, pressed by his financial needs, Harris made a reckless effort to comply. But, concluded Shaw, his constructions and speculations were so far from the truth that "I had to rewrite his book myself on matters of fact" in order that it could be published after his death.[125] Shaw's relation to the Harris book should be viewed with that perspective.

Those familiar with the literary address of Harris on Sex will find it difficult to believe that the celebrated author of *My Life and Loves* composed the quietly, simply, even chastely written passage just cited. I suggest that Harris could not have written it and, by extension, that it owes its existence to GBS. Comparison of the structure of it to Shaw's own account in the *London Music* preface will indicate the ancestry of the quotation from "Harris." It will be noted in both cases that the general approach, sequence and even misspelling were the same. In each account it was G. J. Lee who became Vandaleur Lee, and in both versions the whiskers were replaced by a waxed moustache. The fact that the preface to *London Music* was completed four years after the publication of the Harris book does not invalidate the comparison as the preface itself was based on an earlier account to O'Bolger.

The published, unpublished or anonymous works of GBS were not, however, the only sources for evidence of the Professor's pursuit of Lucy. The memoirs of Lady Hanson also provided affirmation of a romantic Lee. Her mother, she told a Dublin radio audience, recalled that Lucy was about twenty when she left for London and

> had a lovely soprano voice, exquisitely fresh in quality; it had, of course, been well trained by the family friend who, by degrees, became a suitor but Lucy would have none of him.[126]

Unquestionably authoritative, Lady Hanson's mother pointed up the attention Lee accorded Lucy as she matured, raising the possibility that Lucy's "quarrel" with him as a child stemmed from an incident unrelated to the pianoforte.

Collateral evidence supporting Shaw's authorship as well as further testimony of Lee's fancy for Lucy comes from a source which has not been available to the biographers. In his thirty-page letter of February 1916 to O'Bolger, Shaw wrote that while Lee was still coming and going to and from Victoria Grove, he was not the man he used to be.

> G. J. Lee of Dublin . . . . [was now] Vandaleur Lee of Park Lane, London, with his whiskers shaved off and replaced by an imperial (style of Napoleon III), was a charlatan and a humbug.[127]

Comparison of this extract with the Harris and *London Music* treatments will clearly show their common interests and common authorship.

As to the final contribution to the "romance" of Lee and Lucy, its authenticity could be bettered only if attested by the two principals themselves. Speaking of the decline of Lee, Shaw told O'Bolger that as the Professor grew older he became involved, unfortunately, in the more vulgar circles of London society and "developed a certain sexual sentimentality." This, GBS was at pains to point out, was something new with him and asserted that while Lee lived with the Shaws, he had absolutely no time for things of that sort. But

> The first sign he ever gave of having any interests except professional ones was his succumbing to the charm of my sister and becoming sentimental about her. My sister, to whom this new attitude was as odious as it was surprising, immediately dropped him completely and this gave him the possibly very disheartening shock of making him aware that she had not even liked him. He came no more to our house; and as far as I can recollect neither my mother nor my sister ever saw him again.[128]

Shaw's published contention that Lee was *persona non grata* in Victoria Grove because of unfaithfulness to The Method or because he was unable to further Lucy's career is not fully justified by the whole record. Foolishly revealed to O'Bolger, slyly inserted into the Harris book, ignored in *London Music,* Lee's interest in Lucy holds the key to his banishment from the Shaws. Lee's interest in the ladies had never been observed by Shaw until the Professor was captivated by the attractions of Lucy. This new development revolted Lucy; the end effect being that Lee had seen the inside of 13 Victoria Grove for the last time. Equally interesting is what Shaw did not tell. Why did Lee never again return to the Shaws' house? Was it because the offended Lucy told him she never wished to see him again? Was it because the rejected Lee could not bear the scene of his humiliation? The answer, I think, lies within the "Harris" quotation. Mrs. Shaw, it stated, perceiving that her Professor of Music had turned into a Professor of Humbug, wanted no more of him. Moreover, if she had any doubts as to her judgment, her decision was specifically strengthened when Mr. Lee turned an unprofessional eye on her own daughter. Mr. Lee would have to go.

Henderson was not unaware of the triangle of Lucy, Mrs. Shaw and Lee, but he discussed it rather cautiously. Lucy, he asserted, was exceptionally ambitious, adding that GBS had once told him she had broken with the Professor "primarily" because he could offer her no assurance of professional stardom and concluded with the following analysis:

> It was almost the situation of *The Second Mrs. Tanqueray* over again, for Mrs. Shaw in all matters save sexual had been his "willing slave." But the stern "Roman matron," far from committing suicide because her erstwhile "hero" was now courting her daughter, broke with him entirely and never saw him again . . .[129]

Now according to this, Lucy severed her day-to-day relations with Lee for a "primary" cause, thus suggesting that GBS believed there were secondary reasons. Henderson's next pronouncement that Mrs. Shaw had been all things to Lee except his *petite amie* was slightly altered in the sentence that followed. Mrs. Shaw, he informed his readers, observing that her former "hero" was *now* paying court to Lucy, did not give way to hysteria but dissolved their association completely, never to see him again. Having recognized the unmentionable by way of denying its existence, Henderson proceeded to other matters.

Mrs. Shaw's disapproval of the Professor's latest ambition was not a protective mother's disapproval of a suitor twice her daughter's age. I suggest that the real reason for Mrs. Shaw's objections arises from the fact that the association of Lucinda Elizabeth Shaw and George John Lee had extended beyond their cultural interests into a relationship presumably restricted to persons married to one another. Mrs. Shaw would have tolerated Vandeleur Lee the quack and swindler. She could have overlooked his inability to find important professional engagements for Lucy. She might have even endured his philanderings if any, but that he dared to make love to her own daughter—this was beyond all bearing. Mr. Lee had to go.

VII

THE LAST YEARS OF GEORGE CARR SHAW, gentleman and wholesale corn merchant seemed to have been spent in the Bed & Breakfast lodginghouses of Dublin. O'Bolger had written in one of the more defamatory versions of his biography that Mr. Shaw had ended his days in the county workhouse and, of course, got his bruised and bleeding head battered again. He did not die there, replied GBS, but spent the remainder of his life most comfortably in an excellent quarter of Dublin known as the Appian Way.[130] Ervine found it to be 21 Leeson Park Avenue which, upon examination, proved to be one of a number of adjoining red-bricked houses, similar in appearance to the Synge Street houses (about a mile distant) and tucked away near the end of a quaint, twisting *cul de sac*. Ervine was the only biographer to offer something more than a mere statistical notation. On the 19th of April, 1885, in his seventy-first year, George Carr Shaw died of lung congestion. Assuming that some sort of eulogium might be in order, Ervine likened him unto Napoleon Bonaparte's father in that he also died without knowing that genius had sprung from his loins. The deceased, Ervine continued, must have frequently bethought of the pitiless fates that joined him to Lucinda Elizabeth and he wondered if, when George Carr stood before the

Throne of Judgment, whether his Maker should not have stood before him instead?[131]

McNulty was at the bedside of the dead Shaw. But this seemed to be one of the moments in his memoirs when one suspected its author of having suffered from one of his occasional lapses of memory. According to McNulty, "The Hermit" died at the Harcourt Street lodginghouse. He recalled that on the day of his death, a messenger had brought word from Mr. Shaw's landlady to come immediately—

> I hastened there, and was ushered upstairs into a bedroom. The landlady and her husband stood together sadly gazing down at the bed where the poor old Hermit lay dead. He had died in his sleep, and his lips wore a smile; proving, as the landlady sympathetically remarked, that he had, at all events, died without suffering.[132]

Examination of the Death Registrations in Dublin's Custom House bore out the reliability of Ervine's Dublin man. From the Registration Book of 1885:

Death Registered in the District of Rathmines in
the Union of Dublin South in the County of Dublin

Nr. 200 Date: 19 April Page 541

Place	Name	Marital State	Age	Occupation	Cause of Death	Witness
21 Leeson Park Ave.	George Carr Shaw	Married	71	Miller	Congestion of lungs several days. Certified syncope certified. [sic]	R. W. Phillip present at death. 21 Leeson Park Avenue

Death registered: 27 April 1885 Registrar: Rich. M. Hearn

Ervine had the opinion that GBS was not "discomposed" much by the death of his father.[133] Henderson believed "jeer" to have been the best word to describe GBS's comment on his father's interment in the genteel Protestant Mt. Jerome Cemetery. He further recorded that when the elder Shaw died, his daughter Lucy who was unabashedly fond of him, happened to be in Dublin. Henderson did not say whether Lucy was actually present at the death but stated that she did not attend the funeral and suggested that her absence from this ceremony illustrated a characteristic of the Shaws. Lucy, he said, wept not over the death of father, mother or sister.[134] GBS did not give an account of his father's death, but he told MacMahon Shaw that although he did not believe Mr. Shaw ever wanted to see any of his family again, there was not the least bitterness between them. Lucy, GBS continued, happened to be in Dublin when the old gentleman died, and they were on terms which he described as "affectionate." There was nothing in GBS's remarks to indicate that Lucy had visited her father during his several days of illness or that she attended the funeral.[135] As to Mrs. Shaw's response to her husband's death, GBS reported that his passing produced no visible effect upon her.[136] His own reaction to the death of the man he called Papa was almost as invisible as his mother's. He told MacMahon Shaw that no one could hate his father and that when he himself remembered certain instances in the past in which he was unkind or ungracious to him, he understood how Dr. Johnson must have felt when he stood in the rain at Lichfield to atone for his own inconsiderateness.[137]

VIII

VANDELEUR LEE'S UNPOPULARITY with the Shaws of Victoria Grove was not shared by one member of that trio. The arrival of GBS from Dublin heralded the beginning of a relationship which saw Shaw involved with the Professor in one scheme or another (not entirely to their individual benefits) practically to the day of Lee's death. When, Shaw wrote to O'Bolger, the Professor was ejected from their home never to be seen again by his mother and sister, "I remained on friendly terms with Lee." [138]

Study of the ten-year period between 1876 and 1886 cannot fail to impress one with the deep shadows obscuring the Lee-Shaw association and the unlikelihood of its full emergence into the light. Earliest reference was given to Henderson in 1905 and, like the few other published comments, was non-specific in form. Deprived of music in Dublin by the flight of Lee and his mother, Shaw made desperate efforts to create his own music by learning to play the piano. Although he never gained ascendancy over the instrument, he learned enough to "thumb" his way through anything, and at one time, he added, he did a great deal of accompanying.[139] In the preface to *London Music* Shaw located the scene of his musical employments by answering his own question. How, Shaw anticipated the curious reader, did he find himself playing accompaniments in Park Lane? His explanation, however, only accounted for the events leading to his coming to Park Lane and did not give any of the circumstances or particulars.[140]

O'Bolger received the bulk of the details GBS chose to release. Faithful to his Dublin pattern, Lee had organized a musical society called *The Troubadours* which he developed to the point of giving a small number of operatic productions in which Mrs. Shaw took part. With the expulsion of Lee from Victoria Grove, GBS seems to have taken over some of his mother's former duties by acting as the accompanist. In this manner, Shaw continued, he saved Lee the money he would have had to pay a professional accompanist, thus implying that he received little or nothing for his services. Lee's artistic collapse, GBS continued, had by this time begun, although it was not yet noticeable. The fashionable ladies who had flocked to Lee's salon had left him and were seeking fresh thrills elsewhere. For all that, added GBS, there was still a residue of clients for several years who could be termed "high class," although none of them reached Lee's original standards, and these, of course, continued to deteriorate. Latterly, Shaw found himself playing piano accompaniments not to the old Lee repertory of Verdi, Gounod and Mozart but to the Gilbert and Sullivan operetta *Patience* which, he thought, was the final concert conducted by the Professor. At last, Shaw continued, "the domestic isolation" brought on by his expulsion from Victoria Grove "produced a very natural result," and GBS related to O'Bolger the following harrowing tale:

At one of Lee's At Homes one of the young ladies who, like everyone else, assumed GBS to be in some measure responsible for the proceedings, approached him in a manner that promised an uncomfortable moment. "Who," she demanded, pointing to a chair occupied by a nervous, clumsily-dressed and clumsily-powdered and rouged-up young woman, "is that person and is she a member of this society?" Looking in the direction of the irate young lady's pointed finger Shaw recognized, of all people, the housemaid—or, as he put it, "the housemaid!" Well, continued Shaw, after this the end was unavoidable. The girl had to be removed to forestall a general crisis and the performance went ahead. But the problem came up again and this sped the dissolution of *The Troubadours*. There then followed a period during which other musically-inclined people came to Park Lane but only to join in a sort of community-sing of popular opera airs in which no pretenses were made of conducting. This too, soon came to an end and the musical meetings were never resumed. Thereafter he and Lee never saw each other, except on one or two occasions when Lee requested him to draw up a circular.[141] The relationship of the housemaid to Lee was made even plainer at another point in the O'Bolger letter—but at the moment one is still stunned at the implication contained in Shaw's explanation that Lee's association with the housemaid was the "natural result" of forfeiting the domesticity of Victoria Grove.

Shaw's revelations to O'Bolger, while informative, hardly plumbed the depths of his relations with Lee. The many letters from Lee to Shaw illustrate Lee's consistent interest in his young friend's welfare and sometimes, as in the *Hornet* affair, much to his own embarrassment or disadvantage. Unfortunately, as Shaw's replies to Lee are in the possession of the Crown or the Devil, the examples offered here tell less than half the story. At any rate, in addition to Lee's efforts on behalf of Shaw in connection with the *Hornet* and possibly other, unidentified literary work by Shaw for Lee there was Lee's early notion on 23 August 1881 that he and Shaw embark on a third but abridged edition of *The Voice*. According to a note by GBS written on the last page of this letter and dated 24 August 1881 at Leyton where he was convalescing from smallpox in the home of uncle Walter, he agreed to give it a try but refused to go so far as to cause Lee any expenditure. However, he added, if it actually came off the press and it showed a profit he would take a share. To this letter Lee replied to Shaw 26 August from St. Andrews in Scotland. He thought that a pamphlet would not be profitable; it should be, he thought, in a form similar to the original and sell at either two shillings and sixpence or five shillings. He could, he said, get the book favorably noted by Hueffer (probably Francis Hueffer, music critic on *The Times* and editor of *Musical World*) and one other. He offered to send GBS a copy of the original *Voice* for cuttings and concluded, "Of course I intend that you shd have share, & I shall be delighted to arrange that in accordance with your wishes. . . . Ever yours, V. Lee." [142]

On 13 October of the same year, Lee wrote to Shaw from Park Lane that he had arranged an appointment for him with one "Messent" but that he (Lee) would be glad to have his views before going further with the matter. He sent his kind regards to Dr. and Mrs. Gurly from which we may assume that GBS was still recuperating from the smallpox.[143] The fourth of May in 1882 brought a letter to Shaw with a request. Would he be kind enough to write a few press releases in favor of an amateur opera to be produced at the Court Theatre in aid of the impoverished ladies of Ireland? Would Shaw also be able to let him have an article of his on any favorite subject adding, "I have just dined with a man who has good press influence & he has promised to work it if you are so disposed—Sincerely, V.L." [144] An undated letter written on Wednesday inquired whether Shaw would be able to play the piano the following Friday at seven in the evening; the program was to be the fourth act of *Il Trovatore*. Afterward, Lee continued, they would dine with a "Chatteris"—"He is the man with Editorial influence & he will do all in his power to oblige me . . ." and postscripted encouragement to come, as the introduction might be invaluable.[145] On 29 May 1882 Lee requested Shaw to prepare "many strong" press puffs for a program including the third act from *Il Trovatore* and a performance of *Trial By Jury* to be presented at Londonderry House in Park Lane under the patronage of Their Royal Highnesses the Duke and Duchess of Edinburgh. He apologized for pressing Shaw, "but I have almost been worried to death with this affair. Of course I shall be delighted to □ with you for the calligraphy.—Sincerely, VL" [146] Another letter, undated, asked Shaw if he could dine with Chatteris (again?), as Lee wanted to get the financial side of the performance into operation. "If you can give up some time to the matter of course I shall pay. It will not," he added percipiently, "come out of my pocket. The charity must stand it. Try to let me have as many squibs as pos." [147] 16 November 1882: Lee reported he had chosen *Patience* for a performance and would Shaw take the piano at the rehearsal Saturday at 8:30? [148]

The fifth of January, 1883, again saw Lee engaged in an effort to find employment for Shaw in journalism. Lee's genuine interest and friendliness gleam in almost every phrase.

> 13 Park Lane
>
> I have just seen Hueffer—he is Editor of the new Paper 'The Musical Review,' Novello of Berners St— He will give you a regular engagement to contribute if he likes the style. He wished you to write to him stating your speciality in music & if you have any article written also let him have it. If he approves he will write and make an appt. to talk the matter over. He will pay [.] Address The Editor, Musical Review, Messrs. Novello & Ewer, Berners St. Perhaps he might like a series of articles on eminent musicians— Write soon as possible before the ground is taken.
>
> Sincerely
> VL[149]

For a while nothing seemed to come of this effort and on 20 March, Lee suggested that if Shaw were willing, he could earn a guinea for four one-hour visits coaching a Mrs. Bell with her songs.[150] April 25 saw some response from Hueffer who, Lee enthusiastically reported, spoke of Shaw in terms of the highest praise and was looking forward to receiving an article from him. Advised Lee, "I don't think that you shd let him drop [—] you might find him useful in [ ] books a help particularly as he likes you. . . Hope that all are well. Sincerely VL."[151]

An envelope postmarked 21 May 1883 contained an undated note from Lee to Shaw hinting that the Professor could see signs of heavy weather ahead. *Patience*, he wrote, would be performed on Tuesday 19 June especially for his benefit by the Park Lane Musical Society—apparently another Lee creation. Could Shaw drop by during the rehearsal this Wednesday? He would be ever so grateful if Shaw could prepare some good press releases, "as I want if possible to make some cash by the transaction. Sincerely, VL."[152] After a few more odds and ends of correspondence Lee once again opened the subject of another edition of *The Voice* in a letter dated 29 August 1883, but this too languished as a performance of *Pinafore* loomed into view.[153] On October 5 Lee mentioned a "Marshall" as being quite anxious to appear in *Pinafore* as Captain Corcoran. Marshall, he said, also hoped to use the *Pinafore* company as a nucleus for a production of *Don Giovanni* and Shaw was invited to help with the rehearsals.[154] The development of Shaw's talent in musical affairs was recognized by Lee who, on 31 October 1883, asked Shaw to come early for the next day's practice, since Lee might have an engagement elsewhere.[155] On 29 November 1883, Shaw was asked by Vandeleur Lee, Hon. Secretary of Park Lane Musical Society, for assistance in starting *Don Giovanni. Pinafore*, he added, might be given up.[156]

Some attention should also be given to a miscellaneous note and some diary entries from the collection in the British Museum, contemporary with the Lee correspondence. The Social Democratic Federation in 1884 offered a Grand Entertainment at Perseverance Hall in which a G. B. Shaw opened Part One of the Program by playing Beethoven's *Egmont* on the pianoforte and Mendelssohn's *War March* from *Athalie* for the opening of Part Two. Excerpts from the Shaw diaries show that he and Lee maintained satisfactory relations up to shortly before the Professor's death:

15 February 1885: Visited V. Lee from 4:15 to 5:45.

25 May 1885: Met with V.L., [E.R.] Pease, K. and [Sydney?] Lee.
10 January 1886: Examined various books on music and singing and prepared prospectus for V.L.
17 January 1886: Visited V. Lee.[157]

Final letter from Lee was dated 29 August 1886. Combining work and a holiday at the Leith Hotel, Nairn, Scotland, Lee wrote Shaw that he expected to spend a month there, and if Shaw was at loose ends, "it wd do you no end of good to have the sea air. I think that I could make you moderately comfortable. There is good walking over the place. Come if you can—Sincerely, VL." [158]

Such is some of the record of Lee and Shaw in London. If they illustrate anything, the letters of Lee exhibit a continuous, considerate and even affectionate concern with G. B. Shaw and his literary and cultural ambitions. They also demonstrate with unmistakeable clarity that of those who gave a helping hand to GBS George John Lee was the first.

Returning to the period immediately preceding the final fall of the Professor, the rain of golden guineas against the door of 13 Park Lane had ceased, with the disappearance of his pupils, and Lee's situation seemed to grow precarious. Writing in the *London Music* preface, Shaw related that London, which took him up so enthusiastically, finally tired of the "damaged Svengali," and the Professor's income plummeted. Casting about for other sources of revenue, Lee began to rent his rooms to those who wished to give private parties.[159] To Mushlin, GBS wrote that Lee's Park Lane rent became a serious problem, when the supply of ambitious Pattis was exhausted and he was forced to offer his rooms to groups for drinking parties and general merrymaking. He also announced in a circular to the clergy (written by GBS) that he would cure their sore throats, but, Shaw noted, though he could actually cure them, the Church failed to appreciate the opportunity.[160] Lee's offer of aid to the clergymen was interpreted by GBS as a sign that Lee was through as a teacher. He added that the Professor did not live much longer after that and survived by letting rooms out to lodgers and offering his large music room to festive groups with whose conduct Lee did not concern himself too closely.[161]

By January or thereabouts of 1882, Shaw's involvement with the projected new edition of *The Voice* had produced five entirely new chapters, to which was added another—the one that dealt with the physiology of the organs of sound—from the original version. Shaw's original composition was committed to a schoolboy's ordinary lined composition tablet whose pages were numbered in advance by hand.[162] As this little work has been adequately dealt with by Henderson,[163] this study will not be served by reproducing any portion of it.

On 6 June 1883, Shaw started work on Chapter 7, laid it aside and did not pick it up again until January of 1886, when he prepared a prospectus—ostensibly for use by Lee in discussion with publishers. Henderson allowed that it remained unpublished "because Shaw never succeeded in completing it,"[164] which is unintentionally misleading. Shaw's own comment quoted *verbatim* on the same page showed clearly why the work was never published. He had, he told Mushlin, accepted the commission to revive *The Voice* and had completed much of it "when Lee's sudden death put an end to the project" thus finishing forever his role as ghost writer to Lee.[165]

IX

THE BIOGRAPHERS' TREATMENTS supply the background to the story of the death and funeral of George John Lee. Henderson wrote that Lee had failed in all his London adventures and in particular in his despairing scheme, that "preposterous undertaking" of converting aspiring young ladies into Pattis at five dollars a lesson. When this swindle came to an end, Henderson continued, Lee converted 13 Park Lane into a night club and was holding forth there when, on

28 November 1886, he expired in the act of "stepping into bed." An inquest and post-mortem, the biographer added, disclosed that he had brain disease which Henderson believed to be largely responsible for his loss of professional honor. Not one of the Shaws went to the funeral, he concluded, nor did they make any effort to learn its details.[166] Ervine's account gave much evidence of independent research and independent conclusions. He held that Lee's school for overnight Pattis was successful but that it eventually degenerated until it resembled an early ancestor of the night club. Lee had been almost completely out of the Shaws' knowledge, Ervine continued, when on 28 November 1886 his dead body was discovered on the floor of his Park Lane home. The inquest, he said, stated the cause of death to be due to "natural angina pectoris." Ervine's probing, however, did not end there. He further reported that Lee's money matters were in a "mess," that a Julian Marshall, Gentleman, was "one" of the creditors and that Lee's assets amounted to £607, twelve shillings and one penny. "In short," Ervine continued, "George John Vandaleur Lee was bankrupt." In an unexpected burst of sympathy for Lee (perhaps as an excuse to belabor Mrs. Shaw), Ervine deplored the Shaws' callous indifference to the death of the man who had given them so much. Surely, he mused, Mrs. Shaw might have expressed a pang at his passing? Were not the gifts of The Method and Torca Cottage sufficiently important to merit the simple gesture of her being present at the funeral of a bankrupt? Capturing the drama of the moment, Ervine lamented the absence of the Shaws when Lee's corpse was lowered into its grave, and he believed that the only wails to be heard were the wails of irate creditors moaning over unpaid bills.[167]

Shaw's own remarks on the death of Lee were stored in three or four literary depositories. Stripped bare was the 1905 contribution to Henderson. Lee died suddenly in Park Lane and it was then discovered that his health had been left behind in Dublin and that he had none to spare for London.[168] The Professor, Shaw informed his *London Music* readers, was still in Park Lane when the end came—he died while undressing. The post-mortem and inquest which followed disclosed that Lee had a long-standing disease of the brain.

This disclosure pleased GBS because, he concluded, it meant that Lee's deterioration was pathological as well as environmental and, consequently, George John of Dublin had really been a man of honor and efficiency.[169] Elsewhere in this preface, Shaw added that when his mother heard the news that Lee was dead, she did not exhibit the least concern.[170] O'Bolger's allotment was, of course, more generous. Lee had just placed his arm through a sleeve of his nightshirt (Shaw had *the* sleeve) when he fell to the floor dead. The post-mortem which followed revealed that Lee's brain had been diseased for a long time.[171] As he had no relatives, Shaw continued, he presumed that Lee's worldly effects passed into the hands of the young woman who had comforted him in the loneliness of his last days.[172]

The manner in which the news of Lee's death reached the Shaws remained unexplained until the diaries of GBS turned up at the British Museum. Nethercot reported that when the diaries came into the possession of the Museum, the authorities permitted their inspection by a very small number of persons, including Winsten and Ervine, before they were withdrawn for cataloguing.[173] Ervine made good use of them. He reported that for 30 November 1886 the diary contained an entry to the effect that it was Lucy who brought the news, thus raising the possibility that Lucy had visited 13 Park Lane. Ervine also noted that the entry for the following day recorded GBS's visit to Park Lane for the purpose of verifying the news. There he was told by a servant (quite likely Lee's housemaid) that Lee was found dead on Sunday morning of a heart attack, whereupon Shaw returned home to tell his mother prior to his meeting Podmore.[174]

A check of the diary for 1886 showed Ervine to be precise in his quotations—as far as they went. For example, the entry for 30 November added it was Coffin[175] who told Lucy that Lee was dead, thus reducing if not eliminating the possibility that Lucy visited 13 Park Lane. The second entry was, as reproduced by Ervine, complete as well as accurate. Viewed critically, the entry inferred that Lee had been dead for approximately forty-eight hours before the Shaws learned of his death, since Lucy's report was given on Tuesday,

30 November, two days after the body was found. Further to the second entry, GBS visited 13 Park Lane the next day, Wednesday, 1 December, and seventy-two hours after the discovery of Lee's body. According to the servant's story, it may be reasonably assumed that the body had already been removed some time prior to his visit.

Some official particulars of the death of George Vandeleur Lee have been exhumed from the vaults of London's Somerset House and are here reproduced:

CERTIFIED COPY OF AN ENTRY OF DEATH

Registration District St. George Hanover Square

1886. DEATH in the Sub-district of Mary Fair in the County of Middlesex

No. [1]	When and where died [2]	Name and surname [3]	Sex [4]	Age [5]	Occu-pation [6]	Cause of death [7]	Signature, description, and resi-dence of informant [8]	When regis-tered [9]
202	Twenty-eighth Novem-ber 1886 13 Park Lane	George Vandeleur Lee	M A L E	55 Y E A R S	Teacher of Singing	Natural Angina Pectoris found dead on the floor P. Mort	Certificate received from Chas. H. C. Bedford Coroner for West-minster Inquest held 30th November 1886	Sixth Decem-ber 1886

[10]

J. L. Hughes

Signature of Registrar

A glance at column eight of the death certificate will show the inquest was held on 30 November (Tuesday) thus establishing with fair certainty that the post-mortem was performed on Monday. The verdict of the inquest, recorded in column seven, does not bear out Shaw's assertion that Lee's brain was diseased, but this, I believe, has no significance, since death certificates are required to list only the principal or actual cause of death. Still, Shaw's reference to a secondary condition reveals his familiarity with the official report of the autopsy and implies an interest prompted by something more than idle curiosity.

Whether it was because Vandeleur Lee was well-known or because the circumstances of his death were newsworthy, his passing was noticed by at least one section of the London press. Thus the *Westminster Times* for Saturday, 4 December, served its readers up with an interesting account of the last hours of a certain professor of music.

SINGULAR DEATH IN PARK LANE

Mr. St. Clare Bedford held an inquest at St. George's Hospital, on Tuesday, on the body of G.V.Lee, aged about 56, a professor of singing, who was found dead at his residence, 13, Park-lane, on Sunday morning under somewhat singular circumstances. The evidence showed that deceased on Saturday went to dine at a restaurant in Leicester-square, with some friends, and after the dinner he suddenly became unwell. He entered an omnibus, and rode through Regent-street to Park-lane. On arriving at his residence he seemed to feel better. He subsequently retired to rest, and was found at 9 o'clock on the following morning lying dead on the floor. Dr. Wadham, of 14, Park-lane, and senior physician at St. George's Hospital, was called, and pronounced life extinct. A post-mortem was made, and the cause of death was found to be extensive heart disease. The jury returned a verdict of death from natural causes.

Less dramatic but equally informative were the formal public insertions and announcements attending such occasions. The London *Times* obituary column for 30 November 1886 carried what appeared to be an official release from the appropriate city department:

On the 28th, at 13, Park Lane, suddenly, of heart disease, G. VANDELEUR LEE, Esq.

On 2 December 1886, the same paper published what was almost certainly a paid announcement but with no hint as to its mover:

> THE FUNERAL of the late MR. VANDELEUR LEE will take place THIS DAY, leaving 13, Park Lane at 10.30 precisely; the interment will take place at the Woking Cemetery, and the special train will leave Necropolis Station, Westminster Bridge-road, at 11.45 a.m.

In explanation of certain terms in this announcement, it can be taken to mean that "special train" and "Necropolis Station" refer to a train and platform specifically and regularly in use for the transport of the several deceased and their mourners to Woking Cemetery via a private spur track. The wording additionally suggests that the Professor's mortal remains would be deposited in a coffin, removed from the scene of the post-mortem, placed into a hearse and thence brought to (but not necessarily into) 13 Park Lane. At half-past ten in the morning the hearse and the mourners who, on such short notice, cared to join the cortege, would then proceed towards Necropolis Station. Such mourners as there were could board the train and, on arrival at Woking, attend the ceremony. How many there were cannot now be ascertained but might one of them have been GBS?

In an effort to locate Lee's grave, correspondence was initiated with the London Necropolis Company. There was a record of the interment of a George Vandeleur Lee, fifty-five years of age, of 13 Park Lane on 2 December 1886. The representative of the Cemetery regretted that he was unable to track down the one who gave the order for burial as the Deed of Grant to Grave No. 103097 had never been called for, hence there was no responsibility. However, he volunteered, Lee's grave—a "private" one—was located on St. Michael's Avenue and did not now, nor did it ever have, a monument of any sort. The grave itself, he added, was in the most deplorable condition.[176]

There seems to be little doubt that neither Mrs. Shaw nor daughter Lucy attended the funeral of their former hero and counselor. It will be recalled that Ervine reported no Shaw was present, but, he meditated, they may not have been at fault, for it could have occurred without their awareness. However, even had they known in advance, he added, it would have been unlikely for any of them to have appeared.[177] Henderson agreed: the Shaws were not represented at the funeral nor did they trouble themselves to find out the name of the cemetery or who buried Lee.[178] The Harris book reported that at the time of Lee's death, the division between the Shaws and Lee had reached the point where the burial of Lee and the disposition of his effects were matters quite without interest.[179] As for Shaw himself, he wrote in *London Music* that Lee's death produced no noticeable effect on his mother, for, as far as she was concerned, he had been dead ever since he had turned his back on The Method.[180] O'Bolger learned that the news of Lee's death left Shaw's mother entirely unruffled, but she did deem it "odd" to absent themselves from the funeral and leave it to others to bury him.[181] Thus from all sources and accounts it seems that the Shaws were not present when Lee was laid to rest.

Since we know GBS "verified" the news of Lee's death, learned that a post-mortem and inquest had already held and became familiar with the details of the post-mortem, we may assume that he received information from Dr. Wadham in 14 Park Lane or at St. George's Hospital. Because of GBS's visit to 13 Park Lane, it is possible that the Shaws had more notice of Lee's funeral than was given the public. Barring the appearance of fresh autobiographical matter, there is no way of establishing the presence or absence of GBS at Lee's interment. But in view of Shaw's general evasiveness in the matter, his unwillingness to publicly admit his presence in 13 Park Lane at the time, the certainty that he knew in advance when and where Lee would be buried and his own heavy obligations to Lee lead me to believe that his presence in Woking Cemetery on 2 December 1886 was not altogether unlikely.

Ervine's report that Lee was a bankrupt and that his death brought a swarm of angry creditors buzzing about his grave was not supported in any of the documents about the disposition of his estate. In particular, the Letter of Administration (which Ervine cited partially[182]) named Julian Marshall as the sole creditor. According to the documents valuating his estate and effects, the deceased was by no means bankrupt: his cash assets had a period exchange equivalent of $675.00, and his property was valued at $2,360.00. The relative value of these figures should, of course, be realized within the economic frame of the 1880's. Insofar as details of Lee's debt to Marshall, i.e., nature and degree, they could not be ascertained. As a relationship of debtor and creditor was recognized by the Probate Court, it may be taken for granted the Court was convinced—for the record at least—that Lee was obligated to Marshall. Still, the singular coincidence that Lee's assets were almost exactly equal to the limitation of £620 placed on Marshall's claim has the collusive ring about it. In a word, the Court's conditions seemed to have been based on Lee's assets rather than on Marshall's claims.

Finally, the death of George Vandeleur Lee of Park Lane seemed to raise the possibility that he was, *de jure,* the last of the Lees. Whether this was actually true genealogically, cannot now be said, nor is it essential to this inquiry. The dominant question is whether the genius of the George John Lee of Dublin still survived.

X

ALMOST ALONE AMONG BIOGRAPHERS (barring O'Bolger and "Harris") Ervine remained puzzled by the sum of George Carr and Lucinda Elizabeth, querulously inquiring:

> What do your eugenics amount to if a genius can be born to people seemingly so unfitted to be parents as George Carr and Lucinda Elizabeth Shaw? [183]

The deepest waters of the Shaw-Lee household were sounded in the extraordinary extract from a letter quoted below.[184] In response to a direct or implied question by the aggressively inquisitive Harris (possibly spurred on by Scully) Shaw summarized the relations of Lee and the Shaws. When Lee arrived on the scene he, of course, completely shunted aside his father, but GBS denied that this meant Lee substituted for him and, with growing irritation, added that

> ". . . in the end she was more lenient to the husband than to the hero. Is it now necessary to add that my resemblance to my father is quite clearly discernible, and that I have not a single trait even remotely resembling any of Lee's? I do not want my mother to be the heroine of another Wagner-Geyer lie." [185]

Ellis' translation of Glasenapp's six-volume *Das Leben Richard Wagners* ignored Geyer other than to name him as a friend of Wagner's father Frederick. Ludwig Geyer, reported Glasenapp, was an artist-painter turned comedian-actor with the encouragement of Frederick whom he met about 1801.[186] Wagner's autobiography, written at various times during his life was, by his direction, published posthumously. Simultaneously released in both German and English *Mein Leben* finally appeared, twenty-eight years after his death, in Munich and New York. Examination of *My Life*[187] produced no support for Shaw's charge that there was a lie in the Wagner-Geyer association. Wagner's own but brief comments on the presence and relation of Geyer to his family are set forth within the first three pages of the first volume. Born in Leipzig on 22 May 1813 Richard wrote that his father Frederick, a clerk in the police service, had a "passionate affection" for the theatre and had chosen actor Geyer to be one of his closest friends. According to Richard, his father acquired still another passion in the shape of one Fraulein Hartwig which, naturally, saddened Frau Wagner. But, while Herr Wagner disported himself at the theatre or elsewhere, Geyer

> the worthy actor generally filled his place in the family circle, and it seems had frequently to appease my mother, who, rightly or wrongly, complained of the frivolity of her husband.[188]

The early death of Frederick on 22 November[189] simplified matters considerably and, after the respectable lapse of nine months, Ludwig married the widow of his dear friend. Ludwig, reported Richard, grew into "a most loving father" to the seven fatherless children. Loving indeed was Ludwig: Richard was chosen for a signal mark of his affection:

> He wished to adopt me altogether, and accordingly, when I was sent to my first school, he gave me his own name, so that till the age of fourteen I was known to my Dresden schoolfellows as Richard Geyer; and it was not, until some years after my stepfather's death, and on my family's return to Leipzig . . . that I resumed the name of Wagner.[190]

From these extracts (there was no further mention of Geyer in any significant sense) it could be seen that while there were no positive signs of *scandalum magnatum,* Wagner's account could bear any of several constructions without straining credulity. As to the "lie" nourished by Shaw, its precise nature was still to be isolated.

First hint came from Wagner in a letter to his sister Cacilie 14 June 1870. Here the composer expressed his gratitude for her thoughtfulness in sending him a packet of letters from "our father" Geyer to their mother. They proved, he told Cacilie, how deep was the affection they bore for each other and he emphasized how much they owed "our father" Geyer.[191] While Cacilie was born to Frau Geyer sooner than normally expected, I do not think the natural use of "father" in place of the ungraceful "stepfather" has special connotation particularly as Wagner himself termed Geyer a "most loving father."

In 1919, critic at large James Huneker of *The Sun* (New York) reviewed Otto Bournot's *Ludwig Geyer: Stepfather of Richard Wagner.* The author, wrote Huneker, admitted that Geyer and Wagner's mother took "certain secrets" with them to the grave, and he quoted Bournot (from page fifteen of his book) as writing: "The possibility of Wagner's descent from Geyer contains in itself nothing detrimental to the art-work of Baireuth." [192]

Ernest Newman's four-volume study paid a fair amount of attention to the role of Geyer in the fortunes of the Wagner family and sounded the keynote in the opening line:

> On his father's side, the parentage of Richard Wagner is still a matter of dubiety; to the end of time, in all probability, it will never be definitely known whether he was the son of the Leipzig Police Actuary Carl Frederick Wagner or of the actor Ludwig Geyer.[193]

Epilogue

AT ABOUT THE TIME of the establishment of the joint household in Hatch Street, young GBS became aware of the possible significance of Lee's presence. The seeds of doubt as well as the seeds of rancor thus planted grew with time, bursting into full bloom during the London years and marking Shaw's literary works with the twin themes of births of doubtful parentage and of hatred of mothers and motherhood. Like young Cashel Byron, who found that it was unsafe to question who his father was and that his mother was not the angel he thought she was, young Shaw hated his mother because of her liaison with George John Lee. He could understand her total rejection of George Carr—after all, he was hardly the ideal husband. He could forgive her for her part leading to the shame of Marlborough Street—perhaps the Central Model School was the best of a bad lot. He could even understand and forgive her for the tears and deprivations, the motherless, loveless years of neglect—it may have been the making of him. But he would never forgive her for her association with Lee. Because of this alliance and its resultant joint households, the gravest suspicions and the most humiliating questions might arise. Surely, if these circumstances tortured him so, might not others see in them certain curious conditions? Might they not ask themselves the same question which plagued him—"Which George was he named after?" and perhaps leading them to its terrifying mate—"Whose George was he?"

When Shaw of Dublin, in his twenties, threw off the Dublin shackles and translated himself to London, he was still unaware of his true goals in life. Once he became infused with a burning, unquenchable fire to become a great man—no less than the twentieth century's Shakespeare—nothing would stand in his way, except for the conscious and subconscious shadows thrown on his life by his mother. His own name constituted a living remorse, making it no coincidence that George Bernard Shaw of Dublin gradually became G. Bernard Shaw of London. Nonetheless, I believe that Mrs. Shaw was a warm human being and, within the limitations of her maternal development, regarded her son with nothing if not her best wishes for his welfare and would, I am convinced, have gladly added the care and affection she was capable of, had her son been receptive. In short, I believe that Mrs. Shaw with perhaps the worst possible qualifications for motherhood, had the best possible intentions and further, that of this Shaw was fully aware. But GBS refused to sympathize with the motivation of his mother when it endangered his ambition, and he bitterly denied her the right to achieve some measure of purpose even as he seized that right for himself.

I am convinced that Shaw's fears kept pace with his growth and, as he became that marvelous and fantastic figure, G.B.S., he believed that the discovery of his "secret" would shatter that carefully-contrived image. He was absolutely convinced that disaster would follow exposure and that the contumely of a mocking world would silence his voice, cancel his works, nullify his selection by the Life Force as a link in the apostolic succession from Shakespeare and thus destroy forever his claim to immortality. It may be avowed that one of his mighty genius would rise above such petty and insignificant considerations. True—but would the world rise with him? In my opinion, Bernard Shaw was convinced it would not; and the specter of Hatch Street haunted him through nine decades, and it haunts us through his works.

Appendix A / Chronology

Year	Event	Relative Ages of Principals GCS	LES	GJL	GBS
1800	Walter Bagnall Gurly b.				
1802	Robert Lee b.				
1805	Eliza . . . . [Lee] b.				
1809	Charles Robert Darwin b.				
1812	Charles Dickens b.				
1813	Richard Wagner b.				
1814	George Carr Shaw b. 30 December				
1818	Karl Marx b.	4			
1828	Henrik Ibsen b.	14			
	Richard Pigott b.				
	Robert Lee and Eliza . . . . m.				
1829	Walter Bagnall Gurly and Lucinda Whitcroft m.	15			
1830	Lucinda Elizabeth Gurly b. 6 October	16			
	George [John] [Vandeleur] Lee b.				
1831	Walter John Gurly b.	17	1	1	
	[Harcourt] William [Nassau] Lee b.				
1833	Charles Bradlaugh b.	19	3	3	
1834	William Morris b.	20	4	4	
1839	Lucinda Whitcroft Gurly d. 14 Jan. aged 37	25	9	9	
1843	John Whitcroft d. 23 March aged 76	29	13	13	
	Robert Lee d.				
1846	Charles Stewart Parnell b.	32	16	16	
1847	Annie Wood Besant	33	17	17	
1848	Ellen Terry b.	34	18	18	
1849	Henry William Massingham b.	35	19	19	
1851	Henry Stephens Salt b.	37	21	21	

Year	Event	Relative Ages of Principals GCS	LES	GJL	GBS
1852	George Carr Shaw and Lucinda Elizabeth Gurly m. 17 June	38	22	22	
	Walter Bagnall Gurly and Elizabeth Anne Clarke m. 25 May				
	Lucinda Frances c.* June				
	Robert Bonteen Cunninghame-Graham b.				
1853	Lucinda Frances b.	39	23	23	
1854	Elinor Agnes c.*—June	40	24	24	
	Oscar Fingal O'Flahertie Wills Wilde b.				
1855	Elinor Agnes b. March	41	25	25	
	[Frank] James Thomas Harris b. 14 Feb. Galway				
	George Bernard c.*—November				
1856	George Bernard b. 26 July	42	26	26	
	Matthew Edward McNulty b.				
	William Archer b.				
	Hubert Bland b.				
1857	Charlotte Frances [Payne-] Townshend b. 20 January Rosscarbery Co. Cork				
1858	Beatrice Potter Webb b.	44	28	28	2
	Graham Wallas b.				
	Mary Stewart [Payne-] Townshend b.				
1859	Sidney Webb b.	45	29	29	3
	Sidney Olivier b.				
	Henry Hyde Champion b.				
1860	Eliza Lee d. aged 55	46	30	30	4
1862	[Harcourt] William [Nassau] Lee d. 7 May aged 31	48	32	32	6
	Ellen Whitcroft d.				
1865	Beatrice Stella Tanner Campbell b. 9 Feb.	51	35	35	9
	GBS enters school				
1866	*Ménage à trois* established in Torca Cottage	52	36	36	10
	Herbert George Wells b.				
1867	Combined Shaw-Lee residence established in Hatch Street	53	37	37	11
1870	Charles Dickens d. aged 58	56	40	40	14
1871	GBS leaves school. Goes to work.	57	41	41	15
	Thomas Demetrius O'Bolger b. 28 Feb. Kilkenny				
1873	Lee leaves Dublin for London	59	43	43	17
	Mrs. Shaw leaves Dublin for London				

* c: Conceptions assuming normal carriage.

Year	Event	Relative Ages of Principals GCS	LES	GJL	GBS
1874	Gilbert Keith Chesterton b.	60	44	44	18
	Holbrook Jackson b.				
	William Bernard Shaw d. aged 63 in Private Lunatic Asylum, Dublin				
1876	GBS leaves Dublin for London	62	46	46	20
	Elinor Agnes Shaw d. 27 March aged 21				
1877	Archibald Henderson b. 17 June	63	47	47	21
	Harley Granville-Barker b.				
1879	*IMMATURITY*	65	49	49	23
	Albert Einstein b.				
1880	Henry Louis Mencken b.	66	50	50	24
1882	Charles Robert Darwin d. aged 73	68	52	52	26
1883	Karl Marx d. aged 65	69	53	53	27
	Richard Wagner d. aged 70				
	St. John Greer Ervine b. Belfast				
1884	GBS joins Fabian Society	70	54	54	28
1885	George Carr Shaw d. 18 April aged 71		55	55	29
	WIDOWERS' HOUSES begun with William Archer				
	Walter Bagnall Gurly d. 19 December aged 85				
1886	George John Lee found dead 28 Nov. aged 56		56		30
1887	Robert Butterfield and Lucinda Frances Shaw m. 17 December		57		31
1888	Thomas Edward Lawrence b.		58		32
1889	Richard Pigott suicude in Madrid aged 61		59		33
1891	Charles Stewart Parnell d. aged 45		61		35
	Charles Bradlaugh d. aged 58				
	Mary Susannah Payne-Townhend d.				
1892	*WIDOWERS' HOUSES* finished without Archer		62		36
	Sidney Webb and Beatrice Potter m.				
1896	GBS meets Charlotte Frances Payne-Townshend		66		40
	William Morris d. aged 62				
1898	GBS and Charlotte Frances Payne-Townshend m. 1 June		68		42
1899	Walter John Gurly d. 30 August aged 68		69		43
1900	Oscar Fingal O'Flahertie Wills Wilde d. aged 46		70		44
1905	MENCKEN ON SHAW		75		49
1906	Henrik Ibsen d. aged 78		76		50
1907	JACKSON ON SHAW		77		51
1910	CHESTERTON ON SHAW		80		54
1911	HENDERSON ON SHAW (I)		81		55

Year	Event	Relative Ages of Principals GCS	LES	GJL	GBS
1913	Lucinda Elizabeth Shaw d. 19 February aged 83				57
1914	Hubert Bland d. aged 58				58
1915	HAMON ON SHAW				59
1919	O'BOLGER ON SHAW				63
1920	Lucinda Frances Shaw d. 27 March aged 67				64
1923	Thomas Demetrius O'Bolger d. 1 Aug. aged 52				67
1924	William Archer d. aged 68				68
	Henry William Massingham d. aged 75				
1928	Ellen Terry d. aged 80				72
	Henry Hyde Champion d. aged 69				
1931	HARRIS ON SHAW				75
	[Frank] James Thomas Harris d. 26 August aged 75				
1932	HENDERSON ON SHAW (II)				76
	Graham Wallas d. aged 74				
1933	Annie Wood Besant d. aged 86				77
1934	RATTRAY ON SHAW				78
1935	Thomas Edward Lawrence killed. aged 47				79
1936	Robert Bonteen Cunninghame-Graham d. aged 84				80
	Gilbert Keith Chesterton d. aged 62				
1939	MACMAHON SHAW ON SHAW				83
	Henry Stephens Salt d. 19 April aged 88				
1940	COLBOURNE ON SHAW				84
	Beatrice Stella Tanner Campbell d. aged 74				
1942	PEARSON ON SHAW				86
1943	Charlotte Frances Shaw d. aged 86 Sept. 12				87
	Matthew Edward McNulty d. aged 87				
	Beatrice Potter Webb d. aged 85				
	Sidney Olivier d. aged 84				
1946	Herbert George Wells d. aged 80				90
	Harley Granville-Barker d. aged 69				
1947	Sidney Webb d. aged 88				91
1948	SHAW ON SHAW				92
1949	IRVINE ON SHAW				93
	JOAD ON SHAW				
1950	George Bernard Shaw d. 2 November aged 94				
1956	HENDERSON ON SHAW (III)				
	ERVINE ON SHAW				
	WINSTEN ON SHAW				

Appendix B

Facsimile page 40 of 1905 Shaw-Henderson letter

(40)

mother found a refuge from her domestic disappointment. She became
the right hand of an energetic genius who had formed a musical society
and an orchestra (all amateurs — there was no other chance in Dublin). He
taught her to sing; and she sang for him; copied orchestral parts for
him; scored songs &c for him (she had learnt thoroughbass from old
Logier); led the chorus for him; appeared in operas that he got up (she played Azucena in
Il Trovatore, Donna Anna in Don Giovanni, Margaret in Gounod's
Faust, and Lucrezia Borgia in Donizetti's opera of that name; and
as they were all rehearsed in our house, I whistled & sang them from
the first bar to the last whilst I was a small boy, not to mention
all the oratorios got up by the musical society); and, to facilitate
all this, kept house for him by setting up a joint household — a
sort of blameless <u>ménage à trois</u>; for she was the sort of woman
who never troubled herself about gossip, and consequently might have
had a dozen men in her house without more scandal than any hotel
keeper would have raised. As to ordinary domestic mothering and wifing
she was utterly unfitted for the sentiment of it. I was not treated as a
child. I was let do as I liked; and I knew everything that was going
on and was present on all occasions as if I were an adult member of
the family. The fact that one of the men of the house was an artist, a

Appendix C

(For the notes to this appendix, see page 377.)

Year[1]	School	Residence[2]	Press Notices[3]	Torca Cottage	The Voice
1838	O'Connel George Lee	Portland Place			
1853		16 Harrington Lee, G. Jno. (D)			
1854		Same			
1855		Same	George J. Lee (T)		
1856		Same			
1857		Same			
1858		48 Harrington Lee, G. Jno. (D)	George J. Lee (T)		
1859		Same			
1860		Same			
1861		Same			
1862		Same			
1863		Same			
1864		Not listed	7 March (S, A) Mr. Lee 14 March (S, A) Mr. Lee 3 December (S, A) Mr. Lee		
1865		Not listed	6 May (K, N) Mr. G. J. Lee 30 May (I, N) Mr. Lee		
1866		Not listed	17 January (I, N) Mr. Lee		
1867		1 Hatch Street (D) Lee, G. J. Esq.			
1868		Same			

Year[1]	School	Residence[2]	Press Notices[3]	Torca Cottage	The Voice
1869		Same	13 December (I, A) George J. Lee 13 December (I, N) Mr. Lee 24 December (S, R) Mr. Lee 27 December (S, R) Mr. Lee		13 December G. J. Lee & George J. Lee (First ed.)
1870		Same	4 January (I, R) George J. Lee		—G. J. Lee & George J. Lee (Second ed.)
1871		Same	21 23, 28, 30 & 31 January (I, A) George J. Lee 1 & 2 February (I, A) George J. Lee 3 February (I, R) Mr. Lee 10, 11, 28, 29 30 & 31 March (I, A) George J. Lee 1, 11, 13, 15, 17, 19, 20, 21, 22 & 24 April (I, A) George J. Lee 18, 25 & 30 November (I, A) George J. Lee 2 December (I, N) George J. Lee		
			9, 10, 11, 12 December (I, A) G. V. Lee 16 & 30 December (I, A) G. V. Lee Esq.		
1872		1 Hatch Street (D) Lee, G. V. Esq.	12 & 13 January (I, A) G. V. Lee 12 through 31 December (I, A) G. Vandeleur Lee	19 September George V. Lee (Signed Torca lease)	
1873		Same	1 through 11 January (I, A) G. Vandeleur Lee 7 January (I, R) Mr. G. V. Lee		
1874		Ebury Street (L) George Vandeleur Lee			
1875		13 Park Lane (L) Lee, George Bilton[2]			
1876		Same			
1877		13 Park Lane (D) Vandeleur Lee[3]			

Year[1]	School	Residence[2]	Press Notices[3]	Torca Cottage	The Voice
1878		13 Park Lane (L) Vandeleur Lee[4]			
1879		13 Park Lane Lee, George Bilton[2]			
1880		No return address V. L.[5]			
1881		St. Andrew, Scotland V. L.[6]			
1882		13 Park Lane (L) V. L.[7]			
1883		13 Park Lane V. L.[8]			
1884		13 Park Lane (L) Lee, George Bilton[2]			
1885		13 Park Lane (L) Lee, George Bilton[2] (also Lee, Vandeleur)			
1886		13 Park Lane (L) Lee, Vandeleur[2]			

Explanatory Notes for the Bibliography

Since all quotations from Shaw's plays come from *The Complete Plays of Bernard Shaw* [1950] published by Odhams Press Limited, London, no information regarding place of publication, publisher, and date of publication is given after the titles of plays listed separately in the bibliography.

All references, with one exception, to Shaw's Prefaces are for *Prefaces by Bernard Shaw*. London: Odhams Press Limited, 1938. Therefore, the individual bibliographical items do not carry the usual information concerning place of publication, name of publisher, and date of publication. In the exception, however, the entry is complete.

Bibliography

AB *The Admirable Bashville.*
AC *The Apple Cart.*
AD *Adam: International Review* (August, 1946).
AE *Annajanska, The Bolshevik Empress.*
AL Laing, Allen M. (ed.). *In Praise of Bernard Shaw.* London: Muller, 1949.
AM *Arms and the Man.*
AP Maurois, André. *Poets and Prophets.* London: Cassell, 1936.
BB Shaw, Charles Macmahon. *Bernard's Brethren.* London: Constable, 1939.
BC MS., Berg Collection. New York Public Library, New York.
BE Ervine, St. John. *Bernard Shaw: His Life, Work and Friends.* New York: Morrow, 1956.
BG Shaw, Bernard. *The Adventures of the Black Girl in Her Search for God.* New York: Dodd, Mead and Company, 1933.
BH Harris, Frank. *Bernard Shaw.* New York: Simon & Schuster, 1931.
BJ Brown, James D. *British Musical Biography.* Birmingham: Stratton, 1897.
BM MS., Shaw Archive. British Museum, London.
BP Dent, Allen. *Bernard Shaw and Mrs. Patrick Campbell: Their Correspondence.* London: Gollancz, 1952.
BQ Esdaille, Ernest. *Bernard Shaw's Postscript to Fame.* London: Quality Press, 1942.
BS Jackson, Holbrook. *Bernard Shaw.* Philadelphia: G. W. Jacobs, 1907.
BT *Back to Methuselah.*
BW Bekker, Paul. *Richard Wagner: His Life in His Work.* London: Dent, 1931.
BY Bettany, F. G. *Stewart Headlam.* London: Murray, 1926.
CB Shaw, G. B. *Cashel Byron's Profession.* London: Constable, 1932.
CC *Captain Brossbound's Conversion.*

CE O'Casey, Sean. *Sunset and Evening Star*. London: Macmillan, 1954.

CF McNulty, Mathew Edward. "G. B. S. As a Boy." *The Candid Friend* (July, 1901).

CI Rattray, R. F. *Bernard Shaw: A Chronicle*. London: Leagrave, 1951.

CM Duffin, H. C. "Bernard Shaw and a Critic." *Cornhill Magazine,* LVI (1924).

CP Harris, Frank. *Contemporary Portraits* (2nd Ser.). New York: The Author, 1919.

CR *Cymbeline Refinished.*

CS McCabe, Joseph. *Bernard Shaw: A Critical Study*. London: Mitchel Kennerly, 1914.

DA Archer, William. "A Lecture on Shaw." *Drama* (Autumn, 1956).

DC Shaw, G. B. *Doctors' Delusions, Crude Criminology and Sham Education*. London: Constable, 1932.

DD *The Devil's Disciple.*

DL *The Dark Lady of the Sonnets.*

DO Shaw, G. B. *Dramatic Opinions and Essays.* London: Constable, 1907.

DR Hill, Eldon C. "Shaw's Biographer-in-Chief." *Modern Drama,* II (1959).

DW Winsten, Stephen. *Days With Bernard Shaw*. New York: Vanguard, 1949.

EB Shaw, G. B. *Everybody's Political What's What.* New York: Dodd, Mead and Company, 1945.

FF *The Fascinating Foundling.*

FL Shaw, Lucy Carr. *Five Letters of the House of Kildonnel.* London: Lawrence & Jellicoe, 1905.

FN Nethercot, Arthur H. *The First Five Lives of Annie Besant*. Chicago: University of Chicago Press, 1960.

FP *Fanny's First Play.*

GB Hackett, J. P. *George VS Bernard*. New York: Sheed & Ward, 1937.

GF Farmer, Henry George. *G.B.S.'s Sister and Her Friends.* Leiden: Brill, 1959.

GG Chesterton, G. K. *George Bernard Shaw*. London: The Bodley Head, 1909.

GH Henderson, Archibald. *George Bernard Shaw: His Life and Works.* Cincinnati: Stewart & Kidd, 1911.

GJ Robinson, Lennox (ed.). *Lady Gregory's Journal 1916-1930*. London: Putnam, 1933.

GM *Getting Married.*

GO O'Bolger, T. D. MS., "George Bernard Shaw's Social Philosophy." Library of the University of Pennsylvania.

GP Pearson, Hesketh. *A Full Length Portrait* and *A Postscript*. New York: Harper, 1942, 1950.

GR Henderson, Archibald. "George Bernard Shaw Self-Revealed." *Fortnightly Review,* DCCXII (1926).

GW Winsten, Stephen (ed.). *G.B.S. 90*. New York: Dodd, Mead and Company, 1946.

HB Laurence, Dan H. (ed.). *How To Become a Musical Critic*. London: Rupert Hart-Davis, 1960.

HC MS., Hanson Group. Lady Hanson, Dublin.

HG Purdom, Charles Benjamin. *Harley Granville Barker: Man of the Theatre, Dramatist and Scholar*. Cambridge: Harvard University Press, 1956.

IB O'Bolger, T. D. MS., "Influence of Mr. Shaw's Youth on His Views and Personality." Harvard University Library. MS. Eng. 1046.

IC Rattray, R. F. *Bernard Shaw: A Chronicle and Introduction*. London: Duckworth, 1934.

IG Irvine, William. *Universe of G.B.S.* New York: Whittlesey House, 1949.

IH Huneker, James. *Iconoclasts: A Book of Dramatists*. London: T. Werner Laurie, 1906.

IM Shaw, G. B. *Immaturity*. London: Constable, 1931.

IW Shaw, G. B. *The Intelligent Woman's Guide to Socialism and Capitalism*. London: Constable, 1928.

JO John O'Donovan: bibliography and research assistant.

JS Joad, C. E. M. *Shaw*. London: Gollancz, 1949.

JW Winsten, Stephen. *Jesting Apostle: The Life of Bernard Shaw*. London: Hutchinson, 1956.

KC MS., Shaw to Archibald Henderson, 17 January 1905. Francis E. Kettaneh Collection, New York, New York.

LB Shaw, G. B. *Love Among the Artists*. London: Brentano, 1900.

LG MS., Shaw Group. Mrs. Grace Goodliffe, Burnfoot, County Donegal, Ireland.

LJ Jones, Doris Arthur. *Life and Letters of Henry Arthur Jones*. London: Gollancz, 1930.

LL Shaw, Lucy Carr. *The Last of the Kildonnel Letters*. London: Lawrence & Jellicoe, 1908.

LM Wagner, Richard. *My Life*. New York: Dodd, Mead and Company, 1911.

LP Laurence, Dan H. (ed.). *Platform and Pulpit*. London: Rupert Hart-Davis, 1962.

LR Glasenapp, W. *Life of Richard Wagner*. Translated by Ellis. London: Kegan Paul, 1900.

MB *Major Barbara.*

MC McNulty, Matthew Edward. MS., untitled reminiscences of Shaw's boyhood friend. Anonymous Collection, County Dublin, Ireland.

MG MS., Shaw-McNulty Group. Anonymous Collection, County Dublin, Ireland.

MH Henderson, Archibald. *George Bernard Shaw: Man of the Century.* New York: Appleton-Century-Crofts, 1956.

MJ Jones, Henry Arthur. *My Dear Wells: A Manual for the Haters of England.* London: Eveleigh Nash & Grayson, 1921.

ML Shaw, G. B. *Music in London 1890-94.* London: Constable, 1932.

MM McCarthy, Lillah. *Myself and My Friends.* London: Butterworth, 1933.

MP *Misalliance* (Preface).

MR Russell, Bertrand. *Portraits from Memory.* London: Allen & Unwin, 1956.

MS *Misalliance.*

MW Wilson, Richard A. *The Miraculous Birth of Language.* London: Dent, 1942.

NA Shaw, G. B. *Nine Answers by G.B.S.* New York: Privately printed by Jerome Kern, 1923.

NT Campbell, R. J. *The New Theology.* London: Chapman & Hall, 1909.

NW Newman, Ernest. *Life of Richard Wagner.* London: Cassell, 1933.

OC MS., O'Bolger-Shaw Group. Harvard University Library, Cambridge, Mass.

OG MS., Shaw-O'Reilly Group. Courtesy the late Patrick O'Reilly, Esq., Ayot St. Lawrence, Portobello, County Dublin, Ireland.

OH Shaw, Bernard. "Memories of Oscar Wilde," appendix to Frank Harris' *Oscar Wilde: His Life and Confessions.* New York: Brentano, 1918.

OP Webb, Sidney and Beatrice. *Our Partnership.* London: Longmans, Green & Company, 1948.

OR O'Bolger, T. D. MS., "The Real Shaw." Harvard University Library. MS. Eng. 1046.

PA *The Admirable Bashville* (Preface)

PB *Back to Methuselah* (Preface).

PC MS., Central Model Group. Brian Mac Giolla Phadraig, Terenure, County Dublin, Ireland.

PD *The Doctor's Dilemma* (Preface).

PE Shaw, G. B. *Pen Portraits and Reviews.* London: Constable, 1932.

PG *Pygmalion.*

PI *Immaturity* (Preface).

PJ *John Bull's Other Island* (Preface).

PK *The Irrational Knot* (Preface).

PL *Music in London 1890-94* (Preface).
PM *London Music in 1888-89* (Preface).
PO *On the Rocks* (Preface).
PP Henderson, Archibald. *Bernard Shaw—Playboy and Prophet.* New York: Appleton, 1932.
PR *The Millionairess* (Preface).
PS Mencken, H. L. *Prejudices: A Selection.* New York: Knopf, 1958.
PU *The Simpleton of the Unexpected Isles* (Preface).
QQ *Queen's Quarterly,* LVIII (1951).
QW Winsten, Stephen. *The Quintessence of G.B.S.* London: Hutchinson, 1949.
RG Scully, Frank. *Rogues Gallery.* Hollywood: Murray & Gee, 1943.
RH *The Saturday Review* [London] (21 May 1898).
RS Colbourne, Maurice. *The Real Bernard Shaw.* New York: Dodd, Mead and Company, 1940.
SA Winsten, Stephen. *Salt and His Circle.* London: Hutchinson, 1951.
SB Shaw, Bernard. *Bouyant Billions* (Preface). London: Constable, 1949.
SC Winsten, Stephen. *Shaw's Corner.* London: Hutchinson, 1952.
SG Shaw, Bernard. *Shaw Gives Himself Away.* Newtown, Montgomeryshire, England: Gregynogg Press, 1939.
SH *Shadowland* (June, 1921).
SJ *Saint Joan.*
SL Loewenstein, F. E. *Bernard Shaw Through the Camera.* London: White, 1948.
SO O'Bolger, T. D. MS., "Social Satires of Bernard Shaw." Library of the University of Pennsylvania.
SR *The Shaw Review*
SS Shaw, Bernard. *Sixteen Self Sketches.* New York: Dodd, Mead and Company, 1949.
ST Mander, Raymond, and Mitchenson, Joe. *Theatrical Companion to the Plays of Shaw.* New York: Pitman, 1955.
SU *The Simpleton of the Unexpected Isles.*
SV *The Shavian* [The Shaw Society of Ireland] (Spring, 1946).
SW Shaw, Bernard. *Short Stories, Scraps & Shavings.* New York: William Wise & Co., 1932.
TC Hamon, Augustin. *Twentieth Century Molière.* London: Allen & Unwin, 1915.
TS St. John, Christopher (ed.). *Ellen Terry and Bernard Shaw: A Correspondence.* New York: Putnam, 1932.
TT *Too True to Be Good.*
TU Lloyd, J. Henry, and R. E. Scouller. *Trade Unionism for Clerks.* London: Cecil Palmer & Hayward, 1912.
TY Patch, Blanche. *Thirty Years With G.B.S.* London: Gollancz, 1951.

UH Huneker, James. *Unicorns*. London: Laurie, 1919.

UN Shaw, G. B. *An Unfinished Novel*. Ed. Stanley Weintraub. New York: Dodd, Mead and Company, 1958.

UO O'Bolger, T. D. MS., Untitled life of Shaw completed 1919. Harvard University Library. MS. Eng. 1046.

US Shaw, G. B. *An Unsocial Socialist*. London: Constable, 1932.

VL Lee, George J. *The Voice: Its Artistic Production, Development, and Preservation*. Dublin: M'Glashan & Gill, 1869.

WF *Family Letters of Richard Wagner*. Translated and edited by Ellis. London: Macmillan, 1911.

WG West, Alick. *George Bernard Shaw: A Good Man Fallen Among Fabians*. New York: International Publishers, 1950.

WP *Mrs. Warren's Profession*.

YN *You Never Can Tell*.

Notes

INTRODUCTION

1 SS p. 71
2 SG p. 171
3 See section on *Getting Married.*
4 PS p. 29
5 MH pp. 8-9
6 DA p. 34
7 OP p. 38
8 MH p. 896
9 MH p. 173
10 MW p. ix
11 BP 8 Nov 1912
12 BP 7 Mar 1917
13 HG p. 2
14 SH June 1921 p. 41
15 KC pp. 37-38
16 OC Feb 1916 p. 7
17 SS p. 21
18 SS p. 19
19 SO p. 309
20 IH p. 266
21 IH p. 236
22 GF p. vii
23 GP (Postscript) p. 85
24 BE p. vii
25 SS p. 17
26 SS p. 21
27 GF p. 5
28 GF p. vii
29 BH p. xi
30 BH p. 419
31 RG p. 210
32 RG p. 13
33 "The Ghost Talks," SR vol. I No. 9
34 SS p. 182
35 UO p. i
36 BH p. xv

I / GEORGE CARR SHAW

1 IB p. 8
2 BH p. 22
3 OC Feb 1916 p. 25
4 KC p. 39
5 GH p. 74
6 MC p. 14
7 MC p. 14
8 BE pp. 55, 56
9 SS p. 141
10 SS p. 141
11 PI p. 660
12 OC Feb 1916 p. 26
13 PI p. 660
14 SS p. 47
15 PI p. 666
16 SS p. 81
17 SS p. 81
18 GB p. 58
19 BE p. 9
20 GP p. 1
21 GH p. 6
22 BH p. 21
23 GH p. 38
24 PI p. 667
25 BE p. 185
26 SH June 1921 p. 41

27 MH p. 87
28 DA p. 33
29 CI p. 63
30 From a letter 3 July 1960 from G. T. Colton, Headmaster, Kilkenny College
31 SS p. 32
32 The smallpoxed GBS, though inoculated and guaranteed immune for life, was treated by Dr. Gurly in Leyton, 1881.
33 PI p. 667
34 GH p. 18
35 PI p. 661
36 LG 3 Dec 1942
37 PI p. 661
38 LG 3 Dec 1942
39 PI p. 661
40 LG 25 Oct 1949
41 OC Feb 1916 p. 20
42 OC Feb 1916 p. 4
43 PM p. 17
44 BE p. 55
45 MC p. 12
46 OC Feb 1916 p. 23
47 MH p. 34
48 ML vol. II, p. 9
49 PI p. 661
50 MH p. 34
51 NA n.p.n.
52 IB p. 13
53 PI p. 666
54 BH p. 55
55 HB p. 329
56 SS p. 28
57 PI p. 668
58 GP p. 5
59 PI p. 661
60 OC 30 Dec 1919
61 BB p. 126
62 PI p. 660
63 SS p. 11
64 JO
65 SS p. 11
66 SS p. 26
67 OC 9 Feb 1916

II / LUCINDA ELIZABETH GURLY

1 BE p. 11
2 BE p. 12
3 BE p. 11
4 EB p. 51
5 SS p. 23
6 BE p. 10
7 PM p. 7
8 PM p. 7
9 KC p. 39
10 OC Feb 1916 p. 7
11 PI p. 662
12 OC Feb 1916 p. 9
13 PM p. 8
14 ML vol. III, p. 172
15 PM p. 7
16 BE p. 13
17 PM p. 9
18 OC Feb 1916 p. 11
19 OC Feb 1916 p. 11
20 SS p. 26
21 OC Feb 1916 p. 11
22 OC Feb 1916 p. 11
23 SS p. 26
24 OC Feb 1916 p. 10
25 GH p. 7
26 GP p. 2
27 BE p. 508
28 BE p. 13
29 BE p. 13
30 BE pp. 9-10
31 BE p. 19
32 BE p. 17
33 BE p. 59
34 BE p. 12
35 OC Feb 1916 p. 12
36 SS p. 26
37 OC Feb 1916 p. 12
38 SS p. 27
39 OC Feb 1916 p. 12
40 *The* [Dublin] *Evening Mail* 21 June 1852
41 PM p. 9

III / GEORGE JOHN LEE

1 BH p. 38
2 PC 16 June 1947 (Loewenstein's italics)
3 BE p. 29
4 GF p. 23
5 PM p. 10
6 OC 21 June 1915
7 SS p. 168
8 BE p. 27
9 BE p. 22
10 PM p. 11
11 BE p. 29
12 MC p. 13
13 OC Feb 1916 p. 6
14 Shaw has pointed out (ML vol. iii, p. 152) that Dublin, being split into two religious camps, had two cemeteries for the repose of their respective souls, each faction being equally certain its cemetery was the Gate to Glory and the other was the Gate to Hell. *Sleater's Directory* of Ireland for 1856 noted Glasnevin Cemetery as Roman Catholic.
15 BH p. 40
16 BH p. 38
17 OC Feb 1916 p. 25
18 BH p. 38
19 OC Feb 1916 p. 25
20 BE p. 22
21 BJ p. 242
22 PM p. 22
23 OC Feb 1916 pp. 3, 6
24 BH p. 40
25 MC p. 13
26 BE p. 29
27 OC Feb 1916 p. 6
28 OC Feb 1916 p. 12
29 PM p. 16
30 OC Feb 1916 p. 18
31 JW p. 17
32 OC Feb 1916 p. 3
33 BH p. 40
34 BC
35 SS p. 144
36 MH p. 36
37 KC p. 40
38 LP pp. 162-163
39 KC p. 40
40 OC Feb 1916 p. 2
41 PM p. 27
42 PM p. 24
43 PM p. 10
44 PM pp. 15-16
45 PM p. 10
46 PM pp. 10-11
47 ML vol. I, pp. 40-41
48 ML vol. I, p. 41
49 GH p. 17
50 PM p. 11
51 SS p. 30
52 BH p. 36
53 GP p. 6
54 MH p. 945
55 BE p. 22
56 KC pp. 40-41
57 GH p. 17
58 PP p. 45
59 MH p. 36

IV / DUBLIN I

1 Register of Marriages St. Peter's Church, Dublin
2 IB p. 12
3 BE p. 16
4 JW p. 10
5 SS p. 27
6 GP p. 3
7 BE p. 16
8 JW p. 10
9 SS p. 27
10 OC 9 Oct 1919
11 GP p. 3
12 GP p. 3
13 CS p. 5
14 TC p. 39
15 GB p. 60
16 GH p. 17
17 MC p. 13
18 BE p. 19
19 MH pp. 88-89
20 GH p. 17
21 CI p. 11

22 GB p. 60
23 BE p. 16
24 OC Feb 1916 p. 13
25 PM p. 24
26 Divorce restrictions were lowered for a short period in the 1870's but were soon replaced.
27 OC Feb 1916 pp. 13-14
28 MH p. 11
29 GW p. 39
30 SS p. 166
31 It was not possible to find a precise definition of "return room." Architectural and historical sources indicate that it may have been a sort of "withdrawing room" to which gentlemen retired after dinner to smoke.
32 BH p. 43
33 BH p. 43
34 PI p. 660
35 BE p. 9
36 CB Prologue p. 2
37 *Dublin Street Directory* for 1846 (1845): 5 Synge Street, Shaw, Henry—Flour Merchant
38 TC p. 28
39 SS p. 44
40 PM p. 15
41 PK p. 684
42 PM p. 9
43 BB p. 5
44 Hardwicke, Ltd., Ormond Quay, Dublin
45 SS p. 140
46 PK p. 684
47 WILLS 1862 p. 336, Public Records Office, Dublin
48 MH p. 80
49 BH p. 32
50 BE p. 103
51 PI p. 657
52 SS p. 28
53 OC Feb 1916 p. 13
54 King's Inns Dublin
55 OC Feb 1916 pp. 10-11; also SS p. 27
56 MH p. 63
57 GB p. 60
58 BE pp. 19-20
59 BE p. 185
60 BE p. 25
61 BE p. 25
62 SS p. 140
63 UO Chapt. IV, p. 9
64 KC pp. 39-41
65 OC 21 June 1915
66 OC 21 June 1915
67 OC 21 June 1915
68 SS pp. 137-145, passim
69 PM pp. 9-10
70 SS p. 30
71 *Saunders' News-Letter*
72 JW pp. 15-16
73 BE p. 103
74 MH p. 63
75 BS p. 36
76 OC Feb 1916 p. 14
77 SS p. 29
78 PR p. 488
79 GH and courtesy Capt. H. de C. W., Dublin
80 *Saunders' News-Letter*
81 MH p. 29
82 JW p. 12
83 JW p. 19
84 BB p. 61
85 From a letter to the author
86 SS p. 12
87 PM p. 10
88 See also SS p. 12
89 JW p. 16
90 GH p. 8
91 DA p. 33
92 PM p. 11
93 SS pp. 30-31
94 From Shaw's personal copy of agreements with American publishers, now in the possession of the London School of Economics; courtesy JO
95 TS No. XXVII
96 DR p. 171
97 DW p. 13
98 TY p. 115
99 PM p. 10
100 JW p. 16
101 PM p. 10
102 OC 21 June 1915
103 PM p. 10
104 SS p. 168
105 PM p. 15
106 ML vol. II, p. 105

107 SS p. 12
108 JW p. 12
109 Days bracketed by author
110 Text bracketing by GBS
111 JW p. 13
112 HC 8 June 1950
113 HC 28 June 1928
114 HC 20 Mar 1942
115 OG 30 Mar 1949
116 LG 25 Oct 1949
117 TS No. CXXXII
118 PM pp. 12-13
119 PM pp. 12-13
120 Act I *Heartbreak House*
121 BH p. 48
122 SS p. 29
123 PM p. 13
124 SV
125 PP p. 26
126 MH p. 16
127 BE pp. 19-20
128 BE p. 17
129 CP p. 7
130 PI p. 665
131 PI p. 667
132 PM p. 7
133 SS pp. 24-25
134 OC Feb 1916 p. 14 and SS p. 30
135 OC Feb 1916 p. 15
136 SV
137 SS p. 147
138 SC pp. 71-72
139 SV
140 GO p. 57
141 MH pp. 20-22
142 BE pp. 29-30
143 UO Chapt. I, p. 1
144 SS p. 71
145 KC p. 38
146 PI p. 659
147 SS pp. 145-146
148 OC 17 Mar 1915
149 UO Chapt. II, p. 8
150 Omitted from SS p. 138
151 OC 3 Nov 1921
152 SS p. 44
153 Henderson reported (MH p. 20) that one of Shaw's uncles spat on the floor whenever any mention of Catholicism was made, but GBS said it was his maternal grandfather Walter Bagnall Gurly who spat whenever he mentioned "Papist." (Dan H. Laurence, ed., *The Matter with Ireland*. New York: Hill & Wang, 1962, p. 295.)
154 SS p. 145
155 PO p. 367
156 PU p. 636
157 MH p. 11
158 MC p. 13
159 SS p. 28
160 EB p. 71
161 BE p. 21
162 TS No. CXXXII
163 SS pp. 27-28
164 JW p. 12
165 TS No. CXXXII
166 OC 9 Oct 1919
167 SS p. 28
168 RS p. 53
169 SS pp. 167-168
170 MC p. 12
171 CF
172 PM pp. 15-16
173 SS p. 142
174 SS p. 147
175 BH p. 42
176 OC Feb 1916 p. 1
177 UO Chapt. IV, p. 4
178 BE pp. 28-29
179 PM p. 15
180 PM p. 24
181 BE p. 40
182 BE p. 34
183 BE p. 37
184 UO Chapt. II, p. 5
185 UO Chapt. IV, p. 10
186 PE pp. 283-284
187 JW p. 18
188 *Freeman's Journal* 17 Jan 1866
189 HC 5 May 1944
190 BH p. 54
191 UO Chapt. II, p. 7
192 SS pp. 77-78
193 OC Feb 1916 p. 20
194 SS p. 147
195 SS. p. 168
196 LG 25 Oct 1949. "Shaws were of no use . . ." must not be taken too literally. We know (SS p. 168) that Uncle William Bernard Shaw played the ophi-

cleide in Lee's orchestra. This Uncle Barney, the pious voyeur, went mad and "killed himself" in an act just short of suicide (PI pp. 668-669). The history of Barney's last days was dug out of the records of the Private Lunatic Asylum in Finglas (Dublin). First admitted 22 April 1873, he returned as a "volunteer patient" 21 July 1873 and died there 8 June 1874.

197 SS p. 78
198 PI p. 661
199 BE p. 22
200 GP p. 5
201 MH p. 63
202 BH p. 54
203 BH p. 419 (for Shaw's account of revision)
204 OC 24 April 1919
205 OC Feb 1916 p. 20
206 OC Feb 1916 p. 1
207 SS p. 24
208 SA p. 11
209 BE p. 27
210 BH p. 38
211 OC 21 June 1916
212 PM pp. 11-12
213 SS pp. 117-118
214 BE p. 27
215 CI p. 17
216 CI p. 16
217 OC 21 June 1916
218 GP p. 6
219 BH p. 39
220 CI p. 17
221 HC
222 BE p. 27
223 JW p. 17
224 RS p. 53
225 KC p. 40
226 GH p. 18
227 MH p. 35
228 PM p. 12
229 BH p. 39
230 MH p. 35
231 BE p. 39
232 BH p. 44
233 OC 21 June 1916
234 UO Chapt. II, pp. 6-7
235 KC p. 40
236 OC Feb 1916 p. 1
237 PM p. 11
238 PM p. 7
239 WG pp. 1-2
240 CI p. 17
241 BE p. 42
242 OC Feb 1916 p. 1
243 OC Feb 1916 p. 7
244 OC 6 Mar 1921
245 OU Chapt. IV, p. 8
246 OC 14 June 1922
247 BE p. 42
248 CP p. 12
249 BH p. 39
250 BH p. 425
251 MH p. 37
252 SS p. 86
253 GH p. 60
254 GP pp. 20-21
255 BH p. 71
256 BH pp. 203-204
257 CP (*How Frank Ought to Have Done It*); also SS p. 17
258 IM p. 29
259 CB p. 3
260 CB p. 137
261 SS p. 141
262 CB p. 211
263 CB pp. 211-212
264 CB p. 213
265 PA p. 773
266 AB Act II
267 Cf. *Passion, Poison, and Petrifaction*; *The Music Cure*; *The Millionairess*; *Adventures of the Black Girl in Her Search for God*; *The Miraculous Revenge*; *The Serenade*; *To-day* (August, 1888); *An Unsocial Socialist.*
268 US pp. 72-73
269 US p. 32
270 SW p. 36
271 BG pp. 27-28
272 WP Act II
273 AM Act III
274 YN Act I
275 DD Act I
276 CC Act II
277 *The New Statesman and Nation,* 16 Aug 1947 p. 128
278 MB Act I
279 GM Act I

280 FF Act I
281 GP p. 91
282 MH p. 152
283 IH p. 235
284 SS p. 158
285 MS pp. 628-629
286 BH p. xvi
287 DL Act I
288 FP Act III
289 PG Act I
290 First entitled *Annajanska, the Wild Grand Duchess*
291 AE Act I
292 BT Part IV Act I
293 SJ Scene II
294 AC Act I. The statue mentioned in the quotation is of Thomas Coram, founder (1739) of the Foundling Hospital, London.
295 TT Act I
296 SU Act I
297 SU Act II
298 CR Act V
299 MP pp. 90-92
300 MJ p. 272
301 PE pp. 171-179
302 PI pp. 659-660

V / DUBLIN II

1 SS p. 32
2 *T. P.'s Weekly* p. 181
3 MH p. 28
4 EB p. 65
5 *T. P.'s Weekly* p. 181
6 PE p. 86 (*Chesterton on Shaw*)
7 SS p. 37
8 DO vol. II, p. 163
9 SS p. 167
10 JW p. 14
11 MP p. 77. Other examples: *T. P.'s Weekly* p. 181; PM p. 14; SS p. 167; and as reported in *The Spoken Word* (London: Collins, 1955, p. 192) from a B.B.C. broadcast by GBS in 1937
12 PM pp. 13-14
13 SS p. 167
14 SS p. 115
15 BH p. 12
16 GP p. 11
17 BE p. 25
18 MH p. 19
19 Much of the information regarding Shaw's relations with Wesley College courtesy of Wm. J. O'Brien, Bursar
20 MH p. 19
21 EB p. 65
22 EB p. 160
23 EB p. 159
24 BH p. 53
25 JW p. 19
26 SS p. 42
27 James Frederick Halpin Preparatory School 23-24 Sandycove Rd. Glasthule
28 MH p. 20
29 BE p. 39
30 JW p. 19
31 SS pp. 42-43
32 SS p. 39
33 SS p. 43
34 SS p. 43
35 BE pp. 29-30
36 JW pp. 19-20
37 MH p. 21
38 SS pp. 42-43
39 SS p. 44
40 SS pp. 44-45
41 LG 25 Oct 1949
42 SS pp. 50-51
43 SS p. 51
44 MH p. 20
45 JW p. 20
46 BE p. 30
47 According to Henderson (MH p. xxxii) Loewstein's title of "Bibliographer and Remembrancer" was self-styled.
48 SS p. 51
49 BH p. 45
50 VL p. 20
51 SS p. 50
52 MH p. 22
53 The "English" in the full title referred to its sponsoring au-

thority: Incorporated Society for Promoting English Protestant Schools in Ireland.
54 SS pp. 44, 50
55 Republished in *The Shaw Review,* vol. II, No. 3, September, 1957, p. 7
56 BE pp. 31-33
57 Thus it seems young Shaw withheld the information that his previous school was the Central Model.
58 MC p. 2
59 MC p. 4
60 Provincial, Very Reverend John Spratt, D.D., Carmelite Chapel and Convent, 56 Aungier St. Thom's Register 1870 (1869)
61 MC p. 4
62 MC p. 6
63 *Boys of England*—A Journal of Sport, Travel, Fun & Instruction. For youths of all nations. Suscribed to by H. R. H. Prince Arthur, The Prince of France and Count William Bernstorff. Edited by Edwin J. Brett, 173 Fleet Street. Price Twopence. Sample story: "The Spectre of the Lighthouse"; or, "Haunted to the Death."
64 MC p. 7
65 According to records of the Central Model, Shaw was suspended or discharged on 11 September 1869. According to testimonial to Shaw's service with Townshend & Company, he started his employment there on 1 November 1871 (MH p. 61).
66 PI p. 672
67 BE p. 33
68 MH p. 54
69 BH p. 61
70 GP p. 29
71 PI p. 672
72 PI p. 672
73 BH p. 61
74 MH p. 54
75 GP p. 30
76 MH p. 22
77 JW p. 20
78 PM p. 16
79 BE p. 38
80 MH p. 947
81 MH p. 141
82 MH p. 946
83 Founded 1849—Printers to the Catholic Church. See *The Sign of Doctor Hay's Head* by Thomas Wall. "Being Some Account of the Hazards and Fortunes of Catholic Printers and Publishers in Dublin from the Later Penal Times to the Present Day." M. H. Gill & Son, Ltd., Dublin, 1958
84 Henderson (MH p. 945) reported The Method to have been set forth in a "small book" with the author's name as G. J. V. Lee.
85 First edition courtesy of Capt. H. de C. W., Dublin
86 *Saunders' News-Letter,* 27 December 1869
87 BE pp. 38-39
88 VL p. i
89 VL p. iv
90 VL p. 14
91 VL p. 23
92 VL p. 24
93 PM p. 11
94 PM p. 11
95 VL p. 88
96 VL p. 81
97 VL p. 104
98 SS pp. 195-196
99 VL pp. 122-124
100 VL p. 108
101 VL p. 109
102 MC p. 11
103 UN pp. 48-50
104 As editor Stanley Weintraub explained in his notes on the text, the ms. of *An Unfinished Novel* had not been revised, corrected or proofread by Shaw. In preparing it for publication, the editor indicated errors, omissions, etc., by supplying bracketed emendations. With regard to the quotation, Kincaid's reply was contradictory and should have

been, of course, "Lady Laurie is afraid that she will die in the middle of the night if it is left *open* altogether."
105 UN p. 54
106 KC p. 41 and PM p. 18
107 PM p. 18
108 KC p. 42
109 BM
110 BE p. 39
111 PM p. 21
112 MH p. 22
113 KC p. 44
114 BE p. 40
115 PI p. 672
116 BE p. 40
117 JW p. 25
118 According to testimonial of employer, reprinted by Henderson (MH p. 60)
119 PI p. 672
120 GP p. 31
121 BE p. 41
122 BE p. 41
123 BH p. 62
124 MC p. 8
125 MH p. 56
126 KC p. 46
127 TU p. 5
128 SS p. 55
129 PI p. 672
130 SS p. 43
131 PB p. 511 and PD p. 269; also MB Act III
132 SS p. 53
133 KC p. 45
134 SS p. 55
135 KC p. 45
136 KC p. 44
137 PI p. 672
138 MS pp. 629 ff.
139 IM p. 49
140 MH p. 53
141 BE p. 41
142 GP p. 29
143 KC p. 43
144 OC Feb 1916 p. 21
145 BH p. 44
146 PM p. 12
147 OC 21 June 1916
148 PM p. 12
149 PM p. 23
150 MH p. 66
151 For a charming episode of Sonny and Hercules, see GP pp. 27-28.
152 JW p. 24
153 BE p. 38
154 SS p. 30
155 PM p. 22
156 OC Feb 1916 p. 2
157 OC Feb 1916 p. 6
158 KC pp. 40-41
159 PM p. 23
160 *Irish Times* 11 Nov 1871
161 *Irish Times* 13 Nov 1871
162 *Irish Times* 2 Dec 1871
163 *Irish Times* 1 Feb 1873
164 *Irish Times* 12 June 1872
165 *Irish Times* 1 Oct 1872
166 PM p. 21
167 KC p. 42
168 *Irish Times* 7 Jan 1873
169 *Irish Times* 13 Jan 1873
170 *Irish Times* 1 April 1873
171 *Irish Times* 5 April 1873
172 GBS to Adda Tyrrell 14 July 1949; his mother played Marguerite, Azucena and Lucrezia Borgia in Lee's opera productions.
173 *Irish Times* 5 April 1873
174 *Irish Times* 8 April 1873
175 PM p. 21
176 *Irish Times* 15 May 1873
177 *Irish Times* 27 May 1873
178 GBS to Frank Harris 20 June 1930 (BH p. 44)
179 Under Nobility, Gentry and Traders; Shaw, George Carr, 1 Hatch Street. Correction probably overlooked
180 MH pp. 53, 66
181 BE p. 42
182 KC p. 43
183 BH pp. 43-44
184 PM pp. 23-24
185 OC 7 Aug 1919 pp. 4-5
186 SS p. 142
187 OC 14 June 1922
188 MH p. 53
189 MH p. 66
190 BH p. 41
191 GP p. 29

192 BE p. 42
193 KC p. 43
194 OC Feb 1919 p. 21
195 SS p. 140
196 OC 7 Aug 1919 p. 3
197 SS p. 142
198 BH pp. 43-44
199 PM pp. 23-24
200 SS pp. 146-147
201 PM p. 24
202 OC Feb 1916 pp. 20-21
203 MH p. 63
204 BE p. 43
205 GP p. 29
206 BH p. 41
207 MC p. 13
208 Hanley Collection, University of Texas
209 OC 14 June 1922
210 BH pp. 43-44
211 PM p. 24
212 Balmoral Sanatorium; no records available
213 PM p. 28
214 GP p. 29
215 JW p. 26
216 CI p. 22
217 TC p. 41
218 GH p. 20, PP p. 54 and MH p. 53
219 BE p. 43
220 BE p. 49
221 KC p. 44
222 BH p. 44
223 PM p. 24
224 OC Feb 1916 pp. 1-2
225 *Thom's* (actual year)
226 JW p. 28
227 Courtesy JO
228 OC Feb 1916 pp. 20-21
229 BE p. 49 ff.
230 Radio WNYC, New York, Nov 1956: *Books and Voices,* John K. M. McCaffery, Moderator
231 SS p. 58
232 MC pp. 8-9
233 MC p. 9
234 MC pp. 9-11
235 Three or four plays and some short stories, including "How I Robbed the Bank of Ireland" published in *The Weekly Irish Times,* 15 March 1891
236 MC p. 11
237 MG
238 MG
239 BB fp. 136
240 CP p. 7
241 SS pp. 129-130
242 OC Feb 1916 p. 25
243 GH p. 9
244 PP p. 33
245 MH p. 44
246 Chesterton said: "Bernard Shaw comes of a Puritan middle-class family of the most solid respectability . . ." (GG p. 56). For Shaw's comments, see PE p. 87.
247 NT pp. 259-262; see also Warren S. Smith, ed., *The Religious Speeches of Bernard Shaw*. University Park, Pa.: The Pennsylvania State University Press, 1963.
248 OC Feb 1916 p. 18
249 UO Chapt. II, pp. 8-9
250 Joey was Mrs. Campbell's pet name for Shaw.
251 BH p. xvi
252 BH p. 40
253 SS pp. 56-67 and KC pp. 47-48
254 MH p. 61
255 PI p. 673
256 PI p. 674
257 PI p. 679
258 BE pp. 53-54
259 MH p. 61
260 AD p. 12
261 Dated 5 Oct 1879, from Victoria Grove; now in the Hanley Collection, University of Texas
262 PI p. 672
263 SS p. 53
264 SS pp. 56, 62
265 BE p. 55
266 MH p. 63
267 AD p. 13
268 BE p. 56
269 BB fp. 132
270 PI p. 673

VI / LONDON

1 BH p. 44 and PM p. 24
2 *Handel* (*The Great Musician*) by Mrs. Julian Marshall, edited by Francis Hueffer. London: Sampson Low, Marston, Searle & Rivington, 1883
3 OC Feb 16 p. 2
4 OC June 14 1922
5 MH p. 65
6 JW pp. 25-26
7 OC Feb 16 pp. 2-3
8 PM p. 24
9 JW p. 26
10 BE p. 43
11 Courtesy Major Arthur J. W. Fitzmaurice, Carlow
12 BE p. 57
13 MH p. 77
14 KC p. 43
15 PK p. 687
16 PM p. 25
17 LB p. 65 and US Chapt. IX
18 MH p. 62
19 BE pp. 57-58
20 JW p. 24
21 SS p. 169
22 MH p. 63
23 MC p. 16
24 Isle of Wight District Register Office, County Hall, Newport, I. of W.
25 BE p. 24
26 BE p. 28
27 King James Version. Cf. also Douay Version.
28 However, Shaw visited the Isle of Wight on his honeymoon in 1898 (see GP p. 187) and it is possible he ordered the stone and its inscription at that time.
29 PK p. 687
30 BE pp. 100-103
31 MH p. 62
32 GP p. 36
33 AD p. 13
34 BE pp. 59-61
35 BE pp. 61, 64
36 MH p. 93
37 GP p. 36
38 MC p. 15
39 BH p. 72
40 Later reprinted by Rattray (CI pp. 32-33) and reprinted (BE pp. 65-66). Text is in Hanley Collection, University of Texas.
41 HB p. 4
42 HB p. xv
43 BM
44 BM
45 CI p. 28
46 GP p. 36
47 BE p. 61
48 MH pp. 161-162
49 MH p. 946
50 SS pp. 65-66
51 MH p. 163
52 MH, quoted at length, pp. 162-163
53 MH p. 134
54 Ervine gave no source, but cf. MH p. 61 where credit is given to Mushlin.
55 BE pp. 66-67
56 AD pp. 12-17
57 BM
58 PI p. 682
59 One exception: in 1881 Shaw helped count votes in an election at Leyton, for which he earned a few pounds. PI pp. 675-676
60 UN p. 8
61 PI p. 670
62 Many now at the University of Texas
63 PI p. 676; also cf. SS p. 87.
64 PM p. 17
65 See PI p. 685 for his encounters with a beggar and a prostitute.
66 MC pp. 14-15
67 BE pp. 55-56
68 BE p. 22
69 OC Feb 1916 pp. 26-27
70 OC Feb 1916 p. 21
71 SS p. 140
72 BE p. 55
73 BE p. 43
74 PI p. 660

75 PM p. 26
76 BE p. 51
77 MC p. 13
78 EB pp. 75-76
79 Ervine reported that the Curral Collection contained McNulty's uncompleted and often "inaccurate" history of his comradeship with GBS. It was also Ervine's opinion that both Shaw's and McNulty's memoirs had many imperfections. BE pp. 31-32.
80 SS p. 29
81 MH p. 610
82 GM (preface) pp. 28-29
83 CM p. 36
84 PI p. 678
85 GR p. 442
86 OC 30 Dec 1919
87 IW Chapt. 44
88 SS p. 141
89 OC 7 Aug 1919 p. 4
90 BB p. 127
91 SS p. 139
92 PI p. 668
93 BB fp. 39
94 First presented at the Haymarket Theatre, London, 12 May 1908 (ST p. 120). See also MH p. 88 for Mrs. Shaw's attending her son's plays.
95 SS p. 32
96 GF p. 169
97 GF p. 175
98 FL and LL, courtesy Lady Hanson
99 LL pp. 54-64
100 Winsten (SC p. 41) quoted Shaw as saying that his mother used the first planchette to be imported into Ireland.
101 MH pp. 77-78. Shaw said of his mother: "She had plenty of imagination and really lived in it and on it (PI p. 667).
102 BH p. 33
103 GP (Postscript) pp. 84-85
104 SB p. 8
105 BH p. 40
106 PM p. 16
107 SS p. 31
108 OC Feb 1916 pp. 18-19
109 From *The Daily Express* (Dublin) 27 June 1963: [The Collegiate Musical Society with which Lee was affiliated gave a concert that did not come up to expectations] "in consequence of the illness of the lady who had undertaken the soprano parts, some of the most striking features of the program were unavoidably omitted."
110 PM p. 16
111 OC Feb 1916 pp. 18-19
112 Probably suggested by Annie Besant's article "Marriage. As It Was, As It Is, And As It Should Be" (ca. 1878); quoted in FN p. 133.
113 Slattox & Chinnery, sweatshop operators; Edith is interested in improving the lot of the working-class girl.
114 ML vol. I pp. 40-41
115 OC Feb 1916 pp. 2-3
116 BH p. 39
117 PM pp. 22-24
118 OC Feb 1916 p. 3
119 PM pp. 24-25
120 According to Farmer (GF p. 48), who credits Ivo L. Curral
121 BE p. 60
122 BE p. 29
123 MH p. 67
124 BH p. 42
125 SS p. 182. It was for Harris' widow Nellie that Shaw entered into the task of preparing the book for publication.
126 HC. In another place in Lady Hanson's script, the family friend, who had a special method for producing and preserving the voice, was identified as Vandaleur Leigh. When asked about the spelling of Leigh, Lady Hanson declared that as a child she once thumbed through an old picture album and came upon a photograph of a man with large pointed moustaches. At the base of the picture was written Vandaleur Leigh. The

album, she added regretfully, had long since disappeared.
127 OC Feb 1916 p. 2
128 OC Feb 1916 pp. 3-4
129 MH pp. 67-68
130 SS p. 140
131 BE p. 185
132 MC p. 15
133 BE p. 293
134 MH p. 75
135 SS pp. 148-149
136 SS p. 142
137 SS p. 146
138 OC Feb 1916 p. 4
139 KC pp. 52-53
140 PM p. 23
141 OC Feb 1916 pp. 4-5
142 BM (All BM extracts in this section courtesy JO)
143 BM
144 BM
145 BM
146 BM
147 BM
148 BM
149 BM
150 BM
151 BM
152 BM
153 BM
154 BM
155 BM
156 BM
157 BM
158 BM
159 PM p. 22
160 MH p. 946
161 OC Feb 1916 pp. 5-6
162 Courtesy Dr. John D. Gordan, Berg Collection, New York Public Library
163 MH pp. 945-948
164 MH p. 946
165 MH p. 946
166 MH p. 67
167 BE p. 63
168 KC p. 42
169 PM p. 22
170 PM p. 25
171 OC Feb 1916 p. 2
172 OC Feb 1916 p. 6
173 FN p. 219fn
174 BE p. 63. Frank Podmore, an active member of the Society for Psychical Research
175 Hayden Coffin, friend of Lucy and fellow member of the cast of *Dorothy*. See Henderson's reproduction of program (MH p. 71).
176 From a letter 13 July 1960 of E. Robinson, General Manager London Necropolis Company
177 BE p. 63
178 MH p. 67
179 BH p. 42
180 PM p. 25
181 OC Feb 1916 p. 6
182 BE p. 63
183 BE p. 21
184 Undated but ca. 1930
185 BH p. 42
186 LR vol. I p. 37
187 LM
188 LM vol. I pp. 1-2
189 According to Glasenapp
190 LM vol. I p. 3
191 WF p. 279
192 UH pp. 301-303
193 NW vol. I p. 5 (New York edition); p. 15 (London edition)

APPENDIX C

1 Actual year.
2 According to Thom's Registers and *London Post Office Directories;* (D): Dublin; (L): London.
3 (A): announcement; (R): review; (N): news item; (S): *Saunders' News-Letter;* (T): Thom's; (I): *Irish Times.*
4 *London Post Office Directory;* possibly another variation by Lee.
5 Lee to Donald Shaw, 1 June 1878 (in British Museum).
6 Lee to Donald Shaw, 3 May 1878 (also in BM).
7 Lee to GBS, 26 January 1880 (BM).
8 Lee to GBS, 23 August 1881 (BM).
9 Lee to GBS, 29 May 1882 (BM).
10 Lee to GBS, 5 January 1883 (BM).

Index

Side Elevation

Return Room

W. C.

Pantry